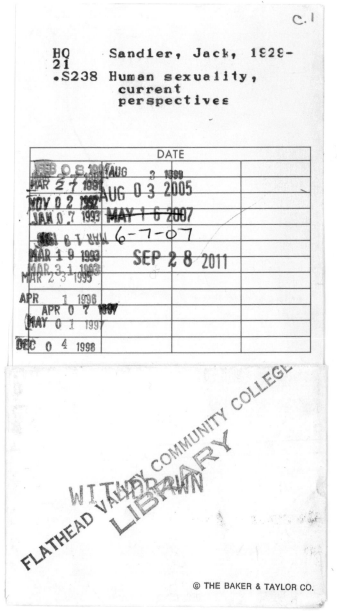

# Human Sexuality: Current Perspectives

# *Human Sexuality: Current Perspectives* c.1

**Jack Sandler, Marilyn Myerson, Bill N. Kinder**
**University of South Florida**

**Mariner Publishing Company, Inc.**

Copyright © 1980 by Mariner Publishing Company, Inc.


All Rights Reserved


Art Work by Eleanor Blair
Cover design by Joe Traina


**Library of Congress Cataloging in Publication Data**

Sandler, Jack
  Human sexuality, current perspectives.

  Bibliography:
  Includes index.
    1. Sex. I. Myerson, Marilyn, joint
author. II. Kinder, Bill N., joint author.
III. Title.
HQ21.S238       155.3′4       80-11080

ISBN 0-936166-01-0

Printed in the United States of America

*This book is dedicated to the current and future generations of students*

# Contents

# PREFACE

Our objective in writing this book was to offer a balanced and comprehensive perspective of the field of human sexuality. How to define balance and comprehensiveness, however, is no simple task.

In our many discussions before and during the course of writing, we ultimately agreed that balance could be achieved by equal representation from several relevant perspectives. Thus, we attempted to create a balance between female and male perspectives of sexuality and between scientific and experiential perspectives. We realize that the task of attaining a perfect balance is an impossible one; however, it is our hope that the final product reflects a serious attempt to achieve this objective. As in the case of any such enterprise, the ultimate assessment of the degree to which we have succeeded rests with the reader.

Comprehensiveness was an even more difficult issue to resolve. There are, of course, a number of topics that appear with great regularity in almost all human sexuality texts. These topics, perhaps, represent the core subject matter of the field. But beyond that, the waters were uncharted. Inasmuch as sexuality may almost be equated with life, virtually any topic related to human behavior may be defined and regarded as germane to the study of sexuality. We opted, instead, for a working and flexible definition that actually (and perhaps appropriately) emerged over the course of writing. Our final effort, then, reflects these differences. Some topics that appear almost universally (for example, a lengthy discussion of the variety of sexual positions) were not included, while other topics that are rarely included (for example, infertility) we considered to be important. Again, an assessment of the degree to which we have succeeded in being comprehensive rests with the reader.

From the outset, we were sensitive to the fact that there would be differences in our writing styles. Such differences were inherent in the writing process of this book for two reasons. The first of these results from the fact that we individually accepted primary responsibility for certain chapters based on our knowledge, professional experience, teaching involvement, and personal interest. The second reason stems from the fact that different content areas lend themselves to different writing styles. A chapter on sex researchers, for example, is best written in a more technical style, whereas a chapter dealing with values and decision making lends itself to a more conversational approach. On the other hand, we each contributed to all of the chapters during the entire writing process. The end result is, indeed, a collaborative effort which, we hope, retains the individual expression of each author.

The final product, of course, is the result not only of our own individual efforts and mutual collaboration but also of the ideas, assistance, and direct contributions of a large number of individuals. It would be impossible to identify each person and his or her contribution, but a number of names are prominent. Perhaps foremost among these is Etta Bender Breit. From the point in time when this book was still in the discussion stage, up to the final revision, Etta was a constant source of support and suggestions, and we wish to gratefully acknowledge her contributions.

There were also others to whom we turned from time to time and to whom we are also indebted for their assistance and encouragement. Certainly this book could not have been written without the encouragement and continued support of Manoug Manougian, the unflagging contributions of our copy editor, Shirley Miller, and our typists Kathy Thielemann, Valerie Smith, and Betty Powell, and the coordination provided by Julie Czaja.

We are particularly indebted to Eleanor Blair, our artist, who responded to a difficult time schedule and the chaos of dealing with three different value systems by translating our ideas into an art form that surpassed our expectations.

A number of reviewers made many valuable suggestions, and we are especially indebted to Minor Chamblin and Jerry Cerny for their efforts. The following individuals also made contributions in this regard: Boyd Duncan, Barb Freesen, Florese Hunt, Valerie Pinhas, Barbara Plager, Libby Tanner, and Lillian Wolfowitz. We also wish to thank Robert Ingram for his assistance in a number of areas and, in particular, for checking our reference sources. Finally, we wish to thank our colleagues in our respective departments for their interest and general support.

Above and beyond the many contributions made by those listed above to the three of us, each of us individually would like to express our appreciation to the following:

to Jeff, Eric, and Alan Sandler for reviewing early drafts of the manuscript and for continuously focusing my attention on issues that are important to college age students;

to Bobbie for her undiminished support, enthusiasm, patience, and good humor throughout the entire project period.

J.S.

to my dear friend and colleague, Etta Bender Breit, for six years of shared exploring, learning, work, and play;
to my extended family Valeria Hendricks, Michael Greeson, Colleen Clark, and Rex Lee for their all-embracing love, enthusiasm, and support;
to the Sunday Night Women's Support Group: Cindy Archer, Mary Ellen Brown, Maxine Hatcher, Mary Jo Hughes, Rusty Penner, Tempie Rendina, Rochelle Yaeger, for their invaluable comfort, inspiration, encouragement, and affirmation; to Bill Robinson, for shared lessons in sight and insight;
to my parents, Nancy and Harry Myerson and Martha Ferrandino, for their continuing interest and love;
to my daughter, Maya Ferrandino for her energy, sunshine, and unabashed affection.

M.M.

to Dan Johnson, David Stenmark, Pat Blakeney and Dan Creson for their personal support, for their influence on my professional development, and, most importantly, for their friendship;
to my parents, Rodney and Nita, and my wife, Carole, for their enthusiastic support, encouragement, and acceptance.

B.K.

There are, no doubt, a number of individuals who also contributed to this book in various ways but whose names are not included in this list of acknowledgments. We apologize for any oversight in this regard. All of the contributors, mentioned and unmentioned, bear no responsibility for any of the book's shortcomings; this responsibility belongs entirely to us.

Our final acknowledgment represents a mutual expression of gratitude to one another. We each of us had strong initial misgivings regarding what we knew would involve questioning, criticisms, and negotiation before establishing collaboration. Whatever else has emerged from this enterprise, we have learned from one another an have acquired a mutual feeling of respect and accomplishment.

# Chapter 1

## Sexuality—A Historical Perspective

## SEXUALITY DEFINED

There is an old saying that man is sexually occupied one percent of the time and sexually preoccupied the other ninety-nine percent. Although these figures may be exaggerated, the adage illustrates our continuous and absorbing interest in all matters related to sexuality.

The question of just how much time is spent in sex-related activities depends on how we define the term sexuality. Some authorities consider sex to be the underlying motive of all human behavior and, consequently, explain every act as an expression of our sexuality. At the other extreme, there are those individuals who restrict the term to just those physical acts that involve the sex organs, for example, coitus, masturbation, etc. Neither of these two viewpoints is entirely satisfactory. The first definition forces us into some rather farfetched conclusions by interpreting everything from international conflict to food preferences as expressions of sexuality. The second definition overlooks all of those human dimensions which, indirectly as well as directly, are influenced by sex. Our position in this book charts a middle course between these two extremes. For us the term sexuality encompasses physical sex, of course, but it also includes the manner in which sex is manifested in society. Sexuality, then, is one of those key concepts that bridges the gap between biology, on the one hand, and psychology, on the other. Although, in the last analysis, sexuality is an individual matter, our definition includes, at least, one's social role, life style, and interpersonal style, as well as one's sexual orientation, attitudes, and behavior. As we shall see, the majority of chapters in this book bear on sexuality in this broader sense, rather than on physical sex per se.

## SEXUALITY THROUGH THE AGES

It seems appropriate to initiate our study of sexuality by considering current sexual values, beliefs, customs, and practices as the end result of a long series of historical influences. Thus, the better we understand these historical factors, the better we may understand our own sexuality.

Although it is impossible to reconstruct completely the sexual expressions of ancient cultures, numerous records are still available which enable us to make some reasonable interpretations of those earlier sexual customs. For our purposes, we will identify four separate lines of influence in tracing the history of sexuality:

1.  The pre-Biblical period
2.  Pagan-polytheistic cultures
3.  Ancient Oriental cultures
4.  Judeo-Christian influences

Of these four, certainly it is the Judeo-Christian tradition which has had the most profound and enduring impact on contemporary sexuality in Western societies. Let us consider the first three lines of influence before turning our attention to the Judeo-Christian tradition. In the discussion that follows, it must

be recognized that sexual values and practices did not remain static within a given culture but changed over time. Any description of Egyptian sexuality, for example, must recognize that the ancient Egyptian empire endured for over 3000 years. Just as our modern sexual values and customs have changed from generation to generation, it is reasonable to assume that changes occurred among the Egyptians over a period of time. What we have described, therefore, are the most salient and durable characteristics for each of the various cultures, to the degree that history enables us to describe these phenomena.

## THE PRE-BIBLICAL PERIOD

Pre-Biblical patterns of sexuality are, of course, obscure and poorly understood. Despite our limited knowledge of this ancient period, it seems reasonable to assume that as social mechanisms such as a form of government, stable economies, and a family network began to emerge, sexual behavior came to be something more than a random, uninhibited event in the lives of these ancient peoples. The earliest artistic expressions of prehistoric societies, European cave paintings dating back some 15,000 to 20,000 years, are apparently sexual in nature, in the sense that human figures are depicted with exaggerated sex organs, in some cases apparently engaged in coitus.

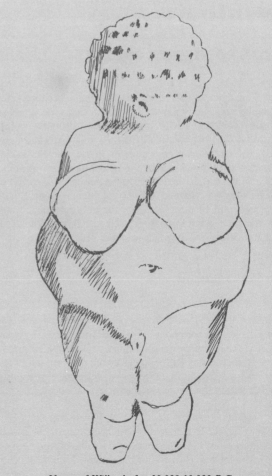

*Venus of Willendorf c. 30,000-10,000 B.C.*
*Museum of Natural History, Vienna.*

Although the exact meaning of these paintings remains unknown, most scholars interpret these efforts as an indication that, even this far back in time, sex was becoming ritualized and modified in the light of social influences (Murstein, 1974). Perhaps, however, one can grasp a clearer conception of the place of sex in ancient times by considering the manner in which primitive man attempted to cope with life in general. Prehistoric peoples had virtually no control over an unpredictable and dangerous environment. Death could occur instantly and without warning from any direction. So as to make some sense out of such chaotic circumstances, primitive man endowed objects and events in his environment with magical supernatural properties and a capacity for independent action, a belief which has been termed *animism*. Animistic thought held that supernatural forces were present in all objects, including those in nature, such as rocks, trees, mountains, streams, etc. It was these forces, then, that controlled the life of primitive man. Cultural practices and rituals were designed to appease these mystical forces, that is, to "ward off the evil events." Even sex was to be undertaken in such a way as to please the gods. In this manner, sex became a sacred act subject to influence, control, and sanction by the shaman or priest who served as the liaison between the ordinary individual and the deities.

In this context cave paintings and the like may be interpreted as an appeal to the gods for fertility or for successful childbearing or as representations of copulation by the gods, to be emulated by the people.

## PAGAN-POLYTHEISTIC INFLUENCES

With the dawn of civilization the association between sex and religion became even more explicit, and a chain was established that has continued up to modern times. Primitive animism evolved into the polytheism of the early Egyptians and Babylonians. By contemporary standards these ancient societies displayed a permissive approach to sexual functions. Within the context of the standards that prevailed during these early times, however, sex was regarded as a natural, human event. But even more important to primitive man, the public sexual rituals of these ancient peoples emphasized their sacred or religious meaning. Later, however, they became more secularized.

### Egyptian Sexuality

Perhaps the clearest example of the sacred nature of sex among these early societies is most apparent with the Egyptians. Explicit sexual representations appear in many cultural artifacts. In these cases Egyptian deities are depicted with clearly identifiable sex organs, and often they are engaged in sex-related activities which the Egyptians themselves practiced.

The Egyptian temple served as the center for many of the sacred sex rituals. Religious rites designed to secure the blessings of the gods often included sexually symbolic events (Sussman, 1976). As was true throughout the ancient Near East, virgins were ritually deflowered in the temple, fertility acts were encouraged by the priests, and all forms of prostitution involving males and females performing every form of sexual behavior

were available in the temple. After the consolidation of the Egyptian empire, royal marriages between brother and sister occurred, in order to concentrate the ruling power. However, there is no reason to believe that incest was widely practiced among the ordinary members of Egyptian society.

Despite these practices, which have, no doubt, contributed to the historical image of open and uninhibited sexuality among the ancient Egyptians, laws prohibiting certain sexual practices were enacted. Although temple sex was available, for example, most forms of adultery were severely penalized. By and large, however, as long as religious requirements were met and the need for producing children was accomplished, virtually all forms of sex were permitted, provided no harm to others was involved. All sexual behaviors from bestiality to anal intercourse to oral-genital contacts are portrayed in tomb paintings; and, though the Egyptians might have disapproved of some activities more than others, their society seemed to be fairly permissive sexually (Bullough, 1976).

The influence of the ancient Egyptians on later sexual practices in Western society is an indirect one. Their impact is more important to the degree that their religious sexuality served as a departure for later Judeo-Christian beliefs.

## Greek Sexuality

Where the Egyptians permitted all forms of sexual expression on religious grounds, the Greeks idealized and secularized virtually every type of erotic activity. For the ancient Greeks, sexuality was woven into every fabric of their society, as revealed by their straightforward references to sex in their literature and in their art (Sussman, 1976). From the doorposts of their homes, which were decorated with an ithyphallicherm (a statue of a male figure with an erection), to the public displays of male and female nudity, the Greeks were constantly reminded of and influenced by their sexual nature (Young, 1964).

Greek religion, of course, was replete with references and myths regarding the sexual exploits of the deities, which included legends describing many different forms of sex with one another as well as with humans. Such references served, no doubt, as examples for the ordinary Greek to emulate.

Some insight into the impact of sex in the daily life of the ancient Greeks might be obtained by considering the sexual experiences of the typical Greek from birth to adulthood. Sexual education for the female started with the celebration of Priapus, a sexual deity with an exaggerated, erect phallus. At varying times during the year, virgins carried the representation of Priapus in religious processions. In many of the Greek cities, males and females were exposed to and accepted nudity as an ordinary event. Boys and girls, for example, frequently exercised together in the nude, and those practices continued into adulthood. Sex exploration and activity, including bisexual behavior, were accepted under these circumstances as natural human behavior. A great deal of emphasis was placed on practices and customs which enhanced erotic appeal — for example, developing a well-proportioned body (still admired today in the surviving statuary of Greek figures), using perfumes liberally to counteract offensive body odors, wearing apparel which facilitated sexual encounter, etc. At certain times of the year, for example the feast of Dionysus, god of wine and fertility, sexual orgies were engaged in by the majority of the adult population. Judging from the art and the accounts of Greek customs that have survived, the Greeks engaged in a wide variety of positions during coitus.

As the average Grecian boy and girl from the citizen class grew to adulthood, they acquired the characteristics of their respective sex roles. Greek society encouraged monogamy. The male adult, however, was expected not only to take a wife and to father children but also to be sexually active in other ways, including having homosexual liaisons with young men and engaging in bisexual practices with slaves and prostitutes (Murstein, 1974).

*Greek Plates , Staatliche Museum, Berlin*

The female sex role was less clearly defined than the male sex role, but women were evidently recognized as active participants in sexual activities. Although Greek society was male dominated, the sexual double standard was apparently less stringently invoked in Grecian times than in modern times; and no doubt many women engaged in sexual activities outside the marriage relationship with no fear of retribution. Again, judging from surviving evidence, women frequently expressed assertive roles during the sex act.

A recognition of alternative female sex roles is also revealed in Greek legend and art. The legend of the Amazons, for example, described a tribe of extraordinary female warriors, who dominated the men in their society. Female homosexuality was also recognized. The famous Grecian female poet Sappho, for example, was reputed to have lived with a group of women on the island of Lesbos, from which the term lesbianism is derived. Thus, although men dominated Grecian society and women had few, if any, legal or civil rights, women's sexual rights were not restricted.

One popular view reflecting the values of certain members of Greek society was expressed by Plato. He argued that the most profound relationships were based on spiritual learning and intellectual attraction. Such "platonic relationships" could be shared only by men as contrasted with heterosexual relationships that were based on physical and sexual attraction and were therefore of lower status. As we shall see, this sentiment influenced later Christian values.

By the fourth century B.C. sexual luxury was identified as a praiseworthy ideal, with Aphrodite (from which the term aphrodisiac is derived) revered as the goddess of sexual intercourse (Flaceliere, 1962). The following statement, attributed to Demosthenes (400 B.C.), perhaps best describes this theme: "We resort to courtesans for our pleasures, keep concubines to look after our daily needs, and marry wives to give us legitimate children and to be the faithful guardians of our domestic hearths."

Despite the highly permissive nature of Greek sexuality, numerous laws and codes governing unrestricted sex were enacted. Athenian laws, for example, specified that rape, adultery, and sexual abuse were punishable offenses (Sussman, 1976). In brief, then, the ancient Greeks actively promoted and enjoyed vigorous sex lives. Sex was considered to be a normal, natural, human activity, to be experienced to the fullest, so long as innocent people were not harmed. The impact of Greek sexuality on later Western customs, however, is a matter of some debate. Certainly, in some respects, Greek influences continue — for example, in Greek art and literature, which is replete with sexual themes that are repeated today, and in many of our words, such as hermaphrodite. Young (1964) argues that the values of Grecian culture are still alive today, although often obscure. At the very least, Greek customs served as a point of departure for Judeo-Christian codes in the sense that Hebrew and the later Christian attitudes can be interpreted primarily as a reaction to Greek attitudes toward homosexuality (Bullough, 1976).

## Roman Sexuality

Although there is reasonable agreement among most authorities regarding the characteristics of Greek sexuality, Roman customs and values are a matter of considerable debate. Conventional wisdom holds that the Roman society was as sexually promiscuous as the Greek; and it is popularly believed that the collapse of the Roman Empire was due, in no small part, to the sexual excesses of its citizens (Canter, 1963). These views have been challenged, however, on the grounds that the sexual excesses of Roman society have been greatly exaggerated and that the accounts of these events are biased and inaccurate (Bullough, 1976). Whatever the actual case, certainly Roman culture was more complicated and multidimensional than Greek society. The Roman Empire endured for a relatively long period of time; and, whereas the Greeks retained their beliefs and customs, Roman culture changed in the light of the changing empire and in the face of continuous exposure to other cultures.

The Romans, of course, shared the polytheistic religion of the Greeks, as well as the sexuality of their deities. Thus, they shared the Grecian religious approval of sex. As Grimal states:

> To love was to obey the gods and achieve one of the requisites of the human condition. Chastity could be required by religious rites in certain cases, but it was not a good thing in itself; not even a desirable thing; it was rather an impairment of what was good and desirable for among the gifts of the gods to man, love is always to be found. [Grimal, 1967, p. xiii]

Although monogamy was the Roman custom, the right to enjoy sex by both men and women was not to be jeopardized by such values. If man and wife proved ill-suited or could not satisfy each other, let them change partners. Even if complications occasionally arose as a result, that was still better than letting sex needs remain unfulfilled (Lewinsohn, 1958).

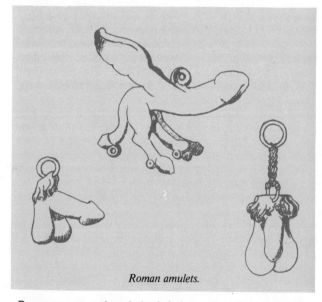

*Roman amulets.*

Roman women shared the inferior status of their Grecian counterparts; however, there were some important differences. Virgins, in particular, were held in high esteem, and the vestal virgins were charged with important responsibilities in temple functions. Religious ritual was attached to the deflowering of a bride, again because of the virgin's mystical powers. Roman women also exerted a strong influence on political life from time to time, although this circumstance occurred primarily behind the scenes.

The range and variety of Roman sexual practices is represented, in part, by the durability of Latin terms which are still in use today. The word *sex* itself is of Latin origin, as is *for-*

*nication,* derived from the word *fornices,* the arches of the Colosseum, which served as a location for prostitutes. Similarly, *fellatio* and *cunnilingus* are Latin terms still in current use, especially in medical and legal contexts.

Despite the persistent belief in Roman sexual promiscuity, Roman codes governing sexual misconduct were, for the most part, quite conservative. Sexual deviations were at least publicly condemned, including homosexuality, which was called the Greek practice and was regarded as unworthy of a true Roman (Lewinsohn, 1958). These laws persisted despite the real or rumored homosexuality of such prominent Romans as Julius Caesar, Augustus, and Tiberius. From these conflicting values, it appears that Roman culture revealed many of the paradoxes of contemporary Western sexuality, that is, public condemnation of certain sexual behaviors that were evidently engaged in by many of the citizens. Perhaps this inconsistency constitutes another reason for the conflicting perspectives on Roman sexuality.

During the latter stages of the Roman Empire, and particularly under the leadership of Caligula and Nero, Roman society and sexual practices took on a harsh, cruel character. Public sexual exhibitions were performed in the arenas, often with unwilling participants, prostitution increased dramatically, and, by some accounts, sadistic practices emerged. The question remains, however, to what extent the sexual excesses of the emperors were representative of the average Roman citizen. Furthermore, the argument which condemns Roman sexuality must be counterbalanced by the poetic and sensitive descriptions of lovemaking on the part of such Roman writers as Ovid, Horace, and Petronius. Ovid, in particular, offered a manual of erotic content which is still admired today for its artistic expression.

---

### Ovid on "The Art of Love"

If dust be on her lap, or grain of sand,
Brush both away with your officious hand,
If none be there, yet brush that nothing thence
And still to touch her lap make some pretence.
Touch anything of hers, and if her train
Sweep on the ground, let it not sweep in vain;
But gently take it up and wipe it clean:
And while you wipe it with observing eyes,
Who knows but you may see her naked thighs.

(From: Pike, E.R. *Love in ancient Rome.* London: F. Muller, 1965.)

---

Most importantly, however, the growing Christian movement focused its attack on what was increasingly seen as the moral dissolution of Roman society, thereby consolidating its own influence. In addition to these external pressures, Roman culture was becoming divided from within by a number of different forces. There were those Roman patriots who were appalled by the corruption of the emperor position, but it was that element in Roman society that rejected all sexuality in favor of asceticism and abstention that had the most profound impact on the Christian movement and, ultimately, Western society.

## SEXUALITY AMONG THE ANCIENT INDIANS AND FAR EASTERN CULTURES

Of the various cultural antecedents that have impacted on Western sexuality, the customs and practices of India, China, and Japan clearly represent a separate and independent tradition. Our knowledge of the sexuality of these cultures has only recently become available and has yet to be properly assessed. For these reasons, we will only briefly mention the most salient features of these cultures.

What we know of the sexual practices and conduct of the Eastern cultures is available from such sources as love manuals, cultural artifacts, and temple sculpture. In general, it would appear that the ancient peoples of India, Japan, and China shared many of the same values as did early Western society, for example, monogamy (although Chinese royalty also engaged in polygamy), prohibitions against incest, adultery, etc., and a religious or sacred context in which sex was embedded. The differences, however, are probably more striking than the similarities. Very clearly, sex was regarded as an important component of life, to be practiced and enjoyed to the fullest extent possible. This thesis is revealed in the now familiar Kama Sutra, a Hindu love manual for young people apparently formulated around the 8th century. The Kama Sutra details every conceivable dimension of male-female relationships, including elaborate descriptions of coitus, even to the point of specifying which positions are best for varying sizes and configurations of male and female sex organs. Clearly, then, Indian custom promoted a form of sex education and encouraged both men and women to become highly skilled sexually.

Similar values prevailed in China and Japan where sex education was promoted through "pillow-books," basically sex manuals for the newly married, usually depicting many different positions and describing the sources of stimulation available in each position. In each of these cultures, the male's responsibility to bring the female to orgasm is clearly recognized. Numerous suggestions are offered in Chinese literature to accomplish this goal. In one such account, for example,

> a man closes his eyes and concentrates his thoughts, he presses his tongue against the roof of his mouth, bends his back and stretches his neck. He opens his nostrils wide and squares his shoulders, closes his mouth and sucks in his breath. Then (he will not ejaculate and) the semen will ascend inwards on its account. A man can completely regulate his ejaculations. When having intercourse with women he should only emit semen two or three times in ten. [Van Gulik, 1961]

From all the available evidence, then, it appears that not only did the Indians, the Chinese, and the Japanese enjoy sex, but they studied it, analyzed it, and ritualized it, for the express purpose of enhancing the sexual dimension of human functioning (Bullough, 1976).

## JUDEO-CHRISTIAN INFLUENCES

As we have suggested, contemporary American and Western sexuality can best be understood as the end result of a long line of historical influences originating primarily with the ancient Jews and elaborated and refined by later Christian ethics and philosophy. Let us begin our analysis of these critical events by reviewing the sexual life of the ancient Jews. The two major sources of information for such a review are the Old Testament

*Woodblock color print: Erotic art of the East.*

and the Talmud. The first five books of the Old Testament (the Pentateuch) describe the early history of the Jews and their "testament" with God. Tradition holds that Moses was the author of the first five books, although many Biblical scholars claim that different sections were written by different individuals over a long period of time and that this portion of the Bible might not have been completed until as late as 800 B.C., some 400 to 500 years after the writings were apparently initiated (Gaer, 1951). Whatever the actual case, it is reasonably certain that the entire Old Testament was written by various individuals and did not realize its final form as we know it today until perhaps A.D. 200.

The Talmud, a series of commentaries, judgments, and guidelines, similarly is the product of various individuals and was collected over a considerable period of time. Whereas the Bible was accepted as God's word to the ancients, the Talmud represented the effort on the part of Jewish scholars to interpret God's word and to establish a set of rules and regulations for governing every last detail of human behavior, including sexual conduct.

Given these two sources of information, then, any description of Jewish sexuality as it emerged and evolved over perhaps some 4000 years is subject to error and at best will probably reflect only a limited perspective of what might be true for any given time and place in Jewish history. With this reservation in mind, let us attempt to reconstruct Jewish sexuality and consider how Jewish customs influenced later Western values and practices.

The overriding feature which distinguished the ancient Jews from their neighboring nomadic tribes was, of course, their rejection of polytheism in favor of a belief in one God. This distinction was of such significance that it colored their views of and reactions to the religious customs of other cultures which, as we have seen, included sexual practices.

A second important distinction was that the Jews, perhaps more so than most ancient cultures, continuously attempted to

refine and stabilize a body of rules and regulations in order to guide Jewish affairs, to resolve disputes, and to serve the ordinary Jew in his daily routine. Because of these two predominant characteristics, Jewish tradition and custom began to diverge from that of their neighbors.

Before this divergence occurred, however, Jewish sexuality was probably not much different from the other tribes and cultures in the Middle East. Tradition holds that the ancient Hebrews dealt harshly with those who deviated from a strict code of sexual morality; and the Bible is replete with references to various "abominations," such as fornication (sex between unmarried persons), adultery, homosexuality, bestiality, etc. There is some reason to assume, however, that the ancient Jews were actually more permissive than is ordinarily believed (Bullough, 1976; Murstein, 1974). For one thing, it seems reasonable to assume that, at least very early in their history, the Jews shared the rather casual sexual practices that were characteristic of all nomadic societies, including polygamy, slavery, concubinage, some form of temple prostitution, and fertility rituals (Bullough, 1976). God's frequent remonstrations, then, may be taken as an index of criticism of a sexually permissive society. Additionally, it may be that the constant concern expressed in the Bible over sexual immorality represented more of a fear that such practices would lead the Jews back to polytheism rather than a concern with the evils of such behavior per se. Finally, the real life circumstances characterizing Jewish life of the times offer some possible clues which may also be relevant in this interpretation. For example, the many injunctions against fornication may actually have been related to the sexual exploitation of children. Since marriage usually occurred at the time of sexual maturity (age 14, 15, etc.) and the ordinary examples of Biblical fornication, that is, sex between older individuals, resulted in relatively mild economic penalties (Exod. 22:17), it may be that the greater sin was to engage in sex with a child below the age of sexual maturity. Of course, these statements are mere speculations, but the basic point remains that the harsh characterization of the ancient Jews insofar as sexual morality was concerned may be an exaggeration by later writers.

On the other hand, as we have suggested, certain Jewish sexual practices, roles, and customs were probably shared by most of the cultures in the area. Thus, theirs was a patriarchal society in which women held an inferior status. And even the male circumcision ritual which Jews continue today as part of their "covenant" with God was probably borrowed from other cultures that emphasized a belief in the phallus's magical properties. Within these restrictions and the various codes of conduct, however, sex was accepted as a natural, human event.

As time went on, however, the importance of sex for procreative purposes became paramount. For Jews, God's directive, "Be fruitful and multiply," was more than just a human injunction; it was God's commandment. Although sex for other purposes was probably tolerated, there was to be no compromise with this divine declaration.

Insofar as male-female roles were concerned, the Jewish culture was clearly male dominated and many statements in the Bible reflect the female's second-class status in their society. The Jewish view of the woman's role, however, was much more complex than in other ancient patriarchal societies. If Jewish

---

### Sex life of the ancient Hebrews

"Though we know little about the actual technique of coitus practiced by the ancient Hebrews, there were relatively few prohibitions about the manner or postures of intercourse. Some rabbinical authorities recommended coitus be performed rapidly with a minimum of foreplay, but others were much more liberal. Sexual relations were permitted during pregnancy and nursing. In general, if the Song of Songs and Proverbs are any indication, the Jews were tolerant toward sexual activity between males and females, as long as penetration took place. Jewish law never indicted sexual relations between unmarried persons, although virginity in a bride was highly prized. Children born either in or out of wedlock were normally regarded as legitimate. Those classed as illegitimate were the offspring of unions impermissible in marriage, such as from incest or adultery, or from a union of a member of a priestly caste and a divorcee."

(From: Bullough, V.L. *Sexual variance in society and history.* New York: John Wiley and Sons, 1976, pp. 77-78.)

women occupied a subordinate status, they were also vulnerable to exploitation and abuse; and Jewish codes protected them from such treatment. Even the earliest Jewish accounts recognized the responsibility of the Jewish male to protect the welfare of the female. In addition to these rights, which Jewish women evidently aggressively pursued, Jewish history clearly reveals a recognition of female sexuality. Sometimes this recognition was cast in negative terms, for example, Eve's corruption of Adam, Delilah's cause of Samson's downfall; and sometimes this was cast in positive terms, that is, women who used their sexuality to promote the welfare of the society. But, if nothing else, the scriptures clearly suggest a recognition that women were sexually active and not simply the target of sexual interest on the part of the male. Further evidence of this position stems from the numerous codes which specified the husband's obligation to satisfy his wife's sexual needs, including the importance of bringing the woman to orgasm before the male achieved it himself (Bullough, 1976).

In this regard, it is also of interest to note that Jewish heritage is traced through maternal lineage rather than paternal ancestry. Thus, in cases of intermarriage, the offspring of a Jewish father and a non-Jewish mother is not considered to be Jewish by birth. These and many other customs and traditions suggest that, despite the clearly subordinate role of women in the place of ancient Jewish society, their status was recognized in a number of important ways.

In general, then, early in their history the Jews shared the permissive sexual values and traditions of other ancient Middle Eastern cultures. Gradually, however, as Jewish culture became more insulated as the result of monotheism, their social codes and customs diverged from those of their neighbors. Increasingly, monogamy began to be emphasized as the norm and the Jews began to condemn certain sexual practices. Prohibitions with increasingly severe penalties against homosexuality, masturbation, prostitution, and nudity emerged. The older concern for affiliation with polytheism was now joined by injunctions against the loss of semen, a theme that appears with increasing regularity in the scriptures. Since procreation was every man's responsibility to God, sexual acts which resulted in the loss of semen (masturbation, bestiality, homosexuality) were regarded as abominations (Lev. 15:16-18). Perhaps it is in this context that the story of Onan (Gen. 38:7-10) (which has often been interpreted as a condemnation of masturbation, although the act described is actually an example of coitus interruptus) can best be understood.

The situation with regard to homosexuality is equally complicated. The earliest mention of homosexuality in the Bible is in Leviticus: "Thou shalt not lie with mankind as with womankind; it is an abomination." What is not clear, however, is whether this warning accurately reflects early Hebrew values or, as we have seen, was actually written at some later stage in Jewish history, after homosexuality came to be considered deviant, and was then inserted in Leviticus. Similar ambiguity exists with regard to the story of Sodom, from which the term sodomy is derived, and is most frequently used to describe homosexual practices. Suffice it to say that, again, the scriptures are unclear as to the exact nature of the "abominations" of the sodomites, despite the traditional interpretation.

Whatever is the correct interpretation of the sexual morality

of the ancient Jews, by the time of the Babylonian exile (400 to 200 B.C.) sexual customs of the Jews had clearly diverged from those of their neighbors. The pleasurable dimensions of sex were still recognized, but they were to be realized only within the context of a monogamous marriage relationship. Certain rituals and codes were imposed on sexual behavior, such as the cleansing rituals and the abstention rituals for women during the menstrual period. However, as long as the importance of procreation was recognized and these various customs were honored, no serious restrictions governing sexual activity were imposed.

In the following centuries, assimilation by other cultures came to be regarded as a threat to Jewish survival, leading to even more rigid distinctions between acceptable Jewish practices and those that were associated with pagan cultures. The most important changes which occurred in this context were the strengthening of prior rules prohibiting intermarriage, which have continued to present times.

## THE CHRISTIAN TRADITION

A consistent and unified Christian code of sexual conduct did not emerge until some 400 to 500 years after the death of Christ. Many authorities credit St. Paul and St. Augustine as having been instrumental in identifying the early dominant themes of sexual morality which ultimately shaped the views of the Church on all matters related to sexual conduct. Paul advocated the emerging ideal of celibacy as the best way to control sexual urges. Marriage was reserved for those who were unable to resist these impulses, as reflected in his message to those who could not attain celibate status: "But if they cannot contain, let them marry: for it is better to marry than to burn." (1 Cor. 7:7-9). Paul's position on this issue appears to be in response to the various pressures to which the growing Christian movement was exposed. On the one hand, the early Christians condemned the sexual permissiveness of the Greeks and the Romans, a criticism that was borrowed from the Jews. Conversely, there was a recognition that complete sexual abstinence as advocated by the ascetics would be impractical and unpopular with the masses. Marriage within the constraints of Church doctrine, then, was offered as a compromise solution.

The theme advocating abstention from sex was elaborated on by a number of other early Christian authorities including St. Jerome and St. Ambrose, but it was St. Augustine (died A.D. 430) who is credited with having the most profound influence on the Church's ultimate position in favor of celibacy as the Christian ideal. After having engaged in a sexually active life up through the age of about 30, Augustine converted to Christianity and accepted sexual continence as the ideal state. In the *City of God* he expressed his views in this manner: "Lust requires for its consummation darkness and secrecy; and this not only when unlawful intercourse is desired, but even such fornication as the earthly city has legalized." Given such strong antisexual opinions by such powerful authorities, small wonder that those who were unable to resist their sexual impulses (that is, the vast majority of individuals) did so at the expense of shame and guilt.

Predictably enough, if even marital sex was suspect, other behaviors such as fornication, homosexuality, and adultery were even more heavily condemned. St. Basil, for example, held that fornicators should be excluded from the Sacrament for seven years, while adulterers as well as sodomists and bestialists should be excluded from the Sacrament for fifteen years.

Bullough (1976) summarizes the position of the early Christian Church in this manner:

> Christians were, in spirit, if not always in practice, ascetics, and justifying sexual intercourse only in terms of progeny meant that any kind of sex not leading to reproduction had to be condemned. It also meant that, even when pregnancy resulted, sex was not something to be enjoyed. The church fathers regarded sex as at best something to be tolerated, an evil whose only good was in procreation. Western attitudes have been dominated by their concepts ever since. [Bullough, 1976, p. 196]

During the next several centuries, these basic views were expanded by Church authorities. Thus, the Doctrine of Original Sin required a baptism in order to cleanse the infant of the sin committed in the conceptual act. A growing sentiment within the Church emerged, requiring celibacy on the part of the priesthood. Bodily urges were increasingly seen as the work of the devil, who was particularly active during sleep. Women came to be regarded as inferior beings and were to be "taken care of" in terms of true Christian charity, because they were incapable of exercising mature and sound judgment. Above all, the antisexual values expressed by Paul, Augustine, and others became even more firmly established in Church doctrine.

To some extent, these views were moderated by later Church scholars. In particular, Thomas Aquinas (1225-1274) in *Summa Theologica* argued that if intercourse was not a proper human function as Augustine claimed, at least it might be justified as a "second class" perfection (Murstein, 1974). He then went on (despite his own lack of sexual experience) to offer a set of rules covering every aspect of sexuality from kissing to coitus, from incest to bestiality, from fantasies to wet dreams (Strong, 1978). In this manner, Aquinas identified a number of sexual vices, the worst being those acts which were directed solely to experiencing pleasure and which excluded procreation: masturbation, bestiality, homosexuality, and deviations from the natural manner of coitus, which, according to Aquinas, was restricted to face-to-face contact with the female on her back (male superior position). Such vices were considered to be sins against God, as constrasted with fornication, adultery, seduction, rape, and incest, which were sins against another individual.

> The definitions of St. Thomas [Aquinas] tended to dominate all thinking on sexual subjects to the end of the Middle Ages with the result that any kind of sexual activity not leading to procreation could be classed as deviant whether it took place inside or outside of marriage. [Bullough, 1976, p. 380]

With the coming of the Renaissance and the Reformation (1400-1650) sexual values and codes changed, at least for those who adopted Protestant views. Martin Luther, in his *Treatise of Good Works,* ultimately rejected the Church's emphasis on celibacy, which he reserved for only those few individuals who were able to resist their sexual impulses. Consequently, and in

*Renaissance erotic art—Gurliv Romano c. 1495-1546 Palazzo del Tè, Mantova.*

contrast to Catholic tradition, sex in the context of marriage was entirely proper. Calvin essentially agreed with Luther that celibacy was not for everyone, and he was even more positive regarding the appropriateness of sex in marriage. No compromise was to be made, however, with the traditional sexual deviations: fornication, adultery, homosexuality, etc. In sum, marital sex became theologically acceptable in the sixteenth century. Although its pleasurable dimensions were still not directly acknowledged, the day when sex was considered intrinsically evil had clearly passed (Murstein, 1974).

With the Reformation, the influence of the Church in sexual morality diminished and the influence of sociocultural ethics grew. The effect of this development was the emergence of an increasing variety of local customs and values. Some countries, such as France, manifested a relative degree of sexual permissiveness, while others, such as Switzerland and Germany, expressed the values of Luther and Calvin. The Church of England, which had broken with the Roman church, came under attack by a growing number of influential citizens who wanted the Church to divest itself of *any* remaining vestiges of Catholicism. Many of these "puritans" left England and settled in several other countries, including New England in the American colonies. Their moral and sexual values were essentially Calvinistic, that is, they accepted sex within marriage but vigorously condemned any deviation from this standard.

> As to sex in particular, the American Puritans held that it was a fact of creation. God had created woman so that men and women together could "cultivate mutual society between themselves," but this was permissible only within the marriage and family. Sex was part of the divine plan, but it was to be confined to the bounds of monogamous marriage and subservient to the community's needs. It was neither to be abhorred nor exalted. Satan tempted the faithful into believing they were polluted by intercourse in marriage and led them to abandon coitus. The marriage could not pollute nor corrupt since marriage itself had been ordained by God as a means of producing offspring and avoiding fornication. Within the confines of the conjugal bed, the wife was equal to the husband and had the same rights he had. [Bullough, 1976, p. 505]

Along with establishing the respectability of conjugal sex, however, the Puritans attempted to persuade civil authorities to establish severe penalties for sexual misconduct such as adultery (so well described in Hawthorne's *The Scarlet Letter*) — which was considered to be an even more serious sin than fornication — sodomy, bestiality, masturbation, and oral-genital contacts. In many cases, this effort was successful. For example, in several of the New England Colonies the penalty for sodomy, bestiality, and adultery was death (Haskins, 1960). In varying degrees, the strict moral code prohibiting sex outside of marriage was accepted by most civil authorities in the United States, even up to recent times. Moreover, Puritanism exerted its influence on the emerging medical sciences. Thus, the famous American physician, Benjamin Rush, claimed that excessive depletion of semen (either through intercourse or more particularly through masturbation) was the cause of many disorders, including mental illness (Bullough, 1976).

Despite the Puritan influences in Colonial America, it is important to recognize that not everyone complied with these demanding requirements. In fact, there are numerous accounts of widespread prostitution and premarital sex, which suggests that the colonists were no different in their sexual practices from their predecessors. Moreover, the nature of Colonial society would have made it impossible to thoroughly implement Puritan values. America was very much a class-oriented culture; and it is doubtful that the Puritan sex codes applied to the lower classes, and they certainly did not apply in those Colonies where slavery was practiced.

At about the same time that pre- and post-revolutionary America was acquiring a sexual ethic in the image of Puritan values, European views were coming under the influence of a number of individuals who were interested in promoting social reform. Perhaps the prototype of this trend was the English writer Mary Wollstonecraft (1759-1779), who advocated marital reform, free love, the redefinition of male-female relationships, and equal rights for women (Sussman, 1976). These views were accepted and amplified by a number of other social thinkers, writers, artists, and philosophers. Although the ideas expressed by these individuals were suppressed for the time being, by the turn of the twentieth century they began to play a role in social reform in the United States as well as in other Western countries.

Of more immediate impact on sexual morality in the United States, however, was the new European morality which came to be termed Victorianism. The central thesis of this code, so named because it characterized the behavior of a large segment of influential English society during the reign of Queen Victoria, was the denial of sexuality, especially where sex came into conflict with one's economic and social responsibilities. The ideal Victorian male was urged to postpone marriage (and, therefore, deny or repress his sexuality) until he had "established" himself. The ideal Victorian female was delicate, pure, and incapable of any sexual feelings.

These values were expressed and elaborated upon in a large number of marriage manuals which served as popular guides in directing the lives of the typical Victorian citizen. Many of these texts relied on the authority of William Acton, a prominent English physician who translated Victorian values into a psuedo-medical context. Where earlier societies had relied upon religion and the concept of eternal damnation for those who engaged in sexual misconduct, Acton and the other "sex experts" of the times substituted the concept of disease as punishment for those who violated sexual morality. In his widely read text, *The Functions and Disorders of the Reproductive Organs,* Acton outlined a whole catalogue of horrible consequences that resulted from sexual deviations. For example, any boy who masturbated could be easily identified, according to Acton, by the following characteristics:

> The frame is stunted and weak, the muscles undeveloped the eye is sunken and heavy, the complexion is sallow, pasty, or covered with spots of acne, the hands are damp and cold, and the skin moist. The boy shuns the society of others creeps about alone, joins with repugnance in the amusements of his schoolfellows. He cannot look anyone in the face, and becomes careless in dress

and uncleanly in person. His intellect has become sluggish and enfeebled, and if his evil habits are persisted in, he may end in becoming a drivelling idiot or a peevish valetudinarian. [Acton, 1839]

The religious views which were responsible for such opinions are even more clearly reflected in Bostwick's very popular *Treatise on the Nature and Treatment of Seminal Diseases, Impotency and Other Kindred Afflictions*, which related anti-Victorian sexual behavior with disease and ended with the stern Biblical admonition: "The wages of sin is death."

It is impossible to determine the total impact that such views had on the sexual customs and beliefs of Victorian American society. However, several effects are clearly apparent. For one, a whole new language structure was devised in order to eliminate any reference to sexuality in "polite company." Ordinary speech was overhauled such that "breasts" became "bosoms," "legs" became "limbs," and even "underwear" was now referred to as "unmentionables." And, of course, no decent individual would employ terms and expressions which described the sex act or biological functions under any circumstances. Every form of art and human communication was censored in order to remove "offensive" stimuli. All literature, from the Bible through Shakespeare to contemporary novels, was censored (or bowdlerized, after Thomas Bowdler, the self-professed guardian of Victorian morality). Ancient art was concealed or transformed, for example, by placing fig leaves over strategic locations, etc. As late as the 1930s and 1940s (and even up to the present time although in a much more moderate manner) various censoring agencies were employed to eliminate any material of questionable taste from public view, with the definition of what constituted questionable taste left to the discretion of the censor. As we shall see in a later chapter, this led to what we might consider today ridiculous extremes. For example, movie scenes showing even a husband and wife sleeping in bed together were prohibited by the Hays office, a movie censoring agency. And when Clark Gable as Rhett Butler in *Gone with the Wind* (1939) uttered the word "damn," the production studio was fined, although the scene was permitted to remain.

In any event, one end result of Victorian practices was that our mechanisms for communicating even healthy sexual values could be expressed only in a negative way. Another result was that the role of female sexuality was totally denied. Whereas men were viewed as being constantly at the mercy of their sexual desires, such that, if not restrained, they would aggressively seek satisfaction, women were urged to be constantly on guard against the male's impulses and, even in marriage, to retain their "purity." The consequence of this disharmony was to cast sex roles in a competitive posture, such that, even under socially approved circumstances, the woman was cast in the role of victim while the man was responsible for placing her in such a degrading position. Inevitably, male-female sexual relationships were characterized by guilt, shame, and anxiety (Bullough, 1976).

A third dimension of influence involved the many practical efforts to eliminate sex completely from society. We have already seen how the Victorian era produced institutionalized forms of censorship, but other examples also abound. In medicine, for example, by 1900 physicians were recommending and practicing castration, clitoridectomy, cauterization of the genitals and prostate, severing the nerves leading to the penis, and the use of various mechanical devices to obstruct access to the genitalia or to make sexual arousal extremely painful (Sussman, 1976).

Finally, sex education went underground, relegated to the streets and to whatever sources of erotic materials could be obtained. For the typical family raised under Victorian influence, the catch phrase that best characterized the extent of parental sex education was, "You should be ashamed."

It would be a mistake to assume that American sexuality remained at the Victorian level after the turn of the century. On the contrary, a number of conditions emerged that produced changes in our sexual ethics and codes. Sex became more acceptable again during the Roaring Twenties, although it was still bad form to make too much of an issue about it; the earlier suffragette movement, which gained the right to vote for women, now began to focus its attention on more substantive social reforms, including female sexual rights as advocated earlier by Mary Wollstonecraft in England; and a sizable body of scientific and professional opinion, represented by the views of Sigmund Freud, was beginning to express concern about the damaging impact of Victorianism on sex, in particular, and human relationships, in general. The stage was set for the modest sexual reforms of the thirties and forties and the "sexual revolution" of the fifties and sixties.

## SUMMARY

Given the extremely diverse nature of society and the many different cultures which have influenced our own values and sexual morality, it would be an oversimplification to draw any direct parallel between the cultures of the past and contemporary sex life in America. Much has been made of the impact of Victorianism on our own sexual attitudes; and at least until the last thirty years, it is probably the case that the *public* morality of mainstream America is most accurately described in Victorian terms. Certainly, ours has been a sexually repressed society, and much of this can be attributed to the influence of the Victorian era. But, as we have seen, the Victorians did not introduce the double standard between men and women. The origin of this custom is lost in antiquity and can be traced back at least as far as the Old Testament. Similarly the sanctity of marriage as the proper and only place for sex has an equally long and complex history. The manner in which we define sexual deviance and our social and legal efforts to control sexual misconduct today are not unlike social mechanisms in a number of ancient cultures. Victorianism then did not initiate these values and customs — it merely lent its particular stamp of approval (or disapproval) to these practices.

In the final analysis, our culture now provides for a very wide latitude of individual expression. Obviously, there are those who are heavily influenced by Protestant values, Catholic values, Jewish values, etc.; and a case may even be made that there are elements in our society who share the values reflected by the ancient Greeks. The manner in which any or all of these influences are joined to determine the sexuality of any one given individual is a matter of further exploration in the remaining chapters.

# Chapter 2

## The Sexual Revolution

# INTRODUCTION

When we compare the status of sex in our society today with that of earlier decades, the obvious differences are quite startling. Evidences of a new sexual morality and a new sense of sexual freedom confront us daily. The nearest bookstore or newspaper rack offers a variety of sex-related features and information. Even such formerly staid standard-bearers of conventional morality as *Reader's Digest, Ladies' Home Journal,* and *Redbook* offer sex information, sex survey reports, and self-administered questionnaires analyzing such topics as masturbation, sexual incompatibility, and so-called frigidity, as well as articles urging every reader to join the "happy orgasm of the week" club. Spend an evening watching television and, without fail, you will see at least one program that features erotic or sex-related content, if only mildly so. On some evenings television seems to be devoted entirely to the so-called T and A (a euphemism for tits and ass) genre.

As we saw in Chapter 1, this open atmosphere did not always prevail. In fact, as late as the mid-forties educational courses in human sexuality simply were not available and the presentation of sex in the popular media would have produced a public outcry. The typical American male teen-ager of the thirties and forties just becoming aware of his own sexuality and subject to the normal curiosity of his age had to rely on his peers for his sex education and often turned to pictures of bare-breasted African women in the *National Geographic* to satisfy his interest in female anatomy. (For some strange reason, the conventional morality of the thirties and forties did not regard such material as pornographic or erotically arousing.) Even fewer sources of information were available to meet the sex education needs of the female teen-ager of the times.

Sex information and materials that were available only in private, if at all, during that time are now as close as the nearest magazine rack. Sex education courses are now offered in many public schools. The public's sexual curiosity has even reached into the White House; the alleged sexual escapades of several presidents have been examined and publicized. However one views these developments, sexuality from 1940 until now has become a matter of serious scientific study and a topic of open public discussion. Because these developments occurred so rapidly, so dramatically, and so radically, they came to be known as the *sexual revolution*.

Public and professional reactions to the sexual revolution have ranged across a broad spectrum. There are those who have welcomed the change as an expression of progress and enlightenment in a previously repressed society. Others have responded to these developments with alarm, viewing them as examples of commercial "sex exploitation." Still others, perhaps the guardians of traditional morality, view with distaste any public expression of a sexual nature. Regardless of one's own particular bias, one thing seems clear: each of us has been affected by the sexual revolution, for better or for worse and in varying degrees. Furthermore, the old standards of sexual morality must now be reevaluated in the light of the new knowledge and demands that characterize contemporary sexuality in America.

In this chapter we will examine the specific changes that constitute the sexual revolution, review the circumstances that have produced those changes, and consider how our lives have been affected as a consequence of those changes. For our purposes, we will equate the start of the sexual revolution with the publication of the Kinsey reports (described in detail in Chapter 4) in the later forties and early fifties although widespread substantive changes in sexual morality and behavior did not emerge until the sixties and seventies. In reviewing the causes of the sexual revolution, it is important to recognize that most of these events were twofold: they were the results of other social forces that produced them and they were the agents which facilitated further social change.

# CAUSES OF THE SEXUAL REVOLUTION

Social scientists are often hard put to explain major social changes, like the sexual revolution, since these changes typically involve many complex and interrelated events. Clearly, many important major social processes were at work. Some of them had emerged long before the sexual revolution became a reality; others emerged during the sexual revolution. One such gradual change was the general decline of religion as an influence on human behavior. Another was the increasing importance of science and improved technology. Although these factors had been operating for several centuries, their maximum impact most clearly emerged in the 1920s; and the process accelerated thereafter. Since such broad social events are difficult to document, what follows is more of an overview of the more obviously dramatic factors at work, rather than a detailed analysis of the series of changes.

Historians generally agree that dramatic social changes often emerge after the termination of a long and intense armed conflict, and surely World War II must qualify as one of the most devastating examples in history. Among other effects, World War II impacted on literally millions of individuals, exposing them to different cultures, different customs, and, of course, different sexual practices. Traditional sexual values, in particular the conventional rigid Judeo-Christian definitions of sexual misconduct, came under challenge from a variety of quarters. American soldiers stationed in the Far East, for example, were exposed to a sexual ethic that was quite different from their own. These men and other Americans came to realize that the traditional definition of sexual misconduct (that is, any sexual activity other than marital sex in the face-to-face position), was not shared entirely by other societies. The global impact of World War II combined with a number of other social and economic forces, all of which contributed to the momentum for change.

## ECONOMIC CHANGE

For a variety of complex reasons that are beyond the scope of this book, Western economic practices changed after the war from what had previously been a conservation-oriented value system to a consumer-oriented economy. Americans, about to realize the greatest degree of affluence in the history of civilization, became, with their increased buying power, a more pleasure-oriented society. Americans now had more things and more leisure time to enjoy them. The self-control, denial, and abstention of the Victorian period gave way to the self-indulgence of the fifties, sixties, and seventies; and sexual gratification was well up on the list in the search for pleasure.

## LITERARY DEVELOPMENTS

A more direct confrontation with traditional sexual morality after World War II was expressed in literary form. Although American novelists such as Edna St. Vincent Millet, Theodore Dreiser, and Sinclair Lewis had challenged conventional sexual morality in the twenties, it was not until the end of the war and shortly thereafter that a number of major breakthroughs occurred. Kathleen Winsor's *Forever Amber* titillated a sexually repressed society in this account of the sexual exploits of a French courtesan, and in *From Here to Eternity* author James Jones described the use of prostitutes by soldiers.

But it was Norman Mailer's book *The Naked and the Dead,* published in 1948, which, for the first time in American literature, vividly and realistically depicted the sexual language, behavior, and fantasies of men involved in armed combat. In addition to the powerful sexual themes described by Mailer, the book introduced the euphemistic term "fug" in the dialogue of male characters, closely reflecting, at long last, the true character of masculine speech under such circumstances. Mailer's book would appear mild in comparison to the completely explicit novels of today, but in terms of the lingering Victorian remnants of the forties it had a revolutionary impact.

With this major breakthrough the literary floodgates opened, and during the next thirty years every facet of sexuality was dealt with in a printed form that was available to anyone with the purchase price. Moreover, many of the classic works of erotica that had been reserved in libraries for research purposes now began to appear in bookstores. By the 1950s, respectable authors were writing about sexual themes previously considered taboo. There was, for example, *Lolita,* by Vladimir Nabokov, which described an erotic relationship between a teen-age girl and a middle-aged man. By the 1960s, there were literally no limits to sexual accounts available in popular novels. In *Valley of the Dolls* Jacqueline Susann described variations in group sex, and in *Portnoy's Complaint* the last barriers were broken by Philip Roth's explicit descriptions of male masturbation and scenes of fellatio and cunnilingus. And, for those readers who were still not satisfied, a vast supply of hard-core pornography previously relegated to underground and illegal sources now became freely available, either through mail-order houses or through bookstores that operated in every major urban center of the country. Now commonplace in almost every popular novel are explicit sexual descriptions, including portrayals of female masturbation and homosexuality (for example, in *Kinflicks*). Moreover, sex manuals (*The Sensuous Woman, The Sensuous Man, The Sensuous Couple, Joy of Sex, More Joy of Sex*) offer a host of suggestions for enhancing sexual pleasure and are freely available in most bookstores.

Along with these changes, as we have seen, even the

mainstream middle class sources of literature, such as news magazines and newspapers, began to reflect these recent changes in sexual expression. These developments were, of course, accompanied by similar changes in other media. Magazine photos have progressed from the bare-breasted *Playboy* bunny of the fifties to complete frontal nudity in *Hustler, Cosmopolitan,* etc.

*Soft-core porn magazine.*

The end of the war ushered in a similar revolution in cinema sex. When Howard Hughes in 1945 featured a daring exposure of Jane Russell's cleavage in *The Outlaw,* over the strenuous objections of the movie censorship office (thereby insuring the movie's box office success), he risked fine and imprisonment as a purveyor of pornography. Only twenty years later, the movie censorship system which had dictated the morality of the movie-going public for the previous several decades, was abandoned in favor of a rating system, in order to accommodate what seemed like an increasing demand for greater sexual explicitness and self-determined morality.

*Still from a skin flick.*

Finally, there were similar important changes in pop music themes and expression. A Cole Porter tune of the thirties, for example, might be risqué or even suggestive but never sexually explicit. All of this changed, however, when Elvis Presley gyrated his pelvis on national television, and the Beatles, Rolling Stones, and other rock artists acknowledged explicit sexual themes in the lyrics of their songs.

These are, of course, the most highly visible examples of the sexual revolution. They are now familiar to all of us and so commonplace that they do not require any further elaboration.

## SCIENTIFIC AND TECHNOLOGICAL DEVELOPMENTS

We have already seen how scientific perspectives gradually emerged as a general source of influence in almost every sphere of human endeavor. Certain scientific and technological developments, however, contributed even more directly to the sexual revolution.

Again, these factors did not emerge overnight but rather exercised their influence over a relatively long period of time. Thus, the explicit acknowledgment of the importance of sexuality by Freud and Havelock Ellis in the early 1900s was followed by the significant work of anthropologists Margaret Mead and Bronislaw Malinowski. Both of these social scientists studied and described in detail the courtship, mating, and sexual behaviors of several relatively so-called primitive cultures, thereby revealing the plasticity and relativism of sexuality. During the next thirty to forty years, other social scientists followed these pioneering efforts, which culminated in the work of Alfred Kinsey and his associates. (These developments are described in detail in Chapter 4.) For our purposes, their significance is highlighted by the claim that the Kinsey report served as a bench mark for the sexual revolution.

As important as these developments were, it was the technological advances in medicine and pharmacology in the late 1960s which perhaps had the most direct impact on the sexual behavior, and ultimately the sexual morality, of millions of individuals. For the first time in the long history of humanity's attempts to regulate conception, a reliable and convenient oral birth control technique was developed—"the pill." Although the pill does not meet all of the requirements of the ideal contraceptive (as discussed in Chapter 8), and research along these lines continues, there is little question that the availability of an inexpensive, effective, and simple contraceptive technique has changed the sexual lives of millions of individuals. Several statistics serve as an index of the impact of the pill: By the middle of the 1970s, 100 million women around the world were using oral contraceptives (Hatcher et al., 1978); and, despite the official opposition of the Catholic church, a sample of approximately 68% of American Catholic women in one study reported using contraceptive techniques, including the pill, other than the rhythm method. While moralists regard the pill as being responsible for increases in premarital sex, teen-age promiscuity, and the increase in the incidence of venereal disease, it is at least equally as plausible to argue that oral contraceptives have changed the sex habits of millions of individuals in constructive ways by virtually eliminating the fear of unwanted pregnancy.

A second pharmacological advance that emerged during the post World War II period and impacted on the sexual revolution was the discovery that penicillin and other antibiotics were effective in treating venereal diseases. However, as we shall see in a subsequent chapter, this development has proved to be a mixed blessing. The major difficulty here is that venereal disease is still regarded as a moral problem rather than as a medical problem (Strong et al., 1978) and for this reason, the full benefit of anti-VD treatment programs has not, as yet, been realized.

*Abortion ads and women's health clinic flyers.*

One final topic that is also relevant in this category relates to the increasing availability of safe abortion procedures, a factor that also emerged since 1960. Although the issue of abortion is still enmeshed in controversy (see Chapter 8), the fact remains that techniques of this nature are achieving increasing acceptance in our society.

## LEGAL DECISIONS

The post World War II period was a time of change in many ways, of course, other than sexual. A number of historical legal decisions were enacted in the fifties and sixties that dramatically transformed American values and affected the lives of all of us in a variety of ways. In particular, several Supreme Court decisions were reached that had a profound influence on American sexuality and that contributed to the sexual revolution. Although these events are described in more detail in subsequent chapters, their importance as both causes and effects of the sexual revolution is discussed here.

The first of these issues, pornography, produced several Supreme Court decisions, dating from 1957 to 1973. These decisions were essentially attempts to resolve the apparent conflict between the First Amendment's guarantees of freedom of speech, on the one hand, and the various State laws prohibiting the sale and distribution of pornographic material, on the other. Although the many complex issues related to this question still have not been resolved, the *practical* effect of the Court's decisions has been a greater availability of pornographic material to the general public with a reduced risk of criminal conviction on the part of the vendor. Most communities, for example, now tolerate X-rated movie houses and "porno shops" as long as they meet whatever the local requirements may be. Moreover, mail-order houses for sales of pornographic material operate with little risk of intervention on the part of the postal authorities.

No doubt a contributing factor to this dramatic departure from American tradition, which had dealt harshly with pornography prior to World War II, was the President's Commission on Obscenity and Pornography, established in 1968. As we shall see in Chapter 12, although the Commission's status was purely advisory, its majority recommendation that "Federal, State, and local legislation prohibiting the sale, exhibitions, and distribution of sexual materials to consenting adults should be repealed" was simply endorsing a posture that was, to all intents and purposes, already in effect at the community level.

A second issue that the courts became involved in was abortion, with results that bear directly on the sexual morality of Americans. Again, these events are described in other chapters, but here we will briefly examine the impact on the sexual revolution of the Supreme Court decisions. In the past, policies on abortion were determined exclusively at the State level, and all States maintained antiabortion legislation, which excepted only those cases where the mother's life was threatened. As a consequence of vigorous scrutiny by the medical profession, various antiabortion groups, and the Catholic church, *legal* abortions were relatively rare in the United States through the forties and fifties, although illegal abortions were apparently quite numerous. As our society changed, however, and more moderate voices within the antiabortion organizations themselves emerged, the rigid definition of legalized abortion changed and became more flexible. Various States, in particular New York and Hawaii, responded by decriminalizing abortion under many previously illegal circumstances. In 1973, the Supreme Court upheld the petition of a Texas resident who had argued that her State's antiabortion law denied her constitutional right of personal privacy, on the grounds that a fetus is not a person and therefore not entitled to constitutional protection. More recently, Congress in 1977, passed the Hyde Amendment which limited federal Medicaid funds for abortions to cases of rape or incest when the crime was immediately reported to the police, and cases in which two doctors certify that a full-term pregnancy would severely endanger a woman's health.

Again, the impact of these decisions still remains to be determined, but very clearly, the Court, at least in the case of antiabortion legislation, has associated itself with the forces of sexual change in our society.

## THE FEMINIST MOVEMENT

We have already described some of the changes in women's status which started in the twenties after women achieved the right to vote. Let us now consider some of these changes in detail and describe their impact on the sexual revolution.

The "new" woman of the twenties became more assertive, increasingly rejecting the role of the pure and sexless Victorian female. She expressed her new-found sexuality much more openly:

The length of her skirts rose during the 1920s from a few inches off the ground to knee height. Corsets, petticoats and cotton garments were cast aside and replaced by flesh-colored rayon and [by] silk stockings; she also took to an array of cosmetics to make herself more alluring: lipstick, rouge, creams, perfumes — all became vital. (Murstein, 1974, p. 419)

These changes were accompanied by a gradual shift in family structure to a less male-authoritarian model. Although the husband continued to maintain his role as the breadwinner and moral authority, the relationship between husband and wife was now one of respect and sharing. By the early fifties the ideal father image had changed from the stern authoritarian of the early 1900s to the kind and understanding type, like television's Robert Young, the father, who, however, still always knew what was best.

During this time a new social phenomenon arose — dating. Ultimately, dating became the normal custom for meeting members of the opposite sex, replacing the traditional family arranged approach to mate selection.

In spite of these changes, however, the new woman of the twenties and thirties still had little sense of her own sexuality. The socialization patterns of the female sex role continued to stress women's emotional dependence on men, men's role as the initiators of sexual activity, and womanly intuitiveness as contrasted with masculine rationality. The importance of fashion and the search for glamour that originated in the twenties did introduce a relative degree of sexual freedom, but the new woman of the twenties was still far from a sexual equal to the man.

The women's movement continued into the thirties and forties with fits and starts, sometimes making progress, sometimes retreating in the face of strong opposition. World War II, by necessity, provided for a whole new range of traditionally unfeminine work experiences for vast numbers of women. From Rosie the Riveter to the women in military uniform, a wide variety of economic and political events confirmed the growing feminist attempt to redefine the role of women in our society. However, with the end of World War II, the feminist movement once again retreated. Many working women were replaced by returning GI's, and the numerous day-care centers that had facilitated women's entry into the work force were closed (Gross and MacEwan, 1971).

The late forties and fifties marked the emergence of what Betty Friedan termed the feminine mystique, a complex of attitudes which encompassed the view that "the highest value and the only commitment for women is the fulfillment of their own femininity" (Friedan, 1963, p. 37). The housewife-mother was held up as the model for all women to identify with and emulate. Friedan documented the changes in the mass women's magazines that reflected and contributed to this traditional cultural ideal. That is, the magazines of the early war years depicted heroines who were independent, self-reliant, and of high spirit and strong character. They were career women who also loved and in turn were loved by men. By the 1950s, however, these same women's magazines no longer presented articles on politics and international issues but instead focused almost exclusively on articles about housework, child care, or

concern of the contemporary women's movement is for political, economic, and social equality. There is also a focus on modifying current sex roles which emphasize woman as sex object and man as success object (Pleck and Sawyer, 1974), with dehumanizing consequences for each. Finally, the women's movement emphasizes the right of self-determination, the right to make one's choices free of the restrictions of predetermined sex roles, including the woman's right to control her own body.

In sum, the contribution of the women's movement is only one of the concerns of feminists. They argue that sexual liberation cannot be achieved in the absence of legal, social, and economic equality. More specifically, with regard to sexuality, in the course of modifying traditional sex roles, the women's movement has demythologized masculine definitions of female sexuality (on the subject of the vaginal orgasm, for example) and asserted the woman's right to define her own sexuality, including the principle that women are indeed sexual, that sex should be pleasurable for women as well as men, and that any remaining vestiges of the double standard of sexual conduct should be relegated to the past.

## GAY LIBERATION MOVEMENT

The most recent social phenomenon to impact on and contribute to the sexual revolution was the gay liberation movement. Kinsey's report that homosexual experiences were relatively common among the heterosexual men and women in his sample, and that approximately four percent of American men and two percent of American women were exclusively homosexual, had a devastating impact on our sexual stereotypes. Prior to that time, Americans pictured the typical male homosexual in terms of the feminine parody, complete with lisp, limp wrist, and a swishy gait. The female homosexual stereotype, although less well-defined, was frequently cast in

*Women's rights demonstration.*

other aspects of this feminine mystique. In the women's fiction of the times, the typical career woman was either in the process of giving up her career to become a housewife or threatening to steal the housewife-heroine's husband away from her. The popularization of Freud's views on female sexuality (see Chapter 4) provided further ideological support for the advocates of the feminine mystique.

Despite the pressures against careers for women and the difficulties encountered by working women, the percentage of females in the work force continued to grow. Along with the other major social changes in the sixties, the struggle for women's rights achieved respectability once again for the first time in almost fifty years. The complexity of events that facilitated the development of this "second wave of feminism" are beyond the scope of this book, but we can point to several prominent circumstances. In 1961, President Kennedy appointed a national commission on the status of women; in 1966, the National Organization for Women (NOW) was founded; and 1967 and 1968 saw the proliferation of autonomous, grassroots women's groups (Freeman, 1979). Many of the women who formed these groups had participated in the social-action movements of the 1960s. While they were struggling for the rights of others, their ·consciousness of feminist issues was spurred by the contradiction of their being treated as second-class citizens (Freeman, 1979; Firestone, 1971; Stimpson, 1971).

The critical issues highlighted by the contemporary women's movement have been extensively discussed elsewhere, and we will present only the most salient features. In brief, the main

*Gay rights demonstration.*

terms of the woman who was masculine in appearance or manner. It became increasingly clear to a previously disbelieving public that there was no simple relationship between sexual preference, on the one hand, and general appearance and behavior, on the other. In fact, the vast majority of exclusively homosexual men and women were, except for this one behavioral dimension, indistinguishable from the most heterosexually oriented (that is, "normal") individuals.

During the 25 years from 1950 to 1975, homosexuals came "out of the closet," organized into a sociopolitical entity, and actively promoted legislation that attempted to end their persecution and establish their rights to practice their own sexual preferences.

In this manner, the gay lib movement joined the general spirit of protest and new thrust for openness that characterized the sixties. The effort to establish homosexuality as a matter of personal preference and to remove it from the category of the unnatural and perverse achieved a measure of success in 1973 when the American Psychiatric Association officially agreed to remove homosexuality from the category of abnormal behavior.

Although it is clear that this judgment has not filtered down to all elements of our society, the gay liberation movement has been instrumental in a general redefinition of abnormal sexuality and in advancing the principle that *any* form of sexual behavior is normal as long as it is engaged in by consenting adults.

## SUMMARY

In the preceding account covering about thirty years of political and social change, we have selected only those events that are generally considered to be of greatest importance in the sexual revolution. Certainly there were additional influences that were related to the sexual revolution. Some of these were more cause than effect, some were more effect than cause; but each in its own way impacted on our changing sexual morality. Such a list would include at least the following: President Kennedy, beatniks and hippies, Bob Dylan, the generation gap, the anti-Vietnam movement, Woodstock, the black movement, civil rights, Marilyn Monroe, the ecology movement, "pot" goes middle class, and blue jeans become the national costume. All of these represented forces of change in our society and as such were part of and further facilitated the sexual revolution. Considered separately, all of these various factors were limited in scope, each one affecting some one segment of our society or group of individuals more than another. In terms of their total impact, however, they made an indelible impression, creating changes that will make it difficult, at least in our time and perhaps for a long time to come, to return to the Victorianism or the Puritanism of the past.

## WHAT ARE THE CHANGES?

### Sex in the U.S.

From two nationwide surveys of female teens, researched by Melvin Zelnik, Young Kim, and John Kantner of Johns Hopkins University, comes this summary on the sex lives of America's young women:

1. By age 16, one in five has engaged in sex relations.
2. By age 19, two-thirds have engaged in sex relations.
3. More than nine out of ten have had sex prior to marriage.
4. By age 17, one in ten has been pregnant at least once.
5. One-fourth become pregnant before age 19.
6. Eight out of ten of these conceive prior to marriage.
7. Blacks are more likely than whites to become pregnant as teen-agers. But between 1971 and 1976, because of their increased sexual activity, the proportion of white teens conceiving increased considerably.
8. By using legal abortion, however, the proportion of whites giving birth declined substantially.

The full survey, "Probabilities of Intercourse and Conception Among U.S. Teenage Women, 1971 and 1976," appeared in the May/June, 1979, issue of *Family Planning Perspectives*.

In order to determine the changes that have been brought about by the sexual revolution, we can turn to two sources of information: those that are immediately apparent and conventionally identified, and those that have been examined through scientific study.

We have already suggested a number of obvious changes that are publicly acknowledged, and in Chapter 4 we will examine in detail the changes in American sexuality that have been scientifically documented. For our present purposes, we will offer a brief overview here of the changing sexual scene in America from the fifties through the seventies and in subsequent chapters we will describe them more thoroughly.

As we suggested earlier, many of the changes effected by the sexual revolution are apparent even to the casual observer; the most visible of these are in the popular media: newspapers, magazines, television, and the movies. Somewhat less evident, but equally important, is the more generally relaxed atmosphere in which sexual topics are publicly discussed. Even our highest government officials now acknowledge that sex is a fact of life; for example, President Carter's statement that he "lusted after women" simply means, in non-Biblical terms, that he finds women sexually attractive.

Many such examples are available from a wide variety of resources and it seems unnecessary to belabor the point: American society in the sixties and seventies is much less sexually inhibited than it was prior to World War II.

But what of the other and perhaps even more important dimensions of a sexually mature society: Has the sexual revolution provided for the sex education needs of our young people?

Has it helped reduce the ignorance and superstition of 2000 years of sexual repression? And, finally, has it contributed to the sexual enhancement and thus the personal enhancement of our citizens? Here, the answers are difficult to determine and require a more penetrating analysis. Simply because a popular TV program satirizes conventional antihomosexual attitudes, or a renowned photographer is deluged with volunteers willing to pose in the nude, does not mean that we are no longer burdened by the guilt and the superstitions of the past; as a matter of fact, many archaic sexual laws are still in effect.

There are other reasons for suggesting that the sexual revolution has not completely resolved the problems of the past. A number of writers have suggested that one effect of our changing sexual morality has been to substitute the present "tyranny of sex" for the earlier fear and hatred of sex (Gagnon, 1977). The pressures to perform, to be sexually sophisticated, to evaluate all human relationships on sexual terms are no less distortions than is the complete denial of sex.

Similarly, despite the heightened public awareness of sexuality, and the apparent general increase in sexual activity, there is still considerable confusion and ignorance. Numerous surveys, even among college students, reveal the perpetuation of sexual myths (one such myth being that masturbation causes insanity) and the existence of a serious lack of knowledge regarding such topics as venereal disease and birth control (see Chapter 4). It may also be the case that the public recognition of sexuality has not been accompanied by changes at the private/personal level. Most surveys continue to suggest that few parents discuss sex with their children and that most adult partners continue to feel inhibited in discussing sex, as we shall see in Chapter 4.

But perhaps most disturbing of all is the lack of progress in the area of sex education. The rationale underlying the efforts of sex educators is that a firm foundation of sexual knowledge will provide the kind of information that will enable people to make sexually responsible decisions based on fact and a positive appreciation of one's sexuality. Typically, the impact of sex education techniques is measured in terms of changes in knowledge, attitudes, and behavior. In terms of these measures, sex education efforts have been shown to be moderately effective in improving knowledge with selected populations. However, they have had little durable impact on sexual attitudes and sexual

behavior (Eisenberg and Kinder, 1979). For example, in one study, college women who had applied for abortion counseling revealed that over seventy percent of them had not engaged in birth control techniques at the time of conception, despite exposure to a sex education course that emphasized contraceptive practices and despite the availability of contraceptive services at their college health center (Monsour and Stewart, 1973). Similar results have been reported by other investigators (Spanier, 1976). Even those cases that claim that sex education has improved attitudes or constructively changed sexual behavior can be called into question because of inadequate scientific methods (Eisenberg and Kinder, 1979). It would appear, then, that even where sex education courses can overcome public and official hostility, their impact is sadly unimpressive. The challenge of the eighties, then, may well be the development of those educational programs that will indeed bring the sexual revolution to a successful resolution by providing more effective sex education.

## SUMMARY

Briefly considered, the sexual revolution may be regarded as a point in time when sex once again was reestablished as a vital human function. Comfort (1972) defines this changing status of sex as one in which we have moved from reproductive sex (sex as parenthood) through relational sex (intimacy between two people) to recreational sex (sex as physical play). Thus, more sexual options are available to each of us. It is now clearly the case that the traditional religious, legal, and social constraints that once determined our sexual decisions have been gradually eroded. Conversely, most of us are now in a much stronger position to exercise our own individual initiatives in determining which sexual options we will select. The question of whether this new-found freedom has enabled individuals to make their sexual decisions on the basis of knowledge, mature judgment, and a concern for the welfare of others — objectives most people would consider of merit — is a matter of some debate. If the importance of the sexual revolution is measured in terms of an emergence of a scientific perspective, then, clearly, considerable progress has been realized. The results of using these same scientific resources to gauge the broader impact of the sexual revolution have not, however, established whether the above objectives have been accomplished.

*Woman doing "man's work."*

*Man doing traditionally "woman's work."*

# Chapter 3

## Cross-Cultural and Cross-Species Comparisons

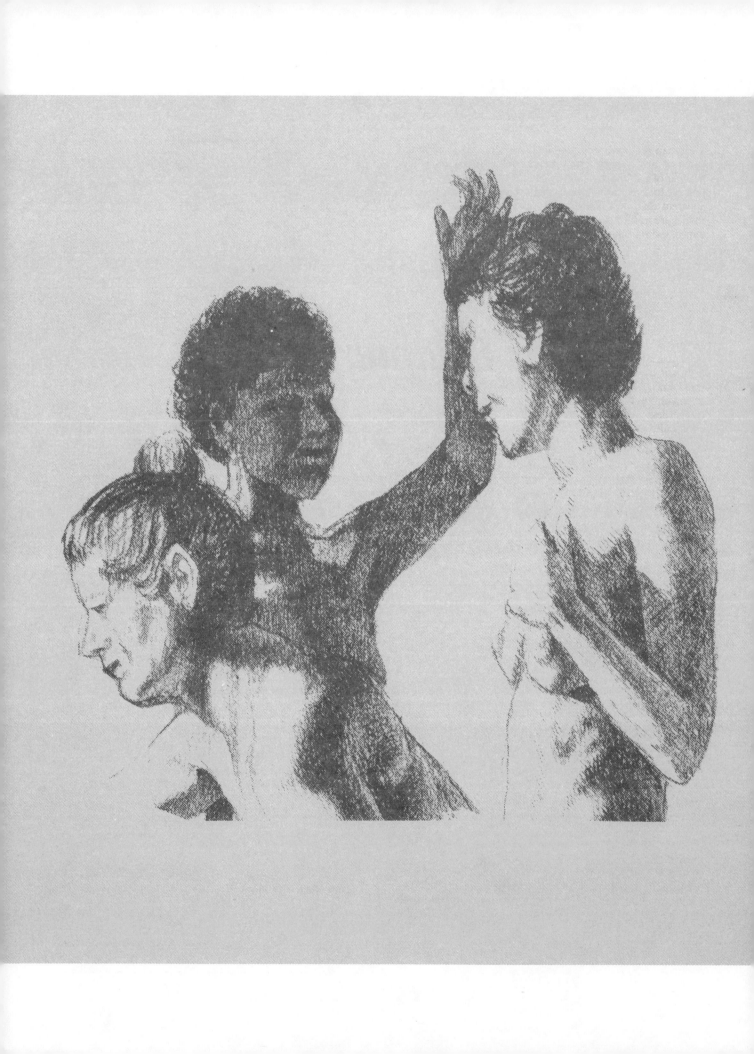

## CROSS-CULTURAL COMPARISONS

Human behavior, including sexual behavior, is an extremely complex and variable phenomenon with an almost infinite number of possible determinants and outcomes. While it is impossible to deny the biological components of our sexuality, it is apparent that most of the variety and flexibility of sexual activities are learned patterns of behavior that are culturally determined and transmitted.

We tend to take our own patterns of sexual behavior for granted. We behave sexually in certain ways with little thought about *why* we behave in those ways. If pressed, few, if any, of us could describe the variety of past experiences which shaped our present patterns of behavior. Moreover, we often tend to judge others in comparison to ourselves and to others like us in our culture; such egocentricity and ethnocentricity often inhibits us from understanding and accepting behaviors which are different from our own. A broader perspective should help us to understand our own sexual behavior patterns, in the light of those of other cultures, in a more realistic context. Thus, in this chapter, we will describe some of the diversity of sexual behaviors among other cultures.

## MORALITY

The kinds of behaviors that are sanctioned or prohibited vary greatly from culture to culture. An individual's decision regarding what is "right" or "wrong" has multiple determinants, such as the ethnic or subgroup culture to which one belongs, religious beliefs, common family structure within a society, and even the sex of the individual.

As we saw in Chapter 2, there have been many changes in the United States in the last several decades with respect to sexual mores. Despite the changes which have occurred in the last thirty to forty years, when we examine moral sanctions and prohibitions in a broad cross-cultural perspective, we find that, in general, our society is actually less permissive than most. For example, in their classic work Ford and Beach (1951) surveyed the sexual behaviors in some 190 different cultures around the world and found that the American culture was more restrictive than most. Likewise, Murdock (1960) studied 250 cultures scattered throughout the world and concluded that the United States was one of only three cultures which placed a general prohibition on intercourse outside of marriage. For most people in the world, some type of formal marriage bond is much less important in determining sexual mores than are other variables, such as kinship patterns or social status (Jensen, 1976).

There are, however, several cultures that are even less permissive than our own. Perhaps the most sexually restrictive culture studied is that of Inis Beag, a small island folk community of some 350 individuals off the coast of Ireland (Messenger, 1969). Any sexual activity outside of marriage is totally taboo, and the residents of Inis Beag marry relatively late in life: women at around age 25 and men at an average age of 36. Within marriage, the husband always initiates sexual activity, and only the male superior position is used. Stimulation of the partner's breasts or penis, passionate kissing, and all forms of

*Young children examining their bodies.*

In contrast to many other societies, children and adolescents in the United States typically receive little formal sex education. Although sex education is a part of the curriculum in many school systems, studies have repeatedly shown that, for the most part, our sexual attitudes and knowledge emerge from more informal influences. Some examples of informal education are: a parent cautioning a two-year-old not to go out unclothed; young children playing "doctor"; an adolescent discovering that genital stimulation is pleasurable; young adults gossiping about sexual topics between classes.

Given these sources of sexual information, the question still remains as to which of these circumstances, formal or informal, are most influential in predicting or shaping our actual sexual behaviors. Recently, the sociologist Graham Spanier investigated the impact of each of these sources of education on the premarital sexual behavior of 1,177 college students. Using statistical procedures, he was able to determine which of these variables best predicted sexual behavior. In males, the single best predictor of premarital sexual patterns was the activity of reading sexually related books and magazines, viewing pornographic materials, and being involved with other sources of erotica. Frequency of childhood sex play and of high school dating were of less importance. For females, being sexually assaulted or exhibited to as an adolescent were the most important predictors of premarital sexual patterns. Perhaps most significantly, the variable of "formal sex education course" was of no utility in predicting the sexual behavior of either males or females. Thus, we gain most of our important sexual information from informal sources, information which is often incorrect and misleading.

(Eisenberg, G. & Kinder, B.N. The impact of sex education programs: a review of the literature. Unpublished manuscript, 1979)

(Spanier, G. B. Formal and informal sex education as determinants of premarital sexual behavior. *Archives of Sexual Behavior,* 1976, 5(1), 39-67)

oral-genital activities are totally prohibited. Nudity is also unheard of among these people; partners keep their underwear on during intercourse and wash only those parts of the body that extend beyond their clothing, for example, face, neck, lower arms, legs, and feet.

One broad generalization does emerge from the studies of sexual behaviors of different cultures: all societies regulate sexuality in some way. Incest taboos, or some prohibition of intercourse between relatives, seems universal. However, the degree of closeness of relationship that defines incest does vary to some extent. Most societies also have some prohibitions against forcing sexual activity on another. But even such prohibitions against rape are not universal. Among the Trobriand Island people of the South Pacific, it is actually socially accepted and even expected for groups of women to rape a man (as long as he is from another village) if he ventures too close to the women's village by himself (Malinowski, 1929).

Determinations about which sexual activities are right and which are wrong seem almost totally culturally determined, with a tremendous amount of variability around the world. As we look now at more specific sexual behaviors and attitudes, we will continue to observe this extreme diversity among the different societies of the world.

## GENDER ROLES

All cultures have assigned certain types of behaviors (or roles) to men and certain types to women, although the specific roles vary greatly from culture to culture. Margaret Mead (1935) was one of the first investigators to document the variety of gender roles among different cultures. Her study of three primitive tribes in New Guinea is representative of the diversity of general behavioral patterns. Among the Arapesh, both males and females have developed what are often termed feminine traits. On the other hand, among the Mundugamor, both sexes seem to closely approximate a masculine stereotype. Finally, the Tchambuli live in what we might call a cross-sexed society: the males tend to take what we would consider feminine roles and the females, more masculine roles.

In recent years, gender roles in our American culture have evolved significantly and are generally more flexible and are much broader than in previous generations. Both women and men today are actively involved in occupations and activities that only a few years ago were identified with only one sex or the other. For example, women are becoming more active in business and politics, and it is not uncommon for men to take a more active role in child-rearing and household tasks. On the other hand, some societies function with very narrowly defined gender roles. Many tribes of the American Plains Indians operated with these strictly defined roles, where the women were exclusively responsible for the care of infants, for cooking, and for other household jobs, and the men were the providers of food and shelter (and were usually also required to be warriors, oriented toward aggression against other tribes).

One interesting phenomenon among societies that hold to such rigidly defined gender roles is that they generally also have some type of specific, alternative roles for those males who do

not or cannot fit into the expected role. For the Plains Indians of North America, this third gender role was that of *berdache,* or "not-man" (LaBarre, 1971). The *berdache* did not follow the traditionally held warrior role but instead dressed in women's clothes and performed traditional feminine tasks. The *berdache* was accepted by members of both sexes. As LaBarre has pointed out, the *berdache* was not necessarily sexually perverse but may be best described as a "social transvestite." Apparently the *berdache* was a relatively common phenomenon and was described by many early explorers of the American West. Recently the role of the *berdache* was very realistically portrayed in the motion picture *Little Big Man.*

There has been some speculation as to the determinants of gender roles, that is, whether these roles are biologically inherent or are for the most part culturally determined. The work of Barry, Bacon, and Child (1957) has been interpreted by some as supporting a biological basis for gender roles. These investigators found certain consistencies among roles in many cultures. Females were found to be generally obedient, responsible, and nurturing, while males were more self-reliant, achievement-oriented, and assertive. Today, however, most investigators emphasize that gender roles are mostly a product of social conditioning. For example, Whiting and Edwards (1973)

> Circumcision, the surgical removal of the foreskin, is a relatively common procedure performed on male infants in our country and other societies. This enables better cleansing of the penis and eliminates the problem of bacteria accumulating under the foreskin. Circumcision has also been a part of Jewish religious practices for thousands of years, symbolizing the covenant between God and the Jewish people. In the majority of more primitive societies, a variety of different types of "sexual surgery" are also performed; in these instances such practices are invariably symbolic in nature and are usually a part of broader social rituals. For example, most Australian aborigine societies perform an extensive circumcision ritual, symbolizing the young man's entry into adulthood. This is a mandatory procedure; marriage is not allowed unless the ritual is performed, and women of the tribe will not have intercourse with an uncircumcised man.
>
> Girls are also subjected to mandatory genital "operations" in many primitive societies. Ritual cutting of the hymen, cutting off part or all of the clitoris, or sewing up the vagina and later reopening it after marriage have all been reported among several African tribes. As in the case of sexual rituals for men, these procedures for women all have strong symbolic components, the most common being transition from one stage of life to another.

(Davenport, W.H. Sex in cross-cultural perspective. In F.A. Beach (Ed.), *Human Sexuality in four perspectives.* Baltimore: Johns Hopkins Press, 1976)

have suggested that the typical division of functions between the sexes has led to different socialization processes for males and females. Women usually have major responsibility for raising children and are thus more likely to stay closer to home; males have more varied interactions with a greater number of different people and in more settings. These investigators have concluded that, while there may be some biological basis for these general task assignments (like child raising), the *specific* resulting behaviors are culturally determined.

## CHILDHOOD SEXUALITY AND SEX TRAINING

As we shall see in other chapters, young children are sexual beings and begin to explore their sexuality at an early age. In spite of this fact, American parents are often upset when they observe their child engaged in sex play; such behavior is most typically repressed or punished by the parents in some way. Additionally, the American culture has no universally accepted way of educating young people about sexuality. Most of what we learn about sex as children in American society is learned informally from friends our own age. Often this turns out to be "the blind leading the blind," and many sexual myths and misconceptions are promulgated in this fashion. This general trend is seen among most so-called modern societies. On the other hand, in many more primitive cultures, some specific pattern of childhood sexual experimentation and education is an intricate part of the socialization process.

Illustrative of such a permissive and structured sexual socialization process is that practiced by the inhabitants of Mangaia, one of the Cook Islands in the South Pacific (Marshall, 1971). The children of Mangaia, like other children, begin sexual experimentation at an early age; instead of being repressed or punished, however, this exploration is accepted as a normal part of childhood. Both sexes regularly masturbate by age nine or ten. At around age 13, boys undergo a superincision ritual in which a slit is made along the top surface of the penis. (It should be noted here that some form of circumcision has been a relatively common practice among a variety of cultures worldwide.) During the two weeks or so that the young boy is

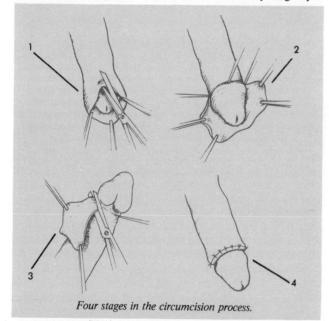

*Four stages in the circumcision process.*

recovering from this operation, he undergoes detailed instruction about specific sexual techniques, taught by the same "expert" (an older man) who performed the superincision. Included are instructions about a variety of sexual techniques. Major emphasis is placed on the ability to bring the woman partner to orgasm several times before the male permits his own climax. After this period of formal instruction, the young boy is permitted a practice exercise in copulation. This introduction to intercourse is with an older, experienced woman during which the

youth receives coaching and practice in those techniques he was previously taught. Girls also receive instruction in sexual techniques, although there is no counterpart to the superincision ritual or actual practice with an older, experienced male.

After such training, both males and females are sexually active during adolescence; it is not uncommon for them to have intercourse every night for several years. Girls tend to have four or five successive steady boyfriends before marriage, while boys tend to have slightly more girlfriends during the same period. During this time members of both sexes are looking for a potential mate, one with whom they can be as sexually compatible as possible.

In contrast are the sexual socialization patterns on the island of Inis Beag, where there is no sex education of the young. Sex is just not a topic to be discussed in that society. While other cultures are not so totally restrictive, there are tribes like the Bola tribe of Africa which have elaborate shame sanctions about many aspects of bodily functions, sexual activities, and nudity (Merriam, 1971). Taken in a cross-cultural perspective, our American culture fits somewhere in the middle. While we are not as restrictive as some cultures, we are much less permissive about different aspects of childhood sexuality and sex training than are many societies around the world.

## SEXUAL TECHNIQUES

Specific sexual techniques or patterns of sexual interaction vary greatly in our American society and also in other cultures. Kissing is common to Western societies and occurs in some form in most cultures. Variations in mouth-to-mouth contact do occur, however, such as among the Trobriand Islanders, who actively suck each other's lips and permit saliva to flow from mouth to mouth. Few societies, such as the Thonga tribe in Africa, do not engage in kissing at all (Ford and Beach, 1951). Some form of oral-genital stimulation is also acceptable in most societies. Attitudes toward masturbation vary widely from culture to culture, with some, like the Mangaia, actively encouraging this practice, and others disapproving, particularly when the activity is performed by adults.

Sexual positions during intercourse also vary greatly, with many cultures (like our own) allowing several different positions. The rear entry position seems more common among other cultures than it is in the United States. Anal intercourse is part of the initiation rites of adolescent males in some preliterate societies. Finally, some societies place certain prohibitions on intercourse during menstruation, or while the female is pregnant or nursing a newborn (Jensen, 1976). It can be seen, then, that it is in the area of these specific sexual practices where we find the greatest degree of variability both among cultures and within individual societies.

## BIRTH CONTROL PRACTICES

Davenport (1976) has pointed out that there is probably no society in the world that does not attempt to use some type of birth control method in certain circumstances. In many primitive societies, these attempts often entail the use of magical or symbolic potions and practices, the effectiveness of which is questionable at best. Abstinence is used by some societies. Even more widespread is the practice of coitus interruptus, or withdrawal of the penis from the vagina just before ejaculation. This practice is also very unreliable. Davenport suggests that one reason abstinence or coitus interruptus is so commonly practiced in many primitive societies is that both methods can become a part of the culture simply by the awareness that conception results from the injection of ejaculate into the vagina. All societies, except perhaps a very few, seem to possess this simple knowledge.

## HOMOSEXUALITY

Some type of homosexual activity has been reported in many cultures throughout the world. Ford and Beach (1951) indicated that homosexual activity was rare, or at least engaged in secretly, in 28 of the 76 societies studied. In general, homosexuality is most likely to occur among adult and adolescent males; female homosexual activities occur less frequently, although Jensen (1976) reports that female homosexuality is more accepted than male homosexuality in all societies throughout the world.

The actual incidence of homosexual activities varies greatly among cultures. In some societies almost all the males have had at least one homosexual experience, and in some societies virtually none of the males have had homosexual experience (Gebhard, 1971). While many societies have (or do not have) laws or customs against homosexuality, these social pressures (or the lack of them) by themselves do not seem to account for the relative presence or absence of these behaviors in any given culture. Homosexuality occurs even in those societies with strict prohibitions against such behavior, although it may be engaged in secretly and participants may be punished if discovered. Conversely, in the Mangaian society discussed above, even though there is little or no social pressure against homosexuality, almost no homosexual behavior is reported in this society. Perhaps the general availability of heterosexual partners, as a result of the high degree of permissiveness toward heterosexuality, explains this low incidence of homosexuality among the people of Mangaia; and the same may be said of other, similarly permissive societies. This explanation, however, is a purely speculative one at present.

Frequency of homosexual activities also varies among societies (Gebhard, 1971). One generalization can be made: exclusive or near-exclusive homosexuality on the part of any one individual is found most often in more complex, highly organized cultures like our own. Such behavior patterns appear to be very rare in simple, preliterate societies. Finally, it should be noted that homosexuality has never been found to be the predominant form, culturewide, of sexual behavior in any of the cultures investigated.

## SEXUAL DYSFUNCTIONS

We have very little data concerning sexual dysfunctions or inadequacies in preliterate or so-called less civilized societies. In the Irish folk community Inis Beag, women apparently do not achieve orgasm (Messenger, 1969) and thus, by modern Western definitions and standards, would be considered dysfunctional. As noted above, however, Inis Beag is a sexually repressive and sexually naive culture, and it is possible that the women of that society are not even aware of the possibility of female orgasm.

Jensen (1976) has reported that impotence, or the inability to obtain an erection, is a common problem in the Mangaian society, where it is given the status of a "disease." As described earlier, sexual intercourse is highly performance-oriented in Mangaia, with the male expected to bring his partner to orgasm several times and to delay his own climax for 15 to 20 minutes. Masters and Johnson (1970) have found such performance expectations to be strongly implicated in impotency among American men, and it is very likely that these same variables are significant in the etiology of impotence among Mangaian men.

## SUMMARY

When we look at the sexual behaviors of various societies throughout the world, we see a great deal of diversity in mores, attitudes, and practices. On the other hand, we see also that all humans seem to have a great deal in common with respect to sexuality. Virtually all of us share a biological sexual drive which, in some fashion, is expressed over a long period of time, beginning in childhood. Sexual activity takes many forms; and the religious, philosophical, and moral assumptions of a society appear to be the most important determinants of that society's mode of sexual expression.

## CROSS-SPECIES COMPARISONS

References have been made in this book to experiments done with animals. It seems appropriate, therefore, to examine briefly selected data from the literature on animal studies, especially as it may relate to human sexuality. The first reason these studies are significant is that much of the data is indeed relevant to humans, for example, certain hormonal and biochemical findings. We must, however, be cautious in generalizing from animal studies to human behavior. Behavior in a lower organism that appears similar to human behavior is not necessarily identical to the human behavior. Such a similarity can be misleading if not examined critically. An animal behavior which is similar to a human behavior can have a very different origin and may be influenced by one or more of a variety of different biochemical, hormonal, neurological, psychosocial, and behavioral variables. For example, sexual behaviors between members of the same sex have been observed in many species. To use such examples as models of human homosexuality, however, simply because of the observed similarities in overt behavior and without consideration of possible origins and other variables, is clearly inappropriate.

A second reason for discussing sexual behaviors in lower organisms is to bring an evolutionary perspective to the study of sexuality. Some similarities between related species may be a function of their common phylogenetic ancestry. As Beach (1976) has stated, "Man is no more a naked ape than chimpanzees are hairy people, but he is a mammal and a primate, and as such shares certain physical and behavioral characteristics with other members of his class and order" (p. 297).

## A CONCEPTUAL FRAMEWORK

Beach (1976) has proposed a conceptual model of mating behavior which can be useful in comparing certain aspects of sexual activity in organisms, including humans. Much previous research with both animals and humans has often investigated small, discrete behavioral sequences and has thus underemphasized the complexity of sexual activity. Beach's model will be useful in this respect. While it still allows us to examine specific parts of any mating sequence, it also emphasizes the relationship and interactional aspects of sexuality and points out that successful completion of any mating behavior requires both stimulus input and behavioral output by both partners involved.

Beach's conceptual model breaks down mating behaviors into the following: sexual attraction, appetitive behaviors, consummatory behaviors, and postconsummatory behaviors. Sexual attraction in humans is a complex process, originating and being influenced by a variety of psychosocial and cultural determinants. Human definitions of sexual "attractiveness" vary greatly from culture to culture and from time to time within the same culture. In nonhuman species, the determinants of sexual attractiveness appear to be hormonal in nature. Most of us have observed the premating behaviors of dogs or other household pets. Male dogs are attracted by the smell of the vaginal secretion of the female when she is in heat. This attraction can be changed either by bringing the female out of heat or by castrating the male. Female dogs in heat prefer the odor of urine from normal dogs to that of castrated dogs; however, once the female completes the estrus cycle, this preference disappears. Similar findings abound with respect to other lower organisms, and it seems clear that sexual attraction in nonhumans is hormone-dependent (Beach, 1976).

Whereas "attractiveness" in nonhumans is an abstract concept, inferred from observed behaviors, appetitive behaviors are more directly observable and take more elaborate and ritualistic forms often termed "courtship." Various forms of pursuit by a male after a female in estrus are examples of these appetitive behaviors. We often think of these appetitive behaviors as primarily male behaviors, with the female of the species taking a more passive, receptive role. Beach's conception of mating behavior is unique in this respect, emphasizing the interplay of the sexes during sexual activity and particularly the fact that, for most species, the female role extends beyond simple receptivity to include active, appetitive behaviors. Again, most of us have observed the "teasing" behavior of a female dog in estrus. She is not just receptive to the male, but she may alternately actively present herself to and then run from her prospective partner. Analogous appetitive patterns are seen in most nonhuman females, and, like attractiveness, these behaviors are basically determined by hormonal variables.

Beach points out an additional function of these appetitive behaviors: that of "screening" with respect to possible incompatibility. Some "selection" of partners obviously does take place in nonhumans, as again evidenced by the commonly observed behavioral patterns in dogs. Several male dogs may congregate around a female in heat, yet the female may be unwilling to mate with some males while being quite receptive to others. While we can only speculate about the possible evolutionary and socialization implications of such a process, it is important to note that some potential for selectivity in mating is not just a human characteristic but also seems to be an integral part of the behavioral patterns of lower organisms as well.

Consummatory behaviors are those responses centered around the actual art of copulation (Beach, 1976). These are usually species-specific and often stereotypical in nature. For males, the principal consummatory behaviors are mounting, insertion of the penis and thrusting, and ejaculation. The female counterparts are the assumption of an appropriate and accessible mating position and the maintenance of this position until intravaginal ejaculation occurs. In almost all mammalians, the female is approached from behind by the male, although face-to-face copulatory patterns are sometimes seen in chimpanzees and apes. Here, of course, humans display much more variability in behavioral patterns than do nonhuman organisms.

*Typical rear-entry animal mating position.*

Postconsummatory behavior refers to the male and female behavioral sequences after ejaculation. Human patterns have much in common with lower organisms in this respect. For example, the human male experiences a refractory period after ejaculation, that is, a period of time during which he is temporarily "impotent," or unable to perform sexually. Similar findings have been reported for all male mammals that have been closely studied to date. The lengths of these refractory periods vary according to age and number of preceding ejaculations in the same sexual episode. On the other hand, female mammals (including humans) are capable of sexual activity over a longer period of time without these refractory periods; and females are, in general, capable of more sexual matings in a given time period than are males of the species.

This conceptual model of mating behavior as proposed by Beach represents an important innovation in the study of sexual patterns of different organisms, including humans. It should serve to emphasize the reciprocity and relationship aspects of sexuality among the nonhuman species, components that have often been played down or overlooked by investigators. The breakdown of mating activities into separate components should allow us to be more specific in our future investigations and at the same time alert us to the fact that mating behavior is actually a long continuum of interrelated and often complex behavioral components. Finally, it provides us with a consistent theoretical framework by which we may compare the sexual activities of different species, including humans. Let us now turn to some comparisons of selected sexual behaviors among different species.

## MASTURBATION

Some form of self-stimulation has been reported in a variety of nonhuman species (Beach, 1976; Chevalier-Skolnikoff, 1974; Rowell, 1972). But not all autogenital stimulation qualifies as real masturbation in the framework of Beach's model since some of these behaviors are not truly appetitive or consummatory. For example, males of many species lick or manipulate their genitals at various times, particularly immediately after mating; these responses then are grooming responses, not sexual responses.

True masturbatory behavior has been observed in several species of mammals. Males typically rub the penis against some object. Monkeys have been observed to use their hands and, because of their body flexibility, can even orally stimulate themselves. Captive female monkeys have been observed to insert a foreign object into the vaginal opening and to move it rhythmically. Many of us have probably observed some kind of self-stimulative behavior in domesticated animals or in zoos. It was once thought that masturbatory behavior occurred only among captive animals, but we now know that it occurs also among feral animals (Beach, 1976; Carpenter, 1942). Masturbation does appear, however, to be more common among captive animals than among those in the wild. Captive male chimpanzees often masturbate, even in the presence of receptive females, a phenomenon Beach (1976) suggests may be due, in part, to the boredom of captivity.

Thus, there are striking similarities among the masturbatory behaviors of humans and the lower organisms, especially the primates. Beach feels that the similarities are so consistent as to conclude that masturbatory patterns of behavior for men and male primates is probably traceable to their shared mammalian-primate origins. He states:

> The self-stimulatory activities of male monkeys and apes are so similar to autogenital behavior in human males that we are justified in provisionally defining male masturbation as a basic primate trait. As far as females are concerned, the evidence is less convincing, but sex differences in frequency seem common to humans and other primates and planned observation of nonhuman species is needed before any conclusion is justified. [Beach, 1976, p. 314]

## HOMOSEXUAL BEHAVIOR

Sexual activity between individuals of the same sex has been reported for many nonhuman species. The typical pattern for both sexes of a given species generally involves the same sexual mounting pattern that is typical for that species. Beach (1968) reports that some type of female-female mounting has been observed in 13 different species and is most likely to occur when one female is in estrus. Among captive male monkeys, attempts at anal intercourse have been observed (Erwin and Maple, 1976). Lorenz (1966) has even reported a long-term homosexual relationship between two ducks, animals that typically form lifelong bonds or relationships.

Again, many apparent similarities have been observed between, on the one hand, homosexual behaviors of humans and, on the other hand, homosexual behaviors of nonhumans. However, unlike masturbation, a critical analysis of the data does not suggest that such behaviors among the several species are, in fact, analogous. Homosexual behaviors in lower organisms have been termed a "temporary inversion of mating roles" (Beach, 1976), explainable in terms of biologically inherent stimulus-response relationships which are to some extent influenced by sex hormones. While the behaviors may "look the same," human homosexuality appears different in terms of both causal mechanisms and the functional outcomes. Consequently, the use of animal data as a model of human homosexuality is not appropriate in the light of our present knowledge.

## OTHER SEXUAL BEHAVIORS

When other human and animal sexual behaviors are compared, we find both similarities and differences. One major difference has to do with breeding seasons. Humans are typically receptive to sexual stimulation at all times, even at those times during the female's menstrual cycle when conception is unlikely. This is not true among lower organisms. Most animal females are truly receptive only while in estrus, thus increasing the likelihood of conception and procreation of the species. Male animals are not likely to make appetitive responses unless a receptive female in estrus is available, although this does occur on occasion.

Most nondomesticated or feral animals have a specific breeding season, thus insuring that the offspring of such matings will be born at a time most suitable to survival (usually late winter or spring). Jensen (1976) reports that this phenomenon also seems to occur among humans, in that there is a slight but significant tendency toward seasonal births. He further suggests that this tendency may be due to meteorological factors, since the two hemispheres of the earth have opposite seasons and correspondingly opposite peaks of birth. The exact reasons for this phenomenon, however, are as yet unknown.

The specific structure of relationship or bonding patterns varies greatly in the animal world (Lorenz, 1966), just as it does among humans. Some species form permanent, lifelong bonds between two individuals. Other species, such as many herding animals, may exhibit a pattern in which one dominant male is involved in mating with several females. In other species, mating is more of a random event, with the female being receptive to the first available male and with absolutely no long-term bond being formed. The female of certain insect species ensures no long-term bonding by eating her mate after impregnation!

One type of relationship pattern, promiscuity, has generally been thought of as a typically human behavior. However, frequent and apparently indiscriminate mating has been reported in at least one nonhuman species. During her observational study of chimpanzees living in the wild, Jane Van Lawick-Goodall (1968) observed one female chimpanzee who mated with a dozen different males in the same number of minutes.

## PHEROMONES AND SEXUAL BEHAVIOR

Pheromones are biochemical substances secreted outside the body (as opposed to hormones, which are secreted internally). Through the sense of smell, pheromones serve as an important means of communication among most animal species (Wilson and Bossert, 1963). The fact that animals make extensive use of the sense of smell has been known for some time. But more recently, many investigators have examined the possible effects of pheromones (Karlson and Luscher, 1959).

Pheromones were first discovered in insects, and many have since been identified in other organisms; several have been produced synthetically. Pheromones have been shown to be one prominent way in which lower organisms communicate sexually. With mice, pheromones have been implicated in the female's choice of a mate (Rogel, 1978). Female mice which have been impregnated have even been found to abort the pregnancy when exposed to the presence of the smell of a strange male mouse (Bruce, 1960), presumably because of the effects of some pheromone.

Comfort (1971) has speculated that pheromones may similarly play an important role in human sexual behavior, especially in sexual attraction and arousal. In 1974, Michael, Bousall, and Warner isolated fatty acids in the vaginal secretions of women which structurally were closely related to similar substances thought to be sex-attractant pheromones in monkeys. Other studies, both behavioral and biochemical in nature, also seemed to suggest a relationship between what might be termed human pheromones and human sexual behavior. However, recent critical reviews of this data (Beauchamp, Doty, Moulton, and Mugford, 1976; Rogel, 1978) have cast considerable doubt on this speculation. No mammalian reproductive pheromone has been definitely chemically identified; there is doubt that the substances tentatively termed human pheromones actually meet the traditional, scientific criteria that have been used to define nonmammalian pheromones. Also, vaginal odors have been found to be very complex, highly individualized, and affected by a variety of environmental factors (including diet, phase of menstrual cycle, and the use of deodorants and perfumes). These findings have led Rogel (1978) to conclude that while olfactory cues may influence human behavior in many ways, it is not likely that any form of chemical communication plays any significant role in the control of human sexual behavior.

## SUMMARY

There are many commonalities among the observed sexual behaviors of humans and other species. However, the determinants of such behaviors, as well as specific behavioral patterns and outcomes, are quite diverse. For nonhuman species, the main determinants of behavior appear to be inherent, instinctual, and hormonal in nature, although some amount of learning is also apparent in animal behavior. Compared to lower organisms, human sexual behavior is determined more by sociocultural and behavioral variables. A review of the cross-cultural literature has served to point out both the great diversity of human sexual behaviors and the significant role that cultural variables play in the actual modes of expression of such behaviors.

# Chapter 4

## The Sex Researchers

# INTRODUCTION

The scientific study of sex is a relatively recent development. The physical and biological sciences have a long history of scientific investigation dating back hundreds of years. The anatomical and physiological aspects of human functioning also have a long history of study, yet within that total body of knowledge there was little data collected regarding sexuality until the nineteenth century. Up to that time, almost everything we knew with respect to the anatomical, physiological, and emotional components of human sexuality was merely the result of speculation and opinion, often inaccurately tied to the political and religious doctrines of the times.

In the last 100 years, human sexuality has finally become an area of legitimate scientific interest and has finally been looked at more objectively. This chapter will discuss the major historical developments in the recent history of sex research, with emphasis on the prominent individuals involved, the general trends that have emerged in terms of the research methodologies, and the general findings that have been reported. Research findings in a variety of specific areas, such as homosexuality, the effects of pornography, and the results of treating specific sexual dysfunctions, are reported in detail in other chapters.

# THE EARLY RESEARCHERS

In the mid to late 1800s, several investigators became interested in many aspects of human sexuality. In most respects, these individuals did not conduct research in the true sense of the word. Little actual experimentation was done; and the case study approach, with all the attendant problems such as lack of generalizability, was heavily relied upon. Also, some of the hypotheses proposed were stated in such a manner as to be essentially untestable. Finally, it must be remembered that all of these early investigators were working and writing at the time the Western world was just emerging from the Victorian era, a time of extreme restrictiveness, repression, and negative values and attitudes toward sexuality. As we shall see, these Victorian values strongly influenced the attitudes and beliefs of some of these investigators, leading to inappropriate and inaccurate conclusions based, not on data, but on religious and philosophical grounds.

## KRAFFT-EBING

Richard von Krafft-Ebing (1840-1902) was a German physician who specialized in forensic psychiatry and was the most noted expert witness of his day in the criminal prosecution of sex crimes. Because of his purported expertise, his ideas about sexuality were accepted as truth by both professionals and lay persons throughout Europe and were of great importance in shaping the sexual attitudes of several generations. Unfortunately, most of his theories, in the light of today's knowledge, were inaccurate or incorrect and added little of scientific value to the study of sex.

His famous book, *Psychopathia Sexualis,* first published in 1886, presented very negative views regarding sex in general and in fact viewed most sexual behavior (except heterosexual intercourse between married adults) as terrible diseases. Intended originally only for professionals, *Psychopathia Sexualis* became a best seller and has been reprinted many times. A series of case studies, *Psychopathia Sexualis* begins with the most lurid descriptions of sex crimes in the classical sense, such as sex murders and crimes against children. Krafft-Ebing then proceeded to describe other sexual behaviors (e.g., voyeurism, masturbation) in this same negative tone. Inaccuracies abound in these descriptions. For example, he saw transvestites, transsexuals, and homosexuals as all "suffering" from different stages of the same "disease." Perhaps his most influential misconception was that he viewed all sexual variations as stemming from two basic causes: masturbation and genetic influences. He gave such weight to genetic predispositions that almost all the case studies began by "documenting" problems (sexual, psychological, or physical) among the relatives of the subject under study.

Krafft-Ebing's writings were very influential for several decades. Not only did he reinforce the negative views and misconceptions of the Victorian age, he added to them. Fortunately, few people today place much validity in the majority of his theories.

---

Krafft-Ebing believed that most "sexual perversions" were strongly influenced by genetic predispositions. Thus, he went to great lengths to "document" evidence of this nature among family members. An example is the case of S., whom Krafft-Ebing incorrectly identified as a hermaphrodite. (S. was a woman who dressed and lived as a man but whose sex organs were clearly female.) The following are only some of the disorders that Krafft-Ebing reported among S.'s family members.

> A sister of the maternal grandmother was hysterical, a somnambulist, and lay seventeen years in bed, on account of fancied paralysis. A second great-aunt spent seven years in bed, on account of a fancied fatal illness. S's mother was nervous, and could not bear the light of the moon. She inherited many of the peculiarities of her father's family. One line of the family gave itself up almost entirely to spiritualism. Two blood relatives on the father's side shot themselves.[1]

Today, few of us would accept any of the above examples as evidence that S. "inherited" her problems from her family. Such beliefs, however, were quite common only a century ago as well as more recently. Also of interest in this case study is the fact that, after documenting the peculiarities in S.'s family, Krafft-Ebing went on to discuss how her father had raised her as a boy and was careful to assure that she was treated "always as a young gentleman" during her adolescence. It is likely, then, that S.'s behavior as an adult was shaped or learned through this set of unique experiences as a child, rather than determined by some hereditary condition.

(Krafft-Ebing, R. von *Psychopathia sexualis.* New York: Stein and Day, 1965 ed., pp. 284-285)

## ELLIS

The views of Havelock Ellis (1859-1939) were in direct contrast to those expounded by Krafft-Ebing. Ellis viewed a variety of sexual behaviors not as terrible deviations but only as variations of normal sexual expression. Furthermore, he viewed sexuality in a relativistic sense. Thus, sexual behaviors that were different from one's own behavior were not necessarily wrong, sick, or perverted. It is indeed remarkable that he, raised in the strictest of English Victorian homes, ever came to hold such enlightened values for himself and others, values that would not seem out of place even today. Undoubtedly, these attitudes were further reinforced by his relationship with his wife, Edith, who engaged in a series of homosexual affairs during their marriage. Ellis apparently accepted her behavior just as he accepted variations in sexual expression in others.

Ellis was a prolific writer throughout his life and, like Krafft-Ebing, gained much of his knowledge through case studies. However, he also attempted to provide empirical verification for a variety of sexual phenomena. For example, Victorian society held very negative attitudes toward nocturnal emissions (wet dreams), thought by many to be closely akin to venereal diseases. Termed spermatorrhea, nocturnal emissions were viewed as a progressive disease, with a rapid increase in the frequency of occurrence if left untreated. Spermatorrhea was said to lead to lethargy, infertility because of abnormal sperm production, and nervous system involvement, ultimately producing death. Like most normal males, Ellis had experienced these "wet dreams" since early adolescence; and, partly out of concern about their effect on his health, at age 17 he began to keep an accurate record of his own nocturnal emissions. After twelve years of record keeping he was no doubt reassured to find neither a progressive increase in frequency nor any of the predicted ill effects on his health.

Because of his empirical approach and his ability to detach himself from the Victorian morality, Ellis' writings contain much accurate knowledge supported by more contemporary researchers such as Kinsey and Masters and Johnson. For example, in dramatic contrast to the popular beliefs of his time, he stated that masturbation was common among both sexes and began at an early age. He further pointed out that most youngsters engage in sexual activities and experimentation until prohibited by parents, who, in the process, instill most of our adult negative attitudes regarding sexuality. Ellis also viewed sexual dysfunctions such as impotence and frigidity as usually stemming from psychological rather than organic sources, and he discussed the similarities between male and female orgasms.

In addition to providing accurate information about many aspects of human sexuality, Ellis was also a social critic and advocated social changes which were quite liberal for his time. His view that most people were extremely ignorant with respect to sexual matters led him to be an early advocate of organized sex education. He was also critical of the place of women in society and worked for equality of men and women in terms of sexuality as well as in a broader sense, as in the labor market. All things considered, Havelock Ellis was extremely influential in shaping the sexual attitudes and knowledge of the twentieth century. While he did not live to see many of his theories confirmed, he laid the groundwork for later researchers and set the stage for many of the social changes that have occurred in the last few decades.

## FREUD

Sigmund Freud (1856-1939) is, of course, one of the most noted men of the twentieth century. The founder of psychoanalysis, his creative and intuitive writings are the basis of modern psychiatry and psychotherapeutic techniques. Freud was a contemporary of Krafft-Ebing and Ellis, and his views might be described as middle-of-the-road in comparison to the views of the other two. Unlike Krafft-Ebing, Freud did not consider sexual deviations as terrible perversions or loathsome diseases, a viewpoint that caused considerable disagreement among these men at the time. For example, Freud thought hysteria had a sexual etiology stemming from early childhood, a theory which Krafft-Ebing publicly denounced as "a scientific fairy tale." On the other hand, Freud was not nearly so accepting of the diversity of sexual behaviors as was Ellis and did view sexual issues as being of etiological importance in many neurotic behaviors.

Freud was correct in agreeing with Ellis that sexual expression begins in early childhood. However, many of Freud's ideas either were stated in such a fashion as to be empirically untestable or were later proved to be incorrect. Additionally, some of his views regarding female sexuality have been labeled

*Sigmund Freud (1922), age 66.*

as sexist in addition to having been proved invalid. For example, he viewed women as being anatomically inferior since they lacked a penis. He also discussed the differences between clitoral and vaginal orgasms and felt that women who were incapable of vaginal orgasm were psychologically immature. Recent research by Masters and Johnson (1966) has indicated that all female orgasms occur in essentially the same fashion, through clitoral stimulation. In spite of such inaccuracies in his observations, Freud's influence has been considerable. Rather than advancing our sexual knowledge to any great extent, however, his greatest impact was in bringing sexuality out in the open and in making it an area of legitimate discussion and research. Thus, Freud can be considered a bridge between the Victorian era with its sexual myths and repression, and the modern era, where sexuality is considered a very important part of people's lives and an acceptable area of scientific study.

## VAN DE VELDE

Theodore van de Velde (1873-1937) was a Dutch gynecologist who occupies a unique place in the history of human sexuality and sex research. Based on his own personal experiences and the reports of his patients, his book *Ideal Marriage,* published in 1926, became an overnight success. This was somewhat unexpected by van de Velde, who evidently anticipated that his vivid descriptions of sexual techniques might bring forth waves of protest. Contrary to his expectations, *Ideal Marriage* was well-received by the public, was translated into several languages, and has been continually reprinted in the United States as late as 1965. This is an interesting book in that, while van de Velde still held with many traditional Victorian attitudes (the book was intended only for married couples in a permanent relationship), in stark contrast to Victorian inhibitions, he described in explicit detail the sexual response and a variety of sexual activities. Van de Velde was concerned with the fact that people were slowly emerging from the Victorian repressiveness and were beginning to view sexuality as a more normal and healthy human activity but at the same time lacked knowledge about sexual functioning. It was to fill just this void that *Ideal Marriage* was written.

*Ideal Marriage* is essentially a "how-to" book, not unlike many of the so-called marriage manuals of today. For example, convinced that simultaneous orgasms were the most pleasurable, he discussed several techniques for reaching this goal. He also described the use of several coital positions to provide variety to the sexual encounter. There are inaccuracies in his factual data in many places, especially in his chapters on anatomy and physiology. For example, he believed the vagina was lubricated by fluid seeping down out of the uterus. And in the description of specific techniques, his Victorian attitudes were apparent, as in his discussion of oral-genital sexuality as a normal and enjoyable technique *as long as it is discontinued before orgasm.* On the other hand, he added to our accurate knowledge of sexuality; and many of his suggestions anticipated present-day thinking about sexual relationships. Van de Velde noted that the male nipple is a pleasurable area of the body and is capable of erection just like its female counterpart. He was a strong proponent of the importance of foreplay, especially in helping females achieve a maximum level of arousal. And throughout the book, van de Velde constantly reiterates the concept of the marital couple considered as a unit, not as two

separate individuals behaving and responding independent of each other. In this vein, he discussed the joys of both giving and receiving sexual pleasure, an attitude that would become an integral part of sexual treatment programs by Masters and Johnson and others several decades later.

Van de Velde is often ignored in discussions of early sex researchers, yet his influence in Western society has been, in many respects, just as great as that of Krafft-Ebing, Ellis, or Freud. His book was widely read and was important in instilling the attitude that sex is a normal, healthy, and important aspect of human behavior. Finally, his emphasis upon communication and upon the couple as a unit has had a great influence on the present generation of therapists who treat sexual dysfunctions.

## SOME METHODOLOGICAL ISSUES

A good proportion of later sex research has been in the form of surveys, especially those based on respondents' self-reports of their own attitudes or behaviors. Before reviewing the information that has been derived from these efforts, let us briefly consider some of the problems that limit our knowledge.

If we are interested in learning the attitudes of American adults toward masturbation, for example, we are unable to ask each and every individual how he or she feels about this topic. Instead, we ask a *sample,* which is some smaller proportion of the total population, to indicate their attitudes. Two concepts, representativeness of the sample and generalizability of the results, are important. When we use the term representativeness, we are asking if our sample is really like the total population as a whole, especially with respect to demographic variables such as age, socioeconomic status, etc. Once we have "sampled" some proportion of the population, we hope that our results will be generalizable, i.e., that they are really an accurate reflection of the results we would have obtained had we been able to question everyone in the entire population. If our sample is not representative, it is highly unlikely that we can accurately generalize our results to the total population. For example, if we question only white males living in dorms on several college campuses, it would be inappropriate to interpret these results as being representative of all Americans in general. Such a sample would be unrepresentative in many respects, most notably in terms of age, education, race, sex, and marital status. On the other hand, we *might* be able to generalize our results to other white college men, but only if we can show that the students we sampled are indeed like the white male college student population as a whole.

Many sex surveys have suffered from a lack of representativeness and are therefore of questionable generalizability. Others, typically those that have assessed more limited populations, such as college students or women of reproductive age, have been shown to be reasonably representative and thus probably have a high degree of generalizability to the specific populations in question.

Another major problem concerns the actual measurement devices used in surveys. A researcher should always question whether the questionnaire is both reliable and valid. In discussing reliability, we are referring basically to the consistency or stability of a test. Let us suppose we ask 1,000 students at what age they began to masturbate. One week later we ask the same question of these same 1,000 individuals. If the questionnaire is reliable, the responses should be the same on both administrations. This is an example of what is termed test-retest reliability, a measure of stability over time. Other types of reliability are also important, such as measures of inter-item reliability, or the internal consistency of a questionnaire. These types of reliability reflect whether the questionnaire as a whole is reliable or if certain parts or questions are likely to be unstable.

Validity is another important concept related to the specific assessment techniques utilized. In very simple terms, a test is valid if it accurately measures what one really wants it to measure. A test cannot be valid if it is unreliable; on the other hand, a test can have good reliability and still not be valid. Many of the sexual surveys are inadequate in terms of both reliability and validity. Investigators usually make up their own questionnaires, a fact that yields almost as many questionnaires as there are studies. Many, if not the majority, of these questionnaires lack any published data as to their reliability and validity and thus must always be interpreted with great care.

Finally, there are several difficulties that arise from the self-report nature of questionnaire and interview techniques. The problem of selection bias is present to some extent in all the published surveys. Some people are willing to respond to sexual questionnaires while others are not; the refusal, or nonresponse, rate has been as high as 90% or more in some studies. Also, many surveys have contained a built-in selection bias, such as those for which the questionnaire was published in a magazine. If one is not a reader of the magazine in question, then one does not have the opportunity to take part in the survey. Thus, in many studies, we have no way of knowing why any one individual chose not to participate. More importantly, we do not know in what ways "nonresponders" may have been different from those individuals who did choose to participate, particularly in reference to the sexual attitudes or behaviors being measured.

In discussing the following survey research, we have tried to point out the strengths and weaknesses of each study and to determine how valid or generalizable the results are. For a more detailed exploration of the theoretical aspects of survey research, the interested student is referred to the work of Anastasi (1976), Babbie (1973), and Kish (1965).

## THE KINSEY REPORTS

Knowledge of the first forty years of the life of Alfred C. Kinsey (1894-1956) would lead few if any of us to predict his great accomplishments in sex research. Born into a Victorian family in New Jersey, young Kinsey grew up in a strict moral and religious atmosphere (even while in college he is reported to have prayed for a friend who had confessed excessive masturbation to him). Kinsey earned an undergraduate degree in psychology and received his doctoral degree in entymology from Harvard in 1920. He then went to Indiana University to teach biology. His research for several years centered on the study of the gall wasp, which, ironically, is one of the few organisms to reproduce asexually. Even early in his career his scientific

*Dr. Alfred C. Kinsey.*

thoroughness was apparent; Kinsey is said to have collected over two million wasps during these years.

In 1937 Indiana University decided to offer a course in sex education and marriage, and Alfred Kinsey was asked to teach the class. In selecting Kinsey, the university had chosen a shy and unassuming person, a conservative and settled family man, a man known for his scientific thoroughness and vigor. Although he knew little about the area of human sexuality, in characteristic fashion Kinsey set out to do his research in the university library; he found there was little factual data available. Most of the available information, such as the writings of Krafft-Ebing and Freud, lacked statistical validity (up to this point, only Havelock Ellis had utilized statistical procedures to any extent in reporting sexual data). Consequently, Kinsey began in 1938 to collect his own data, beginning with the responses of 62 males and females to a preliminary questionnaire. During the next decade Kinsey refined and expanded this questionnaire and his interviewing techniques and, along with his colleagues, interviewed a total of 5,300 males and 5,940 females. The results of this extensive data pool were published in two volumes, *Sexual Behavior in the Human Male* (1948) and *Sexual Behavior in the Human Female* (1953).

While some authorities were critical of Kinsey's research, both on moralistic and scientific grounds, the books were generally well accepted; and, in fact, both became almost overnight best sellers. An in-depth examination of the Kinsey reports is beyond the scope of a text such as this; however, a summary of some of the more important findings follows.

## CHILDHOOD SEXUALITY

The Kinsey researchers found that Freud and others had indeed been correct: sexual expression and behavior begins in early childhood. Many respondents reported memories of sexual experimentation during childhood, with about one-half of the sample having engaged in some form of sex play before adolescence. Even more striking and informative were the reports of respondents' observation of their own very young children. For example, orgasm was observed after self-stimulation in several young children of both sexes before age three. The physical descriptions of these observed orgasms in these children corresponded closely to orgasms in physically mature adults except for the following: (a) orgasm in male infants occurred without ejaculation, and (b) multiple orgasms were fairly common among male infants.

## HOMOSEXUALITY

The data on homosexuality was perhaps the most shocking and controversial information presented in Kinsey's two books. These results indicated that 37% of all males have had or will have had at least one homosexual experience to the point of orgasm sometime during their life. The extent of this homosexual activity varied greatly; that is, some individuals reported being aroused by both sexes at some time in their life, some reported an isolated homosexual experience in adolescence, etc. Nevertheless, 4% reported that they were exclusively homosexual and that they had never been aroused by the opposite sex. One important piece of data often overlooked even today is that Kinsey found that the stereotyped, effeminate behavior often thought to be characteristic of male homosexuals occurred in only about 10% of his homosexual sample.

Data on female homosexuality indicated the same variability of expression, although the percentages of females engaging in homosexual activities were generally smaller than for males. The most significant sex difference was that females typically had fewer partners than did male homosexuals.

## MALE SEXUAL BEHAVIOR

Most males masturbate. Over 90% of Kinsey's sample reported engaging in masturbation at some time during their life. Males from lower educational and socioeconomic levels were more likely to view this activity as perverted or abnormal and reported less masturbatory behavior than those in higher socioeconomic levels. This latter finding illustrates an important conclusion drawn from the totality of the Kinsey data: sexual attitudes and behaviors are often related to educational and socioeconomic factors. Males with less education were much more likely to engage in premarital intercourse than were more well-educated males. That is, about 98% of males with a grade school education had premarital intercourse, whereas about 67% of college-educated males did. Higher educational level males reported being aroused by a greater variety of sexual stimuli and engaged in a greater variety of heterosexual activities (e.g., oral-genital sex) than the less educated males.

Kinsey also pointed out that around 75% of all males ejaculate within two minutes after beginning actual intercourse and that, given this high proportion, it made little sense to continue considering such behavior deviant or neurotic.

## FEMALE SEXUAL BEHAVIOR

The data on female sexuality often parallel the data on males, although percentages and relationships to sociocultural factors differ in many instances. Around 70% of the female sample had masturbated, and around 50% had engaged in premarital intercourse. With respect to premarital intercourse the relationship to educational level was exactly opposite to the male data. Thus, females with more education were more likely to engage in premarital sex than were females who were less educated. Contrary to the beliefs of many people at that time, the majority of married females were orgasmic either through coitus or other sexual activities. Among the younger females (less than age 20) about 20% were not orgasmic, but by age 40 only about 5% reported being nonorgasmic. Kinsey noted that the factor which had the highest correlation with orgasm in marital coitus was premarital orgasmic experience. Very few women in Kinsey's sample (about 2%) reported being totally devoid of any sexual arousal, laying to rest the myth of widespread frigidity among the female population.

## THE KINSEY SURVEYS: CRITICAL APPRAISAL

There can be little doubt that Kinsey attempted to obtain as accurate data as possible. His final questionnaire consisted of some 350 questions which were asked in a one-to-one interview. Kinsey himself performed about half of the more than 11,000 interviews. The interviews were structured so as to obtain the highest degree of accuracy and honesty from the respondents. For example, questions of a more controversial or threatening nature were asked late in the interview to allow rapport to be built between the interviewer and respondent. The questions themselves were structured to encourage the respondents to reveal information. Instead of asking "Do you masturbate?" Kinsey would inquire, "At what age did you begin to masturbate?" (It should be noted that critics suggest that this type of questioning may have led to an overreporting of certain types of behaviors.) Kinsey also sought accuracy by a variety of other methods: he obtained test-retest reliabilities, he interviewed groups of wives and husbands separately, and he checked for accuracy of his coding procedures by having two interviewers rate the respondent's answers in some interviews.

Nevertheless, the validity of the Kinsey data has been a matter of argument since its publication. One common criticism of a nontechnical nature is that the Kinsey reports deal mostly with behaviors and neglect attitudinal components. This criticism appears to have some foundation in fact. The most serious criticisms, however, involve the representativeness of the people sampled. Simply stated, were the persons questioned by Kinsey and his associates really comparable to the adult population at large? If not, then is it appropriate to generalize Kinsey's findings to the population as a whole? Critics (e.g., Cochran et al., 1953) have repeatedly pointed out that the persons questioned in Kinsey surveys in many ways are *not* like the U.S. adult population. Kinsey's respondents were, on the average, younger and better educated than the average citizen. They were also more likely to live in cities and to hold higher prestige jobs. Blacks, Catholics, Jews, and older people were underrepresented in the Kinsey sample. Although Kinsey attempted to adjust for these discrepancies by statistical procedures, his critics warn that systematic errors of unknown proportions may nevertheless femain in the data. Generally cited as examples of such possible errors are: (a) the relationships of various sociocultural and demographic factors to sexual activities and preferences, and (b) the relatively high incidence of many reported sexual activities, especially homosexual behaviors.

Given these concerns, we are required to ask just how accurate the Kinsey data are. There is really no way of proving or disproving the validity of the original Kinsey findings. However, there have been several other surveys since the publication of the Kinsey reports; and Brecher (1971) has noted that the better the methodology employed in these more recent surveys, the more likely they are to support Kinsey's data. Let us turn now to these later surveys.

# RECENT SURVEYS

Since the late sixties there have been literally dozens of surveys of sexual attitudes and behaviors in the United States. These studies vary greatly in the populations sampled, the research methodology employed, and the probable validity of the results. These methodological variations have often led to conflicting results and thus make comparisons between the surveys difficult. Nevertheless, some consistent findings have emerged across several studies, and perhaps the most appropriate manner of evaluating these recent data is to discuss these consistencies rather than to deal in detail with individual survey findings. Before doing so, let us look at the methodology employed in the major recent surveys.

## THE PSYCHOLOGY TODAY SURVEY

A 100-item sex questionnaire was published in the July, 1969, issue of *Psychology Today*; and some 20,000 replies were received, the results of which were later published in the same magazine (Athanasiou, Shaver, and Tarvis, 1970). This study represented the first recent survey to sample a large number of individuals, yet the findings are of very questionable generalizability on a number of grounds. First, only the readers of *Psychology Today* were sampled, and these respondents were quite unlike the population at large. They were more educated and of a higher socioeconomic level than the average American; and they were relatively young, the majority being under 30 years of age. Additionally, most respondents rated themselves as sexually "liberal" compared to the average person. The authors themselves caution that their findings should not be regarded as being representative of the population at large.

## THE HUNT SURVEY

The Playboy Foundation sponsored a major sex survey, the results of which were published in *Playboy* magazine and then in greater detail in Morton Hunt's *Sexual Behavior in the 1970s* (1974). An attempt was made to gather data comparable in some respects to the Kinsey data in order to assess possible changes since the early 1950s. A national market survey research company, the Research Guild, was hired to collect the data. Respondents throughout the country (their names were chosen at random from telephone directories) were asked to participate anonymously in small group discussions of changing sexual behaviors in America, and approximately 20% (N=2026) of those originally contacted agreed to do so. After these discussions, the participants were then asked to fill out a questionnaire; and all 2,026 respondents complied with this request. The questionnaire was very long (over 1,000 items) and covered a variety of demographic and other nonsexual areas. Two hundred of the 2,026 individuals also received interviews similar to those administered by Kinsey and his associates.

Unlike the *Psychology Today* sample, Hunt's respondents were similar to the population at large in many demographic variables including age, race, marital status, education, and socioeconomic status. However, the use of telephone directories to obtain the sample does limit the possible sample in some ways, and it must be remembered that 80% of those originally contacted refused to participate. On the other hand, an analysis of the nonsexual parts of the questionnaire indicated that the Hunt sample was very similar to the population as a whole, lending some additional validity to his data. All in all, the Hunt survey is probably reasonably representative and has been used in comparison with Kinsey's data to evaluate trends or changes in sexual behaviors since the late forties.

## THE REDBOOK SURVEY

The October, 1974, issue of *Redbook* magazine included a 75-item multiple choice questionnaire tapping both sexual behaviors and attitudes. The results appeared in abbreviated form in *Redbook*, and later a more extensive report was published in book form (Tarvis and Sadd, 1975). Over 100,000 women responded to this survey; this represents the largest sample of all the sexual surveys to date. While such a large sample is more likely to be representative than a more restricted sample, the enormity of this data made it prohibitive in terms of both time and money to fully analyze all the questionnaires. Therefore, these investigators used a sample (N=2278) of the larger data pool for most of their comparisons. They also utilized a larger random sample of 18,000 replies for several special comparisons.

Like similar surveys, the *Redbook* study began with a restricted sample, in this case the readers of *Redbook*. For analysis, the sample was further restricted to married or remarried women, since only a small proportion of the respondents fell into the other marital status categories. A comparison of this final sample to married women in general (Tarvis and Sadd, 1975, pp. 21-23) indicated that the respondents closely approximated the national distribution with respect to geographic area, religion, and percentage who were employed. On the other hand, the respondents were younger, better educated, and more affluent than the average American female. Thus, the results of the *Redbook* survey are best interpreted as representative of a somewhat select sample of married women.

## THE HITE REPORT

Shere Hite's survey has been widely publicized as presenting female sexuality from a new perspective. It has also received more criticism from other professionals in the field than any other contemporary survey. *The Hite Report* (1976) is based on responses to an open-ended questionnaire (i.e., respondents wrote their answers in their own words rather than choosing from some multiple choice alternatives). Questionnaire distribution began in 1972 in a series of national mailings to various women's groups such as the National Organization for Women, abortion rights groups, and university women's centers. Notices were later placed in publications, including *The Village Voice* and *Ms.*, informing women where to write for the questionnaire; and the magazine *Oui* carried the questionnaire in its entirety. Of the approximately 100,000 surveys distributed, 3,019 were returned, which Hite states is "more or less the standard rate of return for this kind of questionnaire distribution" (Hite, 1976, p. 23). In reality, however, not only is such a low response rate inadequate for accurate analysis and reporting, but also most scientifically acceptable questionnaire surveys typically obtain response rates of 50% to 70% with even higher rates of response obtained in many instances (Babbie, 1973; Kish, 1965). In addition, many of the returned questionnaires were not completely analyzed for a variety of reasons, further reducing the final sample to 1,844. Demographic data was not specifically requested and was available only when spontaneously reported by the respondents. An examination of the data that was reported indicates the sample is far from being representative; for example, a very large proportion of the women were between the ages of 18 and 30 and fewer than 40% of the women sampled were married.

*The Hite Report* has probably received more publicity than any sexual survey since Kinsey. However, it is based on a limited sample which does not appear to be representative of the population as a whole. Furthermore, the lack of appropriate demographic data leads to additional problems of interpretation; it must be remembered that Kinsey and others found a relationship between sexual attitudes and behaviors on the one hand and several demographic variables on the other. Thus, while the Hite data *may* represent the sexual attitudes and behavioral patterns of a selected group of feminists (because the questionnaire distribution was mostly to such groups or through feminist publications), generalizing these data in a statistical sense to other groups is entirely inappropriate.

On the other hand, the general attitudes and values espoused by the respondents cited in *The Hite Report* should not be overlooked. The extensive quotations do provide excellent examples of the wide varieties of normal sexual expression. For example, the specific descriptions furnished by these women of how they masturbate and of what orgasms feel like is the most comprehensive source of such information currently available (Pomeroy, 1976). Additionally, these women repeatedly indicated that the process and quality of a sexual encounter is more important than orgasm. Because the book presents a wide variation of female responses, numbers of women will find some of their own experiences reflected in the quoted material, which may enable them to better define their own sexuality in a broader and more realistic context.

## THE PIETROPINTO AND SIMENAUER STUDY

The book *Beyond the Male Myth* (1977) by Anthony Pietropinto, a psychiatrist, and Jacqueline Simenauer, a psychiatric writer and editor, reports the findings of their survey of the sexual attitudes of American men. These authors were interested in finding out more about male sexuality, particularly those areas that might be of most interest to women. In light of their criticisms of the previous survey methodology employed by others (they were especially critical of the Hite data), these investigators set out to gain information that might be representative of the male population as a whole. They began with a set of almost 100 questions which they presented to a group of female raters. The results of this procedure indicated that women were more interested in feelings and attitudes than in actual behaviors; thus, most of the items chosen were concerned with feelings and attitudes. The final questionnaire consisted of 40 multiple choice items. In addition a total of 32 longer, handwritten responses were collected from some of the men sampled.

A well-established marketing research firm, Crossley Surveys, Inc., was hired to collect the data, with the goal of analyzing a sample that was as much like the total male population as possible. Data was collected in 18 States and Washington, D.C., from a total of 4,066 male respondents. This final sample is very similar to the U.S. male population in terms of many demographic variables when compared to the 1970 census data. It seems biased to a significant extent only in terms of educational levels; compared to the census data, the sample contained fewer men with a grammar school education or less, while men with some college education were overrepresented. All in all, however, the Pietropinto and Simenauer survey is one of the better surveys with respect to the methodology employed, and the sample closely approximates the total adult male population in terms of most demographic variables.

## SURVEYS OF SPECIAL POPULATIONS

In recent years, there have been several major surveys of the sexual attitudes and behaviors of special, more restricted populations. Two of these surveys (Kantner and Zelnik, 1972 and 1973; Sorenson, 1973) investigated teen-age Americans. Using probability sampling (a technique for maximizing the representativeness of a sample and thus the generalizability of results), Kantner and Zelnik surveyed females between the ages of 15 and 19. Since this sample is fairly representative of the female teen-age population at large, it has provided much useful data with respect to the relationships between various demographic factors and sexuality. Of special import here were the analyses of black-white differences, since about one-third of the approximately 4,600 respondents were black.

Sorenson (1973) surveyed adolescents of both sexes between

the ages of 13 and 19. Using accepted sampling techniques to identify over 2,000 households containing 839 adolescents, Sorenson then sought informed consent to participate from both the adolescents and their parents. This yielded a total sample of 393 respondents. Thus, over 50% of the participants identified initially did not take part in the study, certainly a limiting factor because we cannot know precisely the effects of this selection bias. It should be noted that this high nonresponse rate was due mostly to the parents' failure to give their consent since almost 80% of the adolescents agreed to participate.

As part of a broader study of American women of reproductive age, Westoff (1974) gathered some data on female sexuality. Some 10,000 women were questioned, approximately one-half in 1965 and the others in 1970. Like the Kantner and Zelnik study, Westoff used probability sampling techniques and managed to obtain a sample that was fairly representative of American women in this age group as a whole. Two additional aspects of this study are relevant. First, since most of the questions were of a nonsexual nature, such as attitudes about family size, the questionnaire as a whole would seem to have been much less threatening to the respondents than a questionnaire dealing exclusively with sexuality. Therefore, the women chosen were probably more likely to participate and also to respond in an honest fashion, thus increasing the generalizability of the results. This speculation seems to be confirmed by the fact that the refusal rate for responding to the sexual questions was consistently low, typically less than 10%. Secondly, since the two samples were surveyed five years apart, this study has been useful in assessing possible changes in sexual attitudes and behaviors over that period of time.

## RECENT SURVEY FINDINGS

Let us now turn to the results of these more recent surveys. A complete description of the results from each individual survey is beyond the scope of this book (several of the surveys reviewed above were themselves reported in book length). Furthermore, such a complete description of the results is probably inappropriate because of some conflicting findings. It must be remembered that these surveys were completed in several different decades by different investigators and that most, if not all of the studies, used some questionable methodological procedures. Additionally, it is possible that people today are simply more willing to *report* engaging in certain behaviors than they were earlier. Thus, we must be especially careful about drawing conclusions when comparing these various surveys. Nevertheless, some consistent findings have emerged and we will review them briefly here. The interested student is referred to the original publications for more detailed information.

One general finding is that Americans living in the 1960s and 1970s appear to be more open than twenty or thirty years ago about their sexuality and to engage in a wider variety of sexual behaviors. Open and honest communication about sexual matters, particularly between sexual partners, is more the norm than it was in Kinsey's era. Studies have suggested that the more communication there is in a relationship the more likely that relationship is to be judged as "good" by the participants. More people are also experimenting with a variety of ways of sexual expression, such as oral-genital techniques and anal stimulation.

Although such techniques are far from being universal, they do appear to be more prevalent than they were a generation ago.

Masturbation practices among males seem to have changed very little since the Kinsey report. Almost all males masturbated then and almost all males masturbate in our current society. However, masturbation among females apparently has changed during the last few decades. There is some evidence that masturbation is now more common among women and that it tends to begin at earlier ages. On the other hand, a significant proportion of people, both males and females, still report having some negative feelings, such as guilt or anxiety, regarding their masturbatory experiences.

More individuals of both sexes are engaging in premarital intercourse; and, like female masturbation, premarital intercourse appears to begin at earlier ages. It will be remembered that Kinsey found some rather consistent differences in the occurrence of premarital intercourse among males and females of different educational and socioeconomic backgrounds. Recent findings have suggested that these differences between social classes are becoming smaller.

Some have interpreted the apparent increase in premarital sexuality as evidence of a growing promiscuity among American youth. The data, however, particularly that gathered from adolescents and young adults, suggest that this interpretation is not the case. Premarital sexuality does seem to begin at earlier ages, and Americans as a rule are waiting longer to marry than their counterparts only a generation ago. The latter fact alone has probably led to some increases in reported premarital intercourse. Additionally, the mores surrounding sexual expression during this lengthened premarital period also argue against the promiscuity hypothesis. That is, adolescents and young adults as a rule do not appear to be "sleeping around" with a variety of partners in "one night stands." Rather, they appear to engage in serial "monogamy," perhaps forming several long-term relationships before marriage but remaining sexually faithful to the partner for the duration of each relationship.

Sexual behaviors among married couples also seem to have changed somewhat in recent years. The frequency of intercourse has increased since the publication of the Kinsey reports and appears to still be increasing. The data of Westoff (1974) illustrates this phenomenon particularly well. As noted earlier, Westoff sampled some women in 1965 and others in 1970. Both groups reported higher frequencies of intercourse than did the Kinsey respondents; additionally, the 1970 respondents reported a greater frequency, an average of 8.2 coital experiences in a four-week period, than those sampled in 1965, who reported an average of 6.8 coital experiences in a similar period of time. One hypothesis for this apparent increase in coital frequency is the popularity and use of birth control pills. With the increasing use of this relatively safe and effective method of contraception, one might expect married couples to have less fear of unwanted pregnancies and thus feel freer to have intercourse more often. Although this is probably the case, The Westoff data indicates, however, that this variable alone cannot account for these increases in intercourse. The average coital frequency increased from 1965 to 1970 even among those women who used less effective contraceptive methods or who reported using no contraception at all. Finally, the Westoff data indicates that one general phenomenon is basically unchanged since the Kinsey reports: the frequency of intercourse is highest during the period immediately following a marriage and then gradually declines with age.

The frequency with which married women experience orgasm with intercourse also seems to have increased. The largest increase over the Kinsey figures for incidences of orgasm during coitus is for women married for a relatively short period of time (Hunt, 1974). Not only is this a significant finding in and of itself, it also supports another of Kinsey's findings: a positive correlation between, on the one hand, orgasm with intercourse and, on the other, earlier, premarital sexual experiences. Since women today are beginning premarital activities at an earlier age and are waiting longer to marry, they have, on the average, more premarital experiences and thus might be expected to have a higher frequency of orgasm with marital intercourse.

Extramarital affairs by women probably have increased slightly since Kinsey published *Sexual Behavior in the Human Female* in 1953. (We have little data to make this same comparison for men.) Several studies have suggested such an increase, with the *Redbook* survey reporting that 38% of the women between the ages of 35 and 39 revealed at least one extramarital affair. This does seem to indicate a real change, since in the Kinsey survey only 26% of the women respondents reported extramarital sexual relationships by age 40. There is reason to believe, however, that the validity of this finding is more in question than most of the results concerning other sexual behaviors reviewed previously in this chapter. First, Kinsey himself felt that his data was perhaps not entirely accurate with respect to the frequency of extramarital sex. On this issue he felt he was dealing with a real taboo among the American population of the 1940s and 1950s and that admitting to such behavior might have been much more difficult for his respondents than replying honestly to most of the other questions they were asked. Thus, Kinsey strongly suggested that the incidence of extramarital sexual relationships was probably higher than his data indicated. Secondly, it must be remembered that the *Redbook* sample was restricted to the volunteer self-reports of readers of this magazine and, while a large number of women did reply to this survey, they tended to be younger, better educated, and more affluent that the average American female.

It is really not possible to interpret with any certainty what all this means. Perhaps women today are more likely to have and to report extramarital affairs than they were two or three decades ago for a variety of reasons. The social structure of the American family is changing, with women "allowed" more varied roles and more freedom than in earlier generations. More women are a part of the work force and thus have more opportunities than they previously had to become acquainted with possible extramarital partners. And our society as a whole is now more conscious of sexuality and there is more open and honest discussion of sexual matters. Maybe women today are just more willing to admit to this behavior than were Kinsey's respondents. However, at this time we cannot unequivocally state that women today are more likely to have engaged in extramarital relationships. Perhaps future, better designed studies will yield more meaningful data on this question. Nevertheless, both Kinsey's results and recent surveys do indicate that a significant proportion of both men and women do engage in extramarital affairs at some point in their married lives.

These, then, have been some of the major findings of the surveys of sexual attitudes and behaviors conducted during the last few years. They seem to indicate that sexuality is a topic more open to free and honest discussion than in the past. Married couples and single people are engaging in sexual activities more often, are utilizing a greater variety of sexual techniques, and are beginning these sexual activities at an earlier age. Paradoxically, a significant portion of the population still experience anxiety or guilt concerning their sexuality, although these negative feelings do not seem as prevalent as they were only a few years ago. The overall social and cultural changes experienced by our society seem also to have impacted on the sexual arena. Women have gained more equality both sexually and in other aspects of their lives, with the result that today's male and female patterns of sexual expression are becoming more alike, as will be discussed in Chapter 5. Finally, the differences between the sexual attitudes and activities of individuals of varying socioeconomic strata are diminishing, although some consistent patterns do continue to be related to several demographic factors.

## PSYCHOPHYSIOLOGICAL RESEARCH

The actual anatomy of the sexual organs and the physiology of the sexual response cycle have been studied by several investigators throughout the world in the last 100 years (Brecher, 1971). Kinsey and his associates had observed sexual responses in a laboratory setting and reported these findings (Kinsey et al., 1953) although they did not go into any detail about how these data had been collected. Aware of the criticism his work was receiving, Kinsey probably was wise in not revealing to his critics the added ammunition of admitting that sexual behavior had actually been observed at Indiana University in the 1940s. However, not until Masters and Johnson published *Human Sexual Response* in 1966 did we have really good anatomical and physiological data based on long-term and precise measurement in the laboratory.

### MASTERS AND JOHNSON

Dr. William H. Masters graduated from Hamilton College in 1938 and entered the University of Rochester School of Medicine to prepare himself for a career in research in the biological sciences. During his first year, he began working in the laboratory of Dr. George Washington Corner, one of the world's foremost authorities on the biology of sex. Masters soon narrowed his interest to research in sexuality. Aware of the public prejudice against such research, especially with humans, Dr. Corner suggested three rules that Masters should follow if he expected to successfully carry out his chosen work: he should wait until he was at least forty years old before beginning this line of research; he should, by then, already have established for himself a scientific reputation in another field; and he should wait until he was able to obtain the sponsorship of a major university (Brecher, 1971). Masters followed Corner's suggestions; by the mid-1950s he was an established professor at Washington University School of Medicine in St. Louis and had published many important contributions to the medical literature in obstetrics and gynecology, including a series of

*Dr. William H. Masters and Virginia E. Johnson.*

studies on hormone replacement therapy for older women. Finally, in 1954, Masters launched his comprehensive study of the physiology of the sexual response.

Shortly after beginning the study, Masters posted a routine job announcement with the university placement service, seeking someone to help in obtaining interview data. Mrs. Virginia E. Johnson, with training in sociology and psychology, was hired for the position; and thus began a long-term collaborative effort. Johnson provided many important contributions during the study of sexual physiology and became an even more important part of the research team several years later when Masters and Johnson began their therapy program for the treatment of sexual inadequacies.

The research that culminated in the publishing of *Human Sexual Response* was creative and thorough and was conducted with meticulous care. For almost the first two years, Masters and Johnson worked with a group of prostitutes, gathering interview data from individuals who had been in a unique position to observe many sexual response cycles in a large number of different individuals. Of the original 145 prostitutes, a small number (8 women and 3 men) were chosen for further anatomic and physiologic study. These individuals proved invaluable as subjects during the months of trial and error when the techniques and instruments to study the sexual response were being devised and refined. However, the results that came out of their work with these prostitutes were not included in the final report. Masters and Johnson have described this group as having "migratory tendencies," that is, they frequently moved from place to place, which made it difficult if not impossible to obtain detailed response patterns over a long period of time. More importantly, this group had a high incidence of pathology of the sexual and pelvic organs, making the group unsuitable for research into normal sexual functioning.

The final subjects studied by Masters and Johnson were all volunteers, many from the university community. Subjects were expertly screened to weed out those who were only "thrill seekers" or who had volunteered for other inappropriate reasons. The remaining volunteers were all paid for their time spent in the laboratory. A total of 382 women, ranging in age from 18 to 78 years, and 312 men, aged 21 to 89 years, actively participated to some extent in the project. Included were both married couples and unmarried singles.

For over ten years Masters and Johnson carried on their detailed laboratory study of these subjects, gathering a variety of new data about the human sexual response. Subjects were routinely filmed while engaged in a variety of sexual activities. Also measured were physiological responses such as blood pressure, heart rate, breathing rate, and muscular contractions. One of the most innovative devices to be developed was an artificial penis. Made from clear plastic and containing its own internal light source, this device made it possible for the first time to actually observe the internal changes that take place in the vagina during sexual stimulation and orgasm. By the time this research project was concluded, Masters and Johnson had observed and recorded over 10,000 orgasms, either through masturbation, coitus, or use of the artificial penis.

The individuals studied by Masters and Johnson were not representative of the population at large. The sample was more educated, more affluent, and generally of average or above average intelligence. Almost all subjects were white and all had had some previous sexual experience. This lack of representativeness is probably much less of a problem than it would have been in some of the surveys we have previously discussed in which self-report data was used. Remember that Masters and Johnson were not asking for subjective reports of attitudes or frequencies of any particular behaviors but were observing and measuring actual physiological processes. The assumption made in most research of this kind is that basic physiological processes vary very little among normal individuals. Thus, if a medical researcher sets out to study the digestive process or how antibodies work to fight disease in the bloodstream, the assumption is that these basic processes are much the same in all people and are not affected to any great extent by such variables as education or marital status. If this assumption is true, as it probably is in most instances, then the lack of representativeness in terms of demographic variables probably does not affect the generalizability of these results to most of the rest of the population. However, we must be careful in making statistical comparisons based on these data. For example, it would not be appropriate to state that X percentage of men ejaculate within a certain period of time, since such data would probably be specific to the subject population and the circumstances surrounding a given study and therefore might not be true of the rest of the male population.

The work of Masters and Johnson has provided us with a much clearer picture of what occurs physiologically during sexual activities. These basic findings are covered in detail in Chapter 5. Since their original work, Masters and Johnson have provided much additional knowledge in other related areas, such as the treatment of sexual dysfunctions and, in their more recently published work, on homosexuality. Planned for future publication are studies of sexuality among the aged and of sexual physiology and inadequacies among adolescents (Brecher, 1971). Thus, these researchers have had and will no doubt continue to have a great impact on our knowledge of sexuality.

## LATER PSYCHOPHYSIOLOGICAL RESEARCH

Recent researchers have expanded upon the methodology developed by Masters and Johnson in attempts to further delineate the physiological processes involved in the sexual response and to study the various external factors that may influence sexual responsiveness. Previous researchers in the 1950s and 1960s had utilized a variety of measures they thought might be reflective of the sexual response: GSR (galvanic skin response), skin temperature, heart rate and respiration, and pupillary dilation. While many studies were published using one or more of these measures, this line of research provided little useful information that further enhanced our knowledge of the sex response. The basic problem is that most, if not all, of these nongenital measures reflect *general* arousal and are not specific to sexual arousal. Likewise, self-reports of amount of sexual arousal have generally correlated poorly with nongenital measures of arousal (Zuckerman, 1971). Thus, most recent investigations of sexual arousal have utilized genital measures, such as penile volume and vaginal blood flow and lubrication.

A variety of more sophisticated mechanical and electrical measurement instruments have been used with increasing frequency in the past decade. In one way or another, these procedures measure changes in blood flow or volume in the genital areas, a technique called *plethysmography*. For the measurement in penile changes, instruments have been developed which are attached around the penis. One such device consists of an airtight container (Freund, Sedlacek, and Knob, 1965), with changes in penile volume causing changes in the air pressure in the surrounding instrument which can be measured. Another type of device consists of a small loop of hollow, elastic tubing filled with mercury (Fisher, Gross, and Zuch, 1965). As the penis enlarges and the tubing is stretched, the diameter of the tube interior, containing the mercury, is reduced. This reduction changes the electrical conducting capacity of the mercury, and these changes in electrical resistance can then be monitored.

Measures of vaginal changes have generally been measured by some form of optical plethysmography (Geer, Morokoff, and Greenwood, 1974; Cerny, 1977). These devices consist of a transparent tube, somewhat like the artificial penis developed by Masters and Johnson. Contained in the tube are both a light source and a photosensitive recording apparatus. The light source produces a steady illumination which is reflected from the walls of the vagina and recorded by the photosensitive cell. The reflective characteristics of the vaginal walls change as blood flow increases or decreases during sexual arousal, and these differences are measured through the photosensitive cell.

While these new procedures are innovative and show promise, the art of direct measurement of genital changes is still in its infancy. Many problems have arisen with these measurement techniques. For example, McConaghy (1974) made simultaneous penile recordings by two different types of measurement instrument and found the relationship between the two to be quite variable. While the responses did parallel each other much of the time, on several occasions one device indicated a penile volume increase while the other indicated a decrease. Finally, external variables such as sexual experience (Mosher and Abramson, 1977) or alcohol (Rubin and Henson, 1976) can affect arousal; however, these variables have rarely been controlled and very likely have confounded in unknown ways many if not most of the studies utilizing direct genital measurement.

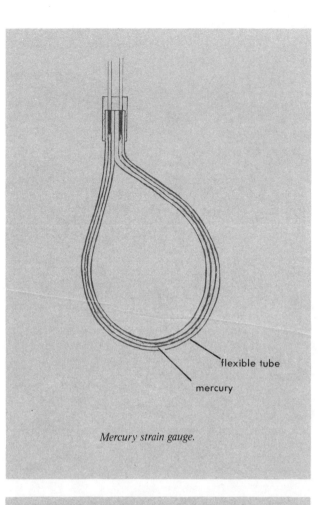

*Mercury strain gauge.*

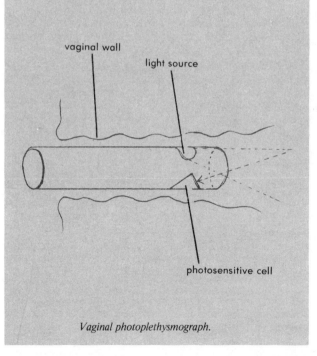

*Vaginal photoplethysmograph.*

# Chapter 5

## Sexual Anatomy and Sexual Response

# INTRODUCTION

A complete appreciation of our sexuality cannot be achieved without an awareness of what our bodies look like and how our genitals function. While this statement may seem to be an obvious one, the unfortunate truth is that few of us are encouraged to explore our bodies in general, and we thus remain sadly ignorant of genital characteristics in particular.

This hands-off attitude, so to speak, can typically be traced back to our childhood. Whereas parents will readily discuss the digestive and respiratory systems, for example, in a straightforward manner, discussion of sexual functions, if it occurs at all, is usually oblique and euphemistic. What *is* communicated to the child, under these circumstances, is a negative perspective that suppresses curiosity and promotes embarrassment rather than healthy self-exploration. Small wonder then that many adults find it difficult to examine their genitals, even for ordinary health and sanitary reasons. Moreover, the secretiveness, shame, and guilt associated with these early experiences causes many people to regard their sex organs as ugly, rather than as a natural and acceptable part of their anatomy.

Sometimes ignorance of our genitals can lead to both physical and sexual problems. Certain disease processes start with detectable changes in the breast or genitals, but an aversion to checking those body parts may result in symptoms progressing to serious stages. A lack of understanding of how our bodies respond sexually can lead to inappropriate expectations and thus hinder sexual expression. Sex therapists, for example, report that a considerable percentage of the problems presented to them are the result of their clients' lack of relevant information or education.

Not only does the lack of suitable education at home and in the schools, coupled with misinformation gathered from peers, foster our ignorance, but also the current attitudes toward sexuality in our culture work to further our misunderstandings. These attitudes create for us a paradox: on the one hand, we are bombarded, through advertising and through the media in general, with sexual imagery; on the other hand, the "official" cultural taboo undercuts our ability to deal with and speak about sexual matters in open, healthy, positive ways.

In order to accept the implications of our sexuality — an awareness of our values, a sense of responsibility for ourselves and others, an ability to take pleasure in our bodies, and an acceptance of and confidence in our own sexuality — we need to have a foundation of basic knowledge.

In this chapter, therefore, we will discuss the anatomy, both female and male, relevant to human sexuality and the process of sexual response.

# FEMALE ANATOMY

## INTERNAL FEMALE ANATOMY

The female sexual-reproductive system is housed in the pelvis; the major internal organs lie behind and are protected by the pubic bone (*pubis symphysis*). These organs are situated in close conjunction with the urinary and intestinal tracts, as are the external openings of these three systems.

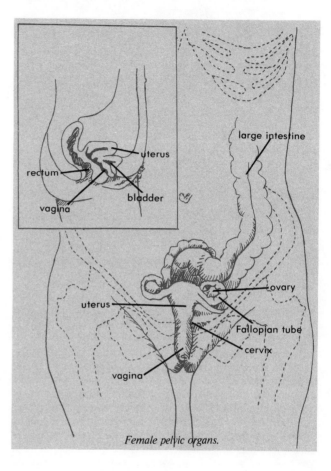

*Female pelvic organs.*

The ovary, or female gonad, is similar in size and shape to an unshelled almond. The human female has two ovaries, one at the left and one at the right in the pelvic cavity. The ovaries perform two main functions: they produce eggs, or *ova*; and they manufacture the female hormones, estrogen and progesterone. When a female child is born, her ovaries contain 200,000 to 400,000 follicles holding oocytes, or immature eggs; this number reduces to 100,000 to 200,000 by puberty. The newborn's ovaries contain all the egg cells she will ever produce. In contrast, once boys reach puberty, their bodies continuously manufacture new sperm. Given that a woman is fertile for approximately 35 years, releasing one egg with each menstrual period 13 times a year, she needs only 450 ova to achieve her maximum reproductive capacity; nature thus provides an overabundance of gamete cells in order to ensure the continuation of the species.

When an individual egg is released at ovulation (see Chapter 7), it pops out through the surface of the ovary and remains momentarily suspended in the abdominal cavity. It is then, generally, "transferred" to the fingerlike ends of one of the two Fallopian tubes. These tubes are muscular canals, each suspended by a ligament, which extend outward from the uterus a distance of four to six inches. Each Fallopian tube curves around an ovary but is not directly attached to the ovary.

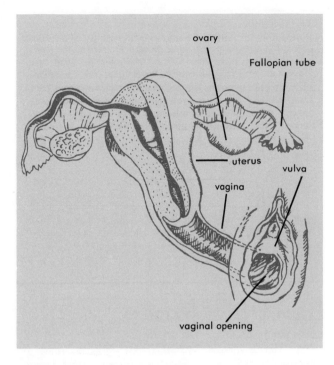

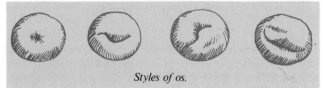

*Styles of os.*

Lying more or less underneath the uterus is the bladder, the reservoir for urine. Projecting from the bladder is a tube called the urethra, the pathway for urine to exit the body. The external opening of the urethra, that is, the opening through which women urinate, is called the urethral opening, or meatus. Positioned behind the uterus is the intestinal tract and the rectum, which opens at the anus.

The connection between the internal and the external sex organs is the vagina, or birth canal. Vagina is a Latin word whose original meaning was sheath; presumably the designation came about in reference to the role the vagina plays relative to the penis in heterosexual intercourse. The vagina performs three separate functions: it serves as the passageway for menstrual flow, it couples with the penis during intercourse and is involved in other forms of sexual activity, and it is the birth canal.

The mechanism by which the egg enters the tube is not fully understood; three theories have been advanced by way of explanation. First, there is the possibility of a chemical affinity, or chemotaxis, between the egg and the entrance of the tube. Secondly, the fringed end of the tube is motile and may engulf the egg in a tentaclelike fashion. Thirdly, the cilia, or tiny hairs, that line the Fallopian tube beat rhythmically in unison, to sweep the egg inward (Cohn, 1974). Once the egg is in the Fallopian tube, it is moved along by the cilia lining the tube and by peristalsis, rhythmic contractions of the tube, in the direction of the uterus. Cases have been reported in the medical literature in which women with only one ovary and one Fallopian tube on the opposite side have nonetheless managed to conceive (Hellman and Pritchard, 1971). In such cases, the expelled egg has migrated from one side of the body cavity to the other, a distance of over six inches.

The Fallopian tubes are connected to the upper "corners" of the uterus, or womb. The uterus is a pear-shaped muscular organ, capable of tremendous expansion (as during pregnancy) and subsequent contraction. (It contracts back to almost its original size in approximately six weeks after childbirth.) The uterus is situated in the midline of the body, above the line of the pelvic bone, between the urinary bladder and the rectum. The uterus, which is held in place in the abdominal cavity by six ligaments attached to the pelvic wall, still retains a good deal of mobility. In some women it tilts forward of the midline position (anteverted), and in some women it tilts backward (retroverted).

The upper portion of the uterus is called the fundus (or body), the lower part is called the cervix (Latin for neck), and the opening of the cervix is known as the os (Latin for mouth). The os is generally quite small; the os of a woman who has neither borne a child nor had uterine surgery resembles a dimple. The os of a woman who has borne a child or which otherwise has been dilated with surgical instruments takes on a different shape: transverse, crescent, etc.

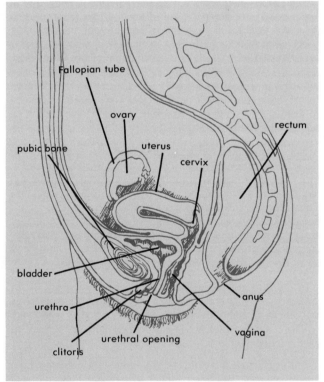

History has its share of myths about the vagina. For example, among certain so-called primitive peoples, it was believed that the vagina was lined with teeth *(vagina dentata)* or other dangerous objects. While we are more enlightened today, stories still circulate in contemporary folklore about vaginal odors (for example, "anchovy paste") and the like.

The vagina resembles a collapsed tube of toothpaste when all the toothpaste has been squeezed out. It is a potential space; it is not always open. When a woman is neither sexually stimulated nor in the process of giving birth, the vagina is closed, with its two walls touching. These walls are composed of soft folds called *rugae*. The vagina is extremely flexible and expandable; it can open to accommodate a finger, a tampon, a penis, or a baby. In its resting state, it is about eight to ten centimeters (three to four inches) long; it tilts at a slightly backward angle from its bottom (external opening) to its top — an anatomical fact of some significance for the woman learning to insert a tampon or a diaphragm.

The upper two-thirds of the vagina has relatively few nerve endings and thus is relatively insensitive to touch. However, this portion of the vagina is sensitive to pressure. The cervix, too, is relatively devoid of nerve endings. Thus, the medical procedure known as the Pap smear, which involves removing cell samples from the cervical os, can be done with minimal discomfort for the woman. (The Pap smear will be discussed more fully in a later section of this chapter.)

The lower third of the vagina, especially around the entrance, is the most sexually sensitive part of this organ. A procedure which can be performed for therapeutic reasons or as part of self-discovery involves thinking of the vaginal entrance as the face of a clock. Having located the relative positions of 12, 3, 6, and 9 o'clock, the woman then explores which areas are most sensitive for her. Some women also locate a sensitive spot on the anterior, or upper, wall of the vagina, which may be related to the clitoral nerve system.

The vagina can have two types of moisture present in it. One is a product of the normal functioning of the hormonal system, for example, cervical mucus, and of the vagina's self-cleansing mechanism. Vaginal discharge is thus a normal product; the amount varies from woman to woman, and the amount, texture, and odor varies with the phases of the menstrual cycle. The environment of the vagina is normally acidic, between 3.5 and 4.5 pH. As we shall see in Chapter 15, this acidity works to reduce the possibility of infection. The other type of moisture produced in the vagina is the lubrication which is secreted as a woman becomes sexually aroused.

The urinary, vaginal, and rectal openings are situated quite close together, thus making women relatively prone to infection. The bacteria which are at home in the anus can be harmful when carried to the vagina or urethra. For this reason, young girls need to be taught the simple procedure of wiping from front to back after defecation.

As these structures are very much interrelated, it can be seen that the urethra can become irritated if intercourse is performed too forcefully or with insufficient lubrication and the tissues "bruised." This can sometimes occur as the woman's body becomes accustomed to a new male partner, a situation which has given rise to the medical term "honeymoon cystitis." (Cystitis is an inflammation of the urinary bladder; the irritation of the urethra leaves it vulnerable to invading bacteria, which then travel up to the bladder.) This is a preventable disorder when there is an awareness of the causes and the simple procedures to prevent them.

The anus and the perineum (skin between vagina and anus) is a sexually sensitive area for some people since it shares the same nervous system as the genitals. If anal intercourse is desired, two factors are important to remember: relaxation and lubrication. The sphincter muscle around the anus, in women and men, cannot heal itself if it is damaged. If the individual is sexually aroused, this muscle will be relaxed; if he or she is unwilling or unready, the muscle will be tense. Unlike the vagina, the rectum is not self-lubricating. A water-soluble jelly can supply the necessary lubrication.

To allay concerns about bacteria present in the rectum, simple precautions can be taken. The man can use a condom over his penis and/or urinate and wash after anal intercourse, thus preventing bacteria from ascending his urethra. If a woman is experiencing anal stimulation, her partner's penis or hand should not go immediately from the anus to the vagina, thus checking the potential spread of bacteria.

## EXTERNAL FEMALE ANATOMY

The external genitalia, known collectively as the vulva, are comprised of the mons pubis, labia majora, labia minora, clitoris, urethral opening, vaginal opening, and the perineum.

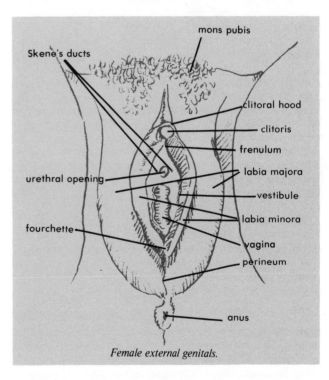

*Female external genitals.*

The *mons pubis* (or *mons veneris*, "mount of love") is a rounded, fatty pad of tissue, which becomes covered with pubic hair at puberty. It lies on top of the pubic bone and is the most visible part of the genitals when a woman is standing up.

The *labia majora* are the fleshy outer lips (in Latin labia means lips). The outer surface of these lips is covered with pubic hair; the inner surface is composed of mucous membrane. Inside the labia majora, and lying parallel to them, are the *labia minora,* or inner lips, which vary widely among women in appearance and color, with the color often varying from pink to brown along their surface. Normal configurations of labia minora include those that remain tucked in under the outer lips and those that protrude and hang down lower than the outer lips. This latter variety has occasionally been a cause of consternation for women with such lips whose only basis for comparison was stylized medical or marriage manual drawings or former *Playboy* type models with airbrushed vulvas showing no protruding inner lips.

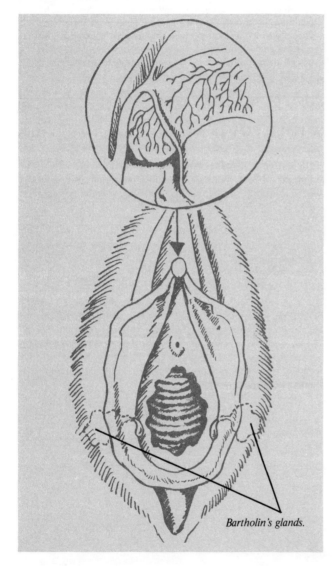

Bartholin's glands.

The labia minora join at the top and divide into two folds which surround the clitoris. The upper fold forms the clitoral hood, and the lower constitutes the frenulum of the clitoris. At their base, the labia minora form the fourchette.

The word "clitoris" (derived from a Greek word meaning "small hill") can be pronounced with the accent on either the first or second syllable, there being no general consensus on pronunciation, since this term lacks the household-word status of its closest relative, the penis (see Chapter 6, prenatal differentiation). The clitoris is a highly specialized and unique organ; its sole function is for sexual pleasure.

The clitoris extends from the hood to the pubic bone, where it is connected by a suspensory ligament. It is composed of two cavernous bodies which are tissues that fill with blood during sexual arousal, causing the clitoris to swell. It has a glans (tip) and a shaft, which feels like a rubbery cord under the skin. The shaft internally divides into two parts which spread out, like a wide wishbone. These parts are called the *crura* (singular is crus) each of which is three inches long and which attach to the pelvic bone. From the place where the shaft and the crura fork, and continuing down along the sides of the vestibule (area enclosed by the inner lips and containing the urethral and vaginal openings) are two bundles of erectile tissue called the vestibular bulbs. These become congested with blood during sexual excitement. The crura of the clitoris and the vestibular bulbs are surrounded by muscle tissue, which tenses during sexual arousal and which is part of the muscular system that contracts during orgasm.

Thus we see that the visible external clitoral structure is like the tip of the famous iceberg or, perhaps more accurately, the volcano (Seaman, 1972); in this case, it is the tip of a complicated internal system of highly responsive sexual tissue. This internal system of the female is in contrast to the male system, where the responsive tissue is mainly external (in the penis). Various African tribes have been known to manipulate the clitoris and labia to enlarge them, since a large size was equated with beauty. However, there is no known correlation between the size of the clitoris and its sexual functioning.

The procedure known as female circumcision involves the removal of the clitoral hood. Apart from its history as an attempt to prevent or curb masturbation, this operation was a minor fad in the early 1970s for the purpose of allegedly enhancing female responsiveness. Similar in intent to the procedure occasionally performed a few decades ago of repositioning the clitoris closer to the vaginal opening, these maneuvers are based on a misunderstanding of female sexuality. They also carry their own risks, for example, development of scar tissue or loss of the protective function of the clitoral hood.

The clitoral hood is derived from the same tissue as the foreskin of newborn boys and uncircumcised adult males. Glands under the hood normally secrete smegma, the same white cheesy substance produced under the male foreskin. Gentle washing of this area removes the smegma, which, if allowed to accumulate, can cause adhesions under the hood. The vulval area is composed of delicate mucous membrane, much like the inside of the mouth. Soap and water, without unnecessarily vigorous scrubbing, are sufficient to keep it clean.

The next structure below the clitoris is the urethral orifice or opening. This opening is sometimes difficult to locate because it is relatively small; a mirror is useful to help locate the urethral opening. This structure is the least important in terms of sexual functioning. Some women like stimulation of the area around this opening; others find it irritating. It is not a good idea to insert any objects (other than for bona fide medical purposes) into this opening.

So-called feminine hygiene products are not only unnecessary but can cause irritation and potential infection (Stewart et al., 1979). The profusion of such products and of douche preparations, ranging from champagne-flavored to expensive concoctions whose main ingredients are water and everyday household vinegar, plays into the cultural negativity surrounding the female genitals. The uncertainty and fearfulness which many women feel about their genitals often start with the lack of appropriate names and education in childhood and is augmented by the folklore about nasty smells and discharges. Advertising for feminine hygiene products and for deodorant menstrual products capitalizes on these themes and proclaims that all women are concerned (or ought to be) about vaginal odor, that vaginal discharge is a problem, that femininity is enhanced by perfumed douches, and so on. The marketing success of such products attests both to the general concerns with body odors endemic to the American consumer and to the widespread lack of knowledge of the normal functioning of the vagina.

An interesting twist on this theme is provided by new products on the market which claim to restore the natural sexual scents to the bedroom atmosphere. Based on the unsubstantiated hypothesis (see Chapter 3) that pheromones, chemical substance with sex attractant properties, are present in normal vaginal secretions which are then removed by douching, these products claim to replicate the functioning of pheromones. Needless to say the avoidance of unnecessary douching would eliminate the need for yet another consumer product of this ilk.

On either side of the urethral opening is a tiny (not always visible) opening to a duct which leads to the Skene's glands. These are small vestigial structures (homologously related to the male prostate gland; see Chapter 6), which may occasionally become infected.

The glands on either side of the vaginal opening are the Bartholin's glands. Before Masters and Johnson demonstrated the self-lubricating property of the vagina (Masters and Johnson, 1966), it was believed that these glands produced the lubrication present during sexual arousal. While they do secrete a drop or two of fluid during excitement, the major portion of vaginal lubrication is produced within the vagina itself. Bartholin's glands can become infected or form cysts; pain in this area, indicative of these conditions, should receive medical attention.

The area of skin and muscle between the vagina and the anus is called the perineum and, as previously stated, has the potential for sexual stimulation in some individuals.

The hymen, or maidenhead, or, as commonly known, cherry, is a membrane which covers the entrance to the vagina. It usually has a small opening in it for vaginal and menstrual discharge. In some cases, a woman's hymen has no opening. The imperforate hymen, as this is called, can be opened by a fairly simple surgical procedure. The hymen has a dubious mythical status, in which it is commonly believed that an intact hymen is a positive sign of virginity. Some cultures, for example, in the Middle East, have employed the ritual of exhibiting the bloodstained sheets on the morning after a marriage ceremony, testifying that the bride has come to the groom in an unsullied state. Some cultures meted out heavy punishment, including death, to the woman whose hymen was not appropriately present. Other cultures have practiced ritual "deflowering" of the bride-to-be by religious figures or older women of the tribe; during feudal times in Europe, this proceeding was the prerogative of the lord of the manor. This practice was known as *droit du seigneur* in French, or *jus primae noctis* ("right of the first night") in Latin.

The relationship between an intact hymen and virginity, however, is not all that simple. In some cases the hymen is highly elastic, and gentle insertion of the penis might not cause it to rupture. In general, the tearing of the hymen may cause bleeding and possibly some pain but is usually not physically traumatic. Conversely, a torn hymen is not necessarily a sign that the woman has had sexual intercourse, since various activities, such as athletics, bicycle riding, and horseback riding, can similarly cause this tissue to tear. Even after the hymen has been stretched and broken, small folds of this tissue, known as hymenal tags, will remain.

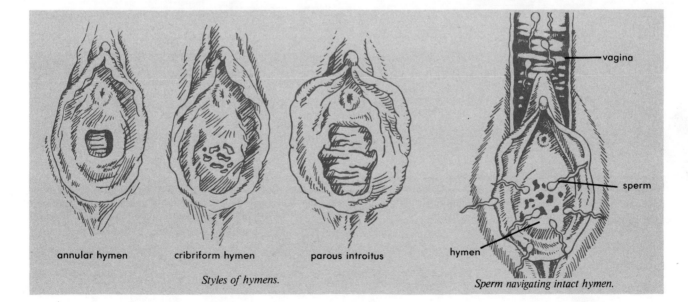

annular hymen      cribriform hymen      parous introitus

*Styles of hymens.*

vagina

sperm

hymen

*Sperm navigating intact hymen.*

The diagram shows several varieties of hymen styles. It also illustrates the manner in which a virgin can conceive a child. Sperm seek an egg like homing pigeons fly toward home. If sperm are deposited on the labia or near the vaginal opening, sufficient numbers for impregnation may find their way through the hymenal opening and thus on the journey to the Fallopian tubes and a possible egg. The same situation obviously holds true for sperm near a vagina without hymenal covering.

The set of muscles of the pelvic floor extend from the pubic bone to the coccyx, or tailbone, and is appropriately called the pubococcygeal muscle, or P.C. muscle for short. Some authorities recommend exercising this muscle to strengthen the pelvic floor (especially recommended after childbirth) and to promote the possibility of achieving a heightened degree of sexual sensation. To locate this muscle, a woman can bear down as if she were going to urinate and then contract her muscles as if to stop the flow of urine in midstream. The muscle thus contracted is the P.C. muscle (it contracts the urethral, vaginal, and anal openings). Other ways to locate this muscle are to practice stopping the flow when actually urinating or to insert a finger into the vagina up to about the first knuckle and then contract the vagina around the finger; the contracting muscle is the P.C.

One exercise used to strengthen this muscle consists of contracting or squeezing the muscle for three seconds, releasing for three seconds, repeating this pattern ten times, and practicing this sequence three times a day at first, gradually adding more sets. It will take a while (several weeks or months) to experience the effects of the exercise. Advantages to this exercise are that it requires no special clothing or apparatus and that it can be practiced in public (while waiting for a bus or watching television, for example) without anyone else's knowledge. This exercise was originally developed by Dr. Arnold Kegel, a gynecologist (and is hence known as Kegel exercises), to treat women with urinary incontinence and to help develop urinary control. Women to whom he recommended it reported to him that it also helped increase their sexual sensations. This exercise is also used as an adjunct in sex therapy, to give women "permission" to concentrate on their genital sensations. New reports claim increased sexual sensations for men who practice a similar exercise, which will be discussed in a later section of this chapter.

There are substantial differences in the size, color, shape, and texture of the genitals, and these features of the individual woman change, too, at different phases of the life cycle, from youth to old age. The basic anatomy is the same, but the appearance of these separate structures, and their relative distance from one another, is quite varied. The configuration of each woman's genitals is as unique as her face. We all have eyes, a nose, and a mouth, and it is to the enrichment of our aesthetic senses that there exists such incredible variety in their relative size and shape. The same holds true for the genitals. Just as the size or shape of our facial organs is not correlated with their sensory functioning, so, too, the size or placement of the genital structures does not affect sexual functioning. Some women have thin outer lips; others, large and puffy. In some women, the inner labia show between the outer lips; in other women they do not. Clitorises vary in size, and the relative position of the urethral opening between the clitoris and the vagina varies, too. Some women's genitals have a thick covering of pubic hair; others, a thinner covering. Also, the color of pubic hair can differ from the color of the hair on one's head.

All too often, women measure how they look against a culturally standardized norm of how a woman *should* look and

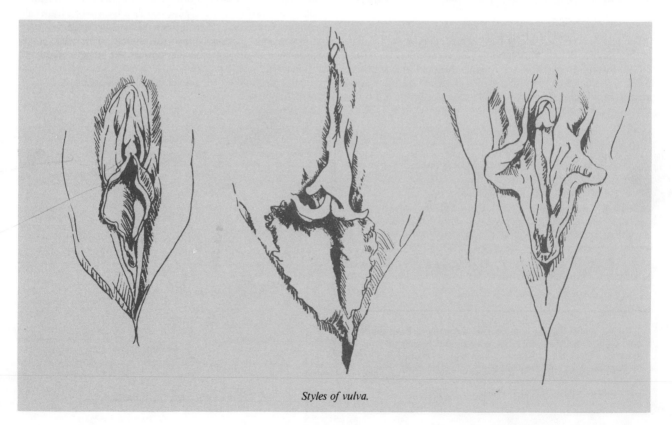

*Styles of vulva.*

find themselves lacking. No matter that the model changes rather rapidly, for example, from Marilyn Monroe to Twiggy to Cheryl Tiegs, the vast majority of women do not resemble the current model. Rather than placing value on the diversity of the human form for its own sake, we tend to want to look like whoever is "in," with support amply provided by the fashion and cosmetic industries. As a result, many women have a negative body self-image and invest a great deal of time and energy into concerns such as excess weight loss. The negative attitudes toward one's genitals, which stem from a number of sources, both contribute to and are reinforced by a general negative self-image.

Perhaps the increasing emphasis on health issues (for example, physical fitness and nutrition), and the growing influence of the women's movement with its message of self-acceptance, will help us to appreciate our bodies for their healthiness and their unique individuality. Knowledge about our sexual appearance and functioning can help to further establish our comfort about ourselves and our self-confidence.

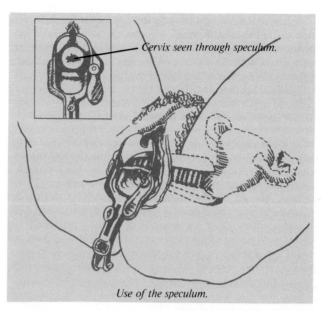

*Cervix seen through speculum.*

*Use of the speculum.*

## The Gynecological Exam

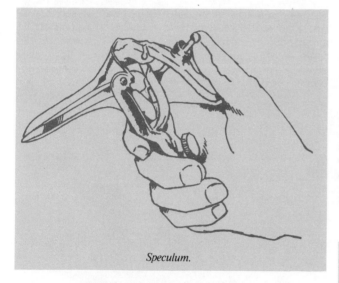

*Speculum.*

The medical procedure performed to check the health of the female sexual-reproductive system is called the gynecological or pelvic examination. For numbers of women, such exams are distasteful or anxiety producing. Lying on one's back with one's legs up in stirrups and one's genitals exposed produces a feeling of vulnerability. If the woman is anxious and tense, a procedure which can otherwise be negligibly uncomfortable can be transformed into a painful and trying event. Since an annual pelvic exam is considered an important part of preventive health

care, it is important to demystify the procedure. The medical practitioner first examines the external genitals. He or she then inserts a speculum into the vagina to look at the vaginal walls and cervix and to take cell samples from the cervix for a Pap smear, a laboratory test for the early detection of cancer. After removing the speculum, the examiner performs a bimanual ("internal") exam. She or he inserts two fingers of a surgically gloved hand into the vagina and places the other hand on the lower abdomen. By applying pressure, she or he can usually locate the pelvic organs between the two hands. In this way, the size, shape, position, and mobility of the uterus and ovaries can be checked. The more knowledgeable a woman is about her anatomy and its functioning, the more she can become an active participant in the exam, with fear and excess anxiety replaced by understanding.

Recent studies suggest that low-risk women need Pap smears only every three years. High-risk women, that is, those from a lower socioeconomic background, those who began sexual activity at an early age and have had many sexual partners, or those who have a history of genital herpes (see Chapter 15), should have annual testing (Marx, 1979a).

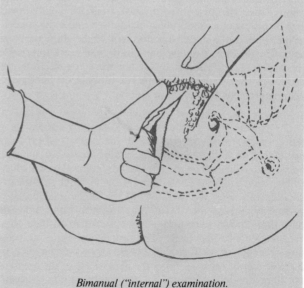

*Bimanual ("internal") examination.*

As the women's movement in the late 1960s focused attention on health-related issues, the concept of self-examination developed. This procedure enables a woman to examine her own cervix with the aid of a plastic speculum, a mirror, and a light source such as a flashlight or high-intensity lamp.

By performing self-examination, a woman can learn to become familiar with the menstrual cycle changes in the appearance of her cervix and in the cervical mucus. She can also learn what constitutes the normal amounts and texture of her vaginal discharge. In this way, she can become aware of unusual changes, detect infections early, and, when necessary, provide a medical practitioner with appropriate information. If the woman has an IUD (intrauterine contraceptive device; see Chapter 8), she can check the placement of the string. Additionally, in some cases, a woman can detect early pregnancy: the cervix will take on a bluish color that is due to increased venous blood circulation. In general, the value of self-examination resides in the demystification of one's anatomy and in the heightened comfort level and self-acceptance it can facilitate.

## The Breast

The breasts, or mammary glands, are also considered part of the sexual system. Breasts are highly specialized sweat glands, whose biological function is to transport milk manufactured in the milk glands through the nipple and into a baby's mouth. The milk-producing glands are saclike structures with ducts that extend to the nipple. These glands are surrounded by connective and fatty tissue. Most women have the same amount of glandular tissue in their breasts as other women; it is the amount of fat and connective tissue that accounts for differences in breast size and shape. The brownish area surrounding the nipple is called the areola. When the nipple is sexually aroused, it becomes erect. Other stimuli, such as exposure to cold, can also produce erection.

In our culture, as in several others, the female breast has acquired the aura of a sex symbol. Fashions in breast display have ranged, over the past three decades, from the pointy-tipped breast sticking out almost horizontally from under the sweater in the fifties to the so-called braless look of the late sixties and seventies. Brassiere manufacturers have been quick to provide the appropriate apparatus to further these trends, from the heavily padded, sculptured bras of the fifties to the lightly padded, natural-look bras of the seventies.

The popularity of big breasts is evidenced by current slang terms which stress large size and by the diversity of products manufactured and advertised (generally falsely) to increase breast size. Women who are influenced by cultural trends which emphasize the desirable breast profile tend to think that breasts come in two sizes: too small or too big. While small-breasted women might envy their D-cup sisters, women with big breasts have been known to complain about the attention their large breasts garner or about related or resultant physical problems (like shoulder or neck strain). Plastic surgery to increase or decrease size or otherwise alter the appearance of the breast is not infrequently resorted to. Such operations are not without their own risks, however; for example, in the early versions of

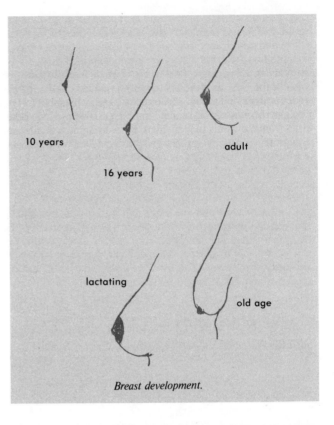

*Breast development.*

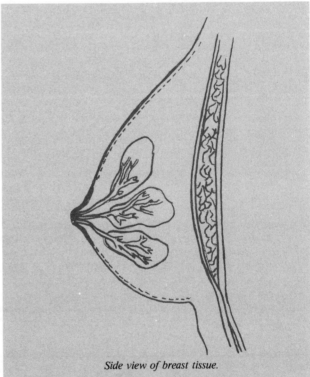

*Side view of breast tissue.*

silicone implants to enlarge breast size, the implants sometimes moved from the breast and caused problems. It must also be realized that sensation may sometimes be permanently lost if nerve endings are severed during surgery.

Although cultural attitudes may value one breast profile over another, women continue to have breasts that vary a great deal in size and appearance from one woman to the next. Often a woman's two breasts, like her two feet or her facial profiles, will also vary in appearance, with the left breast usually being the larger of the two. As is the case with the genitals, the size of the breast is irrelevant to its capacity for sexual sensitivity. The areola is the most sensitive area, but breast response in general varies from individual to individual. In some women, small hairs grow in the cleavage between the breasts or around the areola.

Regular breast self-examination, in order for a woman to become familiar with her normal breast texture and thus be able to detect the appearance of unusual lumps or other changes, is an important element of preventive health care. A woman is less likely to be fearful about or avoid performing this procedure when she recognizes that self-detection (which usually means early detection) of possibly malignant changes depends on her familiarity with her own body.

# MALE ANATOMY

## EXTERNAL MALE ANATOMY

As is the case with the female sexual-reproductive system, the internal male sex organs are housed in the pelvis, which is similar to the female pelvis except that the space between the hip bones is narrower in the male. In discussing the male system, we will start with the highly visible external genitalia.

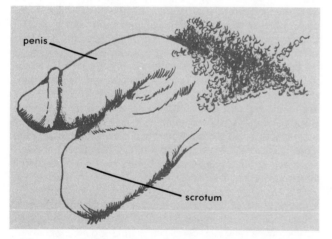

The external male sex organs are the penis and the scrotum, or scrotal sac. The penis, which we will discuss first, is designed to perform three different functions. These functions are, in order of presumed frequency, urination, sexuality, and impregnation.

The penis is a cylindrical organ composed of spongy tissue which is served by a rich network of blood vessels and nerves, and very little muscle. The portion of the penis which is attached to the pelvis is called its root, and the pendulous part is known as the body. The body has two distinct parts: the shaft and the smooth, rounded head, which is called the *glans* (acorn) *penis*. The ridge separating the glans from the shaft is called the *corona* (crown). The glans is richly endowed with nerve

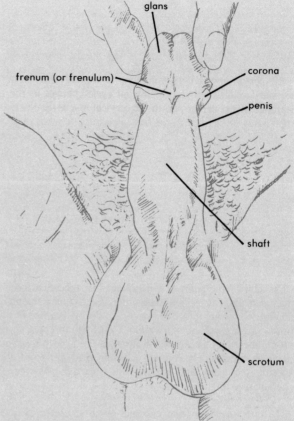

endings, and the glans and corona comprise the most sexually excitable area of the penis. On the underside of the penis there is a thin strip of skin called the *frenum* or *frenulum*, which connects the shaft and the corona. This is usually the most exquisitely sensitive area, although, again, self-exploration can determine what are the areas of particular sensitivity. At the tip of the glans is the urethral opening.

The internal structure of the penis consists mainly of three long cylinders of spongy tissue. The two lying on the top are larger and are called the cavernous bodies (*corpora cavernosa*), and the one lying on the bottom is known as the spongy body (*corpus spongiosum*). The urethra, which conveys both urine and semen out of the body, runs through the spongy body. The glans penis is formed by the free end of the spongy body. These separate bodies cannot be distinguished in the flaccid (nonerect) penis, but during erection the spongy body can be felt as a distinct ridge on the underside of the penis.

As their names suggest, these bodies consist of many cavities or spaces, much like a dense sponge. They are served by an abundant supply of blood vessels and nerves. When the penis is flaccid, or unaroused, these cavities contain little blood. During arousal, they become engorged, or filled with blood, and expand, causing the penis to assume its characteristic stiffness.

The inner tips (*crura*) of the cavernous bodies attach to the pelvic bones. The inner tip of the spongy body expands to form the bulb of the penis. The crura and the bulb together constitute the root of the penis.

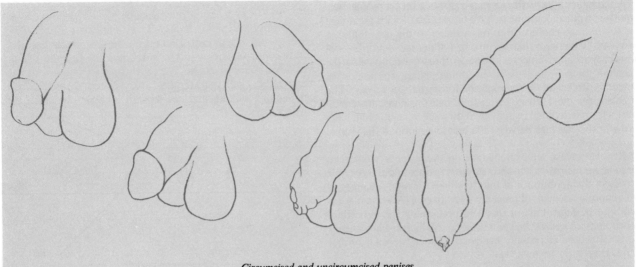

*Circumcised and uncircumcised penises.*

The skin of the penis is hairless and fits somewhat loosely, which permits it to expand during erection. Around the glans, and partly covering it (rather like a loose sleeve), is a fold of skin known as the *prepuce*, or *foreskin*. Under the foreskin, in the corona, are small glands which produce the cheesy substance known as smegma. The foreskin is usually easily retracted, thus exposing the glans and making this area available for appropriate cleaning.

The operation known as circumcision involves the excision, or removal, of the foreskin. This operation has been performed both as a religious ritual and as a sanitary measure. Masters and Johnson (1966) claim that there is no difference in sexual sensitivity between the circumcised and the uncircumcised male.

The practice of circumcision, which is widely performed in this country, has recently become controversial. A review of the indications, other than religious, for this procedure shows that the operation has been justified both on the grounds of mental health and for physical health reasons. The original ground for this practice was a belief in its ability to control "masturbatory insanity." When this "mental health" rationale began to decline in the 1930s, it was superseded by the cancer-prevention rationale. The often-cited study this reasoning was based on (connection between uncircumcised men and cervical cancer in their wives) has long since been criticized on the grounds of fundamental statistical errors; other studies have shown that women who develop cervical cancer are equally likely to be married to circumcised men (Paige, 1978).

Around the world circumcision continues to be widely practiced where it has a religious or cultural tradition, for example, in Israel, Arab nations, and some African tribes. Otherwise, the United States is the only country where this procedure still flourishes widely. There are several indications, however, that the issue is being reevaluated; for example, Dr. Benjamin Spock's latest edition of *Baby and Child Care* says that circumcision is not medically necessary, and in 1975 the American Pediatric society concluded that "there are no valid medical indications for circumcision" in infancy (Paige, 1978).

New research is being developed to evaluate the psychological

and stress consequences of early circumcision. It is believed that this procedure is indeed stressful for the infant, but the potential effects of this stress are yet to be investigated (Paige, 1978). Given that the majority of male readers of this page are circumcised, it is helpful to put this event in context and to realize that many features of the newborn's daily life can produce stress.

The second of the two external male sex organs is the scrotum. The scrotum is the male tissue which is homologous to the labia majora of the female (see prenatal differentiation, Chapter 6). The scrotum is a multilayered pouch, which is at a lower temperature than the rest of the body. This lower temperature is necessary for the manufacture of sperm. The thin, outermost skin layer of the scrotum is generally darker in color than the rest of the body. It contains many sweat glands and becomes sparsely covered with hair during puberty. The second, inner layer contains loosely organized muscle fibers (*dartos* muscle). Although not under voluntary control, these fibers do contract and raise the scrotum closer to the body in response to such stimuli as cold (as some men may have noticed after jumping into a cold body of water for an invigorating swim) and sexual excitement. When the inner thigh is stimulated, the dartos muscle contracts slightly; this contraction is known as the *cremasteric* reflex.

The scrotum, or scrotal sac, contains two separate compartments, each of which contains a testicle (also called testis) and its accompanying spermatic cord. The spermatic cord contains the tube (*vas deferens*) that carries the mature sperm out of the testicle and a supply of blood vessels, nerves, and muscle fibers.

The male perineum and anus are also potentially sexually responsive. This is another area in which self-exploration and/or partner exploration can lead to new knowledge of and familiarity with the range of one's sensitivity.

The functioning of the male reproductive system can be divided into three units: the production of sperm, its storage and transportation, and its delivery. The penis performs this last activity, and the first two are accomplished by the internal sex organs. These organs consist of the testes (or testicles), epididymis, urethra, and the accessory reproductive glands.

## INTERNAL MALE ANATOMY

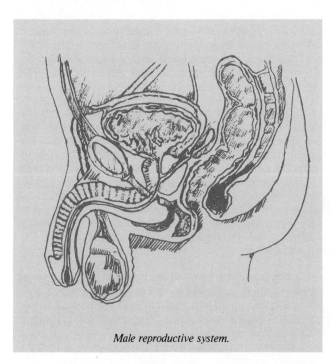

*Male reproductive system.*

The testes, or male gonads, are comparable to the ovaries of the female. Both testes are about the same size; and one of them usually the left one, hangs lower than the other one. Whether the lower one is the right or left one does not seem to be influenced by left- or right-handedness, ethnic background, etc. Like the ovaries, the testes perform two main functions: they produce sperm and they manufacture the male hormone, testosterone. The testes descend from the abdominal cavity into the scrotal sac during the seventh month of prenatal development. It is estimated that about four percent of males are born with undescended testicles (cryptorchidism). If this condition persists, it should be surgically corrected by the time the boy reaches the age of four or five.

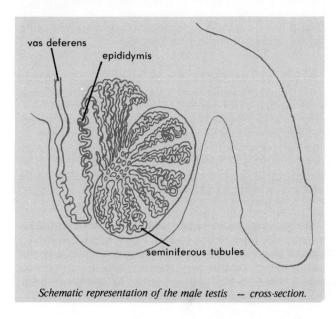

*Schematic representation of the male testis — cross-section.*

Each testis is surrounded by a tight, whitish fibrous sheath (*tunica albuginea*) which divides the testis into many sections or lobules (small lobes). Each lobule contains several winding and tightly coiled seminiferous (sperm-bearing) tubules, the site at which sperm are produced. The cells which are engaged in the manufacture of testosterone are located between the seminiferous tubules and are known as the interstitial, or Leydig's, cells.

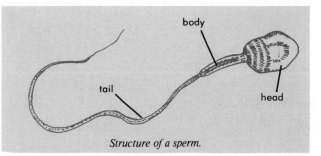

*Structure of a sperm.*

It is the tunica albuginea which accounts for the sterility which may follow a case of mumps in the adult male. When the mumps virus involves the testicles, it causes them to swell. Since the tunica albuginea is tight and does not expand, the pressure of the swelling testicle crushes the delicate seminiferous tubules and impairs their ability to produce sperm. If an adult female contracts a case of mumps, there is no analogous problem because the ovaries are not enclosed in a comparable tight sheath; they swell up and then return to their normal size and functioning.

A male has approximately 1,000 seminiferous tubules, comprising an elaborate system which produces between about 100 and 500 million sperm daily. Each seminiferous tubule is one to three feet long and their combined length measures several hundred yards. Their convoluted and compact structure is a wonderful example of efficient design.

### Spermatogenesis

Mature sperm are called *spermatozoa*. Males are not born with spermatozoa; however, their testes contain a number of undifferentiated cells called *spermatogonia*. Through a complex process known as *spermatogenesis*, which starts during puberty, the spermatogonia undergo subsequent stages of development to become spermatozoa. Up until the nineteenth century it was believed in some quarters that the sperm contained, in miniature, the whole future infant (de Beauvoir, 1961). Perhaps this belief was in reaction to earlier thought, when the role of the male in conception was not yet acknowledged and the woman was believed to conceive through the agency of ancestral spirits (de Beauvoir, 1961; Himes, 1963).

The seminiferous tubules within each testis ultimately converge into a single crescent-shaped tube called the *epididymis*. The epididymis, which reaches a length of twenty feet uncoiled, is a storage place for sperm, where they ripen and mature. The sperm may remain in the epididymis for as long as six weeks, during which time they are nurtured by its lining. If ejaculation does not occur within this time, the sperm are reabsorbed and

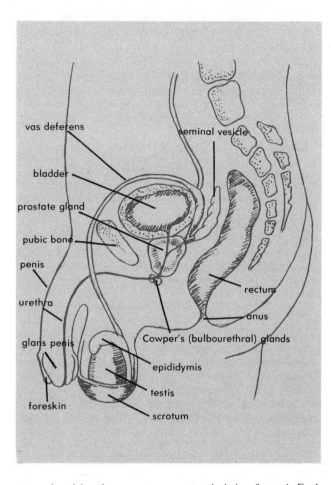

are replaced by the new ones constantly being formed. Each ejaculation contains between 150 and 600 million sperm (Katchadourian and Lunde, 1975); it has been estimated that there are 36 calories per ejaculate.

At the end of the epididymis, the sperm pass into the *vas deferens,* through which they are transported by the action of the cilia lining the vas and by peristaltic contractions, not unlike the journey of the egg. Each vas passes out of the scrotal sac and upward into the abdominal cavity, makes a long arc over the bladder, and descends toward the prostate gland. As it passes through the prostate, it narrows; and its name changes to *ejaculatory duct.* The two ejaculatory ducts then connect with the single urethra.

The urethra serves as the passageway out of the body for both urine and semen. There is a sphincter muscle at the neck of the urinary bladder which closes reflexively prior to ejaculation, forcing the ejaculate out of the penis instead of into the bladder.

The remaining internal sex organs are collectively known as the accessory reproductive glands. The best known of these is the prostate gland. Located beneath the urinary bladder, this structure has the size and shape of a large chestnut. It is composed of muscle and glandular tissue, and it secretes a milky, alkaline substance which comprises about one-third of the seminal fluid, or semen, the medium of transportation for the sperm, and which accounts for the seminal fluid's characteristic odor.

The seminal vesicles, which supply the other two-thirds of the seminal fluid, are two sacs, one on each side, each about two inches long. They empty their contents into the ejaculatory ducts. The secretion which they contribute to the semen is believed to help activate the whiplike movements of the sperm's tail. This portion of the seminal fluid also contains nutrients (fructose) to sustain the sperm on their journey (Mann, 1970).

Cowper's glands, or the bulbourethral glands, are two pea-sized structures located, one on each side, just below the prostate; they empty into the urethra. During sexual arousal, they secrete a clear, sticky fluid which often appears at the tip of the penis before ejaculation. This fluid is alkaline, which serves the function of neutralizing the urethra (urine is acidic) before ejaculation, allowing for safe passage of the sperm. Although not to be confused with semen, this fluid may contain some stray sperm; thus impregnation is possible even if the penis is withdrawn from the vagina before ejaculation.

The amount of seminal fluid per ejaculate is 2.5 to 5 cc., or approximately 1 to 1⅓ teaspoons. The sperm themselves, some 150 to 600 million of them, comprise only a very small proportion of the total volume of semen. The amount and consistency of seminal fluid varies both from individual to individual and in the same man from time to time. Sometimes it is thick and almost like gelatin; other times it is thin and watery.

The semen exits from the body quickly; and, if the penis is in a vagina at the time of ejaculation, the sperm migrate toward the cervix. They can swim quickly, especially considering their microscopic size, and have been known to reach an egg in the Fallopian tube within one and a half hours after ejaculation. Sperm remaining in the vagina will die in several hours, as a result of the unfavorable (for them) acidity of the vagina. Around the time of ovulation, the cervical mucus provides a very hospitable environment for sperm, and they may survive there for a few days. Generally, authorities in the field do not agree on the exact number of sperm which actually complete the journey to the Fallopian tubes. While 2,000 seems to be a reasonable estimate (Katchadourian and Lunde, 1975), the point is that the number represents a minute proportion of the original millions of sperm in the ejaculate.

A male who has had his prostate gland surgically removed can often still experience orgasm but will not ejaculate externally, as the fluid enters the bladder instead and harmlessly exits with the urine. Prepubic boys can have orgasms but do not ejaculate. In a man who has had a vasectomy (see Chapter 8), the volume of seminal fluid without any sperm remains approximately the same as before the surgical procedure, since, as we saw above, the sperm comprises such a tiny proportion of the total volume of the seminal fluid.

Just as there are prevalent standards for female sexual appearance (for example, big breasts, "tight" vagina), so too are there norms for the penis. As Bernie Zilbergeld (1978), author of a demythifying book on male sexuality, puts it, "It's two feet long, hard as steel, and can go all night." According to this fantasy model, male sexuality is a simple phenomenon, concentrated in the penis: men are always ready and willing to perform and sex is entirely the male's responsibility. The socially defined male sex role in our culture equates a great deal of masculinity with the size and performing abilities of the male genitals; for example, strength or aggressiveness is often described in slang terms of reference to the testicles: "He doesn't have the balls to ..." It is thus not surprising that many men experience anxiety about the size and shape of their genitals.

As an example of a humorous approach to stereotyped standards about penis size, look at the following quote:

### HOW..."BIG"...SHOULD A MAN BE?

Don't be shy. It's an important question, and one surrounded by confusion.

The average man's penis is 2½ to 3 inches long. Men substantially larger than this often undergo painful surgery to cure their condition. In thickness, the average man is somewhat larger than a ball-point pen.

(Courtesy of National Lampoon, Inc., O'Rourke, P. J., Kaminsky, P., and Cagan, E., Eds., *Another Dirty Book,* First Edition)

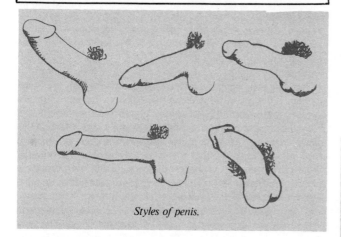

*Styles of penis.*

Casual or furtive glances in the locker room rarely provide helpful information about what other men's penises really do look like and can serve to exaggerate fears. Variation in size and shape of the male genitalia, as is the case for the female genitalia, is the *rule*. Size and shape of the penis (some curve to the left, some to the right) are not related to general body build. A taller man does not necessarily have a bigger penis, nor is penile size correlated with shoe size, straightness or curliness of hair, etc. Variations in the size of the flaccid penis tend to decrease in erection. Generally, the smaller the unaroused penis, the proportionately larger it grows as it becomes erect. The average, that is, composite, flaccid penis is 2.5 to 4 inches (6.4 to 10 centimeters) long; the average erect penis is 6 inches (15 centimeters) in length. Since the penis is basically nonmuscular, it will not grow larger through frequent use, nor with exercise, nor by attaching weights, and so on. Devices similar to those promoted to increase female breast size are being advertised and marketed to increase penis size. A clear understanding of the male human sexual anatomy will help a potential buyer of such a device to recognize its futility.

The size and shape of the penis is not correlated with its ability to provide pleasure for either its owner or his sexual partner, nor is its size a factor in its ability to impregnate. When a man is having sexual intercourse with a woman, her vagina, which is originally "closed" and the upper part of which has few nerve endings, will generally accommodate itself to the size of his penis.

## THE BREAST

The male breasts, like the female breasts, are also potentially sexually sensitive. Since the male breast has not received the same public attention as a sex symbol as its female counterpart, evidenced, for example, by the approval of its nudity in public, some men have not developed an awareness of its sensual or sexual qualities. The actual degree of sensitivity to sexual stimulation of the male breast, like the female breast, will vary from individual to individual. Another similarity between the male and the female is that the male nipple can also become erect during sexual excitement (Masters and Johnson, 1966).

## THE BUTTOCKS

The buttocks of both sexes can add an aesthetic dimension to the appreciation of the curves and lines of the human form. While the buttocks are not directly connected with sexual functioning, many people enjoy stroking and fondling, both giving and receiving, of the buttocks as part of overall bodily sensual or sexual gratification. Indeed, almost any and every part of the body, and the body as a whole, takes pleasure in touching and being touched.

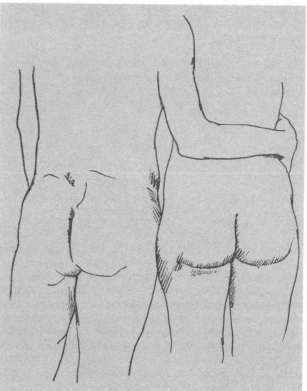

# VOCABULARY OF SEX

In the previous sections of this chapter, we have reviewed the basic anatomy of the human sexual system and the significance of this knowledge to us as participants in our sexuality.

In discussing our bodies, we have generally used standard textbook terminology. This is not the only type of vocabulary that exists to refer to our sexual organs or to sexual activities. In the main, there are four categories of such words: childish (that is, wee-wee, pee-pee), euphemistic (that is, down there, doing it), medical (that is, coitus), and slang or street words. Consideration of this last category can function as a helpful vehicle for insight into some cultural attitudes toward sexuality.

A good number of slang terms which refer to the female are considered by many people to be insulting or contemptuous, while a number of terms which refer to the male connote tools or weapons. Some of the words for sexual activities are either highly idiosyncratic or are also used as swearwords. It is a curious phenomenon that the classical slang word for intercourse can be used both to express contempt or exploitation and to refer to one of the most potentially intimate of human activities. What other words can be used to refer to this activity? "Coitus" is too clinical, "sexual intercourse" seems long-winded and impersonal, "go to bed with" and "sleep together" are quite euphemistic, and "make love" is not always an appropriate description of the context and circumstances. "Have sex with" and "be sexual with" are probably the currently most acceptable terms, yet it is all too obvious that our otherwise highly flexible language lacks a warm, human vocabulary with which to discuss sexuality in meaningful (neither joking nor casual nor embarrassing) ways.

# SEXUAL RESPONSE CYCLE

## INTRODUCTION

Now that we have a background of knowledge about the anatomy of our sexual system, we can explore how this system functions when we are sexually aroused. That the genitals and, indeed, the body as a whole exhibit physiological changes as a result of sexual stimulation has been well-known; however, it is to the work of Masters and Johnson that we owe our current relatively sophisticated knowledge of the physiology of sexual response. Starting in 1954, Masters and Johnson and their co-workers studied men and women masturbating and experiencing heterosexual intercourse in a laboratory setting. Based on their study of 10,000 cycles, they compiled their data and published it in book form, *Human Sexual Response,* in 1966. (For a discussion of their work, see Chapter 4.)

As we shall see, the work of Masters and Johnson not only gives us some fundamental understanding of how our bodies work but also provides a basis from which to reevaluate previous beliefs about sexuality, for example, Freud's theories about female orgasms.

The basic sexual response cycle describes the anatomical and physiological changes in the body as the body participates in the process of sexual stimulation from arousal through orgasm and back to a nonstimulated state. As we discuss in Chapter 17, orgasm need not be the goal of each and every sexual episode; indeed, sexuality as such need not be goal-oriented. A non-goal-oriented perspective suggests the possibility that we direct our attention to the sensations, both physical and emotional, of the moment, keeping our energies concentrated on what is happening with us at this point in time, rather than focusing on the future. Too much emphasis on the future goal, that is, orgasm, might make sexual activity seem more like work than play. Similarly, we can view orgasm as the goal of a sexual encounter, or we can view it as an (albeit exciting) interruption in an otherwise continuous process of pleasurable sensations. Less focus on the necessity for an orgasm as the end result of sexual activity might help reduce performance pressure and anxiety and can help us develop a more open-ended understanding and appreciation of our sexuality. The distinction between affectionate caresses and hugging for their own sake and those which lead to orgasms would not be so rigidly defined. Many of the values of sexual exchange — warmth, affirmation, intimacy — are not necessarily related to the climax itself. We will return to these issues below and in Chapter 17.

Even in our genitals, where men and women are most unalike, there are striking similarities in our response patterns. In fact, the sexual response cycle, as detailed by Masters and Johnson, includes the same basic stages for males and females. These stages are: excitement, plateau, orgasm, and resolution. It is important to note that these phases are not necessarily discrete changes like the shifting of gears. Rather, they represent a flowing process; for example, there is no sharp line between where the excitement stage ends and the plateau stage begins. The two basic body responses that account for the physical changes are vasocongestion and myotonia. Vasocongestion means engorgement or the accumulation of blood in a part of the body, and myotonia refers to muscle tension.

Physiologically, according to the Masters and Johnson model (to state it in the language of the well-known writer Gertrude Stein): an orgasm is an orgasm is an orgasm, whether it occurs during masturbation, intercourse, oral-genital stimulation, fantasy, or any other form of stimulation. Additionally, both men and women may experience orgasm during sleep. The *subjective* experience may, and, indeed, will, differ depending on the situation, but the *physiological* cycle which the individual goes through as she or he builds sexual tension, reaches orgasm, and returns to the initial resting place is similar for all of us.

## FEMALE SEXUAL RESPONSE CYCLE

When a woman is not sexually stimulated, the vagina is closed, and both the inner and outer lips are relatively close together.

As the woman becomes sexually aroused, whether it be through fantasy, contact with her lover, self-stimulation, etc., the excitement phase begins. The first response to effective stimulation is vaginal lubrication. This first sign of excitement in the woman is comparable to the man's penis becoming erect. Vaginal lubrication is caused by a sweatinglike phenomenon. The vagina is lined with a network of blood vessels; as these blood vessels become engorged during excitement, they squeeze out intercellular fluid into the vagina. The presence and the amount of this lubrication is affected by a number of different factors; for example, the fluid can be inhibited by birth control pills, by certain drugs, and for psychological reasons.

> If additional lubrication is desired, a water-soluble jelly is preferable, since it can be washed out of the vagina by the self-cleansing mechanism of the vagina. Petroleum jelly, while a popular source of lubrication, cannot be similarly cleaned out by the vagina and thus remains in the vaginal folds where it can become a possible medium for bacterial growth.

During excitement, the color of the vulva begins to change, becoming more colorful, usually reddish. The tissues begin to get puffier and increase in size; for example, the outer lips begin to open. These changes are due to the engorgement of the tissues with blood, in a way similar to the way our faces turn red when we blush. Internally, the uterus, as a result of myotonia, or muscle tension, begins to move upward into the abdominal cavity.

In the plateau phase, the labia get redder still and the tissues even more puffy. The inner labia increase two to three times in thickness, adding about one centimeter to the length of the vagina. These lips turn shades of color up to bright red, and in a woman who has borne children, they turn a burgundy hue. The walls of the vagina also become a deeper purplish-red.

The clitoris, which becomes swollen during excitement, now retracts and tucks itself up under the hood. This is for self-preservation, since the clitoral glans is now so sensitive that direct stimulation can be painful. At this point, stimulation applied to the hood and the area around it is generally effective.

Meanwhile, during plateau, there are a number of striking internal changes. The uterus has moved up into the abdominal cavity. Vasocongestion may have caused the uterus to increase in size, especially if the excitement and plateau phases are extended in time. Masters and Johnson found this size increase easier to observe in a woman who has borne a child. The upper two-thirds of the vagina balloon out; this is known as the tenting effect. The walls of the lower third of the vagina swell as a result of tissue engorgement, and this narrowed area is known as the orgasmic platform.

If a woman is using a diaphragm for contraceptive purposes (see Chapter 8), it is important that she be fitted with the largest size that is comfortable for her. Since the diaphragm is placed in the upper vagina, if the woman becomes very excited during intercourse, the area that the diaphragm encompasses will expand.

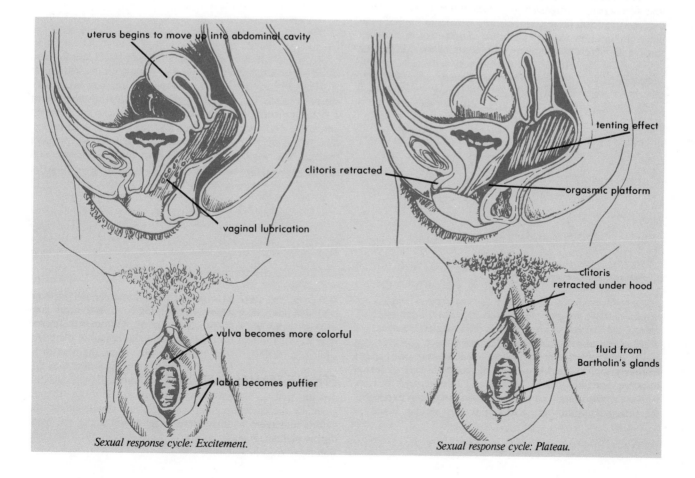

*Sexual response cycle: Excitement.*

*Sexual response cycle: Plateau.*

The whole body responds to sexual stimulation. Muscles all over the body — in the face, thighs, hands, feet, etc. — are tensing; the heartbeat, blood pressure, and respiration rate start increasing in excitement and increase further during plateau. The nipples become erect from muscle tension in the fibers surrounding this structure. This erection phenomenon can also occur in response to other stimuli, for example, cold.

Vasocongestive changes in the breast cause the patterns of the veins directly under the skin to become more visible. As a result of this engorgement, the breast itself increases in size, up to 20% to 25% in the plateau stage. This reaction is more likely to occur in the woman who has not borne a child. During plateau, the engorgement of the areola causes it to project forward, embedding the nipple somewhat and possibly hiding or obscuring the nipple's erection.

Some individuals, women more often than men, may experience what is called sex flush; measle-like spots first appear on the abdomen and then may spread over the breasts and chest. During plateau, the flush may extend to the face, thighs, buttocks, and back as the vessels near the surface of the skin become engorged with blood.

Women generally require stimulation not only up to the point of orgasm but throughout the climax as well. Orgasm is a reflex action and thus cannot be willed or forced any more than a knee jerk can. Orgasm occurs when the mounting vasocongestion and myotonia reach a peak and then release. The reflex action of orgasm is perceived as a pleasurable sensation. The orgasmic platform (lower third of the vagina) and the P.C. and other circumvaginal muscles contract. There may be between three and fifteen contractions that occur every 0.8 second;

the longer the contractions continue, the longer the time interval between them.

Masters and Johnson (1966) report on a variation in female orgasmic expression known as *status orgasmus.* This phenomenon consists of either a series of rapidly recurring orgasmic peaks between which no recordable plateau phase intervals can be demonstrated or a single, continuous orgasm. Masters and Johnson suggest that here the woman is most likely moving with extreme speed between successive climaxes and a base line of advanced plateau-level tension. Status orgasmus may last 20 to 60 seconds.

The uterus also contracts during a woman's orgasm. It is to be noted that these uterine contractions sometimes can help relieve menstrual cramps. The anus may also contract. Finally, there is an extreme amount of variability in the intensity of orgasms, from individual to individual and from time to time in the same person.

The orgasm, like other reflexes, is divided into a sensory component, that is, that which receives the stimulation, and a motor component, that which reacts to this stimulation. In the female orgasm, the sensory component is usually the clitoris, and the orgasmic platform and surrounding musculature constitute the motor component.

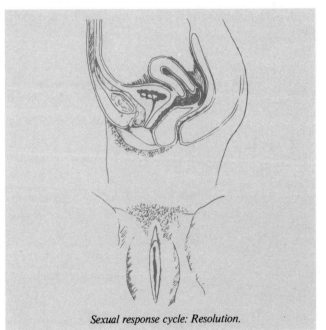

*Sexual response cycle: Resolution.*

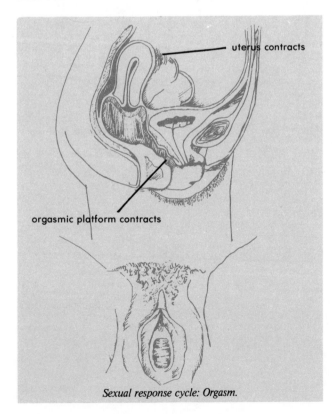

*Sexual response cycle: Orgasm.*

We can also make a further distinction between what is happening in our bodies, which is measurable in the laboratory, and what it is that we are actually aware of. Although the motor response of the orgasm takes place in the orgasmic platform, women sometimes report that they *experience* the orgasm in varying places in the body; that is, the focus of feeling may differ (Seaman, 1972). The area which is stimulated to produce the orgasm, that is, the sensory component of the reflex, though generally the clitoral region, may also vary. Interestingly, the clitoris undergoes its characteristic retraction under the hood during plateau, whether or not it is involved in direct stimulation (Masters and Johnson, 1966).

During the resolution phase, the body returns to its preexcitement state. There is a reversal of the processes that built up during the excitement and plateau phases; the blood vessels become disengorged, muscles relax, and perspiration may appear on the body. The clitoris reemerges within five to ten seconds after orgasm, but its final detumescence (loss of swelling) can take between five and ten minutes and sometimes as long as fifteen to thirty minutes. It may take as long as thirty minutes for the entire body to return to its unstimulated state. If the woman has reached plateau but not orgasm, the massive release of muscular tension and of blood from the engorged tissues which is triggered by orgasm does not take effect, and the resolution phase will last longer.

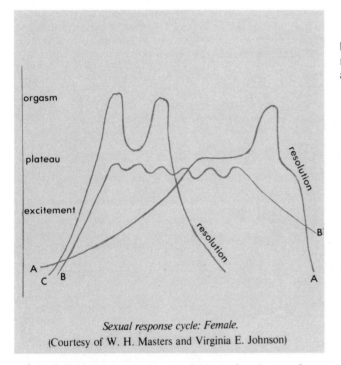

*Sexual response cycle: Female.*
(Courtesy of W. H. Masters and Virginia E. Johnson)

In this illustration, pattern A exhibits a female experience which is most like the typical male experience, straight through from excitement through plateau to orgasm and then resolution. In pattern B, the woman becomes excited, reaches plateau, continues in the plateau stage for a while, does not go on to orgasm, then goes through resolution. In pattern C, once the woman has reached orgasm, if appropriate stimulation is maintained, she will experience another orgasm, and another and another before finally going through resolution.

This last example illustrates the physiological potential of some women to be multiorgasmic as long as there is appropriate stimulation or until fatigue sets in. In such a situation, sometimes the first orgasm is the most intense, sometimes the intensity varies from peak to peak, and other times each succeeding climax grows more intense. The fact that a woman has this potential does not dictate that she must always fulfill it. Nor are numbers of climaxes necessarily correlated with physical, psychological, or emotional satisfaction.

As we saw in Chapter 1, at the turn of this century women were not "supposed" to have orgasms; sometime after that time

they *were* "supposed" to, if the climax was of the "right" kind (Freud's vaginal orgasm); now, in some quarters, women are "expected" to have as many as five to ten orgasms in any given sexual encounter. Transforming a physical potentiality into a performance standard does not serve to enhance sexuality.

Patterns A, B, and C represent but three possible patterns; if a woman were to chart her own experiences, she would most likely discover much more variety.

## MALE SEXUAL RESPONSE CYCLE

During sexual excitement in men, as for women, the whole body responds. The heartbeat, blood pressure, and respiration rate increase; there is tension in muscles throughout the body; and the nipples become erect.

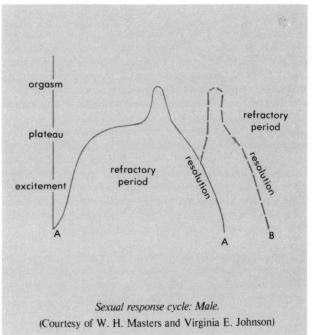

*Sexual response cycle: Male.*
(Courtesy of W. H. Masters and Virginia E. Johnson)

Pattern A in this drawing represents the standard male sexual response cycle from excitement through resolution. Pattern B illustrates a second orgasm following the man's refractory period. As in the case for women, any given man's experience will probably result in a graph with more variations than are pictured here. For example, one such pattern may represent a process of moving from excitement to plateau and back to excitement several times before orgasm takes place.

The first physiological response to effective sexual stimulation, whether it be sensory or psychological, is the erection of the man's penis. The neural message travels from the erection center in the lower spine, via the parasympathetic nervous system, to arterial tissue in the penis, causing this tissue to dilate. Blood flow increases, and the blood sinuses or cavities in the three spongy bodies of the penis become filled. It is believed

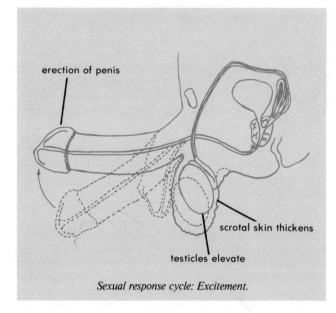

*Sexual response cycle: Excitement.*

During plateau, the mechanism of vasocongestion causes the erect penis to increase in circumference, especially at the head (glans penis). Sometimes the glans will turn reddish-purple, but this change in color is not consistent. A clear fluid may appear in droplets at the urethral opening. This fluid, produced by the Cowper's glands, may contain enough viable sperm to cause pregnancy (as discussed earlier in this chapter). As a result of blood engorgement, the testicles now increase in size by 50% to 100%. If sex flush is going to appear, it may now be visible on the man's forehead, face, neck, shoulders, chest, and thighs. Pulse rate, blood pressure, and respiration rate are increasing.

The general bodily responses to orgasm in the male are similar to those for the female. These may include a potential loss of overall sensory acuity, loss of voluntary muscle control, and massive muscular contractions (due to myotonia); and the heart and breathing rate may be highest now.

that special valves close, constricting the veins, so that blood will enter the tissues faster than it can leave, expanding the spongy bodies to their full capacity (Masters and Johnson, 1966). Thus the penis becomes erect. During excitement, as stimulation varies, a man's erection may subside and be regained a number of times; this process should be no cause for concern.

Sometimes a man may wake up from a night's sleep and find his penis erect. The mechanism underlying this phenomenon of "morning erection" is not fully understood. It is possible that the pressure of a full urinary bladder causes this erection. Since men experience erection (and women's vaginas lubricate) during REM (rapid eye movement) sleep several times a night, some authorities suggest that a morning erection occurs when the male wakes up from a period of REM sleep.

During excitement, the scrotal sac elevates, a result of vasocongestion and thickening of the scrotal skin. The testicles within the scrotal sac also elevate, as a result of contractions in the muscle tissue surrounding the spermatic cord.

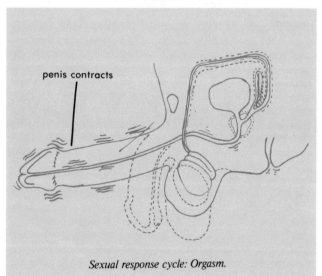

*Sexual response cycle: Orgasm.*

In the male, orgasm is generally equated with ejaculation. Whether this is an accurate equation depends on the definition of orgasm. When orgasm is considered as a total body response, including the individual's subjective interpretation of the experience, then ejaculation is but a part, not the whole, of the orgasm. An interesting example exists in the case of those paraplegic individuals whose spinal lesion is high enough to leave the nerve area responsible for ejaculation intact. These men can ejaculate, but the ejaculation is unaccompanied by the subjective sensation of orgasm.

Reports from men suggest occasional variations in the orgasmic response. Sometimes the excitation before ejaculation is so intense that it in itself feels like a long orgasm. At other times a man may experience a number of peaks, like mild orgasms, before ejaculation (Zilbergeld, 1978).

The process of ejaculation can be divided into two phases, which occur within two to four seconds of each other. The first is emission. This refers to the contraction of the internal reproductive organs in order to collect the various components of the semen, that is, the ejaculate. The vas deferens, prostate,

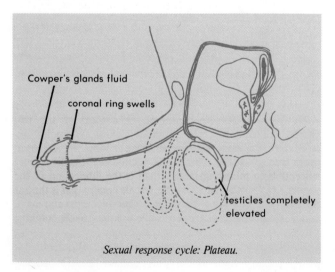

*Sexual response cycle: Plateau.*

and seminal vesicles all contract and pour their contents into the urethra. Subjectively, this is experienced as the time of "ejaculatory inevitability." In ejaculation proper, the semen is expelled out of the penis by vigorous contractions of the urethra and the muscles at the base of the penis and in the perineum. These contractions are subjectively experienced as pleasurable.

The first three or four contractions occur every 0.8 second. As they continue, they are reduced in expulsive force, and the interval between them lengthens. The rectal muscles may also contract. Some men hold their breath, and others breathe rapidly (women also exhibit these varying patterns of breathing). Some men stop moving their penis as they ejaculate, while others increase penile thrusting.

As mentioned earlier, new reports suggest that exercises to strengthen the pelvic muscles used in ejaculation may enhance a man's sensations (Jardine, 1979). Similar to the Kegel exercises suggested for women, these exercises require that the man first locate his P.C. muscles, for example, by stopping and starting the flow of urine several times. Once the man is in touch with these muscles, he begins practicing alternative contraction and release ten to fifteen times, gradually increasing the number of sets he can do. As for women, it takes some time before the muscle is strengthened. It has been reported in the popular press that some men with well-developed P.C. muscles can also learn to stop the flow of semen during orgasm and, with continued stimulation of the penis, can have one or more subsequent orgasms, eventually with ejaculation (Jardine, quoting William Hartman, 1979). It must be stressed that this report is a highly tentative finding and that the substantiation of the male's ability to be thus multiorgasmic needs much further research (see, for example, Robbins and Jensen, 1978).

The orgasmic reflex of the male, like that of the female, has both a sensory and a motor component. The glans and shaft of the penis (homologous to the clitoris) constitute the sensory component, which receives the stimulation and transmits the message; the muscles surrounding the base of the penis (and other internal muscles, like those in the walls of the urethra) constitute the motor component, which react by contracting.

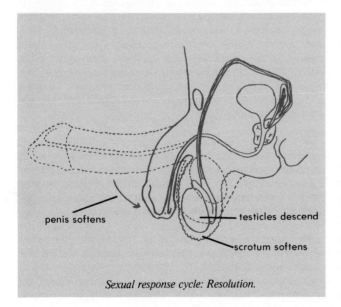

*Sexual response cycle: Resolution.*

During the resolution phase, there is a quite rapid return to the preexcitement state. The penis will detumefy, or lose its swelling. This loss of erection occurs in two stages; the first happens rapidly, as the cavernous bodies empty, leaving the penis still somewhat enlarged. The second stage occurs more slowly, as the spongy body and glans empty. The duration of this second stage depends somewhat on the man's activity. If he remains in close body contact with his partner, it often will last longer.

The testicles revert to their usual size and position, as the scrotal sac lowers. Sex flush, if it appeared, now fades; the body may be sweaty. The nipples lose their erection.

An aspect of the sexual response cycle which is believed to be unique to the male is the refractory period, which immediately follows orgasm and extends into the resolution phase. A refractory period, in general biological terms, refers to the time period in which a cell, tissue, or organ may not respond to a second stimulation until a certain period of time has elapsed since the preceding stimulation. In terms of the sexual response cycle, this means that, regardless of the nature and intensity of sexual stimulation, the male will not respond physiologically, that is, he cannot experience erection and orgasm, until the refractory period is over. There is no precise specification for the length of the refractory period; it will vary with situation, age, amount of alcohol in the system, and other factors.

Women presumably do not have such a refractory period, as evidenced by the ability of some women to be multiorgasmic. Some men, especially younger men, report themselves to be capable of multiple orgasms on occasion; as stated above, this is an as yet unexplored area which calls for further research.

Although we utilize the Masters and Johnson model of the sexual response cycle throughout this book, an alternative conceptualization of the physiological sexual process deserves mention — Helen Singer Kaplan's biphasic model (Kaplan, 1974).

Kaplan conceptualizes a process consisting of two distinct and relatively independent components. The first, or arousal phase, is the "vasocongestive reaction," which causes erection of the penis in the male, and lubrication and swelling of the vagina in the female. The second phase is that of orgasm, produced by reflex muscular contractions. Kaplan offers support for her model by pointing out that these two components are governed by different parts of the nervous system, arousal being mediated by the parasympathetic nervous system, and orgasm by the sympathetic.

Furthermore, Kaplan continues, impairment of the two phases results in distinctly different clinical syndromes. Interestingly, the vasocongestive response is more vulnerable in males than in females. That is, the erection of the penis is more susceptible to inhibiting factors than is the lubrication of the vagina. On the other hand, it is the female orgasm that is the less reliable. Once erection of the penis has been achieved and maintained, the male sexual response cycle will most likely continue on to orgasm. The female sexual response cycle is more vulnerable, and the attainment of orgasm is quite easily interrupted.

## ORGASM

There is a whole gamut of behaviors associated with the actual experience of sexual activity and with orgasm. Each person reacts differently. Some reactions are physiologically based. A person may experience carpopedal spasms (contractions of the muscles in the hands and feet). The face may be contorted in a grimace, though not as a sign of pain. The muscles of the arms, legs, thighs, and back may contract. All of these, when they occur, are involuntary reflexive actions.

Other behavioral reactions will vary depending on both the individual and on the situational context — whether the person is alone or with a partner, the relationship with the partner, the physical setting, psychological factors, the intensity of the orgasm, and so on. Some people are quiet; others make various kinds of noises. Some people thrash around; others remain relatively still. Nor are an individual's reactions necessarily consistent from episode to episode, since there exists such a wealth of situational variables. There is no particular behavioral pattern that we *ought* to exhibit, nor should we assume that a louder or more obvious display necessarily indicates a more pleasurable experience.

The emphasis in our society on performance or goal-oriented sexual activities has led some women to fake orgasm. This can be learned with relative ease by following common media models (visual or literary). Men presumably cannot fake ejaculation, but they can counterfeit the intensity of the orgasmic experience. There are many reasons why a person may choose to fake an orgasm: to please one's partner, to indicate one's prowess, and so on. When faking becomes habitual, however, it may be an indication that the person needs to reassess his or her understanding of sexuality and his or her needs.

A great deal has been written about orgasms and about differences between the male and female experience. Recent studies have shown that panels of readers, students, and profes-

sionals in fields related to sexuality could not distinguish with statistical significance between those descriptions of their orgasm written by men and those written by women (Proctor, Wagner, and Butler, 1976).

A great debate has existed about the nature of the female orgasm. This debate originated with Freud's dual orgasm theory. Early in this century Freud wrote that for the young girl the clitoris was the main seat of sexual sensation. As the female matured, her task was to transfer her erotic sensitivity from her clitoris to her vagina and henceforth to experience adult feminine sexuality. This experience, according to Freud, consisted of vaginal orgasms, that is, orgasms achieved through intercourse. Acknowledging that some adult women persisted in experiencing orgasms through clitoral stimulation, Freud termed these women frigid and neurotic (Williams, 1977). After Freud's death, the traditional school of psychoanalysis reinforced his beliefs, which were then popularized and set up as the standard for female sexuality. Freud's thesis radiated out into a wide number of fields, including the popular press, and into medicine. Gynecology textbooks continued to reiterate Freud's teaching even after contradictory information had become available (Scully and Bart, 1973).

So the woman who was concerned about her sexual response would find the Freudian model to compare herself to, whether she entered analysis or read marriage manuals or pornographic or erotic literature. Given the general milieu of embarrassment and secrecy surrounding the subject, she probably could not ask for or receive helpful information from her peers.

Then came the work of Masters and Johnson, demonstrating only one physiological entity known as an orgasm, and not two separate types. Both the clitoris and the vagina play a role in producing the orgasm: the clitoris as the sensory component, the locus of sensory nerve endings, and the vagina as the motor component, the locus of the orgasmic reflex contractions.

A composite description of the female orgasm, derived from the subjective reports of the women in Masters and Johnson's study, starts with the recognition of a sensation of suspension for an instant (according to the sexological literature, some women experience this sensation as a scary phenomenon somewhat like falling off a cliff; Barbach, 1976, Seaman, 1972). This suspension is accompanied, or followed immediately, by intense sensual awareness, originating in the clitoris and radiating upward into the pelvis. Some women report a concomitant sensation of bearing down. The woman then experiences a feeling of warmth spreading through the pelvis and throughout the body and a sensation of throbbing in the vagina or pelvis.

The subjective report of the onset of orgasm seems to be associated with an initial spasm of the orgasmic platform two to four seconds before this area begins its regularly recurrent contractions. This provides an interesting parallel to the two- to four-second interval between the phases of the male ejaculation.

Some women who have borne children while awake and undrugged report a degree of similarity between the beginning of orgasm and the sensations of delivery. Since there are many parallel reactions between these two phenomena, including breathing patterns, possible vocalization, facial expression, and uterine contractions (Newton, 1973), these reports are not entirely surprising.

So an orgasm is an orgasm; what varies is the type of stimulation which an individual woman requires in order to experience orgasm, and this stimulation need will vary even for the same individual, from episode to episode, depending on the specific circumstances. Some women attach considerable importance to breast stimulation, many others require extensive clitoral stimulation, and still others require succeeding stimulation of different areas. Since the clitoris is the main organ of excitation, Masters and Johnson (1966) hypothesize that those women who climax during intercourse do so because the movements of the penis provide sufficient traction of the vulval area, and the labia minora in particular, which in turn pulls the clitoral hood so that it moves back and forth, stimulating the clitoris itself. Whether this movement of the inner labia also stimulates the frenulum of the clitoris and whether this stimulation would be of significance has not yet been investigated, nor has the role of penile friction transmitted to the engorged vestibular bulbs been determined.

Pressure from contact with the partner's pubic bone (more easily attained if the woman is on top of the man during intercourse) may also increase clitoral stimulation. Seaman questions whether a woman's ability to experience an orgasm induced by intercourse is necessarily entirely dependent on her body. A woman's anatomy may be so constituted that certain characteristics of the penis — its shape, circumference, length, etc. — might variably affect the ability of the penis to provide sufficient traction on the labia minora to produce effective stimulation of the clitoris via its hood (Seaman, 1972).

A different model of the female orgasmic response has been suggested by Singer and Singer (1972). According to this hypothesis, the climax described in Masters and Johnson's study, with its essential vaginal contractions, is but one kind of

orgasm, which Singer and Singer term a vulval orgasm. It occurs during masturbation of the clitoris and may also occur in intercourse. A second kind is what the Singers call uterine orgasm. This kind is produced during intercourse when penile-cervix contact and the thrusting of the penis cause the uterus to stimulate the peritoneum, the tissue which covers the abdominal organs. There are no accompanying vaginal contractions with this orgasm. Leading up to the orgasm, the woman's breath comes in gasps, she then experiences apnea (involuntary holding of the breath), and the climax then coincides with forceful exhalation of the breath, followed by a feeling of sexual satisfaction.

It is further postulated that a third type of orgasm is also possible, a so-called blended orgasm, a combination of the vulval and uterine types (Singer and Singer, 1972).

As Juanita H. Williams, in her book *Psychology of Women,* points out, the Singers' theory has not been tested in the laboratory, and, consequently, it does not have the same empirical backing as does Masters and Johnson's work. Additionally, not only have these latter researchers provided objective descriptions of the physiology of orgasm, but it is also the case that the immediate subjective experiences reported by the women in their studies are consistent with the objective description of the orgasmic event (Williams, 1977).

At this point, we can pause to conjecture about the role of learning in the subjective experience and interpretation of orgasm. If a woman has learned to recognize what constitutes an orgasmic experience and the signs thereof, in accordance with the Masters and Johnson model, is it possible that she might experience what the Singers term a uterine orgasm without being able to identify it as an orgasm *per se*? Even if she does feel satisfied, relaxed, or completed, if she has not been aware of vaginal contractions, she may not be prepared to acknowledge her experience with the honorific label of "orgasm." However, to repeat, while awaiting empirical substantiation or refutation, the conjectural nature of the Singer's theory must be stressed.

Women who do not have orgasms during intercourse still generally experience the activity as pleasurable. It is important to distinguish between those sexual activities which are orgasm producing and those which are pleasurable and desirable for their own sake, as, for example, kissing.

Kaplan (1974) reports that fewer than 45 percent of American woman climax during intercourse. (Hite [1976]) has claimed that the number who do is much lower.) These data lead to the necessity for a reevaluation of what constitutes normal female sexuality. Unfortunately, our culture tends to value one kind of experience over another, and the "no-hands" orgasm ("Look, Ma, no hands"), that is, climax during intercourse, is considered to be the ultimate achievement. One consequence of this attitude is the tendency for a woman to devalue her own experience, to rate an orgasm achieved by clitoral stimulation as "not as good." If a woman believes that her male partner values "vaginal" orgasm, then she may be afraid to let him know how her body likes to be stimulated.

We also need to reevaluate the common notion of what constitutes "the sex act." The pattern of "foreplay/intercourse/

afterplay" puts the main focus on vaginal intercourse. If we move from talking about the sex *act* to talking about sexual *activity*, we can incorporate the notion of process. If intercourse is part of any given sexual interlude, then a woman can have an orgasm (if she is so inclined and able) during intercourse by penile thrusting, during intercourse by accompanying clitoral stimulation (by self or partner), or before or after intercourse (by manual or oral stimulation). From this perspective, any of these patterns is part of the "normal" range of female sexuality, and there is no juncture at which an orgasm is any the more appropriate.

Another experience our culture places on a pedestal is that of the simultaneous orgasm, that is, both partners experiencing orgasm at the same moment during intercourse. Again, not only is this quite difficult to achieve physically, but the idea that this is the "best" leads to both performance pressure and a devaluing of other types of experience. A more satisfying notion is that of mutual orgasm, wherein each partner orgasms at his or her own pace. Rather than losing the experience of sharing one's partner's orgasm because one is so wrapped up in one's own, this process allows for each partner to both experience his or her own orgasm and to give attention to the partner's gratification.

An important issue for the further understanding of our sexual expression concerns the relationship between orgasm and peak sexual experiences. An orgasm is not necessarily always a peak experience, nor the be-all and end-all of a sexual interlude.

Sometimes the warm, tingly sensations running through the partners as they both anticipate and participate in close body contact, the sensations of body movement, the good feelings that make them feel so much alive, can be at least as valuable and meaningful as an orgasm.

In our desire to be adequate and normal, we may tend to set up Masters and Johnson's laboratory findings as *the* goals toward which we must dutifully strive (for example, "What's wrong with me? I don't have sex flush.") But laboratory findings do not take into account feelings, psychological parameters, and the interpersonal context of partner response and interaction. These factors can be very meaningful components in the overall sexual experience, and variations in them may well be important in facilitating a peak or an especially ecstatic sexual experience.

## SUMMARY

In this chapter we have reviewed the anatomy and physiology of the female and male sexual systems and the sexual response cycle. We have discussed the significance of such knowledge for an understanding and appreciation of our sexuality. Within the context of biological explanation, we have stressed the range of diversity and uniqueness of how our bodies look and how we experience our sexual expression.

# Chapter 6

## Psychosexual Development

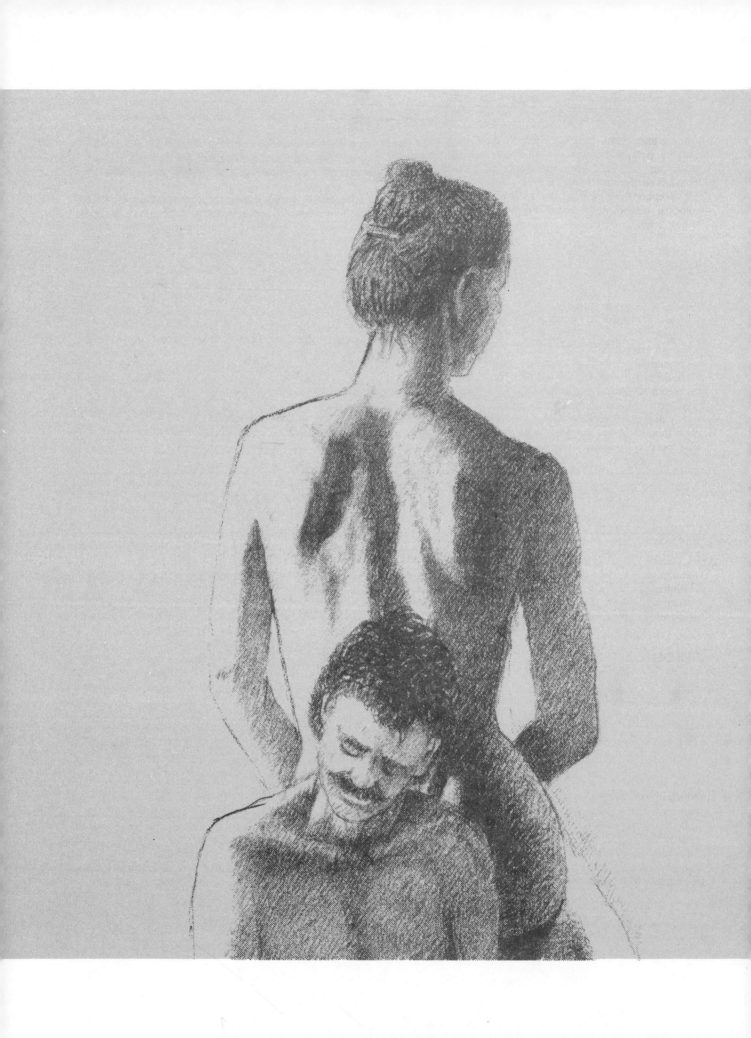

# INTRODUCTION

Of the many fascinating issues related to the study of human sexuality, perhaps the most intriguing centers on the manner in which our individual sexual orientations, preferences, and behaviors emerge and change over the course of a lifetime. With rare exceptions, we all enter the world at birth with the basic biological equipment of either the male or female gender. Almost immediately, however, we are exposed to a variety of familial, social, and cultural influences that continuously shape and mold our sexual identity into what will become later in life a relatively fixed pattern which may vary markedly from individual to individual. Thus, while we cannot deny the physical and biological determinants of sexual behavior, it is also true that the form, quality, and frequency of our sexual behaviors are conditioned or learned as a function of environmental circumstances.

The manner in which this "transformation" from a biological or unlearned basis of sexuality to a social or learned basis occurs has been a subject of great interest and study. Various theories have been advanced, numerous investigations have been conducted, and much debate has ensued regarding the manner in which this change comes about. In this chapter we will examine this process of psychosexual development.

# THEORIES OF PSYCHOSEXUAL DEVELOPMENT

Virtually all of the theories that have attempted to explain psychosexual development recognize the contribution and interaction of both biological determinants and environmental determinants in terms of the final outcome. An arbitrary distinction can be made, however, on the basis of which of these two components is emphasized by the various approaches.

## BIOLOGICAL THEORIES

Although Freud may be more accurately described as an interactionist, the biological emphasis of sexuality is usually attributed to him for at least two reasons: first, because it was Freud who recognized the importance of infantile sexuality, thereby challenging the prevailing Victorian notion of childhood sexual innocence; and second, because his explanation of psychosexual development focused on a sexual drive or instinct (the libido) that was the motivating force behind human behavior. Although Freud recognized the importance of social influences on psychosexual development (in fact, he clearly articulated the significance of parental influences on the process), it was his theory of the innate drive to achieve sexual gratification, or one's libido, that occupied his attention and characterized Freud's biological orientation.

Freud believed that the newborn child enters the world with a diffuse and unstable reserve of energy. The term *libido* was applied to these instinctual forces. Sex, in this context, referred to *all* pleasurable experiences, including, but not limited to, erotic

activity. These libidinal forces constantly sought release or expression since the tension they created was subjectively unpleasant and the release of the tension was experienced as pleasurable. For Freud, the manner in which this libidinal need was met during sexual development determined the adequacy of psychosexual adjustment, influenced the personality, and impacted on the individual's general life adjustment ability.

According to Freud, during the varying stages of development from infancy to sexual maturity, various body areas provide a source of pleasure, in the sense that they serve as erogenous zones (that is, they are particularly sensitive to erotic stimulation), thereby channeling the libido's source of sexual gratification. During the first year of life, the mouth is the most prominent source of tension reduction and the libido is said to center around the oral cavity during this *oral stage*. If the child's oral needs are appropriately satisfied during this stage (that is, he or she is not overindulged, or weaning is accomplished without difficulty), libidinal energies shift from the oral area to the anus during the next two years of life (the *anal stage*). Eliminative processes serve as sources of tension reduction; and again, if toilet training is accomplished without undue stress, the child is prepared to enter the next stage of psychosexual development. During the fourth and fifth years of life the libido is centered in the genital region. Erotic expression becomes more clear-cut, for example, through masturbation, examination of the genitals, manifesting sexual curiosity, etc. It is during this *phallic stage* that the opposite-sex parent is identified as an object of sexual gratification and the same-sex parent as a rival (the Oedipus complex in boys and the Electra complex in girls). This conflict is ordinarily resolved when these incestuous impulses are repressed and the child comes to "identify" with the same-sex parent, that is, adopts an appropriate heterosexual orientation. In this fashion, the child incorporates the same-sex parent's behaviors, attitudes, and values and the path is clear for the assimilation of those attributes that are necessary for "normal" sex-role behavior.

Following the phallic stage, the libido is channeled into a variety of general social activities, and, according to Freud, little advancement of psychosexual development occurs during this *latency period*. With the onset of puberty, however, and the further progression of sexual maturity, the libido again focuses on the genitals for sexual gratification and the release of tension. The individual who has reached this *genital stage* with libidinal reserves intact is now free to further develop a "normal" sexual adjustment and enjoy a genuine heterosexual adjustment. During this time, sexuality increasingly encompasses the concept of love and the establishment of a healthy, genuine heterosexual relationship.

In any of the stages described above, but in particular during the childhood stages, normal psychosexual development may be impaired as the result of insufficient or excessive libidinal gratification. Either of these experiences will hamper the adequate transition to the next stage and, ultimately, adjustment in the adult and may result in a neurosis or sexual difficulty. Thus, the many cases of inadequate adjustment or neuroses were inevitably interpreted as the end result of an unresolved libidinal or sexual conflict during childhood. For example, as we shall see in Chapter 10, homosexuality was regarded as a perversion resulting from an unresolved conflict during childhood psychosexual development.

Although this is a necessarily abbreviated description of Freud's explanation of psychosexual development, the importance of biological determinants is clear. Many authorities (including some of his own followers) criticized the theory on a variety of grounds. In particular, Neo-Freudians have attempted to de-emphasize the libidinal determinants of psychosexual development in favor of a more socially oriented explanation. Moreover, social scientists in general have argued that Freudian theory neglects to recognize that sexual behavior is manifested within the context of the socially defined characteristics of masculinity and femininity.

## ENVIRONMENTAL THEORIES

Advocates of an environmental explanation for psychosexual development vary across a broad spectrum; but they all agree in their belief that sexual attitudes and behavior are primarily determined by familial, social, and cultural experiences and that biological factors are of less importance in this connection. This approach is roughly equated with the learning theory position which argues that our sexual styles are learned as a consequence of psychological and social experiences.

Learning theorists have not advanced a unified theory to specifically account for psychosexual development. Rather, this approach has focused on learning principles which are broad enough to explain many examples of behavioral change (including sexual behavior). Moreover, learning theorists interpret psychosexual development in the context of the overall socialization process, that is, the manner in which social expectations, roles, and attitudes are conveyed to the child and the manner in which social mechanisms "shape" the child in a given socially approved direction. The learning approach to understanding sexual development argues, then, that although each of us is obviously sexually influenced by physical and biological characteristics, we develop our own cultural sexual styles. Furthermore, within that culture, our own unique, idiosyncratic sexual style is a function of the way in which these social forces impact upon, and interact with, these other influences. The process is continuous, dynamic, and subtle, starting shortly after birth and continuing thereafter throughout the individual's lifetime.

This approach can, perhaps, be reduced to two comprehensive principles. The first of these represents an extension of reinforcement theory as proposed by B. F. Skinner (1953). Skinner did not attempt to explain psychosexual development in the same manner as Freud. However, he described certain principles which are assumed to govern the acquisition of complex behavior, including sex roles, sexual identity, and sexual values.

Skinner argues that human behavior is heavily influenced by the consequences of our actions. Stated in its most elementary form, this principle asserts that those behaviors that are intrinsically pleasurable or are rewarded by outside agents (parents, peers, etc.) tend to be repeated, while those behaviors that are unrewarding or punished tend not to be repeated. These contrasting behavior-consequence relationships are roughly equated with the popular terms reward and punishment. Thus, the child who finds genital stimulation to be pleasurable will repeat the behavior. If, however, the behavior is punished, it may cease.

The second principle invoked by learning theorists to explain psychosexual development involves observational learning (Bandura and Walters, 1963). Thus, children acquire "appropriate" sex role characteristics by observing and imitating the behavior of others. Good "matches" are rewarded, while inappropriate imitations are punished.

This is, of course, a simplified version of learning theory and its analysis of psychosexual development. Although a great deal remains to be discovered regarding this complex process, the discussion that follows is formulated in a social learning-interactional context, since we feel that this framework best explains what is known about psychosexual development up to this point in time.

# SEX, GENDER, AND SEXUALITY

With this brief theoretical discussion as background, let us now turn to the manner in which the psychosexual process emerges from biological antecedents, on the one hand, to the final sociocultural results, on the other.

The phrases "sex" and "gender" and the paired expressions "male/female" and "masculine/feminine" are often used ambiguously or interchangeably. In this section, we will define these terms and investigate their significance in psychosexual development. The word "sex" refers both to the anatomical structure of the sexual organs and to sexual behavior. The expression "gender" is a psychosexual category, with both biological and psychological components; "gender identity" is the individual's self-identification as a member of one category or the other, male or female. One's sense of gender identity generally leads to the adoption of a behavioral gender role, or "sex role," that is, the patterns of actions, beliefs, attitudes, and expectations considered appropriate to the respective gender, and which are determined within the social context. Thus, "male" and "female" refer to biological sex and to gender identity, while "masculine" and "feminine" refer to sex role. The connections between gender identity and sex role will be explored below.

## PSYCHOSEXUAL DIFFERENTIATION

Psychosexual differentiation, or the formation of an individual's sexual identity, starts at conception and continues through early childhood. This process involves the interaction of two separate but intimately related components: biological sexual differentiation and sociocultural influences. As humans we are sexually dimorphic, that is, male and female are biologically separate forms. The elements involved in the process of biological sexual differentiation are the genes, gonads, hormones, internal reproductive structures, and external genitalia.

The chromosomal or *genetic* sex of an individual is determined at the moment of conception. The genetic material contributed by the ovum consists of 22 autosomes (non-sex chromosomes) and an X sex chromosome; the sperm contributes its complement of 22 autosomes and either an X or a Y sex chromosome. Thus, the fertilized zygote contains 46 chromosomes and is designed as either 46, XX (female) or 46, XY (male). Contrary to the common belief that the sex of the embryo is now ineradicably set and that male and female embryos immediately differ, the process of sexual differentiation has at this point been *initiated* but is by no means complete, and in the first few weeks, the male and female embryo are identical in appearance.

> In certain rare cases, errors occur which result in abnormal patterns, several of which have been identified and studied. Sometimes a fertilized egg will contain either 45 or 47 chromosomes. Turner's syndrome is the name given to the condition in which an individual has only 45 chromosomes, one of which is an X, that is, the pattern of 45, XO. An individual with this syndrome differentiates as female, although the gonads do not develop and she is thus sterile. Without ovaries, she produces very little estrogen. With appropriately administered female hormones, however, she will develop female secondary sex characteristics and will menstruate. The possession of an X chromosome appears to be an absolute biological necessity, since an embryo which is 45, YO will not survive (Money and Ehrhardt, 1972).
>
> One example of a 47 chromosome pattern is Klinefelter's syndrome, in which an individual is 47, XXY. As a result of the presence of the Y chromosome, this individual differentiates as a male. However, as a result of this chromosome pattern, his genitalia are undersized, and he is sterile.

In order for an XY embryo to develop into a male, certain substances must be produced to accomplish this differentiation. The two requisite substances thus far identified are a hormone which acts as a Mullerian-inhibiting substance, and the hormone testosterone, both of which are secreted by the embryonic gonads. The Y chromosome influences the development of the embryonic gonads into testes; without this chromosomal action, the gonads will later become ovaries. The sixth week of prenatal development is believed to be a critical period in sexual differentiation (Money and Ehrhardt, 1972); it is at this point in time that the testes must begin to develop in order to ensure normal male differentiation. If this process is obstructed, the XY embryo will develop as a female. Additionally, if the gonads of either genetic sex embryo are absent, the individual will follow the pattern of female sexual differentiation. For these reasons, several researchers have suggested that nature's basic pattern is female (Money and Ehrhardt, 1972).

Under the influence of secretions from the testes, the precursor of the internal male reproductive structures begins to differentiate. This precursor is known as the Wolffian ducts. All embryos have both Wolffian ducts and Mullerian ducts, the latter being the precursor of the female internal reproductive system. In the XY embryo, however, the Mullerian-inhibiting substance suppresses the growth of the female system, and testosterone promotes the development of the Wolffian ducts into the epididymis, vas deferens, and seminal vesicles. In the XX embryo, the Wolffian system degenerates and the Mullerian system proliferates into the Fallopian tubes, the uterus, and the upper portion of the vagina.

The action of testosterone also promotes male differentiation of the external genitalia. The external genitalia of the early human embryo consists of a genital tubercle, genital folds, and a genital swelling. Under the continued influence of testosterone, these basic structures differentiate into the male penis, skin of the penis, and scrotum. In the female, without this influence of testosterone, these structures develop into the clitoris, labia minora, and labia majora, respectively.

At this point, it is of interest to note that many features of the male and female systems are *homologous*, that is, they develop from the same embryonic tissue. Thus, it would appear that even in our sexual-reproductive systems where we would seem to be most dissimilar, males and females are quite alike at these early stages of development.

> ### Homologous Organs
>
> | Female | Male |
> | --- | --- |
> | clitoris | penis |
> | clitoral hood | foreskin of penis |
> | labia minora | skin of penis |
> | labia majora | scrotum |
> | ovaries | testes |
> | Skene's glands | prostate gland |
> | Bartholin's glands | Cowper's glands |
>
> (Jones, H.W., Jr. Development of genitalia. In A.C. Barnes (Ed.), *Intrauterine development*. Philadelphia: Lea & Febiger, 1968.)

In temporal sequence, the last influence which plays a role in psychosexual differentiation is the sex of assignment and rearing. When a baby is born, it is assigned to a sex category (female or male) on the basis of the appearance of its external genitalia and is generally reared in accordance with the attributes which are socially ascribed to this sex. At this point in time, although biological determinants continue, environmental contributions to gender identity begin to exert their effect and eventually supersede biology (Money and Ehrhardt, 1972).

We have stated that sociocultural influences are a more powerful determinant of gender identity than is biological structure. Most of the evidence in support of this position comes from case studies of individuals in which natural or human error interrupted the normal pattern of development. Most of these cases involve pseudohermaphrodites, that is, individuals with gonads of one sex or the other, but with ambiguous external genitalia. (Pseudohermaphrodites are to be distinguished from true hermaphrodites, that is, individuals who possess gonads of both sexes. True hermaphrodites are most commonly 46, XX, although occasionally a small part of a Y chromosome is present and is attached to an autosome. True hermaphrodites are exceedingly rare.)

Two categories of these cases involve genetic females who had been exposed to the action of androgens, that is, male hormones, during fetal development, with the result that their external genitalia took on a male appearance. In one, the "adrenogenital syndrome," the XX fetus was exposed to excessive amounts of androgen produced by malfunctioning adrenal glands of the fetus. In the other, "progestin-induced hermaphroditism," progestins administered to pregnant women (to prevent miscarriage) acted like androgens, thus affecting an XX fetus in the same way as high dosages of this male hormone would. Individuals in both of these categories have been variously sex-assigned at birth: some were reared as girls, some as boys (Money and Ehrhardt, 1972).

To investigate the potential behavioral effects of androgen, a study was conducted on a group of fetally androgenized girls, all of whom had been given corrective surgery and hormone therapy and all of whom had been raised as girls. Results of this study indicated that these girls were more likely to be tomboys, for example, they showed high levels of physical energy expenditure, but that their psychosexual identity was unambiguously female and also heterosexual. It is possible that their tomboyishness was a result of "masculinization" of certain pathways in the brain. This result remains speculative, however, and the behaviors characterized as tomboyish are also very common for girls in our culture (Williams, 1977) and are readily incorporated into a female identity (Money and Ehrhardt, 1972).

The closest reverse situation to fetal androgenization of genetic females is the "testicular feminizing," or "androgen-insensitivity" syndrome. In this case, an XY embryo produces the requisite supply of testosterone, but, as a result of a genetic defect, the body tissues are insensitive to the male hormone. The internal reproductive system does not develop; the testes usually remain undescended, and the external genitalia have a female appearance. At puberty, such individuals will develop female secondary sex characteristics, because the small quantities of estrogen produced by the testes (a normal condition in the male) are not counterbalanced by the effects of testosterone. Again we are reminded that without testosterone, the female development pattern has primacy. Individuals with this syndrome are usually assigned and successfully reared as females (Money and Ehrhardt, 1972).

An example of human error which resulted in sex assignment contrary to genetic sex is furnished by the case of the seven-month-old boy, an identical twin, whose penis was accidentally burned off in a circumcision procedure (Money and Ehrhardt, 1972). In this case, corrective surgery was performed, with more surgery and hormone therapy required at puberty; and the child's parents were counseled to raise their offspring as a girl. Follow-up studies have indicated their success, with each of the twins demonstrating the appropriate "little girl" or "little boy" behavior.

In all of these cases, with the adjunct of corrective surgery and appropriate hormone therapy as indicated, it is the sex of rearing, and the attendant sex role socialization process, that will be most important in determining the child's gender identity. The factor of age seems to set the only limitation. At around the age of eighteen months, children begin forming a strong concept of gender identity which usually crystallizes by the age of two and a half (Laws and Schwartz, 1977). It is during this period that the child also develops language skills, and Money emphasizes a correlation between these two processes, since the child's ability to utilize gender words will be crucial to his or her identity formation (Rosenzweig, 1973). In order for the cultural

aspects of the sex assignment or reassignment to be successful, then, this process probably should be initiated prior to eighteen months of age. On the other hand, the physical adjuncts of corrective surgery and hormonal administration often involve a series of steps — during infancy, at puberty, and, in the use of hormone therapy, throughout adulthood. In sum, the investigation of these irregularities promotes further understanding of the complexity of the process of psychosexual differentiation and emphasizes the commanding role played by environmental factors.

## SEX DIFFERENCES

The basic irreducible elements of sex difference are constituted by women's capacity to menstruate, gestate, and lactate, and men's capacity to impregnate. As such, these differences refer to biological functions and do not imply that the behavioral dimensions of "mothering" and "fathering" are likewise determined by sex (Money and Ehrhardt, 1972), even though this distinction is often overlooked. Women can and do assume the traditional "father" role of provider, and men can and do exhibit "maternal" nurturing behavior (Trause, Kennell, and Klaus, 1978).

The question arises whether, beyond reproductive functioning, there are any innate differences between the sexes which are relevant determinants of behavioral or personality characteristics. Recent studies have challenged traditional assumptions about psychological and behavioral sex differences (Maccoby and Jacklin, 1974; Williams, 1977). While behavioral differences have been observed in newborns, it has not been demonstrated that these differences are biologically determined; absolute differences in cognitive functioning and in social behavior in the first two years of life also have not been conclusively demonstrated (Williams, 1977). Several differences in cognitive abilities emerge in middle to late childhood; for example, girls show greater verbal abilities while boys reveal better spatial abilities and, to a lesser extent, mathematical abilities (Maccoby and Jacklin, 1974). The relative weight of, on the one hand, sex-linked genetic factors and, on the other, socialization patterns in the determination of ability and performance differentials is as yet unclear. With a possible exception in the case of a component in spatial ability (Williams, 1977), there is no evidence of genetic transmission of cognitive abilities which is sex-linked. At the same time, it is known that these abilities are affected by sociocultural factors. The magnitude of the differences in question, however, is not great; that is, there is considerable overlap between the sexes and, perhaps most importantly, differences within each sex as a whole are greater than the differences between the sexes.

One sex difference that appears in all cultures studied is that boys display aggressive behavior more than girls do. While aggression thus may have a biological component, it is also accurate to say that aggressive behavior is learned behavior, and it has been argued that boys are more biologically prepared to learn it (Maccoby and Jacklin, 1974). In addition, girls generally learn to use more oblique or covert forms of aggression, such as verbal "injury," rejection, or manipulation (Bardwick, 1971), and do not always put into practice what information they do have about aggression, possibly because of negative social pressure (Maccoby and Jacklin, 1974). What is important is that the aggressive behavior of both males and females can be modified (Maccoby, 1973), again attesting to the malleability of human behavior.

In sum, such sex differences in behavior which may be innate are few in number, and we must direct our attention to the socialization process to explain our culture's dichotomy between femininity and masculinity.

## SEX ROLE SOCIALIZATION

As we saw in Chapter 3, cross-cultural studies provide ample evidence that the differing sets of attitudes and behaviors associated with males and females vary tremendously. Our concern in this section is to illustrate the different ways in which a child in our culture learns to express sex role behavior. Drawing on the concepts of learning theory discussed above, we can see that in our society boys are typically reinforced, that is, encouraged and praised for engaging in "masculine" activities and discouraged or ridiculed for engaging in "feminine" activities. A similar process describes the manner in which typically "feminine" behavior is "shaped up" or refined in girls. These influences operate in various and subtle ways and are implemented by many social institutions. All of these rewarding and punishing experiences coalesce and result in the gradual acquisition of typically masculine characteristics in boys and feminine characteristics in girls. In this manner the process of sex role socialization may be explained solely in terms of differential behavioral consequences. Repeating "appropriate," (that is, normal) same-sex behavior is rewarded, while "inappropriate," cross-sex behavior results in punishment ("No, silly, boys don't play with dolls!").

Within this general framework, the specific manner in which each child is exposed to these learning experiences is highly idiosyncratic. Thus, although the "norms" of society are advanced in this fashion, each individual will acquire his or her own special learning history which will ultimately be reflected in his or her sexual preferences, orientations, and behavioral characteristics.

As stated earlier, Bandura and Walters (1963) have added a second component to reinforcement theory which they also consider to be important in explaining the development of sex role behavior. Their position argues that a good deal of social learning occurs solely by observation. Thus, the child observes the behavior of the parent (the model) and then imitates the behavior. When the child makes an appropriate imitative response, she or he is rewarded (reinforced) by attention, praise, affection, etc. When the child displays an inappropriate imitative response (for example, a boy repeating a "feminine" behavior), she or he is scolded or approval and love are withheld.

The process is, typically, initiated in the home but by the age of three of four generalizes to other situations. For example, Fagot and Patterson (1969) analyzed the manner in which adults and children reinforced (or punished) the sex-typed behaviors of preschool age children. First, the play patterns of four-year-olds were grouped in terms of masculine patterns and feminine patterns. Then, the number of rewards (praise, ap-

proval, etc.) administered by both teacher and peers for sex-typical play and sex-atypical play was assessed. The teachers (all female) rewarded more feminine type behaviors in both boys and girls, but, in the peer group, boys mostly rewarded boys and girls mostly rewarded girls for appropriate sex-type play. Among peers, reward for opposite-sex behavior was not observed, and, in fact, the one boy who exhibited feminine behavior was criticized more by his peers and played with less than any other boy.

We will now investigate several of the specific mechanisms through which sex role socialization is implemented. The process is initiated at birth, with pink and blue wrappings and congratulatory cards which emphasize boys' future career possibilities and girls' physical attributes. The language used to refer to babies and young children — girls are pretty, delicate, petite; boys are tough, strong, active — reflects sex role stereotypes and provides expectations and models for the child.

Different styles of dress and adornment for young children follow sex role patterns, though young girls generally are allowed more latitude in styles than are boys; for example, a girl may wear overalls, but a boy cannot easily wear fingernail polish unless he is immune to both adult and peer disapproval. Being a tomboy is generally tolerated and may even be fashionable, but we have no parallel word for boys; the available expression "sissy" is a term of ridicule and a hurtful label.

Considerable differences exist in the objects to which girls' and boys' attention is directed and in the activities to which they are exposed. "Masculine" toys are more varied; they are relatively more complex, involve social interaction, and promote muscular development and coordination. "Feminine" toys are simpler, involve less activity, and are more often for solitary use. Creative and educational toys are considered "neutral," yet it is boys who receive the most intricate items in this category (Jacobsen, 1976).

The educational system is quite influential in the further development and consolidation of socially appropriate sex roles. A recent report showed that 73% of the books for use by young children are written about boys (Jacobsen, 1976). In another survey (U'Ren, 1971), it was noted that adult females rarely appear in children's textbooks, though adult males are quite visible; and stories about girls are shorter, less interesting, and more

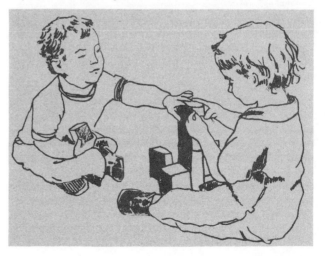

stereotyped than stories about boys. Stock characters in children's books include the following: the girl who sits around being passive and submissive; the highly adventurous boy; the adult male as problem-solver or hero; the adult female as housewife or assistant. Male characters are endowed with physical and moral strength and perseverance; females are more often depicted as lazy, selfish, incompetent, or the butt of jokes.

Although some changes have been made, curricular differences such as home economics and industrial arts ("shop") classes segregated by sex and girls' limited sports opportunities are further formative pressures for the development of "feminine" or "masculine" skills and attitudes. Guidance and career counseling complements and consolidates the lessons that males and females behave differently and are destined for different kinds of life choices once they have graduated from school. Achievement is reinforced and valued more for males, and girls are often told that they must choose between marriage and a career, with the former being preferable (Osofsky and Osofsky, 1972).

Role models for masculine and feminine behavior are constantly available in the child's environment in the form of parents, other family members, the peer group, teachers, etc. The impact of the media in furnishing models must not be underestimated. In comic books, popular music, advertising, television, and movies, stereotyped images of male and female behavior and interpersonal relationships abound (Jacobsen, 1976).

In "X: A Fabulous Child's Story," writer Lois Gould (1976) provides an intriguing illustration (in this fictional story) of the extent to which personality and behavioral characteristics are linked to gender. As part of a scientific experiment, a Mr. and Ms. Jones give birth to a child whom they name X and whose sex is not revealed. The Joneses provide X with both sturdy pajamas and flowered underwear, they give it all sorts of toys, and they teach it both how to play ball and what to serve at a doll's tea party. They allow X to cry when it gets hurt, and they do not scold it for getting dirty. From X's infancy on, however, other people are confused by their ignorance of X's sex. They do not know what kinds of words to use to describe the child, nor what kinds of presents to give it. X's peers at school come to accept and to enjoy X. They decide that X is having twice as much fun by being good at both boys' and girls' skills, and these children want to develop themselves likewise. Their parents, however, are not pleased and pressure the school principal to have X tested. The examining psychiatrist determines that X is very well adjusted and says that X's sex will become obvious in due time. The story concludes with the birth of the Joneses' second child, named Y.

One of the major problems with the sex role approach to human nature is that this dichotomy obscures the greater intragroup differences and variability (Bernard, 1974). Additionally, the conventional concepts of sex roles provide stereotypes by which we tend to prejudge others and confine expectations for ourselves, circumstances which affect both our self-image and our motivation (Bem and Bem, 1970). Both females and males can be handicapped by conforming to the sex role norms, if this limits the expression of their individuality and the maximization of their individual potential (Money, 1977).

Interestingly, conventionally defined femininity and masculinity can prove to be dysfunctional even within the prescribed sex roles. For example, women's training to be dependent and passive does not equip them with the assertiveness necessary for effective child rearing, or for single parenthood, and they may be easily exploited, victimized, etc. Similarly, the adoption of the machismo image and the repression of emotionality inhibits a man from being an effective husband and nurturing father (Maccoby and Jacklin, 1974).

One further dimension of sex role socialization must be considered. Inasmuch as the child's primary socializer is usually a woman, a boy's development of identity is often constituted by a process of differentiation: being masculine is frequently defined in terms of being *not* like a female (Chodorow, 1971). Society in general tends to devalue women and women's work (Chodorow, 1971), and little boys soon learn to regard themselves as superior to girls (Gagnon and Henderson, 1975).

Emphasis on the relative values and virtues of being one sex rather than the other may perpetuate alienation between the sexes and hinder effective communication. Both individual self-esteem and interpersonal relationships would benefit from an emphasis on the appreciation of oneself for who one is, including the enjoyment of one's maleness or femaleness for its own sake.

Not only can conventional sex roles not be easily defended in terms of such concepts as equality or justice, or even efficiency (Myerson-Ferrandino, 1977), it is also the case that benefits are to be derived from a loosening of sex role definitions. These changes are already happening, and individuals are seeing that, once freed from the restrictions of socially coded roles, they have more options and alternatives from which to choose. People can be freer to develop their skills and talents in accordance with their individual abilities and interests. Women can have more opportunities and be more effective outside the domestic sphere, and men can have more latitude in expressing their interests and emotional selves.

## SEX ROLES AND SEXUALITY

Since the concepts of masculinity and femininity have such a powerful effect on our beliefs about ourselves and others, it is no surprise that sex roles are prime determinants in psychosexual development. Just as we pattern our other behaviors, we learn to express our sexuality by means of sex roles. We will now examine the dynamics of how we learn about the sexually related behaviors traditionally associated with femininity and masculinity.

In discussions of anatomical differences, young girls are generally informed that the counterpart to possession of a penis is their future ability to have babies. In such situations, reference to the clitoris is omitted, and the reproductive aspects of sex are stressed over the idea of sexual pleasure *per se*. As the girl becomes physically mature, parental and social stress on the importance of virginity sets up a situation whereby girls are made responsible for setting the limits in teen-age sexual activities. The conventional notion of the eagerness of male sexual desire ("guys always want it") means that it is up to the female to keep it in check. The premise of the existence of female sexuality in its own right is absent. As we will see in the section on adolescence in Chapter 7, popular education materials reinforce these messages.

The sexual socialization of males stresses the ability to perform on desire or request and emphasizes the role of the male as the initiator of sexual encounters. It has been suggested that, if they follow the popular media models, men are going to learn to objectify women, to fixate on various parts of the female anatomy, and to "score" (Litewka, 1977). One implication of this dynamic is that the machismo image, with its stress on aggressiveness, does not facilitate the development of sensitivity and intimacy or the free expression of warmth and playfulness and nonsexualized body contact (Pleck and Sawyer, 1974).

If individuals follow these traditional patterns, men will tend to be conditioned to be aggressive and aroused, and women, to be passive and unaroused. When two such people are together in a heterosexual context, the man may believe he is expected to try to "get" what he can, and both individuals believe that it is up to the woman to say no. Further, when these partners do engage in sexual activity, the man is expected to know everything the woman wants — where, when, and how. Since women are generally deterred from taking responsibility for their own sexual needs, the woman may not have discovered what constitutes the most effective stimulation for her or she may have been discouraged from being assertive enough to communicate her needs.

Stereotyped masculine or feminine sexual behavior may thus provoke anxiety and may be precursors to sexual dysfunctioning. For example, a narrow focus on pressure to perform can set the stage for premature ejaculation (Gagnon and Henderson, 1975) or erectile dysfunction in men (Kaplan, 1974; Zilbergeld, 1978). Similarly, lack of permission to explore one's genitals and a belief in passivity (nonassertion, not taking responsibility) can inhibit women from becoming orgasmic (Barbach, 1976).

## ANDROGYNY AND SEXUALITY

The traditional cultural and psychological models present masculinity and femininity as a single, bi-polar dimension ranging from extreme masculinity at one end to extreme femininity at the other. It has been argued, however, that individuals of both sexes possess, in varying degrees, a combination of masculine and feminine characteristics. Consequently, the dichotomy of femininity and masculinity does not truly reflect human personality, nor do psychological tests which are based on this rigid model. Sandra Bem has been a pioneer in conceptualizing a model in which masculinity and femininity are seen as two independent dimensions. She elaborates the view that each individual can possess a balance of traits heretofore labeled as masculine and feminine, for example, assertiveness and nurturance, and she uses the term "androgynous" to refer to such a person (Bem, 1974). She suggests that the androgynous personality theoretically represents the very best of what our culture presents as masculine and feminine (Bem, 1977), that is, a more balanced, fully human, and effective individual. Evidence suggests that androgynous men and women are more flexible in their functioning than those who are sex-typed

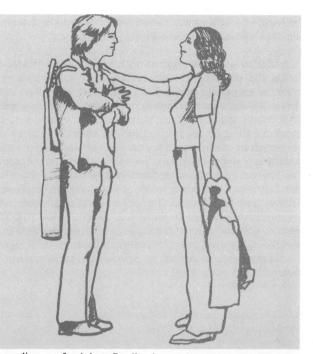

masculine or feminine. Studies have also suggested that androgynous subjects acted more independently (traditionally a masculine trait) than feminine subjects and were more nurturant (traditionally a feminine trait) than masculine subjects (Bem, 1975). In addition, the adoption of an androgynous sex role has been related to healthy psychological adjustment. Androgynous individuals of both sexes have shown high levels of self-esteem (Spence, Helmreich, and Stapp, 1975; Wetter, 1975) than sex role stereotyped individuals, as well as a higher level of self-actualization (Cristall and Dean, 1976).

If it is the case that an androgynous sex role orientation is conducive to better psychological adjustment, it would seem sensible to propose that androgynous individuals would also exhibit better sexual adjustment. A recent study (Walfish and Myerson, 1980) points in this direction. It was hypothesized that androgynous males would have more positive attitudes toward sexuality than masculine males, based on the belief that an androgynous male would be less focused on his role as performer and would be able to be more receptive, less pressured, and more into his "experience." Similarly it was hypothesized that the androgynous female would have more positive attitudes toward sexuality than the feminine female, based on the view that an androgynous female would be less inhibited (Bem, 1976) and would be more able to be assertive and to see herself as a sexual being.

The results of this study indicated confirmation of the hypotheses: individuals who have adopted an androgynous sex role have more positive attitudes toward sexuality than those with more traditional sex roles (Walfish and Myerson, 1980). Although the implications of an androgynous identity for sexual behavior are, at present, speculative and need greater exploration, we can advance several hypotheses for further research. Researchers Walfish and Myerson suggest that the flexibility associated with the androgynous personality would provide this individual with the ability to view sexuality as involving a reciprocity of giving and receiving. The androgynous individual would thus theoretically be able both to listen empathically and be sensitive to his or her partner's needs and to be assertive about expressing his or her own.

Additionally, an androgynous man might not feel pressed to follow the stereotyped model of "going to bed" with every potential sex partner he spends time with, unless he felt genuine desire to share sexual energy. The androgynous woman theoretically might feel freer to initiate sexual encounters, instead of waiting for her partner to do so. We can only speculate on the effects of this type of female behavior. Some writers contend that a woman's assertiveness and initiation may increase her male partner's anxiety and performance fears. On the other hand, Masters and Johnson (1975) argue that more women entering into heterosexual situations as equal, responsible, and responsive participants might help to diminish male performance anxiety and fears of failure. Individuals do not operate in a vacuum, however, and, as Masters and Johnson (1975) argue, sexual emancipation depends on personal and social emancipation.

## SUMMARY

In this chapter, we have attempted to describe psychosexual development as a dynamic, continuously changing process. From conception to shortly after birth, biological and physical determinants play the major role in this process; but shortly thereafter, the impact of socialization, family, and culture exert an ever-increasing influence on psychosexual development.

The structure, form, and character of these converging determinants ultimately result in a relatively fixed pattern of psychosexuality in the adult. Even here, however, the process of psychosexual development does not end since our sexual values, orientations, and behavior continue to evolve throughout the life cycle.

Although the general model of psychosexual development that we have described is largely accepted by the scientific and professional community, admittedly there are still many questions that remain to be answered. Most of us would agree that psychosexuality is a highly diverse and idiosyncratic phenomenon, but there are still no adequate explanations regarding the manner in which these individualized patterns emerge. Although a great deal is known about the basic biological mechanisms underlying psychosexuality, the manner in which these variables interact in any given person with familial, cultural, and societal influences is still obscure. Thus, there is still no clear understanding of why identical twins, for example, recipients of the same genetic endowment and biological determinants and exposed to apparently the same environment, may develop different sexual orientations later in life. There is still no clear understanding of the factors in psychosexual development that result in sexual problem behaviors (see Chapter 13). There is still no understanding of how differences in psychosexual development determine sexual activity or inactivity later in life. These are just some of the more obvious questions related to the study of psychosexual development which are still unanswered.

# Chapter 7

## Sexuality Through the Life Cycle

# INTRODUCTION

The process of psychosexual development introduced in Chapter 6 continues, of course, throughout the entire life cycle. The issues that are related to such a process are diverse and complex. In this chapter we will attempt to encompass as many of the relevant issues as possible. Although the main focus of this chapter is the manner in which various biological and social factors continue to exert their influence throughout the various stages of individual development, many related topics are also described. In the process of determining which topics should or should not be included in this discussion, some arbitrary decisions were made. For example, we present the discussion of menstruation between adolescent sexuality and adulthood, since menstruation begins in adolescence and continues thereafter. The discussion of how the various factors of psychosexual development interact at each stage is complete in itself and can be read either separately or in sequence.

# CHILDHOOD

Infants engage in diffuse body exploration including genital play. Moreover, they apparently enjoy the general sensual pleasure derived from being handled, cuddled, and rocked. Children of both sexes are capable of orgasm from an early age, although, of course, prepubertal boys do not ejaculate. Children also engage in crude forms of sex play with peers of both sexes. The "homosexual" behavior that emerges in such instances is probably a reflection of the child's general homosocial orientation, that is, the predominant interactions with same-sex peers.

In general, then, early childhood development is characterized by a varied sexual history: sexual exploration and experimentation with oneself and with peers of both sexes (Laws and Schwartz, 1977). These activities, initially, are not "sexual" in the same sense that adolescents and adults attach such a label to similar behaviors. They lack the motive, the connotations, and the complex set of meanings that are invested in such behavior by adults (Gagnon and Henderson, 1975). By virtue of parental and other social influences, however, various associations develop in relation to such behavior which often lead to modesty and guilt. The prevailing view of childhood asexuality in our society often leads a parent into misinterpreting childhood sexuality as inappropriate and abnormal (Laws and Schwartz, 1977). In the face of these common parental reactions, the natural expression of childhood sexuality is changed into other forms. Thus, children learn to disguise or hide their activities and interest, but the context of sex play as forbidden and the necessity for secrecy may exert an enduring effect. When masturbation is disapproved of, for example, the child may develop a sense of shame or guilt, and its covert status may prevent the child from integrating this behavior into his or her developing sexual identity in a positive way (Elias and Gebhard, 1969; Laws and Schwartz, 1977). Girls seem to be affected by such experiences more than boys, since boys are more likely to masturbate in a group and thus receive peer validation for such behavior.

Given the confusing and conflicting values about sex that characterize our culture, it is not surprising that most parents are unprepared and uncomfortable in dealing with sex in their children. Even where no major issue is made over childhood sexuality, however, silence, denial, or evasiveness still conveys a powerful message that sex is dirty and shameful (Laws and Schwartz, 1977).

In brief, then, the findings in this area strongly suggest that, although parents agree that it is their responsibility to provide their children with a healthy sexual atmosphere (Gordon and Dickman, 1977), most young people rate their sex education as very inadequate (Laws and Schwartz, 1977). Moreover, as we saw in Chapter 4, the bulk of our sexual knowledge stems from inadequate, unreliable, and misleading sources of information.

There are, of course, a number of things parents can do in creating a healthy sexual atmosphere for their children. In general, parents can let children know that they are "askable," that they are willing to answer questions about sex-related topics and bodily functions in general. Even if the communication consists of acknowledging one's discomfort or admitting to ignorance about a specific issue, such honesty builds trust (Gordon and Dickman, 1977).

---

## Children's knowledge about sex and reproduction

Anne Bernstein, a social scientist, analyzed the manner in which children develop their knowledge about sex and reproduction. She asked a number of children of various ages, "How do people get babies?" The answers reflected six levels of understanding. Level one answers, revealed by 3- and 4-year-olds, were concrete: "You go to the hospital." Level two responses were in terms of "manufacturing": babies are constructed or built. Level three responses were transitional. Children at this stage knew some of the facts concerning sexual relationships and physiology, but the facts were not combined in an integrated manner. Level four responses reflected an understanding of cause and effect relationships, with physiological explanations cast in terms of sperm, or seeds, or eggs. The response of level five children recognized that the sperm and the egg unite but also revealed a belief that one component contained a preformed baby and the other unit provided food or energy to promote the baby's growth. At about the age of 12, children offer a level six explanation, with an accurate understanding in terms of physical causality.

Bernstein suggests that by asking a child open-ended questions about reproduction, parents can determine the child's level of understanding. Explanations can then be offered that are one level beyond the child's present state of knowledge.

(Bernstein, A.C., How children learn about sex and birth. *Psychology Today,* January 1976, pp. 31-36; 66.)

More specifically, answers should be formulated in terms that are understandable to the child. Rather than ridicule a child's fanciful beliefs, it is important to support the child's attempts to learn without confirming misinformation.

# PUBERTY

Puberty is a process of physical development in which the human body experiences rapid growth, the appearance of the secondary sex characteristics, and the maturation of the sexual-reproductive system. The process of puberty, from initial growth spurt to final development of fertility, takes several years to complete. The psychological and cultural dimensions of this transition from childhood to maturity will be examined in the section on adolescence. For present purposes, we will review the relevant physical changes.

The age of onset of puberty varies; the process for girls begins, on the average, around the age of eleven—in general, one or two years younger than the male puberty experience. The initiation of puberty is believed to be a function of the hypothalamus. This is a structure in the interior of the brain which receives input from the central nervous system and which is connected by nerve fibers and blood vessels to the pituitary gland, located at the base of the brain. The pituitary, while small in structure, is the most complex gland in the endocrine (ductless) system. It secretes hormones which travel through the bloodstream to stimulate the other members of the endocrine system to produce their specific hormones. By virtue of its connections with the hypothalamus, the activity of the pituitary is subject to control by the nervous system. Thus, certain physical and psychological events, for example, stress, which affect the organism in general, can have an effect on the pituitary and thus influence processes, such as menstruation, which are ultimately regulated by or dependent on pituitary activity.

## HORMONES

The process of puberty begins when the hypothalamus produces certain chemical substances which stimulate the pituitary to release hormones. These hormones, in turn, induce the gonads to begin the production of gamete cells and to secrete the sex hormones which, in their turn, are responsible for the development of the secondary sex characteristics, for example, breast enlargement in girls (and most boys) and facial hair growth in boys. The relevant hypothalamic substances are known as the follicle-stimulating hormone-releasing factor (FSH-RF) and the luteinizing hormone-releasing factor (LH-RF). These names appropriately indicate the pertinent connection between the hypothalamus and the pituitary, for the pituitary substances in question are called the follicle-stimulating hormone (FSH) and the luteinizing hormone (LH). In males, the latter is also known as interstitial cell-stimulating hormone (ICSH). These pituitary hormones are collectively termed the gonadotropins because of their function as gonad stimulators. FSH derives its name from its function in the female, which is to stimulate the ovarian follicles. These follicles (small sacs) contain immature eggs and are the site of production of the hormone estrogen. In the male, FSH stimulates the

seminiferous tubules in the testes to develop sperm. In the female, LH triggers ovulation, the process whereby a matured egg bursts out of its follicle. Under the influence of LH, the matured follicle now develops into a microscopic gland, called the *corpus luteum*, hence the name, luteinizing hormone. LH then stimulates the corpus luteum to produce the hormone progesterone and some additional estrogen. LH or ICSH in the male stimulates the interstitial cells of the testes to produce testosterone (the primary male sex hormone, or androgen). Secondarily, ICSH is necessary for the maturation of sperm.

The hormones estrogen, progesterone, and testosterone belong to the family of chemical substances called steroids (another well-known member of this group is cortisone, produced in the adrenal glands). These hormones are closely related in chemical structure, and all three are manufactured by both sexes. Both the gonads and the adrenal glands are responsible for the production of the small amounts of opposite-sex hormones (Money and Ehrhardt, 1972). Thus, an individual's hormonal sex is not an absolute but is rather a matter of ratio or proportion between the greater and lesser amounts of the appropriate hormones.

## PHYSICAL DEVELOPMENT

In girls, puberty begins with increased growth, the development of breast buds, and the growth of pubic hair. As the process continues, the girl's voice deepens and her body develops its characteristic contours. Breast tissue grows, and the hips and buttocks become rounded. It is primarily the differential distribution of fat tissue and the muscle-fat ratio which distinguish the "average" adult female and male body shapes. FSH causes the ovaries to grow, and estrogen stimulates the growth of the uterus, vagina, and external genitalia; the clitoris enlarges under the influence of androgens. Menarche, the first menstrual period, occurs as a later event in the developmental process, usually when the girl has attained a critical weight, ranging from 94 to 103 pounds (Weideger, 1977a).

As noted earlier, puberty begins later in boys and lasts longer. Male puberty also begins with an accelerated rate of growth and the appearance of pubic hair. Testosterone stimulates growth of the penis and testes and of the internal reproductive structures. By age 13 or 14 the typical boy will first experience ejaculation during orgasm and will begin to have "wet dreams" (see Chapter 9). The larynx ("voice box") grows, causing the characteristic deepening of the voice, and facial hair begins to grow. About 80% of pubertal boys experience temporary enlargement of the breasts. This phenomenon is probably induced by the small amounts of estrogen produced in the male body.

In both sexes, axillary, or armpit, hair begins to grow. Various changes in the skin and increased activity of the sebaceous (fat-secreting) glands and sweat glands commonly result in acne. The rapid increase in height experienced by both sexes during puberty results from the action of the growth hormone, which is another substance produced by the pituitary gland. This hormone stimulates growth of the bones of the arms and legs, called the long bones. Eventually, the female's estrogen or the male's testosterone counteracts the influence of the growth hormone, and bone growth slows down.

The age at which any specific stage in the process of puberty occurs, or the specific time interval between any of the stages, varies considerably from individual to individual. Genetic factors, nutrition, and the general physical environment all play a role in the process. The first ejaculation of seminal fluid is the boy's biological analogy to the girl's menarche. Both are landmark events that signify reproductive maturation. They do not indicate fertility, however; it is not until at least a year or two after the onset of ejaculatory ability or menarche that mature sperm appear in the ejaculate or that menstrual cycles regularly become ovulatory.

# ADOLESCENCE

By definition, adolescence represents a process, a time of transition and change, as we learn to rehearse and prepare for adult roles. Adolescence is a major turning point in the life cycle. As we learn to put away the toys and pursuits of our childhood, we must learn to develop and incorporate the requisite skills and preoccupations of early adulthood. These tasks are of considerable proportion. As we move from dependence to relative self-sufficiency, we pass through various stages of rebellion, experimentation, value changes, "identity crises," and other life circumstances as we seek to understand our changing selves and the expectations and responses of our peers, our parents, and our culture.

As we attain the social status of adolescence, we are for the first time publicly recognized as sexual beings. Although as a group adolescents are not yet socially permitted to express their sexuality, we are exposed to considerable teaching about our appropriate adult sex roles. There is no strong relationship between preadolescent sex play and adolescent sexual behavior. The mediating factor which most intently influences adolescent sexuality is our sex role behavior.

Although sexual expression is generally discouraged in early adolescence, the reality is such that this *is* the time when people begin having sexual experiences. The sex play carried on in childhood takes on different meanings and significance in adolescence, as we learn to define these and new activities as explicitly sexual. We simply did not have these connotations and interpretations in our childhood.

The typical pattern for heterosexual behavior evolves though four levels of involvement: kissing, light petting, heavy petting, intercourse (Kirkendall and Rubin, 1974). The age at which any given individual begins this pattern and the rate at which he or she passes through these successive steps varies considerably. The availability of opportunities for practicing these behaviors, and various socializing influences, will affect the individual's progression through these sexual activities.

In a 1973 study, Sorensen found that, by the age of 16, 90% of adolescents had had some sexual experience. At ages 16 through 19, 72% of boys and 57% of girls had experienced sexual intercourse. Zelnick and Kantner's (1977) study included a similar finding, that, by the age of 19, 55.2% of girls had had intercourse. A more recent study adds new dimensions to our concepts of adolescent sexual behavior. Haas (1979) reports data on 15- to 16-year-olds; in this age group, 28% of the boys and 7%

of the girls had had ten or more sex partners; 80% of the males and nearly 50% of the females said that they masturbated at least once a week.

---

## The role of the parent in adolescent sexuality

Although it is true that peer influences come to equal and even supersede parental values during adolescence, the responsible parent recognizes his or her role in providing information and in recognizing the sometimes overwhelming sexual changes that occur at this time. The concerns of adolescents are related to their actual and potential experiences. Virtually every relevant sexual topic is a matter of curiosity, if not concern. Thus, there are questions related to such issues as penis and breast size (because of the importance placed on them in our society). Adolescents are also curious about arousal, masturbation, homosexuality, intercourse, birth control, venereal disease, abortion, etc. (Gordon, 1976; Laws and Schwartz, 1977). In addition, of course, the fact of menstruation requires some kind of acknowledgment of sexual development that cannot be ignored.

The responsive parent may provide information on these and related topics and also focus on and explore the broader dimensions of interpersonal relationships (for example, caring, trust), as well as discuss the issues involved in responsible decision making.

Parents generally agree that they want to provide sex education for their children but are often hesitant and uncomfortable in this role (Gordon and Dickman, 1977). Some of this hesitancy is attributable to lack of adequate knowledge; some of it stems from parents' uneasiness or unresolved feelings about their own sexual experiences or sexuality in general. Given the confusing attitudes about sex that characterize our culture, it is not surprising that parents often feel unprepared to fulfill this function. Appropriate sex education courses for adults and programs that teach parents how to teach their children about sexuality might help to remedy this lack. In addition, it may be easier for parents to discuss sexually related topics with their children if the parents are able to discuss sexuality with each other and to be sensitive to their own feelings (Gordon, 1976).

---

## MALES

Whether it is accurate or not, it has been commonly remarked that adolescent males are intensely sexual (Kaplan, 1974), or , as otherwise phrased, "horny all the time." Their sexual focus is primarily directed toward their genitals. Males' comparatively greater awareness of their genital responsiveness, as compared with that of females, starts in early childhood because it is so easy to see and touch one's penis. This awareness is now strengthened during adolescence by the visible and tangible evidence of the ejaculatory fluid which the penis produces.

Masturbation is the major sexual occupation of male

adolescents. In addition to the obvious physical gratification afforded by this activity, it often also carries an aura of some degree of guilt and anxiety (see Chapter 2). Resulting from general social disapproval of masturbation, concern with acknowledging oneself as a sexual being, and possible worries about the content of one's sexual fantasies, this guilt and anxiety often contribute to the intensity of feeling which is then often attributed to sex itself (Simon and Gagnon, 1969).

Sex role models teach adolescent males that it is appropriate for them to be sexually active and aggressive. Sexual activity often becomes a symbol of masculinity and a way to attain this desired status. For some males, this message carries a double edge: if a boy is concerned with not being exploitative in his sexual relationships, he may be judged by his more sex-typed peers as lacking in "masculinity."

## FEMALES

As we have seen, the general script for female rehearsal of socially prescribed adult roles places more emphasis on acquiring social skills and less on competence and achievement. Socializing influences such as educational materials and counseling, along with omnipresent media images, help to construct and support this version of appropriate role behavior. There is a double edge here, too: while girls learn to direct their attention away from competitive achievement to success in interpersonal relationships (Bardwick and Douvan, 1971), they learn important skills such as caring, being expressive, being supportive. These are genderless, human responses that can be equally valuable in boys' developing repertoire of skills.

As the predominant social patterns emerge, males move from developing familiarity with their sexual responsiveness to later acquisition of social skills, while the female process traditionally

### Teen-Age Pregnancy

It is estimated that 1,000,000 adolescent women become pregnant each year. Of this number, 60% deliver their children, accounting for 21% of all births in the United States. Of these mothers, 94% elect to keep their babies; and they are all too often ill-prepared for the tasks of parenthood, in the context of disadvantageous economic and emotional situations. Some of these young women choose to become pregnant, in order to have a defined identity, since both their perception, and the concrete reality, of their situations offer them few alternatives to satisfy their human needs for achievement (Fosburgh, 1977).

Pregnancy for a woman in her young teens may be associated with higher physical risks; and, in many cases, pregnancy means voluntary or involuntary withdrawal from school. Consideration given to the provision of satisfactory contraceptive education and to the development of desirable life options would perhaps offer these women a broader range of choices.

develops in reverse. Girls' awareness of sexuality is directed outward. Since a major goal is marriage, it is of crucial importance to become sexually attractive, but not overtly sexual (Simon and Gagnon, 1969).

Young adolescent girls do not have the same "permission" to be genitally sexual as do their male peers (Simon and Gagnon, 1969). Traditional educational materials stress the reproductive aspects of the female sexual system, while the clitoris may be omitted completely from the text or anatomical diagrams (Breit and Myerson-Ferrandino, 1979). Fewer girls than boys masturbate; in contrast to the male experience, only two-thirds of girls will report ever having masturbated. Additionally, it has been indicated that about half of the females who do masturbate practice this activity only after having initially experienced orgasm in a partner-sex situation (Simon and Gagnon, 1969).

## MENSTRUATION

### THE MENSTRUAL CYCLE

While menstruation is an essential experience of both adolescent and adult females, this natural process is often surrounded by myths and misinformation. In this section we will describe the physiological dynamics and the cultural ramifications of menstruation.

First of all, it is important to understand the menstrual cycle in the context of other natural events. We are well acquainted with solar, lunar, and seasonal cycles, but we often fail to recognize the cyclic nature of many human processes. Nevertheless, it seems clear that many human events are characterized by rhythmic patterns, or cycling. For example, the various stages of sleep exhibit a rhythmic pattern. Similarly, many physiological processes—for example, body temperature, blood pressure, respiration, hormone production—rise and fall in twenty-four hour, or circadian, rhythms. Although such patterns have been studied more extensively in other animals, these findings can have practical utilization at the human level; for example, the timing of the administration of various medications appears to affect their action in the body (Luce, 1973).

While there appears to be no exact male analogy to the physiological events of the menstrual cycle, men do have cycles. For example, biweekly to monthly cycles in beard growth, body weight, and pain threshold have been found (Hoyenga and Hoyenga, 1979). Testosterone production follows a circadian rhythm, and several studies (Hoyenga and Hoyenga, 1979) have also found longer cycles in some men. Since testosterone production is also sensitive to external events (for example, environmental stress lowers testosterone levels [Rose, 1969]), evidence of recurring monthly patterns is inconclusive.

The phenomenon of menstrual bleeding is an integral part of a hormonal cycle which recurs approximately every twenty-eight days, with common variations between twenty-five to thirty-four days. For the first few years after menarche, a young woman's cycles may vary considerably in length and usually assume her own characteristic rhythm by the late teens. The cycle is orchestrated by a hormonal feedback system between the hypothalamus, the pituitary, and the ovaries. Counting the first day of menstrual flow as day one, we will outline the main events in the process.

Responding to the low level of ovarian hormones circulating in the bloodstream during the first few days of the cycle, the hypothalamus produces FSH-RF, which causes the pituitary to secrete FSH. This substance acts on the ovary to initiate maturation of several ovarian follicles, which then begin to produce estrogen. This estrogen promotes egg maturation and stimulates the development or proliferation of the endometrium, the uterine lining, to prepare to receive a possible fertilized egg. This is known as the *proliferative* phase of the cycle and is of varying length. The estrogen also stimulates mucous glands in the cervix. As ovulation (discussed in the next paragraph) approaches, the cervical mucus becomes plentiful, clear, elastic, and stringy, resembling raw egg white in texture. This ovulatory mucus facilitates the passage of sperm and contains nutrients for their use (Hafez, 1978).

As the level of estrogen in the bloodstream reaches a peak, the pituitary responds by depressing its production of FSH and by initiating its secretion of LH. In combination with the estrogen, LH causes the final maturation of one of the developing follicles and the others regress. The action of LH triggers ovulation, that is, the matured egg bursts out of its follicle. Some women experience *mittelschmerz* ("middle pain") at ovulation, which consists of intermittent cramping in the lower abdomen or lower back, and some women occasionally have "staining," or light bleeding, at this time.

LH causes the ruptured follicle to develop into the glandular structure known as the *corpus luteum* ("yellow body"). Stimulated by LH, the corpus luteum produces progesterone and additional estrogen which cause further development of the endometrium. The progesterone also inhibits the flow of cervical mucus. The post-ovulatory sequence is called the *secretory* phase of the cycle because the glands in the endometrium are now secreting nutrient fluids for the potential zygote, or fertilized egg. Regardless of the length of the overall cycle, ovulation occurs approximately fourteen days before menstruation.

As the secretory phase unfolds, the pituitary responds to the high levels of estrogen and progesterone by closing down its production of LH. Without continued stimulation, if the egg is not fertilized, the corpus luteum degenerates and its hormonal output stops. With the subsequent decline in the hormones necessary for its maintenance, the endometrium breaks down and is shed, much like a tree sheds its leaves in autumn. This shedding constitutes the menstrual flow. This menstrual flow consists of approximately two ounces, or sixty milliliters, of blood, together with mucus and endometrial tissue. The flow generally lasts for three to seven days. The decrease in estrogen level at this time initiates the hypothalamic stimulation of the pituitary, and the cycle continues.

If the egg is fertilized, the corpus luteum continues to secrete its hormones to maintain the pregnancy. As mentioned above, the output of LH declines in response to the high levels of ovarian hormones in the secretory phase. In the pregnant woman, the developing placenta (described below in the section on pregnancy) secretes human chorionic gonadotropin (HCG), which assumes the role of the now depleted LH to provide continued stimulation of corpus luteum activity. (The function of

pregnancy tests is to determine the presence or absence of HCG.) Present evidence suggests that HCG chemically resembles LH, so that their functional similarity is not surprising (Stewart, Guest, Stewart, and Hatcher, 1979).

The feedback system of the menstrual cycle is not entirely self-contained; that is, it is subject to outside influences. As discussed earlier, the activity of the pituitary can be affected by other bodily occurrences or by external events (which are perceived via the brain and central nervous system). Thus, a variety of factors—for example, malnutrition, illness, certain emotional states, and significant changes or stress-producing events such as leaving home to go to college, vacations, airplane travel—can affect the rhythms of a woman's menstrual cycle.

In this connection, the phenomenon of synchronous menstrual cycles is intriguing. Women who are roommates, who work together, or who are close friends sometimes find that they menstruate at the same time. For example, McClintock (1971) found that women living together in college dormitories developed synchronous menstrual cycles in the course of an academic year. Beyond the recognition that a shared environment can affect women's experience of menstruation, this phenomenon is not well understood, and the possible role of emotional factors has not been investigated.

## MENSTRUAL PROBLEMS

Many women experience some degree of menstrual discomfort somewhere in their menstrual history, though the occurrence and the extent of discomfort is highly variable. Menstrual discomfort is sometimes experienced for a few days before the actual onset of the flow. Such premenstrual symptoms include excess water retention, feelings of bloatedness, breast tenderness, heaviness in the lower abdomen, and tension; and they usually disappear when bleeding starts. It has been estimated that between 25% and 100% of women experience some of these symptoms, depending on how the symptoms are defined and what population is being studied (Williams, 1977).

Painful cramping during the period itself is termed dysmenorrhea and is experienced by 50% of women at some time during their reproductive years. Several hypotheses have been advanced to explain dysmenorrhea, including an excessively tight cervix, hormonal activity, and uterine muscle contractions (Stewart et al., 1979). Accumulating evidence suggests that overproduction of prostaglandins may be responsible for severe cramps. Prostaglandins are chemical substances that are produced by many tissues of the body and which have a number of physiological effects. At issue here are the prostaglandins which are produced in the uterine lining and which stimulate the uterus to contract to shed this lining during the menstrual phase of the cycle. Excessive increases in prostaglandin concentrations in the menstrual fluid of women who have primary dysmenorrhea (that is, dysmenorrhea not caused by any other organic conditions) indicate a connection between this substance and cramps. In clinical trials, various drugs which inhibit the synthesis of prostaglandins, while not suitable in all cases, have been shown to provide relief from symptoms (Marx, 1979b).

There are a number of remedies for "everyday" menstrual

discomfort that are suggested as alternatives to medication. Some authorities advocate a dietary approach, for example, adequate protein and vegetables and a reduction of refined foods. Vitamin and mineral supplements such as vitamin B complex, vitamin C, and calcium and magnesium are also recommended for menstrual discomfort. For premenstrual problems, a reduction in salt intake and an increase in potassium (for example, bananas) may counteract water retention (Stewart et al., 1979). Various forms of exercise, yoga, and lower back massage all have their adherents, and studies have found that athletes have fewer menstrual difficulties (Weideger, 1977a). Orgasm, experienced alone or with a partner, may relieve cramping because it helps to relax the uterine muscle and decreases pelvic congestion (Stewart et al., 1979). There is no consensus on either the cause or the cure of menstrual difficulties, but some of these suggestions may help. It may be necessary to experiment with a number of these proposed treatments before finding one, if any, that is suitable for any given individual.

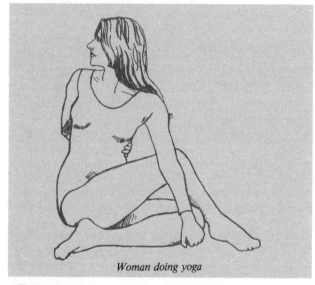

*Woman doing yoga*

Endometriosis is a condition that can affect women in their childbearing years, particularly in their thirties and forties. While symptoms can vary, endometriosis is usually associated with severe, repeated, and increasing menstrual pain. What happens in such cases is that some endometrial tissue becomes implanted outside the uterus, for example, on the ovaries, in the bowel on the outside of the uterus, or on other pelvic structures (American College of Obstetricians and Gynecologists, 1979). This displaced tissue acts like uterine endometrium and thus breaks apart and bleeds during menstruation. Body tissues surrounding this local bleeding become inflamed and develop into scar tissue. Endometriosis may lead to infertility if the ovaries or Fallopian tubes become blocked by scar tissue or through other mechanisms which are not well understood as yet. Treatment for endometriosis may involve hormonal therapy or surgical removal of extrauterine endometrial tissue. Endometriosis stops progressing at menopause, as declining levels of estrogen remove support for the development of the endometrium (Boston Women's Health Book Collective, 1976; American College of Obstetricians and Gynecologists, 1979).

Another menstrual problem is amenorrhea, the absence of menstruation. Primary amenorrhea is the term used when a woman has never had a period, and secondary amenorrhea refers to periods missed after the woman has experienced at least one. Pregnancy is a common cause of amenorrhea; other causes include malnutrition, disease, stress, absence of ovulation, problems in the hypothalamus, or congenital defects (Stewart et al., 1979). It is not unusual for a woman to skip a period now and then, but continued amenorrhea is an indication for medical consultation.

While, as we have seen, organic causes are often responsible for menstrual problems, research suggests that the effects of our feelings or attitudes on our menstrual experience are also important. For example, Paige's (1973) research indicates that women who subscribe most strongly to unfavorable religious or cultural attitudes toward menstruation tend to have more frequent and intense menstrual complaints (cf. Levitt and Lubin, 1967). The social and personal context in which a woman experiences menstrual sensations may influence her perception of their intensity (Weideger, 1977a). For example, if a woman believes that menstruation is an illness or expects to have considerable discomfort, she may experience ordinary uterine activity as uncomfortable and, if she tenses against it, may induce pain. On the other hand, if a woman feels positively about menstruation, she may interpret her sensations as an awareness of a natural bodily process and not experience tension. The generally negative attitudes toward menstruation in our culture lead to the hypothesis that the phenomenon of menstrual discomfort may be related not only to physical conditions but also to social dimensions, thus providing another illustration of the ways in which culture influences biology.

## CONTEMPORARY MENSTRUAL TABOO

| | |
|---|---|
| George is visiting | On the rag |
| My friend is here | Onion soup |
| Falling off the roof | Sick time |
| Sat on the butcher knife | The curse |
| That time of month | Red tide |

These expressions are some of our society's ways of referring to menstruation. These phrases reflect some common attitudes toward this bodily process: negativity, avoidance, and denial. Women have been socialized to, at best, tolerate their monthly flow and, at worst, resent it. In past ages, most cultures and societies treated menstruating women as unhealthy or unclean outcasts. Paula Weideger's book *Menstruation and Menopause* (1977a) provides extensive details of these rites, which stemmed from a belief in the ability of menstruating women to pollute. To avoid contamination, bleeding women were variously isolated in menstrual huts, restricted from contact with others, were sexually taboo, and could not touch food or weapons. Although we no longer visibly practice similar rituals, recent literature suggests that there still exists in our current American culture a taboo on menstruation (Weideger, 1977a; Delaney, Lupton and Toth, 1977; Breit and Myerson-Ferrandino, 1979).

One of the main effects of the taboo is the widespread insistence on keeping menstruation hidden or secret. Not only do we use euphemisms to disguise the fact that women menstruate, but it is also the case that menstruation-related products help to conceal and misrepresent this process. Both the packaging and the imagery used in advertisements reinforce the belief that menstruation is something secretive. For example, pictures of women in white, confirmationlike dresses and ads which proclaim "no smells, no bulges" add to women's fears that someone will know when they are menstruating. Ads for menstrual products have begun to appear on late night television, but they avoid the use of words referring to menstruation and discuss the function of their products in vague and euphemistic ways which almost depend on a secret code between advertiser and viewer. (A recent ad for a new product claimed the product has a new shape, but the product is neither shown nor described.) This masquerade exemplifies another way in which women are socialized to reject an integral part of themselves and their functioning.

Another manifestation of the menstrual taboo is the fact that, even today, many girls are inadequately prepared for the menarche (Laws and Schwartz, 1977). Additionally, sex and health education literature for adolescents often reinforces the message that menstruation is a chore and something to be hidden (Breit and Myerson-Ferrandino, 1979).

## Menstruation and Sexuality

Don't go swimming.              Don't wash your hair.
Don't go barefoot.              Don't get a permanent.
Don't get a tooth filled.       Don't have sex.
Don't play sports.              Don't take a bath.

Menstruation is a disease.
When you menstruate, your insides are falling out.
Menstruation is God's punishment to women.
A menstruating woman is messy, smelly, and crabby.
A menstruating woman is like an unripe fruit—leave her
    alone for a few days before you eat her.

(These examples were provided by male and female
    students in the undergraduate courses taught by one of
    the authors.)

It has been proposed that these beliefs and attitudes, which are in common circulation, may tend to inhibit women's behavior and prevent them from experiencing menstruation as a normal bodily function (Weideger, 1977a; Delaney, et al., 1977; Breit and Myerson-Ferrandino, 1979). A crucial research dimension which is still in the pioneering stages is an exploration of the effects of the menstrual taboo on women's self-image and sexuality. As long as menstruation is considered unclean and something to be hidden, so may women's genitals be considered unclean; if menstruation is feared or considered unattractive, so may women's sexual organs. This prejudice by association is further enhanced by the cultural and religious taboos on sex during menstruation. Studies cited by Weideger (1977a) suggest that it is more often a male partner's attitude that enforces this taboo. If he has never received adequate education about menstruation, this is perfectly understandable. Whether or not to express sexuality during menstruation is the same issue as it is at any other time; it depends on the individual's choice. There exists no medical reason for avoiding sex during menstruation, and some women experience strong sexual feelings at this time.

The existence of cyclical variation in sexual desire varies considerably from woman to woman. Individual women might ex-

perience no such variation, might experience a peak in desire premenstrually, or might feel more aroused at ovulation, and the same woman might experience all these patterns from menstrual cycle to menstrual cycle. For women who do report cyclic alteration in sexual feeling, the majority feel most aroused just prior to the menstrual flow or during and just after it (Weideger, 1977a). Other women report heightened interest at ovulation (Weideger, 1977a), which may be correlated with increased feelings of well-being at this time. Increased sexual feelings premenstrually may be a function of the higher base line of pelvic vasocongestion present at this time. Since vasocongestion is related to sexual arousal, premenstrual women can be viewed as being in a mild state of sexual excitement (Sherfey, 1973). However, this phenomenon is rarely recognized as such. It is interesting to speculate to what extent self-reported irritability preceding menstruation may be due to unrecognized sexual feelings. Since a premenstrual sexual peak may continue through the flow as well, it is ironic that this is a time of culturally enforced asexuality. As one of the author's students once reported in class, the two menstrual beliefs she was most familiar with were: "A menstruating woman is extra sexual" and "A menstruating woman should not engage in sex *at all."*

The considerable variation in levels and peaks of sexual interest from individual to individual seems to indicate that phases of the menstrual cycle are less important determinants than are situational factors.

---

### Daily Log

Moods—intensity and range    Appetite; eating behaviors
Weight                        Sexual feelings
Body feelings                 Energy levels
Body changes                  External factors and
                                  influences

By keeping a log of their daily experiences in these areas, both women and men can come to a better understanding of themselves. Women can add the factors of days in menstrual cycle, breast changes, and so on. For example, we can learn whether certain emotions or behaviors follow rhythmic patterns and how we are affected by situational factors. The more we learn about ourselves, the more we can appreciate our individual uniqueness.

---

## Research

Traditional research on menstruation often presents a model whereby psychological problems and maladjustments are used to explain the variations of menstrual experience. Another popular theme is the association between, on the one hand, premenstruation and menstruation and, on the other hand, poor performance, commission of crimes, and psychiatric hospital admissions. Recent research (Sommer, 1973) has provided a comprehensive critique of these older studies and uncovers implicit unfounded assumptions and biases that were built into these efforts. Social expectations about menstrual disabilities have been shown to affect both the subjects' self-perceptions and the researchers' postulates. The traditional studies tend to focus on negative aspects. For example, the Moos Menstrual Distress Questionnaire (MDQ), probably the most widely used instrument for measuring menstrual experience, focuses predominantly on negative factors, includes feelings of well-being in only one of its categories, and asks no questions about sexual feelings, fantasy, or activity. The conspicuous absence of a Menstrual Satisfaction Questionnaire is to be noted (Breit and Myerson-Ferrandino, 1979).

In contrast to the usual assumption, recent investigations have failed to discover the menstrual-related decrements in performance. Neither cognitive nor physical performance have been shown to be affected by cycle phase; for example, women in all phases of their cycles have broken world records and won Olympic gold medals (Ruble and Brooks-Gunn, 1979).

Similarly, beliefs about the intensity of negative moods before menstruation have not been substantiated. Golub (1976) reports that, while anxiety and depression may be higher at this time, these changes are, on the average, small and are to be sharply differentiated from psychiatric illness or reactions to unusual stress. Persky's (1969) findings substantiate this idea, by indicating that there is little change in such negative moods as anxiety, depression, or hostility across the menstrual cycle. Further, the average values for the psychological variables obtained from Persky's subjects closely resembled those obtained from their male classmates. In a study comparing men, women taking oral contraceptives, and women non-pill users, Schrader, Wilcoxon, and Sherif (1975) found that stressful events accounted for more of the variance for the negative mood factors than did menstrual cycle phase. Sommer, in turn, on the basis of a recent study (1975), presents the perspective that self-reported negative affect remained at a low level throughout the subjects' menstrual cycles, while positive affect showed a cyclic variation with a peak at ovulation. Similarly, Paige (1973) reports that women feel the most optimistic and competent at ovulation. However, we have no shared beliefs or appropriate terminology for the feelings of well-being which seem to be a common occurrence at ovulation (Laws and Schwartz, 1977). Taken together, these findings suggest the desirability of an alternative conceptualization of the menstrual cycle. Rather than concentrating on a nadir in mood before menstruation, refocusing suggests the idea of a zenith achieved at ovulation, an extra boost in positive mood (Sommer, 1975).

## "Celebration Menstruation"

As women feel more comfortable with their bodily processes, they may discover that, at times, menstruation is no different from any other phase of the cycle. At other times, their experience of their period may be different because of specific external circumstances and influences operating then. At still other times, a woman might find that menstruation has a special quality: menstruation may be perceived as a time of increased sensitivity, of new insights and creativity. For some women, menstruation represents a time for communion with the self, or to meet an experienced need for quiet or meditative time.

Elimination of the menstrual taboo and its replacement with positive attitudes toward menstruation can be seen as a preventive mental health measure. Positive attitudes can help to facilitate the process of full acceptance, understanding, and appreciation of one's body and sexuality in all its modes of functioning and expression and the integration of sexuality into the total life process. Additionally, recent research suggests that attitudes about menstruation can be changed through the process of awareness and education (Breit and Myerson-Ferrandino, 1979).

# ADULTHOOD

From adolescence we "graduate" into adulthood. We now expend our energies in the familial, occupational, and social spheres and in pursuit of our avocational and creative interests. The nature and forms of these activities will evolve as our selves and our situations change over time. As the other chapters amply demonstrate, adult sexual expression takes on many forms and styles. Each individual's responses are influenced by a constellation of biological, psychological, cultural, and idiosyncratic factors. Each one of us has our own unique and special learning history which will affect our sexual behavior.

One significant event in the sexual history of the vast majority of both women and men is pregnancy and childbirth. In the following sections, we will discuss the physiological, psychological, and cultural dimensions of these experiences.

## PREGNANCY

The motivation for having children is strong. Despite financial pressures, life style changes, and concerns about population growth, people continue to desire children; and a study has shown that only 2% want only one child or none (Pohlman, 1970). Additionally, many people value the idea of children as an extension of the self, as an avenue to immortality, especially in the face of the transitory nature of life (Williams, 1977). Cultural and especially religious values often view producing children as a moral duty and not having any children as selfish. Parental pressure, peer pressure, the idea of children as a sign of virility, or a desire to "fix up" a relationship are further contributing factors.

In addition to cultural influences, our personal values are crucially important. We might want to experience the excitement, sheer wonder, and awe of witnessing and participating in a baby's development from a helpless infant into an autonomous being as it acquires life skills. For many of us, this is a source of delight, joy, and immeasurable enrichment.

The decision to parent not only concerns the question of if but also the issue of when. Recently, numbers of couples have been waiting until their mid or late thirties to decide to become parents, after the women's career has been established or other goals attained (Daniels and Weingarten, 1979). Having accomplished certain goals of personal and professional development, or finally feeling clear about really wanting a child, many people now feel ready to become parents.

While there are advantages to a woman's waiting till she is 35 or older to become pregnant (in medical terms, "advanced maternal age"), there is also the question of potential risks. Although the absolute risk remains low, the incidence of several complications of pregnancy does increase with advanced maternal age. For example, one study of the rate of spontaneous abortion during the first 12 weeks of pregnancy (early pregnancy) indicated that this event occurs in approximately 40 per 1,000 pregnancies for women in their twenties and 150 per 1,000 pregnancies for women 35 and older. Similarly, women over 35 are twice as likely as women in their twenties to miscarry in later pregnancy (Daniels and Weingarten, 1979).

One of the major complications of later pregnancy is hemorrhage, usually the result of *placenta previa*, an abnormality of the placenta (see below under the section on conception and early embryonic development). The rate of frequency of this kind of hemorrhage in first pregnancies is 1.9 per 1,000 for women aged 15 to 24, and three and one-half times higher, 7.0 per 1,000, for women over 35. Additionally, as we shall see below, the risk of birth defects caused by chromosomal abnormalities can be correlated with advancing maternal age (Daniels and Weingarten, 1979).

In sum, the risks of advanced age are relative. All other things being equal, age is often a less important indicator for the development of complications than general health status, standards of nutrition, and access to medical care (Daniels and Weingarten, 1979).

---

## Beliefs about Pregnancy

It was not until the twentieth century that scientists demonstrated that a sperm and an egg must unite to initiate a new being, although the general connection between vaginal intercourse and conception had been known for some prior thousands of years. However, the facts that many episodes of intercourse do not result in conception and that some women who have the social status of virgins become pregnant do not make this connection any the easier to comprehend. Earlier "primitive" or small-scale societies possessed a variety of beliefs about the origins of life, and some of these beliefs have been carried into modern times.

One such alternative explanation of pregnancy was the belief that a spirit enters a woman, from the wind, water, stars, moon, trees, or birds; in other cultures, conception was believed to be a result of certain foods eaten by a woman (Stannard, n.d.). Even in some cultures where there was an understanding of the association between intercourse and conception, it was a prevalent belief that other external factors were necessary for an episode of intercourse to result in pregnancy, for example, the appropriate phase of the moon. Some peoples believed that each new child born into the group was a reincarnation of a deceased member of the tribe.

---

## Conception and Early Embryonic Development

The uniting of an egg and a spermatozoon (commonly called sperm in both singular and plural) is a result of a complicated process. Sperm travel on a comparatively long journey from the testes out through the penis and into the vagina. Some sperm pass out of the vagina through the force of gravity if the woman has been on top of her partner during intercourse or if she gets up immediately afterward. For those sperm which remain in the vagina, the surrounding environment must have an appropriate pH (not too acidic) to ensure their survival. If the woman has recently ovulated, there will be an egg in one of the Fallopian tubes. The sperm "swim" toward the cervix, up through the uterus, and into the Fallopian tubes, where half of them will enter the tube that does not have an egg in it. The sperm continue their journey against the "current" created by the wavelike motion of the cilia which line the tube. During their travel in the female genital tract, sperm undergo a final maturation process called capacitation. Induced by exposure to certain substances in the vagina and uterus, this process is necessary before sperm can fertilize an egg (Sawin, 1978). Out of the original 150 to 600 million sperm in the ejaculate, approximately 2,000 will reach the egg, and only one unites with it. Contrary to the common belief that fertilization occurs in the uterus, this process actually takes place in the Fallopian tube and generally occurs within 48 hours of ovulation for the egg to be viable.

The egg is surrounded by a thin, gelatinlike layer known as the *zona pellucida*. All the sperm in the vicinity secrete an enzyme called hyaluronidase, which serves to dissolve the zona pellucida, and one sperm enters the egg. The mechanism by which the sperm enters the egg—possibly the most important element in reproduction—remains as yet a mystery. Also unknown are the details of the process whereby the egg then becomes impervious to further sperm, once one sperm has penetrated it. The nucleus in the head of the sperm and the nucleus in the egg fuse, and each contributes its 23 chromosomes to produce the necessary 46. The egg's sex chromosome is always an X. If the sperm carries an X, the resulting XX is genetically female; if the sperm carries a Y, the resulting XY is genetically male. The chromosomes are tiny structures, each of which carries several thousand genes, biochemical compounds which determine or influence characteristics of an individual.

The fertilized egg, now known as a zygote, begins to travel up the Fallopian tube, drawn toward the uterus by "currents" produced by the cilia and the slow peristaltic contractions of the tube. Within 36 hours, the zygote begins the process of cell division. The journey to the uterus takes about three days; the mass of cells, now termed a blastocyst, floats around in the uterine cavity. Five to seven days after fertilization, it begins to make contact with the uterine wall. The action of enzymes digests the outer surface of the endometrium, so the egg can reach the blood vessels and nutrients in the inner lining. This process is called implantation and is usually complete by the tenth to twelfth day after fertilization.

The implanted blastocyst begins to develop different structures: the embryonic disk from which the organism, now known as an embryo, grows and the beginnings of the placenta, amnion, and yolk sac, formed from the remaining cells. The placenta is an organ of exchange through which the embryo receives oxygen and nutrients and discharges waste products. Formed by tissue from both the blastocyst and the uterus, the blood vessels of the placenta connect to the maternal circulatory system through blood vessels in the uterine wall and connect to the em-

## Sex Ratio

While common sense may dictate that the male-female ratio of embryos conceived and children born be equal, statistics show that this is not the case. It is estimated that 120 to 150 males are conceived for every 100 females (Rasmuson, 1971; Rhodes, 1965; Shettles, 1961), while the ratio at birth is 104 to 107 males for every 100 females (Peterson, 1968). The reduction in this ratio probably reflects the greater vulnerability of unborn males. The sex ratio continues to decline with age; the proportion is equal at age 18 and declines to one male to two females by age 87 (Lerner, 1968).

It appears that males, as a group, are more vulnerable to a variety of problems than females at all ages. For example, additional genetic material on the second X chromosome offers some protection for females against sex-linked disorders such as hemophilia and colorblindness. There is a lower incidence in girls of congenital neurological abnormalities as reflected in lower rates of such conditions as mental retardation, learning disabilities, and so on. In addition, girls exhibit comparatively advanced developmental maturity, which can be considered as facilitating their earlier learning and socialization. Whether through biological advantage or differential adaptation to the environment or a complex intermeshing of both these factors, women at all ages are less susceptible to the major causes of death than are men (Williams, 1977).

bryonic circulatory system through the blood vessels in the umbilical cord. The placenta also functions as an endocrine gland, first secreting human chorionic gonadotropin (HCG) to stimulate production of progesterone by the corpus luteum during the first three months of pregnancy, and then manufacturing progesterone and estrogen itself, hormones necessary to maintain the pregnancy.

The amnion is a membranous sac which contains the embryo and amniotic fluid; it serves to equalize pressure and absorb physical shock. The yolk sac is a vestigial organ which serves the purpose of storing nutrients for animals that hatch from eggs; it seems to be insignificant for humans. After eight weeks, the embryo has developed the principal features of human structure and is now called a fetus.

### Variations

In this section we will discuss some variations in the normal process of pregnancy. *Pseudocyesis,* or "false pregnancy," is a phenomenon in which a woman believes she is pregnant, often experiences pregnancy symptoms including cessation of menstruation and the sensation of fetal movements, but is *not* pregnant at all. Pseudocyesis is a rare condition—0.1% of women who consult obstetricians (Katchadourian and Lunde, 1975)—and is usually a result of various emotional factors, for example, an intense and unfulfilled desire to become pregnant

(Hellman and Pritchard, 1971). There are records of nuns in medieval convents who interpreted their marriage vows with Christ in literal fashion and believed they were carrying Christ's child (Katchadourian and Lunde, 1975). Pseudocyesis is another fascinating illustration of how emotional or psychological states can affect our physical functioning.

*Spontaneous abortion*, or *miscarriage*, occurs most often during early pregnancy. The first sign is vaginal bleeding, and then the product of conception is usually expelled. This phenomenon is commonly estimated to occur in 10% to 15% of pregnancies. However, a very early miscarriage will often be undetected, especially if it is mistaken for an unusually heavy but otherwise normal menstrual period. A later miscarriage is usually recognizable and is accompanied by cramping. A revised estimate suggests that perhaps as many as 50% of pregnancies become spontaneous abortions, usually before the first missed period (James, 1970). An early spontaneous abortion is usually the result of a defective ovum, sperm, or errors in fertilization or early cell division. A miscarriage in later pregnancy is usually the result of "environmental" factors, such as transmission of a contagious disease from mother to fetus (Daniels and Weingarten, 1979).

An *ectopic* (literally, "out of place") *pregnancy* happens when a fertilized egg implants and begins developing in a location outside of the uterus. This occurs in about 2% of all pregnancies (McLaren, 1972), and 96% of ectopic pregnancies occur in the Fallopian tube and are thus known as tubal pregnancies. This might occur if the egg's pathway to the uterus is obstructed, for example, by scar tissue. The embryo may spontaneously abort, or it may be released into the abdominal cavity either through the opening of the Fallopian tube or through a rupture in the wall of the tube (Gray, 1959). If the egg continues to develop in the Fallopian tube, within a few weeks it will have grown beyond the tube's ability to expand and the tube will rupture. Early diagnosis of an ectopic pregnancy is difficult because a woman's symptoms will indicate only the existence of pregnancy, not its specific location. Usually the first sign of an ectopic pregnancy is a sharp pain in the abdomen. If this goes untreated, the tube will burst and cause internal bleeding. This is a serious medical condition; if it is neglected, the woman may go into shock and die. Treatment involves removal of the Fallopian tube.

The phenomenon of an abdominal pregnancy is *very rare* (one in 15,000 pregnancies [Willson, Beecham, and Carrington, 1966]) and may be an embryo which started developing in the tube and was then released into the abdominal cavity where it was able to re-implant. If the embryo attaches to tissue which can provide nourishment—for example, ectopic endometrium—it might continue normal fetal development and would need to be delivered surgically, although the survival of such a fetus is rare (Hellman and Pritchard, 1971).

Sometimes a woman is pregnant with more than one fetus. The most common occurrence is twins, one in 90 births in the United States (Hellman and Pritchard, 1971). There are two types of twins: *Identical* twins result when a fertilized egg subdivides into two, with identical genetic information; identical twins usually share a single placenta. *Fraternal* twins result when two separate eggs are fertilized during the same ovulation period; fraternal twins usually have separate placentas. It is biologically possible for fraternal twins to have different fathers. Two out of three sets of twins are fraternal twins.

The occurrence of triplets is one in 9,000 births, and quadruplets, one in 500,000. Higher-order multiple births, that is, quintuplets or sextuplets, are extremely rare and usually attract worldwide attention because they are so far removed from the normal range of human experience. The use of drugs such as Clomid, which contain synthetic gonadotropins as an infertility remedy (see Chapter 8), can stimulate the ovulation of more than one egg and thus result in multiple fetuses, usually twins. More medical risks are associated with multiple births, because of the smaller size of each infant and the potential for premature delivery.

## The Experience of Pregnancy

The experience of pregnancy has been conceptualized as a developmental crisis or turning point for women, similar to puberty and menopause. The physical process of pregnancy is accompanied by emotional and psychological changes as well. This developmental stage begun by pregnancy extends past delivery and into the postpartum period, well after the child is born (Bibring, 1975).

A woman's psychological adaptation to her pregnancy depends on many factors—possible ambivalence about pregnancy; physical health; stresses in her environment, such as work, finances; her relationships with significant others, for example, her partner, her mother. In addition, we must remember that the pregnant woman does not live in isolation; social parameters are also important influences on psychological state. Cultural attitudes, expectations, and responses, her relationship with her medical caretakers—all are important factors. Each woman is a unique individual, and her reaction to any and all of these sources of influence will be individually determined.

The vast majority of attention given to the pregnancy experience focuses on the woman, and, of course, it *is* the woman's experience. But the inability to experience pregnancy does not exclude the father's participation. Indeed, a father can be intensely involved in the process and may experience profound psychological reactions himself. He may display considerable interest in his partner's process through pregnancy and delivery, and he may directly share some of her concerns; he may be concerned about the baby's health, his own parenting ability, life style changes, finances, and so on. A man's reaction and level of involvement will be highly individual, depending, in part, on his self-perception of his role as father. The father's role in birth is often stereotyped as pacing the floor of the hospital waiting room. With the growing popularity of "natural" or educated childbirth, more fathers are becoming directly involved in the labor process. Research has indicated that, when fathers are given the opportunity to be alone with their newly born infants, they react as mothers do, spending almost exactly the same amount of time holding, touching, and looking at their babies (Trause, Kennell, and Klaus, 1978).

The duration of pregnancy is usually nine calendar months (266 days), or 280 days from the last menstrual period (LMP), with variations of a few weeks in either direction being relative-

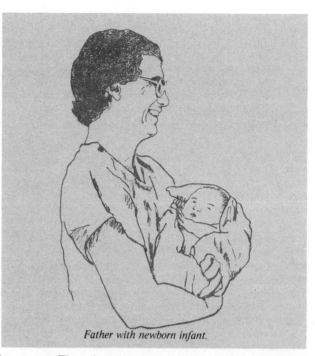

*Father with newborn infant.*

ly common. The estimated due date of birth is usually calculated by subtracting three months from the date of the last menstrual period and adding seven days; for example, if a woman's last period started on December 13, the due date would be September 20. The nine-month process is usually divided into three-month periods called trimesters.

The usual indication of pregnancy is a missed menstrual period. This is not always a reliable sign, however, because, as discussed earlier, other factors can produce this phenomenon. Additionally, some 20% of pregnant women experience "spotting," or vaginal bleeding, during pregnancy (Hellman and Pritchard, 1971). This bleeding may occur during the implantation process, or it may recur for the first two or three months, resulting in light "periods." In addition to a skipped period, other *presumptive* signs of pregnancy are growth and tenderness of the woman's breasts with darkening of the areola; "morning sickness"; more frequent urination; and unusual fatigue. Occurrences of these changes are not necessarily conclusive proof of pregnancy, and their incidence varies from individual to individual.

Around the sixth week after conception, pregnancy can be detected by physical examination. A "blue" cervix, a result of increased blood vessel growth, and Hegar's sign, the soft consistency of an area between the cervix and the body of the uterus, are *probable* signs of pregnancy (Boston Women's Health Book Collective, 1976; Hellman and Pritchard, 1971). *Positive* signs, which are not perceivable until later in the process, are the detection of the fetal heartbeat, active fetal movements, and X-ray observation of the presence of a fetus (Hellman and Pritchard, 1971). This last step may involve risk to the fetus and is usually limited to special cases.

Pregnancy tests can be performed after 42 days from LMP, or two weeks after a missed period. These usually involve testing the woman's urine for the presence of HCG and can be done in a professional laboratory or, since testing kits are now available over the counter, in the home. New procedures have been developed which can detect pregnancy even earlier. These tests check for the presence of HCG in the blood serum and can very reliably detect pregnancy as early as one week after conception, that is, one week before the next period is due (Stewart et al., 1979).

During the first trimester, the woman's physical changes will include the above-mentioned presumptive symptoms of pregnancy, such as changes in her breasts. During the second trimester, her waist will become thicker and her abdomen will grow. Around the fourth or fifth month, she will begin to feel fetal movements. By mid-pregnancy, her breasts may secrete a thin, yellowish fluid, colostrum, the precursor of breast milk. During the third trimester, the woman can feel and see fetal movements from the outside as well, as ripples or slight protrusions in her abdomen. Near the end of pregnancy, the heaviness of the uterus will put pressure on the bladder and urination becomes more frequent. She may also experience Braxton-Hicks contractions: painless sensations of the tightening of the uterus. These contractions are believed to strengthen the uterine muscles, preparing them for the intense work they will perform during labor (Boston Women's Health Book Collective, 1976).

During the process of pregnancy, a woman may experience a variety of emotional responses. She may experience some negative feelings, especially in the first trimester, such as depression, anxiety, or confusion. These feelings are both relevant and natural, as the woman seeks to come to grips with her changing reality. Some of the positive emotional responses associated with pregnancy include feelings of well-being, specialness, and creativity and great excitement, and she may also feel new energy.

## Prenatal Care

Good prenatal care includes regular medical consultation, as a form of preventive medicine, exercise to develop and strengthen the body, and attention to good nutrition. The general consensus of obstetricians and exercise physiologists is that women can, and should, continue most sports activities and exercise during pregnancy for as long as they feel comfortable (Kelly, Leavy, and Northrup, 1978).

Ample supplies of protein along with fresh fruits and vegetables, as well as other essential nutrients, are very important. Poor nutrition is considered by some experts to be a major cause of toxemia, a serious complication of pregnancy, although this condition is not yet fully understood (Boston Women's Health Book Collective, 1976). Toxemia can occur after the twentieth to twenty-fourth week, usually late in pregnancy. Characterized by high blood pressure and excessive water retention, toxemia that goes untreated can lead to coma and death. If detected early in its development, it can be effectively treated.

A woman obviously will gain weight during pregnancy. This weight is accounted for by the weight of the growing fetus itself, uterine and breast enlargement, the amniotic fluid, and retained fluid and fat. An excessive weight gain is to be discouraged since it can cause medical complications. In the 1960s, physicians advocated a small weight gain, but this has been recently questioned because of problems associated with low infant birth weight.

## Pregnancy and Sexual Activity

Traditional medical advice recommends abstinence from intercourse six weeks before and six weeks after birth. Of even greater importance, however, for partner decision making, is an awareness of specific individual conditions which would indicate refraining from intercourse during pregnancy. These include: pain, bleeding, ruptured amniotic membranes, and history of or present threatened miscarriage. Apart from these unusual conditions, intercourse and other sexual activities are not generally harmful during or toward the end of pregnancy (Masters and Johnson, 1966). A recent study (Naeye, 1979) has indicated a statistically significant but very small increase in the number of amniotic-fluid infections in women who reported intercourse once or more per week during the last month of pregnancy. The reasons for the association between intercourse and amniotic-fluid infections are not as yet known.

In their laboratory studies, Masters and Johnson (1966) noticed several changes in the sexual response cycle in pregnant women. There was increased vascularity in the pelvis as new blood vessels grew to support the pregnancy, and increased levels of sexual tension by the end of the first or beginning of the second trimester, continuing well into the third trimester. Toward the end of the first trimester, an increase in vaginal lubrication was observed, which continued through the pregnancy. There was a marked increase of interest in sexual activity during the second trimester. Vasocongestion of the pelvis was not always completely relieved by orgasm, and residual vasocongestion continued during resolution, resulting in continued levels of sexual tension.

## Pregnancy and Drugs

Since the placenta functions more as a sieve than as a barrier, it is advisable for a pregnant woman to avoid the use of all drugs, to prevent their transmission to the fetus. In some cases, however, a drug is medically necessary, for example, to treat a bacterial infection such as syphilis, in which case the balance of the benefit over the risk is significant. The early embryo is at the highest risk as the major organ systems are now developing. However, this is also the time when a woman might not yet know that she is pregnant. Recent studies in the United States and Europe have indicated that drug use, including nicotine and alcohol, is the norm, rather than the exception, during pregnancy (Martin, 1976). The effects of various drugs on embryonic and fetal physiological functioning are being investigated, but effects on developmental and intellectual functioning are still relatively unexamined (Martin, 1976). In this section, we will discuss some of the known effects of various drugs.

Nicotine reduces the blood flow across the placenta. Smoking one or two packs of cigarettes a day during pregnancy has been associated with lower birth weight babies, higher risk of miscarriage, stillbirths (babies born dead), and premature births. Apparently, the risk increases if the pregnant woman is black (Martin, 1976).

If a pregnant woman is an alcoholic or a heavy drinker, she has an increased risk of giving birth to a child with birth defects. The infants who are most severely affected are described as having the "fetal alcohol syndrome," characterized by retarded growth, minor facial feature abnormalities, heart defects, and developmental and motor problems. Recent research suggests that some abnormalities, for example, decreased birth weight and poor sucking, are associated with moderate drinking as well (Streissguth, 1979).

If a woman takes birth control pills while she is already pregnant, there is a risk of various abnormalities in the child (see Chapter 8). Also, hormone administration for medical purposes during pregnancy, for example, to prevent miscarriage, is now being challenged. As pointed out in Chapter 8, DES (diethylstilbestrol) has produced vaginal cancer and male reproductive abnormalities. The use of progestins as a pregnancy test or to prevent a threatened miscarriage can cause heart defects or limb abnormalities (FDA Drug Bulletin, December 1978-January 1979).

The so-called minor tranquilizers, for example, Valium, may be associated with malformations, for example, cleft lip (Ray, 1978). Some antibiotics are also under scrutiny. For example, tetracycline can produce effects in the fetus, such as discoloration of teeth as they are being formed in the gums (Henninger, 1971).

Whether marijuana causes any effects on the fetus is controversial; research has not produced consistent results. Nonetheless, it is advisable to be cautious and avoid complications when possible. It is known that marijuana can produce lowered, though still normal, testosterone levels in males, but it is not known what dosage level might adversely affect a male fetus (Ray, 1978).

If a pregnant woman is a heroin addict, there is a high risk of stillbirth or premature delivery. Most babies born to addicts develop withdrawal symptoms within twenty-four hours after birth. If they are not treated, the death rate is high (Martin, 1976).

It is advisable to avoid the use of aspirin, especially during the last three months of pregnancy. The anticoagulant activity of aspirin increases the time it takes for blood to clot, and this may present complications during pregnancy (Ray, 1978).

## Fetal Development

Fetal development is an incredibly fascinating process. The simple embryo develops all human organ systems in rudimentary form by the eighth week after fertilization, and the embryo is now called a fetus. During the first few weeks, the embryo bears close resemblance to embryos of other vertebrate species, for example, it has traces of gills. As development proceeds, most of these vestigial organs disappear. Between the eighth and twelfth weeks, the fetus increases in length from about one and a half to four inches, and, at twelve weeks, it weighs about two-thirds of an ounce. At the end of the first trimester, the fetus has a definite human appearance. Further fetal development consists primarily of the continued differentiation of existing structures and of overall growth. The average weight of an infant at birth is seven pounds, and the average length is twenty inches, although these dimensions vary considerably.

The predetermination of fetal sex is a concern as old as recorded history; for example, Aristotle recommended having intercourse in a north wind if a boy was desired and in a south wind for a girl. Recent efforts have focused on differences between X-bearing and Y-bearing sperm. The technology has been

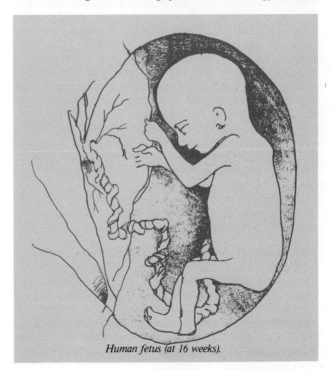

*Human fetus (at 16 weeks).*

developed for the process of separating X-sperm and Y-sperm in seminal fluid, to be used with artificial insemination (Colligan, 1977). "Do-it-yourself" technology has been recommended by arranging the timing of intercourse relative to ovulation and by douching to produce appropriate pH of the vaginal environment to favor either X-sperm or Y-sperm (Rorvick and Shettles, 1970). Although it was claimed that this method is 85% accurate, later evidence has not borne this out, and the assumptions behind the method have been challenged by new research (Colligan, 1977).

## Complications in Fetal Development

As indicated earlier, a considerable number of fertilized eggs and embryos can have serious developmental defects. When these are severe enough to be incompatible with life, the product of conception is spontaneously aborted. In other cases, fetuses with developmental problems survive and are born with what are called birth defects. Some of these defects are devastating; others are relatively minor, with little or no effect on the person's life. It has been estimated that one out of sixteen children is born with some kind of birth defect. It is difficult to compile comparative statistics, however, because of variations in which conditions are considered to be birth defects and whether or not they are detected at birth (Daniels and Weingarten, 1979).

Some cases of birth defects are caused by environmental trauma to a normally developing fetus, for example, by transmission of a contagious disease from the maternal system, harmful effects of certain drugs taken by the mother, or exposure to radiation. Other defects result from flaws in the genes, and 3% to 5% of serious birth defects are caused by defects in the chromosomes themselves (Daniels and Weingarten, 1979). In this section, we will first discuss environmentally caused fetal problems and then review genetic and chromosomal defects.

The best-known example of a connection between maternal illness and damage to the fetus is the case of German measles (rubella). The virus that causes this disease passes from the mother to the fetus; the earlier in pregnancy this happens, the greater the risk of damage. When German measles is diagnosed, especially in early pregnancy, a therapeutic abortion may be recommended. In the first month of pregnancy, there is a fifty percent chance that the rubella virus will produce deafness, cataracts, central nervous system defects, or heart defects (Hellman and Pritchard, 1971). The risk then declines to about ten percent after the third month. If a woman had rubella as a child, she will be immune to contracting it as an adult. If she is unsure whether she has ever had it, or knows definitely that she did not, she can be vaccinated against the disease, preferably well before becoming pregnant.

The virus that causes the venereal disease *herpes simplex II* (see Chapter 15) can also cause damage. If a woman has an active occurrence of herpes around the time of delivery, a Caesarian section can prevent the newborn from contracting the disease (which can lead to severe illness or death) by direct contact with a lesion during vaginal delivery (Stewart et al., 1979). However, it has been suggested that the herpes virus may also be transmitted directly to the fetus in the uterus (Witzleben and Driscoll, 1965).

Other venereal diseases can also cause serious problems. If a pregnant woman has syphilis, the bacteria is able to cross the placenta after the fourth month and enter the fetal system. This is why it is so important to have a blood test for syphilis as a routine part of early prenatal care. If syphilis is detected early, the mother can be cured and the fetus unaffected. After the fourth month, untreated maternal syphilis will most likely cause congenital syphilis in the fetus, which can lead to impaired vision and hearing and bone and teeth deformities, or can lead to fetal death (von Haam, 1971). If a pregnant woman has gonorrhea when she is going into labor, the infant can acquire a gonorrheal infection in the eyes as it passes through her vagina. This infection can produce blindness, and thus the prophylactic use of silver nitrate drops in all newborns' eyes is hospital routine.

Another important part of routine early prenatal care is a blood test to check for the presence of the Rh factor, a substance in the blood in about 85% of the population. If the Rh factor is present, the blood type is known as Rh positive (Rh+); if it is absent, the blood type is Rh negative (Rh-). There is no problem when the mother and the father are both Rh positive or both Rh negative; nor is there a problem when the mother is Rh positive and the father is Rh negative. However, when the mother's blood is Rh negative and the father's blood is Rh positive, then the fetus' blood has the Rh positive factor present and medical intervention is necessary to prevent problems for the fetus from Rh incompatibility. In this disorder small amounts of the baby's blood pass through ruptures in the placenta into the mother's blood, which then develops antibodies against the alien Rh factor. These antibodies are then transmitted back to the fetus where they attack the fetus' red blood cells, causing a kind of anemia which is potentially fatal. The first child of such a union is usually not affected because ruptures in the placenta do not develop until labor. But this leaves a legacy for subsequent pregnancies because the woman's body will now form antibodies. In cases of Rh incompatibility, the drug *rhogam* is administered to the woman within 72 hours after birth of the first Rh positive child, or after an abortion, to prevent the formation of antibodies. If Rh incompatibility develops in a fetus, there is a fifty percent chance of spontaneous abortion (Daniels and Weingarten, 1979). If the fetus survives, and the problem is diagnosed (for example, by amniocentesis [see below]), the fetus can be given blood transfusions.

Some causes of genetic birth defects are known; others are not. Of those that are known, some can be prevented by prepregnancy testing. It is advisable for black people to have prepregnancy blood tests for sickle-cell anemia, a potentially disabling form of anemia, and for Jews of Russian or Polish descent to be similarly screened for Tay-Sachs disease, a fatal hereditary blood disease, since these disorders occur with the most frequency in these respective population groups. A carrier of these genetic conditions may not have the disease herself or himself, but two carriers can produce an affected fetus and should thus seek genetic counseling.

Some other conditions can be detected only during the pregnancy itself. The special procedure by which this is done is called *amniocentesis*. This procedure is quite safe (the complication rate is only 1%), and its diagnostic accuracy for known defects is 99.2% (Daniels and Weingarten, 1979). This procedure is performed between the fourteenth and sixteenth weeks of pregnancy and involves the insertion of a needle into the pregnant woman's abdomen and the collection of about two tablespoons of amniotic fluid. The cells shed by the fetus into the amniotic fluid are studied and therapeutic abortion considered if a defect is detected.

The category of birth defect of primary concern for older pregnant women is chromosomal abnormalities. The most familiar and most frequently diagnosed is Down's syndrome (formerly called mongolism). This defect occurs in approximately 1 in 2,000 live births when the maternal age is 20 and escalates to 1 in 20 when the maternal age is over 45. If the woman is in her early thirties, the risk has been calculated variously as 1 in 750 to 1 in 870; in the late thirties, the risk is 1 in 300 (Daniels and Weingarten, 1979). The availability of amniocentesis and therapeutic abortion can help to ease concerns for the older woman.

New research suggests that maternal age is not the only factor implicated in Down's syndrome. For instance, paternal age has been indicated as a significant factor in the etiology or origin of a special type of Down's syndrome. New research which does not focus on age but on other factors found that 24% of Down's syndrome births were a result of a chromosomal error in the father's sperm. Thus, statistics which include only maternal age in connection with Down's syndrome are in need of revision (Daniels and Weingarten, 1979).

Advanced paternal age is implicated as a casual factor in fresh gene mutations. It has been hypothesized that the longer a man lives, the greater the chance for gene replication errors and mutations in sperm formation, perhaps influenced by environmental factors such as radiation or certain chemicals. The chances of these errors occurring are, fortunately, rare (Daniels and Weingarten, 1979).

The discussion of amniocentesis leads to the broader issue of external interference in the process of fertilization and pregnancy. Artificial insemination, a process whereby sperm are introduced into a woman's body by artificial means rather than through intercourse, has been successful for many years. The technology now exists for external fertilization (so-called test-tube babies) in which the union of egg and sperm is accomplished *in vitro* (literally, in glass) and the fertilized egg is then implanted into the uterus. While these techniques are not always successful, the recent birth of such a child in England (in July, 1978) made worldwide headlines. The issue of external fertilization raises special ethical questions. Can the techniques involved in this process lead to fetal damage? Will this process lead to selective breeding (as in *Brave New World*), surrogate mothers (fertilized eggs implanted in the uteri of women who were not the original egg donors), or genetic intervention, that is, changing the content of genetic material? This also raises the theoretical possibility of cloning, a process whereby the nucleus of a body cell is implanted into an egg whose own nucleus has been removed, thus replicating the genetic characteristics of the body-cell donor (Grobstein, 1979). These are issues of applied genetics; while the technological and practical obstacles are many, and much of this kind of research still in its infancy, the moral and ethical questions are still very relevant.

## Childbirth

Childbirth takes place in three stages: labor, delivery of the baby, and delivery of the placenta. Labor is the process during which the uterus contracts to produce dilation, or opening, of the cervix. When labor is complete, the process enters the next stage as the baby passes through and out of the vagina, or birth canal. This stage is followed shortly by the third stage, the delivery of the placenta, or afterbirth.

The first stage, labor, is the longest and can last anywhere from 2 to 24 hours (Boston Women's Health Book Collective, 1976); it is usually shortened in subsequent pregnancies. During this stage, the woman will experience some discharge tinged with blood, expulsion of the cervical mucus plug as the cervix dilates. Also, the phenomenon of the "breaking of the waters," that is, the rupture of the amniotic membrane and resulting release of amniotic fluid, usually occurs spontaneously during this stage. Uterine contractions are experienced as a tightening of the muscles in a wavelike pattern. These contractions are 15 to 20 minutes apart in early labor and last 45 to 60 seconds. After the cervix has dilated to 8 centimeters (complete dilation is 10 centimeters), the woman enters transition. This transition between labor and delivery, the second stage, is the hardest part; the contractions occur quite close together, but this phase is usually relatively short (one-half hour to two hours). Delivery lasts anywhere from half an hour to several hours. If the woman is awake, she can now work with her contractions to help push the baby down the birth canal. Some women experience the intense energy exertion of this activity as joyful, as they help their baby's passage out into the world (Boston Women's Health Book Collective, 1976). When the baby is born, it is attached to its mother by the umbilical cord. Once the blood has emptied from the cord into the baby's system, the cord can be tied and then cut. Uterine contractions continue, in order to deliver the placenta; this process, the third stage, is usually brief.

Current hospital procedures for labor and delivery have been subject to considerable controversy. Techniques which may be regarded as lifesaving in abnormal births are also used as routine procedures in normal births (which represent 90% of all births). Some authorities have suggested these procedures may produce unnecessary interference in the natural process of birth, which may lead to psychological or physical harm (Arms, 1975), and the question of the balance between benefits and disadvantages or risks must be carefully considered. For example, the use of analgesics (pain-killers) and anesthesia, without necessary indication, in labor and delivery will affect the baby's respiratory system and may have long-lasting effects. Fetal heart monitoring, which is conducted either externally, via electronic devices attached by straps to the woman's abdomen, or internally, via electrodes attached to the baby's scalp, was originally intended for use in those cases where the baby is known to be at risk (Arms, 1975). However, fetal monitoring, particularly the external procedure, is now increasingly used in routine labors; for example, many hospitals are now using this procedure in about 75% of all labors (Corea, 1978). The soundness of this procedure has been questioned, since it can interfere with the mother's birth process. The fetal heartbeat is best transmitted in

this procedure if the woman lies flat on her back and remains almost immobile for many hours. Not only is she thus curtailed from moving her body into whatever position is most comfortable for the appropriate phase of her labor process, but long-term immobility may cause "supine hypotension" (Arms, 1975). In this condition, the mother's blood pressure is lowered and less oxygen is available to the baby. Nevertheless, fetal monitoring has proved to be a useful and lifesaving procedure in many cases.

The induction of labor, with the synthetic hormone pitocin, is also becoming increasingly common, occurring in up to 20% of hospital births (Rich, 1976). There are occasions when induced labor is necessary, for example, when the amniotic membranes have ruptured but labor does not begin spontaneously, or in pregnancies lasting considerably beyond nine months. Many induced labors, however, are done primarily for convenience, not for medical reasons (Arms, 1975). The results are the following: induced labor may occur before the baby is ready to be born and he or she may be premature; induced labor produces contractions of increased intensity, thereby possibly necessitating the use of drugs for pain which then pass into the baby's system; and other complications are also possible (Corea, 1978).

Various routine procedures may be necessary annoyances, for example, shaving the pubic hair. Performing an episiotomy, that is, a surgical incision of the perineum, which then requires stitching to repair after birth, is usually justified to avoid tearing. However, the vaginal opening in a pregnant woman is capable of extensive stretching. If the birth is proceeding without complications, in some cases the birth attendant may massage and gently restrain the perineal tissues around the baby's head to minimize the risk of tearing (Arms, 1975).

The standard "lithotomy," or supine position, for delivery, that is, the woman lying flat on her back, may create unnecessary interference in the process of delivery. It has been argued that this position is not very efficient, since it does not take advantage of the force of gravity and it is not the most comfortable position for the woman. Additionally, in the standard lithotomy position on the delivery table, the woman's legs are widely extended and strapped into stirrups. In this position, there is increased tension on the perineal tissues and they can become tight and inflexible, thus increasing the need for an episiotomy (Arms, 1975).

Caesarian section, the removal of the baby through a surgical incision in the woman's abdomen and uterus, is a lifesaving procedure in certain medical situations, for example, if the mother's pelvic structure is too small to accommodate the baby's passage into the birth canal. A Caesarian section is major surgery, and, as such, its risks should be balanced by medically valid indications. Although such indications exist in only 2% to 4% of births (Arms, 1975), the Caesarian rate has increased in the last few years to at least 11%, with higher rates reported in some large teaching hospitals (Larned, 1978).

Finally, the separation of the infant from the mother immediately after birth, only to be reunited according to the hospital's feeding schedule, deprives them both of significant physical intimacy and may interfere with the development of the parent-child bond (Arms, 1975).

As the increasing use of technology in normal births and the impersonality of the hospital experience are being questioned, people are looking to alternative approaches. Childbirth practices in various European countries are being studied in this connection. For example, in the Netherlands, hospital personnel attempt to bring the atmosphere of a home delivery to the hospital setting; they do not routinely administer drugs unless the mother specifically requests one, and they do not induce labor or perform an episiotomy or separate mother and newborn unless there are definite medical indications for these procedures (Sones, 1974). The use of trained midwives in childbirth clinics is another alternative being explored (Norwood, 1978). The alternative of home birth, with a trained midwife in attendance, offers the advantages of familiar surroundings, comfort, and emotional security; these advantages must be weighed against the risk of unpredicted complications and the lack of access to emergency medical care. A possible model (and such programs are already underway) would be along the lines of the European experience: patient-centered maternity care in a hospital or a clinic specializing in birth. Desirable features would include an attitude of respect for the woman and an appreciation for her feelings and choices, presence of the father throughout labor and birth when so desired, and the option of "rooming-in," where the infant remains with the mother (Sones, 1974).

Important changes in the direction of more humanistic childbirth practices have occurred in recent years. The most important of these is the growing popularity of "natural" childbirth. More appropriately called educated, trained, or prepared childbirth, these methods, the most popular of which is Lamaze, provide education, exercises, and tools to help the woman be in control of her labor process. Grantly Dick-Read, the British physician who published *Childbirth Without Fear* in 1932, learned from watching his patients that fear produces tension, and tension adds to pain. To break this fear-tension-pain cycle, he contributed the idea of the importance of education and of relaxation and exercise techniques. The French doctor, Fernand Lamaze, developed his specific techniques after observing childbirth practices in Russia. The Lamaze, or "psychoprophylactic," method was introduced in the United States by the publication in 1959 of the book *Thank You, Dr. Lamaze* by Marjorie Karmel, who had her first baby in Paris with Dr. Lamaze. Childbirth preparation classes are now available in a majority of places in the United States.

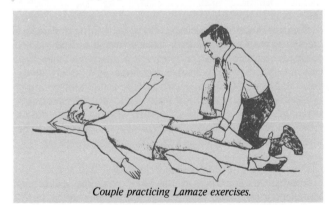
*Couple practicing Lamaze exercises.*

The emphasis in prepared childbirth is not so much on the elusive goal of a painless labor but on the idea of being in control of the process. Education about the labor and delivery process is emphasized, prebirth exercises are practiced to learn relaxation and to strengthen the muscles used in pushing. The pregnant woman also regularly practices the breathing exercises she will use during labor contractions (the phrase "labor pains" is avoided) to help her relax, to increase the oxygen supply to the uterine muscles, and, primarily, for the psychological effect of

disassociation from the uterine contractions. The structure of these exercises becomes progressively complicated as the contractions increase so that the woman's attention is focused on her breathing patterns. She also directs her vision to a preselected spot and moves her hands across her abdomen in rhythmic patterns (*effleurage*). In this way, the sensation from the uterus is felt more on the periphery of awareness, rather than being given total attention, which would be more likely to cause increasing pain as the woman tenses against it. These childbirth methods are often associated with a drugless labor but, again, that is not the main focus. What is of crucial importance is that the woman understands what is going on, and, if she feels that she needs a pain-reducing agent, she can actively choose it rather than being a passive and ignorant recipient. The father (or a chosen friend) plays an active role as breathing coach and provides necessary emotional support throughout the experience.

While methods of prepared childbirth concentrate on the mother's labor process, the LeBoyer method focuses on the experience of the newborn and seeks to ease its transition out of the womb and into the world. This method involves a change in the usual delivery room atmosphere of bright lights and loud voices to one of dim light and softened tones. Immediately after birth, the baby is placed on its mother's stomach, is massaged, and may then be placed in a warm bath.

## Postpartum

As stated earlier, the developmental crisis of pregnancy extends into the postpartum period, the period following childbirth, as the woman adjusts to her changes in life style after the baby's birth. Some women experience various degrees of postpartum depression, or "baby blues." This phenomenon is a result of a combination of physical, psychological, and social factors. The woman's hormonal levels are in a state of disequilibrium, although this is not the sole cause; adoptive parents and fathers have been known to experience this depression (Boston Women's Health Book Collective, 1976). Another important physical factor is the loss of substantial periods of uninterrupted sleep. The early days and weeks with a newborn present the parents with almost overwhelming responsibility and considerable changes in life style. Parents may experience feelings of inadequacy and resentment. Because of the cultural myth of "instant motherhood," that is, that the new parent will automatically know how to meet the infant's every need, the parents may not be adequately prepared for the intensity of the overall parenting experience or given "permission" to acknowledge and thereby work to resolve negative feelings. It is important for the parents of a newborn infant to have material and emotional support.

As in the case with medical injunctions against intercourse before birth, the same situation applies after birth; it is important to evaluate each woman's situation individually. Once the postpregnancy uterine bleeding (lochia) has stopped and the episiotomy incision or local tears have healed, which may take approximately three weeks, the woman's own interest in sexual activity becomes the determining factor. Masters and Johnson (1966) found that many of their postpartum subjects reported low interest in sexuality due to such factors as fatigue. Those women who were nursing their babies reported the highest level of sexual interest. These women described experiencing sexual arousal, occasionally even to orgasm, induced by suckling their babies, although one-fourth of them reported guilt around this experience and were interested in a rapid return to partner sex.

Another phenomenon related to postpartum and later sexuality is the "pregnancy effect." Williams (1977) discusses the fact that pregnancies increase the amount of vascular tissue in the pelvic region and thus enhance the capacity of sexual tension since there is more tissue to become engorged with blood during sexual arousal. It is thus suggested that this phenomenon improves orgasmic intensity, frequency, and pleasure.

## Lactation

If a woman chooses to breast-feed her infant, it is advisable, when possible, to put the baby to the breast while the woman is still on the delivery table. Not only is the suckling reflex strongest right after birth, but this activity will stimulate contractions of the uterus, which help it to return to its prepregnant state (Boston Women's Health Book Collective, 1976). The colostrum which is available in the breast provides protein and some antibodies for the infant. On the third day after birth, the breast secretes milk. Infant formula can closely resemble breast milk, but it cannot replicate the antibodies present in the mother's body; and infants are occasionally allergic to cow's milk. Breast-fed babies are less likely to suffer digestive disturbances and have a slightly lower rate of respiratory infections (Nelson, Vaughn, and McKay, 1969). Physical and emotional closeness can be shared with the baby, whether it is breast-fed or bottle-fed; the ultimate decision depends on the woman's choice and life style.

## Sexual Responsiveness, Birth, and Breast-Feeding

Newton (1973) explores the fact that the reproductive behavior repertoire of women involves three intense interpersonal activities: partner sex, childbirth, and lactation. She discusses similarities between undisturbed, undrugged childbirth and sexual excitement, such as breathing patterns, vocalization, facial expression, uterine reactions, and central nervous system reactions. She quotes Masters and Johnson's (1966) reports of several of their subjects who experienced intense orgasmic sensations during childbirth. She then compares breast-feeding and sexual excitement, in terms of uterine contractions, nipple erection, skin changes, emotional reactions, and so on, and mentions the women in Masters and Johnson's study (1966) who experienced high levels of sexual stimulation while breast-feeding.

## CLIMACTERIC

Just as adolescence is a major turning point, since it marks the transition between childhood and adulthood, so too the process from middle age to old age constitutes another crucial developmental step in the psychosexual life cycle. The climacteric is the name given to this stage; and, appropriately,

the name literally means "rung of the ladder." During this period, from approximately age 45 to 60, we experience gradual changes in all body systems (Weideger, 1977a). From the psychological perspective, this is often a time when people experience what has been popularly termed a mid-life crisis. This is a time at which we are confronted with very real fears about aging, losing our faculties, and dying. Like birth and sex, death is often considered a taboo topic. It is only in recent years that educational and popular materials about the dying process have become more accessible to the public. The euphemisms we use to express that someone has died, and the isolation of the terminally ill, indicate the hesitancy with which this subject is generally approached. So we do not always have peer or social permission to openly discuss or even acknowledge our experiencing of these fears and concerns. Depending on the extent to which an individual man or woman has adhered to his or her respective sex role script, he or she will experience additional concerns and pressures related to this stage of life.

In a culture that generally stresses the linear development of adulthood as a process of "settling down" in the twenties and continuing this pattern uninterruptedly till death, the concept of an authentic period of crisis and reevaluation is not always acknowledged. The one event that is generally associated with mid-life is the female menopause, and it is often shrouded in negative imagery. Inasmuch as men do not menstruate, they do not experience menopause *per se*, but, as is not well known, they do experience specific physiological hormonal changes. In the following sections, we will discuss the physical, psychological, and cultural dimensions of the female and male climacteric.

## Females

Menopause refers to the permanent cessation of menstruation. While the climacteric may extend for 15 to 20 years, menopause itself is of much shorter duration, usually one or two years. When a woman has gone through twelve consecutive months without a menstrual period, she has completed menopause. In the United States, the average age for the occurrence of menopause is 50 (Weideger, 1977b). During the process itself, a woman's periods may become irregular and widely spaced over a gradual span of time, or, less commonly, they may cease abruptly. Since a woman cannot know whether any given period is her last, if she is heterosexually active and does not wish to conceive, she is generally advised to practice contraception until twelve consecutive months without a menstrual period have gone by. Once a calendar year has passed without menstrual bleeding, a woman's fertility is generally ended.

The underlying physiological mechanism is that the ovaries become less and less responsive to FSH, ovulation ceases, and there is a correspondingly reduced output of estrogen and progesterone. Some estrogen supply continues for many years as a result of the following: the ovaries continue a lessened but variable output, the adrenal glands still manufacture this hormone (Cherry, 1976), and other tissues, notably adipose (fatty) tissue, can continue to make estrogen (Marx, 1979c). "Hot flashes" and changes in the vagina are the two basic physiological responses that are a direct consequence of the hormonal levels seeking a new equilibrium, until the pituitary eventually "gets the message" not to make demands on the ovaries.

A hot flash or flush has been described as a sensation of warmth spreading over the neck, face, and upper part of the body and lasting up to two minutes. The woman experiencing a hot flash may look as if she is blushing, and she may sweat more than usual during an episode. Some women experience considerable discomfort while others have none at all. It has been estimated that 60% of women may have hot flashes, generally without the need for medical treatment (Cherry, 1976). Although it is generally believed that the lowered levels of estrogen play a major role in the development of hot flashes, the actual underlying physiological mechanisms have remained undetermined. Recent research suggests that the initiation of a flash is related to the pulsating pattern by which the pituitary releases LH. It was found that LH pulses were not always accompanied by a corresponding flash, but, conversely, each recorded flash occurred in the presence of an LH pulse. The investigators concluded that there is a link between central neuroendocrine mechanisms that initiate episodic hypothalamic release of LH-RF and those mechanisms that initiate hot flashes (Casper, Yen, and Wilkes, 1979).

The standard medical response to the discomforts of menopause has been to recommend "E.R.T.," or estrogen replacement therapy. On the basis of highly inflated claims that estrogen could keep women "feminine forever" and restore youth, this became a popular remedy in the 1960s. Subsequently, however, studies were published indicating that women who take estrogen have an increased risk of endometrial cancer. Since 1977, the FDA (Food and Drug Administration) has required labeling on estrogen products to warn about this association (FDA Drug Bulletin, February-March, 1979).

Alternative approaches to prevention and treatment of possible menopausal symptoms emphasize the importance of adequate nutrition. Poor eating habits and excessive stress conditions can deplete the ability of the adrenal glands to produce their supply of estrogen during menopause (Heidi, 1976). Although there is as yet no conclusive research data, some women and medical personnel report that the use of vitamin E may alleviate hot flashes (Weideger, 1977b).

Although depression in middle-aged women is generally attributed to the hormonal changes of menopause, this link has been persuasively disrupted (Williams, 1977); and this phenomenon is best understood in light of the other dimensions of the middle-aged woman's life. A common cause of this depression is the "empty-nest syndrome," that is, when the children have grown up and left home and the woman has no provision for an alternative role (Bart, 1971). In some instances, a woman derives her sense of self-worth entirely from others, and when these others are gone from her, her self-esteem suffers. This lowered self-esteem, possibly accompanied by unexpressed anger at those who have left her, leads to depression (Bart, 1971). In addition, since the primary cultural definition of a woman is that of wife and mother, when a woman loses her ability to reproduce, she may feel as though she has lost social status. There is an interesting parallel between, on the one hand, the conclusion that women who most closely adhere to social definitions of the female role are the ones to experience considerable depression (Bart, 1971) and, on the other hand, the finding that those women who most strongly adhere to menstrual taboos are those who suffer the most difficulty with menstruation (Paige, 1973).

It is important to remember that menopause is not a disease but a natural process. It is also important to demystify menopause since all women will experience it. Both the medical model and the cultural attitudes promote negative images. Advertisements in medical journals for estrogen products typically include pictures of middle-aged women looking incredibly distraught. Cultural stereotypes of the menopausal woman are hardly any brighter. In general, the conventional image of the menopausal woman is an exaggerated version of many of the devalued characteristics traditionally associated with women, for example, emotionality, irritability, irrationality (Laws and Schwartz, 1977). As Pauline Bart (1971) has said, "There is no *bar mitzvah* for menopause."

A wide variety of reactions to the climacteric are reported; and despite the extent of negative publicity, women in good health generally move effectively through this phase of the life cycle (Williams, 1977). According to a survey conducted by the Boston Women's Health Book Collective (1976), women aged 25 to 40 checked off, or acknowledged having, more "symptoms" than any other age group, and women over 60 reported the fewest. About two-thirds of the menopausal and post-menopausal women felt either neutral or positive about their changes. Similarly, in a study by Neugarten (1963), only 12% of the women studied were unable to see any positive value to menopause; and some women reported positive changes in mental and physical health, and increased energy and well-being. Post-menopausal women were less concerned about its significance than younger women, who saw it as an ordeal (Boston Women's Health Book Collective, 1976).

Rather than considering menopause as the "beginning of the end," more attention should be given to the post-menopausal zest and sense of well-being which many women experience in the later climacteric and early old age. For some women this period ushers in an increased sexual appetite (Kaplan, 1974). Freed from conception worries and from the responsibilities of daily child care, many women welcome this time as a time for pursuit of one's own interests and projects, a time to rediscover oneself.

Attitudes toward menopause vary cross-culturally. Some societies accord greater social freedom and even attribute supernatural powers to the post-menopausal woman. In China, the older woman is released from male dominance and is treated with respect (Griffen, 1977). Interestingly, it has been reported that Chinese women have fewer menopausal symptoms. Among the Mohave Indians, menopause is considered a sign of achievement, and the post-menopausal woman is free to work and to be wise (Delaney et al., 1977). It has been hypothesized that the magnitude of symptoms associated with menopause is correlated with the paucity of roles available to the older woman (Griffen, 1977).

## Males

Most research studies have indicated that men also experience hormonal changes during the climacteric; the rate of testosterone production gradually declines (Kaplan, 1974), and sperm production also gradually declines, although fertility is generally maintained in old age. However, a recent study (Marx, 1979c) found that testosterone levels are no lower and may even be slightly higher in older men than in younger men. A noteworthy feature of this study is that its subjects were better educated and more prosperous than the general population. These facts suggest that these men tended to take better care of themselves and to receive better medical attention. Additionally, all the men in this study were exceptionally healthy, with no cardiovascular disease, obesity, excessive drinking, or other health problems. Perhaps it was the subjects' general good health that accounted for the discrepancy between the results of this study and the previous research. If this is the case, it becomes reasonable to propose that a decline in testosterone production need not be inevitable, provided good health can be maintained.

In addition to the general fears about aging which we confront at this stage of life, males also have to deal with fears about sexual potency and the extent to which they have fulfilled the socially prescribed male goals of success. A critical review of one's past accomplishments, the extent to which one has realized one's goals and dreams, and a sense of the time limitations now imposed on one's desired achievements can be unsettling. Dissatisfaction with one's job or career and a desire to change occupations, or a setting of new and different goals, do not always meet with support in a society that decrees a narrower path. Additionally, since the machismo image prescribes toughness and rationality, along with the repression of emotionality, it may be difficult for a man to acknowledge and come to grips with his concerns and fears.

There is considerable individual variation in the ways in which men react to this "mid-life crisis." Some men become irritable or depressed or experience mood swings (Kaplan, 1974; Williams, 1977). Some make abrupt changes in their life style or seek out a much younger woman in an attempt to recapture a sense of youth and to "prove" they are still virile. Other men are able to effectively integrate their changing sexuality and sense of self into their lives and relationships. Again, as is the case for women, a man needs adequate psychological resources to deal with this developmental crisis and successfully adapt to this new stage in the life cycle (Kaplan, 1974).

# AGING

A basic cultural dictate is often that sexuality is not for older people. This represents a confluence of two sets of attitudes: beliefs that old people are useless and the religious heritage which approves only procreative sex. Inasmuch as old people are past the cycle of reproduction, it is believed that they no longer have a need for sexual expression and that sexual feelings that linger into old age are quite inappropriate. The idea of older people being sexually active and the idea that sexual capacities disappear with age are often the subject matter for jokes (Puner, 1974). Many birthday cards sold for this age group reinforce these themes, for example, a card whose cover states "Here is what to do about sex after 50," and whose inside is totally blank.

Old people thus have to deal with generally negative cultural attitudes, physical changes they may not understand or appreciate, and the attitudes of their peers and their children. Children often deny the sexuality of their parents and often look at the idea of a new marriage for older people as foolish and inappropriate. If parents pass on nonpermissive attitudes about sex to their young children, the children will find it difficult to think of their parents as sexual beings. If parents and children do not discuss their sexual activities with each other, this furthers the mystique. Additionally, the predominant stereotype of sex, amply reinforced by media images, is that it is an activity primarily for the young. A recent survey showed that college students' estimates of their parents' sexual behavior is usually very low compared with Kinsey's data (Pocs, Godow, Tolone, and Walsh, 1977).

Furthermore, old people who are in institutions for the elderly, or even a hospital or another care facility on a temporary basis, are treated like children with regard to their sexuality. There appears to be a general policy that old people should be finished with sex, and the lack of privacy and rigid segregation of the sexes are practices which concretize this attitude.

Old people often believe these messages, from a variety of sources, which admonish them not to be sexual. In the following sections, we will examine the phenomenon of ageism, outline the physical changes in sexual functioning, and explore positive directions for sexuality and aging.

## Ageism

Wine and cheese are considered to age well and are valued for this attribute. However, in our culture, old people are often considered to be used up and burdensome. Ageism refers to this discrimination on the basis of age. While it is the case that older people as a class are socially devalued, there is a double standard attached to the aging process itself. Older women lose their social value earlier than men (Sontag, 1976). Since women often derive their social status from their physical attractiveness, which is associated with youth, and from their reproductive capacities, when they are beyond these stages, they lose esteem. Men, on the other hand, are valued more for what they do; and the financial status, or power, of the older man still stands him in good stead. This double standard is manifested in regard to physical changes. Up to a certain point, older men are distinguished; they have character lines in their faces, and a touch of gray at the temples can be elegant. Meanwhile, older woman are dowdy; they have wrinkles and are admonished to "cover that gray." It is popularly believed that one of the nicest compliments for an older woman is that she is "well-preserved," or, in other words, she still looks youthful. Thus, it is not surprising that a woman might be tempted to lie about her age. Additionally, our language has no male term equivalent to "old maid" or spinster; men continue to be eligible bachelors.

The double standard of aging is also indicated in the different responses to an older man and a younger woman as a couple, and an older woman and a younger man as a couple. The first couple, for whom there are models in popular movies and among celebrities, seems plausible, and often some special virility or charm is attributed to the man. The second couple is usually greeted with disapproval; rather than the woman being admired for her vitality, she is most likely to be scorned or accused of robbing the cradle. She may even be condemned as predatory or exhibitionistic, or even pitied for senility (Sontag, 1976). 1976).

## Sexuality and Aging

In general, when compared with changes in other body systems such as muscular stength, changes in the sexual system are functionally minimal and do not necessarily lessen an older person's pleasure in sexual activity; indeed, some changes may actually help to increase it. It is important to remember that, with rare exceptions, sexual capacity is *lifelong*. Even if and when certain sexual activities can no longer be performed because of infirmity, the needs for other aspects of a sexual relationship, such as closeness, sensuality, intimacy, being valued, persist. Indeed, since all too often we consider that a sexual encounter is the only way we can give and receive affection and physical closeness, by negating the sexuality of older persons, we are also denying them the simple and important joys of hugging and stroking.

Sometimes older people stop expressing their sexuality because they have followed cultural attitudes, or because they are not knowledgeable about the standard physiological changes that occur with age. For example, if a man begins to experience a reduction in frequency of erections and does not understand that this is a normal pattern, he may erroneously assume that his erectile functioning is going to come to an abrupt halt. If poor communication patterns exist in a relationship, partners may react to physical changes by withdrawing from sexual activity without discussion. Another problem for older people is the relative lack of availability of sexual partners. Masters and Johnson (1966) have indicated various other factors which can contribute to a decline in male sexuality. These include monotony within a relationship, preoccupation with career, fatigue, overindulgence in food or drink, infirmities of self or partner, and fears about performance.

Masters and Johnson have argued that it is the regularity of sexual expression or continuity of active sexuality that directly affects our ability to maintain sexual capacity and effectiveness. Contrary to the idea that a sexually active youth "uses up" our sexual powers, the direct opposite seems to be true—regular use keeps the system functioning well. It is to be noted that masturbatory activity, as well as partner sex, is one way to maintain sexual expression.

Research has shown that people's interest in sexual activity continues well into the later years. One such study revealed that one out of every six persons interviewed reported a steadily increasing rate of sexual interest and activity as they got older (Lobsenz, 1975). In a study of the relationship between age and sexual activity in married men, Foster (1979) suggests that older married men may be more sexually active and derive more pleasure in sexuality than had been suspected, provided that sexual activity is defined in broader terms than just genital contact. Additionally, large numbers of older people masturbate (although they may feel it is "wrong"), and individuals in their seventies and eighties can maintain their capacity to experience orgasm.

## The Aging Woman

Although there is considerable individual variation as to when and how women's sexuality alters with age, the major physiological changes involve the following: there is a thinning of the vaginal walls, due to lessened stimulation by estrogen, and vaginal lubrication is slower and diminishes somewhat. The vagina shortens and becomes narrower and less elastic. These are not necessarily negative changes; it is just that the older vagina has different characteristics from the younger one. The standard medical terminology refers to the "atrophic" vagina, which has unpleasant connotations; Reitz (1977) suggests substituting the phrase "venerable" vagina, which is much more congruent with a positive attitude toward aging. Masters and Johnson (1966) found exceptions to the phenomenon of diminished vaginal lubrication in older women who had maintained regular sexual activity. In any case, the use of water-soluble jelly may provide a satisfactory supply of lubrication at any age.

In older women, the labia majora lose some fatty tissue and some elasticity, and the thickening of the labia minora due to vasocongestion during arousal is somewhat reduced. While a younger woman will experience five to ten contractions of the orgasmic platform, in an older woman, there will be three to five contractions. Again, Masters and Johnson found that older women who had maintained active sexual expression were exceptions, to this general rule, experiencing four to seven contractions. Additionally, older women remain capable of experiencing multiple orgasms. A few of the women in this study reported that the uterine contractions during orgasm were painful. Other observed changes included less frequency of sex flush, less marked tenting effect and uterine elevation, and a more rapid resolution phase.

## The Aging Man

A major change in the sexual response of the older male is that it takes longer for the penis to become erect, and there will characteristically be a longer span of time between initial stimulation and ejaculation. This means that the man has improved ejaculatory control and that sexual activity can last longer. With advancing age, the sensation of ejaculatory inevitability will not always be experienced. Ejaculation occurs with less force, and the older the man, the fewer the contractions of orgasm. Detumescence of the penis usually occurs quite rapidly. The refractory period lengthens with age; by the late fifties and sixties, this phase may last 12 to 24 hours. Sometimes an older man will achieve a second erection relatively quickly but may not experience a corresponding urge to ejaculate. As orgasm itself becomes less of a focus, there can be opportunity for exploration of more generalized sensuality.

As the labia majora become less elastic in the older woman, so too does the scrotal skin in the older man. After the age of 60, the vasocongestive effects are reduced, along with the phenomenon of testicular elevation. Again, as is the case with women, sex flush occurs less frequently. For men, as for women, Masters and Johnson (1966) underscore the consistency of regular sexual activity as the most important factor for maintaining effective sexual capacity.

## Positive Directions

The effects of the physiological changes in the sexual system have only an indirect effect on sexual interest and activity. In many ways, the quality of sexual pleasure becomes better; with the person being freed from the need for quick release, sexuality can be more diffuse and imaginative. As individuals adapt to their overall physical changes, they can integrate new modes of sexuality and sensuality. To counteract the negative effects of cultural attitudes, we need general reeducation about aging and we need sex education and counseling for the aged and for those who are concerned with them and who live and deal with them (Lobsenz, 1975).

# SUMMARY

In this chapter, we have attempted to provide the reader with some sense of the changes that occur in sexuality over the life cycle. We have seen how one's sexuality begins in infancy, progresses through adolescence, and continues to evolve during adulthood and advanced age. We have also explored the manner in which physical, psychological, and cultural variables are relevant at each stage of the process. As children, we enjoy sexual play, though these behaviors do not yet acquire the complex meanings of adolescent and adult sexuality. Adolescence signals the public recognition of our sexuality, and it is during this period that we begin to explore sexuality within the framework of interpersonal relationships. As adults, our sexual activity may assume diverse forms, and our capacity for sexual response is lifelong.

It should be recognized that sexuality is a dynamic, constantly changing human dimension. Thus, the description of the various stages of sexuality is merely a necessary convenience which lends itself to a sequential analysis. In fact, however, each new experience, each new event, moderates each previous phase and, in turn, influences the changes that occur in the next stage.

# Chapter 8

## Birth Control and Infertility

## INTRODUCTION

The typical heterosexually active, nonsterile woman has an eighty percent chance of becoming pregnant during any one year (Stewart, Guest, Stewart, & Hatcher, 1979). The fact that such a high probability event may occur despite the individual's wishes to the contrary has led to a continuing interest in preventing, or at least regulating, pregnancy. In this chapter, we will explore the various birth control techniques that have been employed throughout history, as well as the social and political circumstances that are related to such practices.

The term birth control refers to the prevention of birth. There are four procedures that may be followed to achieve this end. These are abstinence (avoidance of heterosexual intercourse), contraception (methods that prevent conception), sterilization (surgical procedures that render an individual infertile), and abortion (termination of pregnancy).

While the term birth control has traditionally been equated with the prevention of unwanted pregnancy, the failure to achieve desired pregnancy may also be a matter of equal concern. Consequently, the issue of infertility will also be a subject of discussion in this chapter.

## PRELIMINARY ISSUES

### HISTORY OF THE BIRTH CONTROL MOVEMENT

In contrast to most other animals, humans will and do engage in heterosexual vaginal intercourse on a noncyclical basis, that is, without respect to the female's fertility status. There are many factors at play in the approach to each episode of intercourse: intention (for example, expression of affection, obligation, conquest), emotional state (as love, fear, anger, excitement), level of inebriation or sobriety, physical setting (for example, the back seat of an automobile or the elegant bridal suite of a hotel). In any and all of these circumstances, however, the reproductive capacity of our bodies remains the same; intercourse can and does lead to conception, even in the face of one's desire to avoid this reproductive event. Despite the fact that the means or the immediate motivation to act on this desire is all too often absent, it is still reasonable to assume that the vast majority of acts of intercourse are not pursued for reproductive purposes.

This reasonable assumption about human sexual life, that most acts of intercourse do not equate sex with procreation, presents a problem for those who do equate sex with procreation. Moreover, the vast range of other sexual activities engaged in by both heterosexual and nonheterosexual partners and the autoerotic activities practiced emphasize the further denial of this equation in human sexuality. The very nature of human sexuality, then, cannot be constrained by arbitrary restrictions. As we saw in Chapter 1, advocates of the sex-procreation equation however, have long exercised authority in the realms of public (church and State) and private morality. Their influence has been felt in the attitudes and values of individuals and in the

more public areas related to the development and distribution of contraceptive information and technology.

The conflict over birth control has a long and bitter history in the United States. Anti-birth control advocates achieved a major victory in 1873 when Congress enacted the Comstock Law (after Anthony Comstock), which made it illegal to mail birth control information as well as contraceptive devices. In addition, individual States and communities enacted their own anti-birth control statutes. Although such laws have gradually been diluted by Supreme Court decisions, there is little doubt that American policy and opinion were heavily influenced by and reflected in these actions.

Conversely, the struggle to provide contraceptive information has been accomplished only with great difficulty. For example, the pioneering efforts of Margaret Sanger (1883-1966) were impeded by the Comstock Law. As a public health nurse in New York City, Sanger witnessed the effects of unchecked reproduction: anxiety, illness, poverty, and excessive maternal deaths from continuous childbearing or from illegal abortions. In her desire to make contraception available, she traveled to Europe to learn about birth control techniques, published her findings, and opened the first birth control clinic in the United States in New York in 1916. As a result of these activities, Sanger and her colleagues were arrested several times.

Despite these obstacles, the publicity generated by Sanger's efforts aroused the public's interest in birth control. By the 1920s there was considerable support for birth control programs. Within the next decade, medical interest grew, and the Planned Parenthood Federation of America was founded (Sharpe, 1972). It is now safe to say that the proponents of birth control are just as numerous as those who oppose it.

Proponents of birth control in this country have had differing intentions. Many, like Margaret Sanger at the beginning of her career, were motivated by moral concerns and health issues. Others sought to use birth control programs to limit the growth of certain populations, for example, within poor or black communities at home and in underdeveloped, Third World nations abroad. These latter efforts have been aided by funds from the Federal government (Sharpe, 1972; Cherniak and Feingold, 1975). The issues and ethical implications of population control continue to be a source of controversy. Our position in this book is that birth control information and devices should be made widely available, thereby enabling individual decisions to be made on the basis of fact and personal judgment.

### HISTORY OF CONTRACEPTIVE TECHNOLOGY

As long as human beings have been concerned with the process of reproduction, they have also employed methods to limit their number of offspring. The conscious desire to control conception has a lengthy history in human affairs and has been documented for at least the last 4,000 years. Various magical rites and formulas as well as genuinely clever techniques have been employed to prevent pregnancy. While we lack substantial knowledge of how many of these methods were integrated into the actual practice of sexuality, we do have a lengthy list of examples. Himes (1963) has documented the use of many substances, including: vaginal insertion of crocodile or elephant dung, honey and cedarwood oil mixed with fig pulp, tannic acid (which still rates high as a spermicide), and hollowed-out pomegranate half; and douches concocted of garlic and wine mixed with fennel. The ancient Greeks advocated a mixture of honey, vinegar, and lemon juice as a vaginal spermicide. The literature of the ancient Hebrews contains references to the use of an intravaginal sponge for contraceptive purposes.

The manufacture of rubber in the nineteenth century led to the development of both the condom and the diaphragm, both made from this substance. While references to devices implanted in the uterus to prevent pregnancy are. found throughout history, the first significant practical application of this method occurred in the early twentieth century. (These devices will be discussed later in this chapter under the section on contraception.)

It is also the case that humans practiced contraception not just for themselves but also for their animals (for example, the intrauterine insertion of pebbles in camels [see below in the section on contraception]), thus testifying to the high level of human ingenuity.

## CONTEMPORARY PERSPECTIVES

Recent developments have dramatically impacted upon the traditional negative attitudes toward contraception. The growing concerns about overpopulation, the availability of improved and practical contraceptive devices, and a generally more relaxed sexual atmosphere have all contributed to a more contraceptively oriented climate of opinion.

Despite these changes, however, cultural forces preventing meaningful education and frank discussion on the pros and cons of contraception continue to exist. Thus, critics of contraception continue to equate sex with procreation in their argument that such information will lead to promiscuity. The mechanisms in our society to deal with such issues, for example, the family, the school system, the medical profession, have not yet taken the initiative in providing appropriate contraceptive information.

The lack of available contraceptive information has profound implications for our society. It has been estimated that of the 11,000,000 teen-agers who are sexually active, no more than 20% use contraception on a regular basis (Byrne, 1977), and this has contributed to our current epidemic of unwanted pregnancies. Furthermore, studies have indicated that, in general, the individual with a negative attitude toward sex is less prone to practice contraception than is a "sex positive" individual (Bryne, Jazwinski, DeNeiro, and Fisher, 1977).

It seems clear, then, that despite the relative availability of contraceptive information and techniques, many individuals continue to deny themselves access to these resources. Perhaps there are deeper psychological issues involved in choosing to or choosing not to engage in contraceptive practices, issues which are complex and multifaceted and remain to be explored. Whatever the case, appropriate decisions certainly cannot be made without the relevant information.

Once the decision to use contraceptive techniques is made, the next step is to acquire information on the types of birth control methods that are available and decide the purposes that are to be served by contraception. For example, if the primary issue is the avoidance of pregnancy (and if abortion is not an acceptable alternative), then the accent will be on the effectiveness of the method utilized. If a concern over possible jeopardy of health as a result of adverse side effects is extremely crucial to the potential user, then the relative safety of the various contraceptive methods will be a determining factor. When deciding upon a contraceptive, one might also want to consider how often it will need to be employed, the physical setting in which one is likely to be sexually active (for example, a diaphragm might not be totally convenient in all settings), and the feelings of comfort, physical as well as psychological, associated with the use of particular method. One might also want to consider which partner is responsible for birth control, perhaps the concept of "taking turns" (for example, alternating the use of condoms and a diaphragm), and the context of sexual activity, for example, short-term versus long-term relationships.

While the issue of contraception, in both its personal and public aspects, is of general concern, there are various considerations that are of particular importance for women. Physical and health concerns are, of course, paramount—it is to prevent the event of pregnancy in the woman's body that contraceptive devices are utilized, and it is, in most cases, the woman who uses the actual contraceptive. Beyond these issues, however, contraception has other implications of significance for women.

The cultural definition of women as primarily wives and mothers is losing its strength and tenacity. The technology of reliable birth control, and thus the capability to make pregnancy an individual choice rather than an inevitable biological event, gives a woman the opportunity to view childbearing as one of the many separate options of her life, rather than its determining characteristic.

## EFFECTIVENESS

Since there is no absolute failure-proof contraceptive technique, we can evaluate each of the various techniques in terms of their percentage of effectiveness. Thus, the statement that method X has a failure rate of 5%, or, equivalently, is 95% effective, means that of 100 women using this method for a year, 5 will become pregnant. There are two approaches from which the rate of effectiveness can be determined. One is called "theoretical effectiveness" and refers to the highest possible effectiveness of the method, when it is used all the time (that is, for every sexual encounter), without error, and exactly according to instructions. The other is called "use effectiveness" and refers to the rate at which a given method prevents pregnancy when it is *actually* being used by a spectrum of consumers. Some will use it without error; others will use it carelessly or improperly. When use effectiveness is thus averaged out, it is generally lower than theoretical effectiveness; that is, the failure rate is higher (Hatcher, Stewart, Stewart, Guest, Stratton, and Wright, 1978). For example, the theoretical failure rate for condoms is 3%, and these three pregnancies might be a result of manufacturing defects in the product. On the other hand, studies of average couples who actually use condoms indicate a 10% failure rate. This higher rate of pregnancies may have been caused by the use of an old, brittle condom that ruptured, a condom that slipped off either during intercourse or as the man withdrew his penis after ejaculation, or failure to use a condom "just this once" (Stewart et al., 1979).

One factor, among many, that may influence a prospective consumer in her or his choice of contraceptive method is the information received from medical authorities. A recent study suggests that family planners bias their responses to their patients' inquiries in favor of birth control pills and IUDs (discussed later), by quoting the theoretical effectiveness for these methods. They likewise indicate the less favorable use effectiveness rate for methods such as condoms, the diaphragm, or spermicidal foam, thus turning patients away from three safe and effective means of contraception (Hatcher et al., 1978).

## ABSTINENCE

Abstinence, or the avoidance of sexual activity, has historically been advocated for a variety of reasons. As we saw in Chapter 1, the Christian Church favored abstinence for the health of the soul. During the nineteenth century, abstinence was promoted for the health of the body, to conserve semen, and to avoid debilitating diseases (see Chapter 2). Individuals who deliberately practice abstinence today do so usually for religious or moral reasons.

Abstinence, in the form of refraining from vaginal intercourse, provides the only absolute guarantee against pregnancy. While this practice has its merits as a method of birth control, its use in this regard is often unsatisfactory for people who wish to express their sexual feelings in heterosexual settings. Partial abstinence, that is, the practice of vaginal intercourse only under certain conditions, is a more frequent practice. Two varieties of partial abstinence are the rhythm method and *coitus interruptus*.

### RHYTHM METHODS

The rhythm method dates from the 1930s as a result of the discoveries by Kraus in Austria and Ogino in Japan that ovulation occurs approximately 14 days before menstruation. This method is thus based on the premise that a woman's menstrual cycle contains both fertile and nonfertile ("safe") days, determined by the time of ovulation. Sperm are generally considered to live up to three days once they proceed into the cervix and uterus, and the egg is viable for 24 hours. Fertility would then range from three days before ovulation to one day after ovulation. As an added precaution, a few extra days are included (for a total of eight days of abstention). Thus, if a woman ovulates on day 14 of her menstrual cycle, based on a 28-day cycle (counting the first day of menstrual flow as day 1), her fertile period would be days 10 through 17. The woman using the rhythm method to

avoid pregnancy abstains from vaginal intercourse on her fertile days.

The traditional rhythm method is known as the calendar method. If a woman has a consistent history of a 28-day menstrual cycle, all she need do is mark days 10 through 17 of her cycle on a calendar and thus keep track of her fertile period. However, it is a rare woman who has such a regular pattern, and two-thirds of all women are too irregular to be able to depend successfully on this method (Brayer, Chiazze, and Duffy, 1969). The problem with this technique, of course, is that it is not possible to determine actually *in advance* when ovulation will occur. The best that can be done, using the calendar method, is to base predictions on past events.

There are two additional techniques for supplementing the calendar method: the basal body temperature (BBT) method and the sympto-thermal method. To use the BBT method, a woman records her body temperature upon waking up each morning, using a special thermometer. Prior to ovulation, the temperature will remain at a fairly constant level. Then, 12 to 24 hours before ovulation, the temperature will drop slightly and then rise the day after the egg is released. The change in temperature is actually quite small; in addition, factors other than ovulation, for example, infections, can cause variations in temperature, thus affecting the reliability of this technique.

The sympto-thermal method, also called "natural birth control" or the Billings method (after its developers, the Australian doctors Evelyn and John Billings), is based on the idea that a woman can learn to recognize changes in her body that indicate when ovulation occurs. The prime focus is to detect the relevant changes in the cervical mucus, which changes from white and cloudy to clear, stringy, and slippery (rather like raw egg white) at ovulation. This technique increases in effectiveness when combined with both the calendar and BBT methods and with other pre- and post-ovulatory signs that a woman may be able to identify, for example, *mittelschmerz* (ovulatory pain experienced by some women) and breast tenderness.

Some advantages of the rhythm method are the minimal expense involved (cost of the thermometer) and the avoidance of specific chemical or mechanical birth control devices (if abstinence is maintained during the fertile period). It is this latter, "natural" aspect of this method that has led to its acceptance by the Catholic Church as the only permissible technique, other than total abstinence, for birth control. Interestingly, recent studies suggest that American Catholics and non-Catholics exhibit little difference in their choices of birth control method (Witters and Jones-Witters, 1975; see Chapter 2).

The main disadvantages of the rhythm method include the discipline involved in record-keeping (on the other hand, for some individuals, this is a positive learning process), the potential strain engendered by periodic abstinence, and the relative lack of effectiveness. On the other hand, if abstinence from vaginal intercourse is preferred to using a contraceptive device during a woman's fertile period, there still exists a variety of sexual activities that can be enjoyed. These include shared or mutual masturbation and oral-genital play.

There is as yet no clear-cut indication of effectiveness rates for any of the various rhythm methods. The research literature

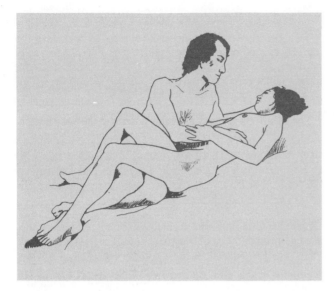

indicates considerable variance among the studies that have been conducted. Two large studies on couples using the calendar method show effectiveness rates of 70% and 85% (Stewart et al., 1979); studies of the BBT method report ranges of effectiveness from 80% to 99.7% (in this latter study, the couples had intercourse only after ovulation had clearly been indicated; Stewart et al, 1979). Reliance on changes in cervical mucus to determine ovulation shows effectiveness rates ranging from 75% to 98.7% (Stewart et al., 1979). Causes of failure can include errors in calculation or observation, nonobservance of appropriate fertile intervals, and unpredictable cycle variations. Using the sympto-thermal method to combine all three techniques should theoretically increase effectiveness. A recent Federally financed study indicates an 89.1% effectiveness rate (Nelson, 1979). It is difficult to determine a specific rate of effectiveness because many women do not have regular periods, clear BBT patterns, and clearly detectable mucus changes (Stewart et al., 1979). With any of the individual or combined rhythm methods, effectiveness will improve if a woman engages in unprotected intercourse only after it has been determined that ovulation has occurred.

It has been suggested that some women are "reflex" ovulators, that is, they might ovulate independently of menstrual cycle factors. Some events that theoretically might trigger such ovulation include intercourse (Clark and Zarrow, 1971) and high levels of sexual excitement (McCary, 1978). While verification of "reflex" ovulation is lacking, unexpected variations in regular ovulation do frequently occur. A position of extreme caution would dictate that there is really no "safe" period at all, not even during the menstrual flow itself (McCary, 1978).

Although the major focus of the rhythm method has been primarily in terms of contraception, it can also be used to help plan a desired pregnancy (see section below on infertility). Finally, and independently of its use to achieve or to prevent conception, this method can help women learn a great deal about the functioning of their bodies.

## COITUS INTERRUPTUS

The other variety of partial abstinence which is used as a birth control method is *coitus interruptus*, more popularly known as withdrawal. In this case, the definition of abstinence is modified to refer to the avoidance of "completion" of an act of intercourse. Intercourse proceeds until the man feels he is about to have an orgasm, at which point he withdraws his penis from his partner's vagina and ejaculates outside of it.

*Coitus interruptus* is one of the oldest and most widely used birth control methods. However, it is a relatively unreliable method, with the theoretical failure rate being 15%; in actual usage, however, it fails 20% to 25% of the time (Hatcher et al., 1978). The main sources of failure include the possiblity of viable sperm in the preejaculatory fluid (see Chapter 5), and the potential of ejaculated sperm entering the vagina if they are deposited in the near vicinity, for example, on the labia minora.

Use of this method requires both the male's ability to be highly alert to his excitation process and the self-control necessary to withdraw his penis at a moment when deep penetration might otherwise be preferred. Another disadvantage is that the need to interrupt intercourse can cause anxiety and psychological strain for both partners.

The relative advantages of this method are that it is always available, it requires no advance preparation, it utilizes no extraneous devices, and it thus involves no monetary expense. Some couples use *coitus interruptus* as their only attempt at birth control. Others employ this method from time to time, or as an adjunct to other methods, for example, to supplement at ovulation time the use of a diaphragm or an IUD. Another variety of this method involves withdrawal of the penis prior to ejaculation, fitting a condom on the penis, and then resuming intercourse. This will have no contraceptive effect, however, on sperm in the preejaculatory fluid already deposited in the vagina.

# CONTRACEPTION

Contraception can be achieved in any of three ways: prevention of the production of gametes (egg, sperm), prevention of fertilization (union of egg and sperm), and prevention of implantation (embedding of fertilized egg in uterus). The various methods currently available interrupt the process of pregnancy at these three various stages and will be discussed according to this scheme of classification. Each method will be considered from the perspectives of its mode of action, its use, its relative advantages and disadvantages, its effectiveness, its side effects, and its availability.

## BIRTH CONTROL PILLS

As we saw in Chapter 2, oral contraceptives, or birth control pills ("the pill"), are very popular. It is estimated that they are presently used by about 80 million women throughout the world, including six to seven million in the United States (Stewart et al., 1979). The most common birth control pills contain synthetic formulations of the female sex hormones, estrogen and progesterone (known as progestin) and are thus called combination pills. Sex hormones were first synthesized in the 1930s and 1940s, and their initial use as contraceptive agents was tested on laboratory animals. In 1956, the first human trials were conducted on 132 women in Puerto Rico (Seaman and Seaman, 1977). In 1960, the FDA approved the first pill, Enovid, for use on the American market. Since then, the pill gained popularity as the most effective contraceptive available. Its theoretical effectiveness rate is 99% or better, and its use effectiveness is generally 98%, with lower rates reported among women who are less consistent or careful pill users (Stewart et al., 1979).

In addition to diminished fear of pregnancy, the pill offers the advantages of minimizing menstrual cramps, reducing menstrual flow, and, in some cases, curing acne (Stewart, et al., 1979). The pill is obtained by prescription from a doctor or family planning clinic. This method of contraception is highly convenient and offers continuous protection, thus effectively preventing the temptation to pass it up "just this once."

The continuously high levels of hormones in the pill work in the woman's body to suppress the production of the pituitary hormones (FSH and LH) which ordinarily stimulate the process of ovulation. Since the event of ovulation is not triggered, no egg is released for possible fertilization.

Pills generally come in packages of 20 or 21, to be taken one each day, starting on day 5 of the menstrual cycle. When the last pill of the package is taken, and the hormone levels subsequently diminish, the uterine lining disintegrates and the woman experiences "withdrawal bleeding" (considered by some authorities not to be "true" menstruation because ovulation has presumably not taken place). This flow is generally less than a regular menstrual period because the progestin in the pill inhibits the normal development of the endometrium.

While the main mode of action of the pill is to prevent ovulation, the synthetic hormones also act to provide various "back-up" effects. These include changes in the cervical mucus which render it hostile to sperm, and endometrial changes unfavorable to implantation (Hatcher, et al., 1978). In summary then, if a woman is "on the pill," sperm cannot navigate past her cervix; if they do, there is no egg to be fertilized; and if there is, the fertilized egg will be unable to implant itself in the uterine lining.

Since the high hormonal levels of the pill mimic pregnancy, several of the more common side effects of the pill are similar to pregnancy symptoms. These include nausea, water retention, weight gain, and breast tenderness and pain. These symptoms tend to disappear after a few months. Other common side effects associated with the pill are breakthrough bleeding (that is, bleeding between periods) or spotting, heavier than usual vaginal discharge, decreased resistance to vaginal infections (including venereal disease [Seaman and Seaman, 1977]), and cervicitis (inflammation of the cervix). In addition, some women experience chloasma (dark skin patches on the face) or loss of scalp hair. Possibly as a result of such side effects, 25% to 55% of the women who begin using the pill will discontinue its use within the first year (Hatcher, et al., 1978).

Some pill users experience depression and irritability; and changes in libido, or sex drive, have also been reported. Some women feel more free in their sexual expression because of the reduced fear of pregnancy whereas others experience diminished sex drive because of pill-related changes. In a related vein, some women experience decreased vaginal lubrication during sexual arousal (Seaman and Seaman, 1977).

The pill affects virtually all organ systems in the body (Hatcher et al., 1978) and causes several changes in body chemistry. For example, various laboratory tests, such as glucose tolerance, may be slightly altered. In addition, women on the pill have lower levels of vitamin C and several of the B vitamins, whereas, on the other hand, their vitamin A and iron levels are higher. Some researchers believe that if a serious vitamin $B_6$ deficiency results, it may lead to depression (Stewart et al., 1979).

In the following paragraphs, we will discuss the risks and complications of the pill. There has been considerable research conducted in this area, but no two studies report exactly the same rate of complications. It is difficult to weigh the obvious benefits of the pill against the potential problems, and it is even more difficult to know how much attention to give to the as yet unsubstantiated risks, for example, a risk of cancer. What is important is that the consumer be adequately informed, so that she may make a knowledgeable choice in the context of her own needs and situation. To this end, each packet of pills is now accompanied by an FDA-approved leaflet which explains the pill's benefits and risks in detail.

The most common cause of serious and fatal pill complications are blood-clotting disorders. If a woman is on the pill, clots can occur more readily than is normal and can be especially serious if they involve the brain, heart, or lungs. While clotting disorders are rare to begin with, use of the pill significantly increases this risk, especially if a woman takes a high-estrogen pill (over 50 mcg.), if she uses pills for more than five years, if she smokes, and if she is over 35 years old (Stewart et al., 1979). If a woman is over 40, the risk of fatal complications from pill use is higher than the risk of death with a full-term pregnancy; consequently, pills are not safe for women in this age group, and many clinicians prefer to lower this limit to age 35. Women who have a history of clotting disorders or sickle cell anemia should not take the pill.

The risk of death from a circulatory problem (including blood-clotting disorders) is 4.7 times higher for pill users than non-pill users in the 15 to 34 age group. That is, the risk for a non-pill user is one in 50,000, and for a pill user, the risk is one in 12,000. The risk of a fatal heart attack for a woman aged 30 to 39 who neither takes pills nor smokes is one in 100,000; for pill users, the risk is one in 50,000; and, if the pill user also smokes, her risk increases to one in 10,000 (Stewart et al., 1979). Examining concrete statistics such as these can help the consumer make an informed decision about pill use.

Other rare but serious complications that have been reported for pill users include the following: a higher risk of developing hypertension (high blood pressure); double the risk of developing malignant melanoma, a serious form of cancer involving skin pigment cells; double the risk of developing gallbladder disease; inflammation of the optic nerve with accompanying vision problems; and lowered resistance to infections, including bladder and kidney infections. The pill has been known to cause, in rare instances, tumors of the liver which are generally benign but which may cause fatal hemorrhaging. The pill appears to aggravate conditions which are influenced by water retention, such as migraine headaches, asthma, and epilepsy (Stewart et al., 1979).

With the exception of very rare liver cancer and rare melanoma, there have been no definite studies citing the birth control pill as a causative agent in the development of cancer. However, it has been known for some time that estrogens can induce cancer in laboratory animals (Stewart et al., 1979); and other forms of reproductive hormones have been linked with increased cancer risk in humans, for example, estrogen used for menopausal symptoms and uterine cancer. Additionally, it has been suggested that women with benign breast disease have an increased risk of breast cancer when they take the pill (Stewart et al., 1979). Because there can be an extensive lapse in time between exposure to a cancer-causing agent and evidence of the disease, it is not yet possible to ascertain these long-term effects of pill use.

A relatively new area of research concerns the effects of interaction between oral contraceptives and other drugs. Drugs such as phenobarbital, ampicillin, antihistamines, sedatives, and tranquilizers may reduce the effectiveness of birth control pills. Conversely, the pill can affect the action of such substances as insulin and anticoagulants (Hatcher et al., 1978).

Studies of the effects on the offspring of women who take oral contraceptives during pregnancy indicate a suspicion that the pill increases the risk of congenital heart defects, limb defects, and abnormal female reproductive tract development. About one in 1,000 fetuses thus exposed showed evidence of such defects. Thus, women who discontinue the pill are urged to wait a few months before attempting to conceive. Women who are nursing should avoid taking oral contraceptives, since the hormone will decrease the amount and quality of the milk, although it is not yet known whether the breast-fed infant would be affected by the hormones. Nursing or lactation itself can provide some contraceptive action in that the resumption of ovulation following childbirth is delayed (Hatcher et al., 1978). However, the return of ovulation is unpredictable and may occur before menstruation begins again; thus, lactation is not a very reliable means of birth control.

In some rare cases, women stop taking birth control pills and do not resume ovulation and menstruation for six months or more (Cherniak and Feingold, 1975). This "oversuppression syndrome," as it is known, is more common in women whose menstrual cycles were irregular before they went on the pill. However, this condition can be treated by drug therapy (Hatcher, Stewart, Guest, Finkelstein, and Godwin, 1976).

The list of possible complications associated with the pill is potentially overwhelming. It is important to put this in perspective by emphasizing that serious complications are rare and the chances of any one individual developing any specific problem are quite low. For women under 40, the risk of death from the known pill complications is lower than the risk of full-term pregnancy and childbirth. On the other hand, use of a barrier method of contraception (diaphragm, condoms, foam) with abortion as a back-up method, presents the least risk of all

(Stewart et al., 1979). Recent reports suggest that pill use has begun to decline in this country—from 64 million prescriptions filled by pharmacists in 1975 to 49 million in 1978—while use of methods such as the diaphragm has increased—503,000 prescriptions for diaphragms filled in 1975 to 1,205,000 in 1978 (Colen, 1979). However, a barrier method with back-up abortion is not always an acceptable option, and safety is not the only factor to consider; the effectiveness of the pill is an important element for many women. A woman can potentially minimize the risks by paying attention to any early warning signs of problems, for example, chest or leg pain, severe headache, vision changes, or severe depression and by having routine medical examinations including pelvic and breast examination and blood pressure check.

As mentioned at the beginning of this section, the pills we have been discussing are known as combination pills. From 1965 to 1976 another formulation of oral contraceptives was available. These were known as sequential pills, and they provided a dose of synthetic estrogen for the first 14 pills and a mixture of this estrogen and progestin for the remaining 6 or 7 pills. Although this was believed to more closely mimic the body's natural production of hormones, the sequential pills were not without their problems. They were less effective than the combination pills and caused similar side effects. In 1976, the FDA recalled sequentials because of a suspected link with uterine cancer (Johnson, 1977).

Two other products that provide hormonal contraception for women have been developed; these are the "mini-pill" and Depo Provera. The mini-pill, which is taken every day, contains small doses of progestin only. These pills do not necessarily inhibit ovulation, but they do create sufficient changes in the cervical mucus, in the sperm's ability to penetrate an egg, in the egg's rate of movement in the Fallopian tubes, and in the endometrium to provide a concerted contraceptive effect. The theoretical failure rate for the mini-pill is 1% to 1.5%; the use failure rate is 5% to 10% (Hatcher, et al., 1978). Pregnancy rates are highest for the first six months of use, so a woman may choose to use an additional birth control method for this period of time. Women who take mini-pills often experience irregular menstrual cycles and/or breakthrough bleeding.

Depo Provera or "the shot," is a long-acting progestin injection. One advantage of Depo Provera is that it is administered only once every three months. Irregular (and often extensive) menstrual bleeding often occurs in the first nine to twelve months of Depo Provera therapy, followed by temporary amenorrhea. Weight gain is not uncommon, and decreased sex drive, headaches, and dizziness have also been reported. Infertility for six to twelve months after the discontinuation of the injections is often observed (Hatcher et al., 1978). The use of Depo Provera has been associated with breast cancer in beagle dogs (Hatcher et al., 1978) and with cervical cancer in women (Pembrook, 1977). It was banned for use in the United States by the FDA in 1978. It is still being used by approximately one million women in other countries (Hatcher et al., 1978).

## Male Birth Control Pills

The achievement of a contraceptive effect by interfering with the production of male gamete cells (that is, sperm) is currently under investigation. Attempts have been made to interrupt the processes of sperm formation, maturation, and transport, by pituitary inhibition or by direct action in the testes. Estrogen, progestin, and testosterone are several of the substances which have been tested for their contraceptive effects; however, these trials produced complications and undesirable side effects such as impaired liver function and increased risk of cardiovascular disease (Camp and Green, 1978).

One of the problems with using synthetic hormones for male contraception is that, in order to be effective, they must be administered in considerably higher doses than those in the pill taken by women. Researchers are now investigating a combination of testosterone and progestin in smaller doses; both of these chemicals can interfere with spermatogenesis, and it is hypothesized that complications can be minimized by the lower dosages (Bremner and de Kretser, 1975). Adequate testing will most likely take several more years.

## CONDOMS

The condom, also called a rubber, prophylactic, or sheath is a cover worn over the erect penis. The historical record first shows penile sheaths in early Egyptian art; those, however, were probably used for decoration. Gabriel Fallopius, the sixteenth century Italian anatomist for whom the uterine tubes are named, prescribed a linen sheath to protect against venereal disease. Casanova, during the eighteenth century, helped to popularize the condom. The vulcanization of rubber in 1844 provided for the development of the mass production of latex condoms.

Currently, condoms are the most popular contraceptive method in England, Sweden, and Japan (Arditti, 1976). In Japan, condoms are made in a variety of shapes, colors, and textures and are marketed as a device that will enhance sexual pleasure; women sell them door-to-door (Levin, 1976).

The popularity of the condom in the United States has been decreased by the advent of the pill, by lack of promotion by medical authorities, and by negative attitudes. The condom has historically been associated with prostitution and with the efforts of the armed forces to promote its use as a means to avoid venereal disease. In addition, various States have laws which restrict the advertising, display, and sale of these devices (Arditti, 1976). Despite these factors, 15% to 20% of American couples who practice contraception use the condom (Levin, 1976), and one billion are sold annually in this country (McCary, 1978).

The condom is quite easy to use. Either partner simply puts the condom on the man's erect penis before it comes into contact with the vagina. Thus, when the man ejaculates, the semen is deposited in the condom, rather than in the vagina, thereby avoiding impregnation. The condom may slip off the penis as the penis becomes flaccid after ejaculation, so the man should withdraw after his orgasm, with either partner holding the rim of the condom against the penis until it has exited from the vagina. It is not recommended that condoms be reused.

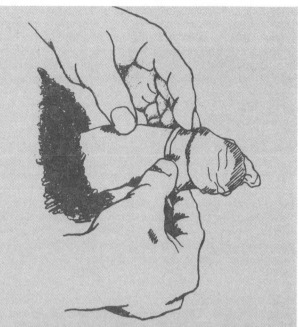

Use of the condom does not have to affect the process of sexual activity, since its application can readily be integrated into sex play and it can be applied by either partner.

There are many different condoms available on the American market. Most condoms come rolled up in individually sealed plastic or foil packages and are available in lubricated or nonlubricated varieties; some are contoured, and some are textured. Most are made of latex; a few brands are manufactured from lamb intestine (a centuries-old product) and are popularly called "skins." These reportedly transmit body heat better than the latex condoms but are considerably more expensive. Latex condoms are themselves quite thin and sensitive. Some models of condoms have a nipple-shaped or reservoir end, to catch the force of the ejaculation. If a condom does not have a reservoir tip, a space of about one-half inch should be left at the end as it is placed on the penis. The quality of latex condoms is carefully controlled by the major manufacturers and by the FDA, so the chances of a hole or another manufacturing defect are quite small (*Consumer Reports,* 1979). If a condom does break during use, an application of spermicidal foam (see Vaginal Spermicides below) should immediately be inserted into the vagina.

There are many advantages to condoms: they are harmless and simple to use; they are available without prescription; they offer protection against both pregnancy and the transmission of venereal and other genitourinary disease. Their failure rate is low: most authorities quote a theoretical rate of 3% and an actual use failure rate of 10% (Hatcher et al., 1978). Recent studies conducted in Britain indicate greater effectiveness: the use failure rate was 4% and, when statistics were recalculated to eliminate those pregnancies resulting from misuse or nonuse of the condom, the failure rate was 1% (*Consumer Reports,* 1979). There are as yet no American studies demonstrating comparative results. When a condom is used, together with spermicidal foam, the combined use failure rate is 1.5% (Stewart et al, 1979).

Diaphragms come in a variety of sizes from 50 mm. to 105 mm. (2 to 4 inches); and a woman must be properly fitted by a physician or other medical personnel, for example, a nurse practitioner. It is important that the prescribed diaphragm be the largest size that fits comfortably, since the woman's vagina will expand somewhat during sexual excitement. A diaphragm can be fitted for a woman who has not yet experienced intercourse, unless the presence of the hymen hinders the fitting. She should be refitted some time later, since intercourse will stretch the vagina somewhat.

At the time of fitting, a woman should also be taught the correct procedure for inserting her diaphragm. After the method has been demonstrated for her, she can then show the examiner whether she has learned it, or she can practice the technique at home and then return for a recheck by the examiner to be sure she is inserting the diaphragm properly. Once she becomes familiar with this new skill, she will be able to insert the diaphragm with ease and rapidity. An appropriate level of comfort with touching one's genitals will influence the choice of this method.

As with the condom, use of the diaphragm need not disrupt sexual expression. Either partner can insert the device and this can be effectively integrated into the couple's lovemaking style. If intercourse is repeated before it is time to remove the diaphragm, an applicator of fresh spermicide needs to be inserted into the vagina for each subsequent act, or the couple can switch to condoms.

The condom is the only reliable, nonirreversible male method of birth control. Use of condoms, or alternating between condoms and a female use method such as the diaphragm, can meet the needs of couples who prefer to have the male partner physically involved in the process of contraception. Additionally, regardless of the method a couple actually chooses, participation in effective communication about contraception can also provide a meaningful way for them to share responsibility.

## DIAPHRAGM

When the modern diaphragm was invented in 1882, it represented a major breakthrough in contraceptive methods for women. It was quite popular until the advent of the pill and the IUD (discussed below) in the 1960s; and it has been estimated that, at one time, up to one-third of American couples practicing birth control used this device (Boston Women's Health Book Collective, 1976). Contemporary concern about the possible serious side effects of the pill and the IUD is facilitating new interest in the use of the diaphragm.

The diaphragm is made of soft rubber, in the shape of a shallow cup or dome, with a flexible spring rim. It fits into place over the cervix, with its front rim behind the pubic bone and the back rim in the posterior fornix, the pocket behind the cervix. When correctly used with an application of spermicide, the diaphragm functions as both a mechanical device (covering the cervical os to prevent the entry of sperm) and a chemical one (the spermicide will kill sperm that manage to "swim" into the diaphragm).

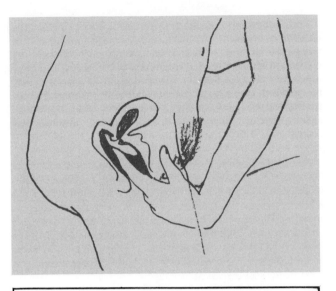

To use a diaphragm, spread about one tablespoon of spermicidal cream or jelly in the side of the dome that will cover the cervix and around the inside of the rim, and pinch (or squeeze) the edges of the rim together. Insert the thus-folded diaphragm into the vagina, following the downward angle (that is, toward the small of the back) of the vagina (which will be familiar from experience with tampons) as far as it will go. Tuck the front rim up behind the ridge created by the pubic bone. The diaphragm should now be in place. To check its position, insert a finger into the vagina to feel that the cervix is covered with rubber. The diaphragm can be inserted in a variety of positions, with one foot propped up, squatting, lying on the back, etc., and can be put in place by either partner. When a proper size diaphragm is correctly in place, the woman should not feel it or be aware of its presence.

Many clinicians have recommended that, for maximum effectiveness, the diaphragm should not be inserted more than two hours before intercourse. However, in a recent study which demonstrated high effectiveness rates for the diaphragm, users were encouraged to insert the device up to six hours before intercourse (Stewart et al., 1979). If more than six hours elapses, an applicator of spermicide can be inserted into the vagina. The diaphragm should be left in place after the last intercourse for six to eight hours, to ensure that the sperm in the vagina have all died (as a result of the acidic pH of the vagina); it can be left in place for up to twenty-four hours.

Removal of the diaphragm is accomplished by hooking a finger behind the front rim and gently pulling downward. The diaphragm is then washed with mild soap and warm water, dried, dusted with cornstarch to preserve the rubber, and returned to its container. Exposure to light and heat can cause the rubber to deteriorate, as can talcum powder. The diaphragm should be checked for holes each time it is used, by holding it up to the light or filling it with water and watching for leaks. A damaged diaphragm should, of course, not be used.

With proper care, a diaphragm should last for two years. Refitting is necessary after childbirth or an abortion or after a weight change of 10 to 20 pounds. The only side effects of the diaphragm are occasional irritation caused by the spermicide (in which case the brand can be changed) or a rare allergy to rubber, in which case a plastic diaphragm may be obtained. Recent studies suggest that the spermicide offers some protection against venereal disease and vaginal infections (Seaman and Seaman, 1977). When used during menstruation, the diaphragm serves to contain the menstrual fluid and is even occasionally used for this purpose by women practicing other methods of birth control. As with the condom, using a diaphragm can confer an immediate sense of taking responsibility for one's own sexuality.

The theoretical failure rate for the diaphragm is 3%, and the standard use failure rate is cited as 17%. Recent studies in the United States and Britain, however, report use failure rates of 2% and 2.4%, respectively (Hatcher et al., 1978). These studies were conducted with highly motivated diaphragm users.

As Masters and Johnson (1966) have demonstrated, the upper vagina expands during high levels of sexual excitement (see "tenting effect" in Chapter 5), which can cause the diaphragm to fit more loosely. This may also happen when the woman is on top during intercourse. In these cases, the spermicide is still protecting the cervical os.

Another device similar to the diaphragm is the cervical cap. It is thimble-shaped, smaller in size than a diaphragm, and made of rubber (latex) or plastic (older versions were made of metal). It fits over the end of the cervix, being held in place by suction. The metal or plastic cap could be left in place for days or even weeks, being removed at the appropriate time to allow for menstrual flow. The latex cap needs to be removed after 24 to 36 hours, to prevent infection. This method is much more popular in Europe than it is in America, where few clinicians prescribe it.

## VAGINAL SPERMICIDES

Spermicides are preparations which are inserted into the vagina, before intercourse, to kill the sperm. They are available in a variety of forms: aerosol foam, creams, jellies, and suppositories. These products consist of a spermicidal agent in an inert base and work both mechanically (block cervical os) and chemically (kill sperm). Deposited deep in the vagina near the cervix, the spermicide is distributed by the movements of the penis during intercourse.

A vaginal spermicide should be inserted no longer than fifteen to thirty minutes before intercourse. Some authorities recommend using a double dose of the product in order to increase its efficiency (Hatcher et al., 1978). Application must be repeated for each subsequent act of intercourse, or the couple can switch to using condoms. If the woman wants to douche, she should wait six to eight hours after intercourse, to ensure that all the sperm are dead.

The advantages of spermicides are that they are available without prescription, they are relatively quick to apply, they are

> To use a spermicide, fill the plastic tampon-shaped applicator with the product (some brands are available in preloaded applicators) and insert it into the vagina. If foam is being used, shake the can twenty times to create an abundance of the bubbles that form the cervical barrier. It is recommended that a foam-user keep an extra can available, since it is unpredictable when the can will be empty or inoperative. The spermicidal suppositories (not to be confused with so-called feminine hygiene products; see Chapter 5) are bullet-shaped wedges, which should be inserted deep in the vagina, where they will dissolve in about fifteen minutes.

harmless, and they may help to prevent venereal disease and vaginal infections (Stewart et al., 1979). They can also be used as a supplementary method with condoms or an IUD. Their disadvantages include their taste during oral sex (if this is a problem, the foam can be inserted after oral sex and before intercourse) and the possibility of allergy or irritation of the vagina or penis (in which case, again, the brand can be changed).

Foam is considered to be the most effective of the vaginal spermicides, because it is the most reliably distributed over the cervix. The theoretical failure rate for foam is 2%. Actual use failure rate has not been specifically determined; various studies report an average of 15% (Stewart et al., 1979).

## INTRAUTERINE DEVICE (IUD)

An IUD is a small plastic device manufactured in a variety of shapes (loop, coil, etc.), which is inserted into the uterus to prevent pregnancy. Such devices were known to the ancient Greeks and mentioned by Hippocrates. For centuries, Arab camel drivers inserted pebbles in the uteri of their female camels to prevent pregnancy on long desert treks, and similar devices are still used on camels in the Sudan and Tunisia. In the nineteenth century, various intrauterine devices were used for both contraceptive purposes and to treat gynecological disorders. Richter's use of a device made from silkworm gut was the basis of the first published report on IUDs, in 1909. Grafenberg used a similar circle of gut and later added silver and copper wire to hold the shape. His work was published in 1930, but his device fell into disrepute because of its complications. These included expulsion, infection, and damage to the uterine wall (Hatcher et al., 1978). In 1957, reports from Israel and Japan documented the contraceptive effectiveness of the IUD; and in 1960, the first American model, the Lippes Loop, was marketed.

An IUD must be inserted by a physician or nurse practitioner; the application cannot be done by the user herself. Most IUDs are packaged with an inserter barrel. Once in this tube, the IUD is stretched out into a straight line. The inserter is passed through the cervix into the uterus, and, once the plunger is depressed, the IUD resumes its appropriate configuration and rests in the uterine cavity. Insertion is often accompanied by cramps and bleeding; the pain will be greater for a woman whose cervical os has not been stretched before (for example, by childbirth). Some authorities recommend that an IUD be inserted during a menstrual period when the woman will already

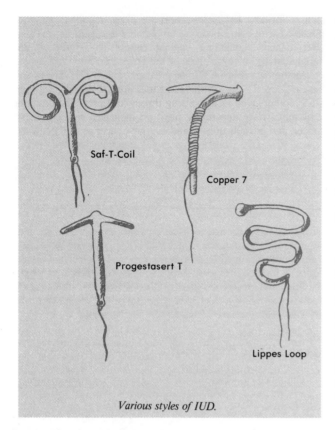

*Various styles of IUD.*

which also negatively affect implantation and, further, render cervical mucus hostile to sperm (Stewart et al., 1979).

The major advantages of the IUD are that they are very convenient and that there is nothing to remember to do in association with this method, other than periodically check the string. The side effects most commonly associated with this device are heavy menstrual bleeding, cramping, spotting, and spontaneous expulsion, at a rate of 5% to 20% in the first year (Stewart et al., 1979). Probably for these reasons, 8% to 10% of women fitted with an IUD have them removed during the first year. Although there are problems, for example, the number of expulsions, medical removals, and failures (that is, pregnancies), 37.5% of the women wearing IUDs report that they are still using them after two to three years (Cherniak and Feingold, 1975).

The potentially serious complications arising from the use of an IUD are infection, uterine perforation, and pregnancy. The presence of an IUD may cause an infection, aggravate existing uterine or tubal infections, or increase susceptibility to pelvic infection. Untreated infection can lead to pelvic inflammatory disease (PID), which can result in an increased risk of ectopic pregnancy (see Chapter 7) or sterility. Rarely, a woman might be allergic to the copper in a copper IUD or have an allergic reaction with a Progestasert T device. Perforation of the uterine wall by an IUD is most likely to happen during insertion and is relatively rare; reported rates of perforation vary from fewer than one to about nine in 1,000 (Stewart et al., 1979).

A woman who becomes pregnant with an IUD in place has a greater chance of having an ectopic pregnancy than a non-IUD user. If the fertilized egg does implant in the uterus and the IUD is not removed, there is an approximately fifty percent chance of a spontaneous abortion or miscarriage, with a possible risk of a septic (or infected) spontaneous abortion. If the IUD strings are visible, the device can be removed by gentle traction, and the risk of spontaneous abortion is reduced to thirty percent. If the IUD strings cannot be located for removal, the risk of serious infection is such that therapeutic abortion should be considered (Stewart et al., 1979). If the pregnancy is maintained, there is a slight increase in the risk of premature labor (Hatcher et al., 1978). Harmful effects for the fetus from the plain plastic or copper IUDs have not been indicated, although the total number of fetuses which have been exposed to copper is quite small. It is not yet known whether the progestin in a Progestasert T device would cause the same fetal deformities as can oral progestin (Stewart et al., 1979).

As noted above, if a woman with an IUD in place becomes pregnant, her chances of miscarrying are one in two; and, if an infection results, it can develop into a life-threatening illness in a very short time (Stewart et al., 1979). The risk of death from an infected or septic spontaneous abortion is about fifty times greater if the woman has an IUD than it would be for a normal pregnancy (Cates, Ory, Rochat, and Tyler, 1976). Seventeen deaths from septic spontaneous abortions in IUD users in the United States were reported between 1972 and 1974 (Stewart et al., 1979). Eleven of these deaths occurred among users of the Dalkon Shield, which had been used by two million women since 1970. Several features in the design of this device have been considered in an attempt to explain its greater capability to cause serious infection than other IUDs. Unlike most other models, the Shield is not inserted through a tube. Thus, as the

be bleeding, when she will not be pregnant, and when her os will be slightly more open (Boston Women's Health Book Collective, 1976). Other medical practitioners claim that this is not the best time for insertion, because of a higher possibility of susceptibility to infection (Hatcher et al., 1978).

The end of the IUD has a string attached which passes through the cervical os, to facilitate removal and as a means of checking that the IUD is still present. The woman should check for the presence of the string periodically, to make sure that the device has not been expelled.

There are two types of intrauterine devices: non-medicated (Lippes Loop, Saf-T-Coil) and medicated (Copper 7, Progestasert T). The mechanism of action of the IUD is still a matter of controversy. IUDs have different effects in different species (Katchadourian and Lunde, 1975). For humans, the consensus of opinion seems to be that they work by causing an inflammation of the uterine lining, which makes it unfavorable for implantation of a fertilized egg. The large number of white blood cells found in the uteri of IUD wearers may be toxic to the sperm, the egg, or the implantation process (Boston Women's Health Book Collective, 1976). It has been suggested that the use of antibiotics or aspirin by a woman wearing an IUD may lower the effectiveness of the IUD by minimizing the inflammatory reaction. Under these conditions, a back-up birth control method such as foam or condoms may be considered (Boston Women's Health Book Collective, 1976).

The medicated intrauterine devices offer other contraceptive effects. The Copper 7 is wrapped with copper wire which works to alter the functions of the enzymes involved in implantation. The Progestasert T slowly releases small amounts of progestins device is pushed through the cervix, it may introduce more bacteria than other IUDs (Hatcher et al., 1978). Secondly, again unlike other styles, the Shield has a polyfilamented string. This "tail" may act as a candlewick, permitting the passage of bacteria into the uterus. Thirdly, the toothed edges of this device increase the likelihood of uterine infection (Hatcher et al., 1978). There is still no consensus about the cause of the Shield's danger, and it is possible that it caused more deaths because of a higher pregnancy rate or because of its wide use among young women (Stewart et al., 1979). In 1974, the FDA withdrew the polyfilamented tail model from the market, and in 1975, the manufacturer, A. H. Robins, stopped the distribution of this device.

How effective is the IUD? Its theoretical failure rate is 1% to 3%, and its use failure rate is 5% (Hatcher et al., 1978). Since pregnancies are more common in the first few months of use, an IUD's effectiveness will improve from year to year. The release of copper or progestin in a medicated IUD eventually declines, thus lowering its rate of effectiveness. It is recommended that a copper IUD be replaced every three years and that a Progestasert T be replaced every year. Some authorities suggest using an additional back-up birth control method for the first three months after an IUD has been inserted (Boston Women's Health Book Collective, 1976).

## POST-COITAL METHODS

We have discussed up to now methods of protecting against pregnancy by interfering with the processes of gamete production, fertilization, and implantation. The question arises whether there are any effective methods of post-coital contraception. One such method that is commonly used is douching. This involves flushing out the vagina with water or other solutions. Douching, besides being inconvenient and possibly disruptive to the vaginal environment, is highly *in*effective as a birth control method. Some sperm can reach the cervix within a minute or two after ejaculation and will not be touched by the douche (Stewart et al., 1979). In addition, the pressure of the douche will inevitably force some sperm up through the cervix.

In the case of unprotected intercourse believed to have occurred at ovulation, medical authorities have offered several possible options. First, an IUD can be inserted. This procedure should be done as soon as possible after coitus (that is, within a few days), to prevent the fertilized egg from implanting (Hatcher et al., 1978). Secondly, a menstrual extraction can be performed (see below under Abortion). A third route is the oral administration of DES.

DES (diethylstilbestrol) is a potent synthetic estrogen. For use as a post-coital contraceptive, 25 mg. of DES is taken twice daily for five days, starting within 72 hours after intercourse. The user will often experience nausea and vomiting. Since this regimen contains a massive dose of synthetic estrogen (Hatcher et al., 1978), users should be cautioned to watch for serious symptoms such as severe headaches, sudden loss of vision, severe leg pains, or shortness of breath.

If the DES therapy is not effective, the pregnant woman should consider having an abortion. DES is known to have possible harmful effects on the fetus that will appear in the child after puberty, including vaginal cancer in females (DES daughters) and abnormalities of the testes and impaired sperm production in males (DES sons) (Stewart et al., 1979). The possible carcinogenic risks to the adult user are unknown, although DES mothers who took the drug throughout pregnancy to prevent miscarriage apparently have an increased risk of breast cancer, and possibly uterine and ovarian cancer as well (Stewart et al., 1979). DES's history and recent questions about its effectiveness have led one group of physicians to label this therapy as "relatively unattractive" (Hatcher et al., 1978).

# CONTRACEPTION—FUTURE METHODS

Researchers continue to develop and investigate alternative methods of contraception. Some of these are variants and attempted improvements of existing techniques; others are relatively new. In this section we will review the spectrum of these possible methods of the future.

## MALE CONTRACEPTION

Most of the new birth control methods that are for use by men and that are under investigation depend on interfering with spermatogenesis (sperm development). As discussed earlier, the site to be affected can be either the pituitary or the testes themselves. In addition to experiments with various combinations of hormones (see above discussion of male birth control pills), researchers are working with a substance called inhibin, which is believed to block pituitary FSH secretion without affecting LH, thus blocking spermatogenesis without impairing testosterone secretion (Bremner and de Kretser, 1975). Other directions of research include disrupting the function of the epididymis (Bremner and de Kretser, 1975; Rosenfeld, 1977); altering the chemistry of the seminal fluid; and immunological approaches which would make a man "allergic" to his own sperm, that is, his body would manufacture antibodies which would attack the sperm (Rosenfeld, 1977).

A different route to the same end—interference with spermatogenesis—takes advantage of the fact that this manufacturing process requires a temperature a few degrees lower than body heat. If testicular temperature can be raised, sperm production will stop. Experiments using heat and ultrasound are being conducted (Rosenfeld, 1977). Such methods have the advantage of avoiding systemic ingestion of chemical substances, although the long-term effects of exposure to ultrasound waves are not known. Perhaps the use of heat (for example, hot baths, insulated scrotal supporters) would entail fewer risks.

Along other lines, a new type of condom is being investigated. This is a condom containing a soluble spermicidal drug which is designed to dissolve during coitus. Its effectiveness will remain in question until sufficient trials have been conducted (Camp and Green, 1978).

According to a recent report in *Scientific American* (1979), there is one chemical antifertility agent for men that has moved out of the laboratory into extensive clinical trials, in China. This substance is gossypol, isolated from cottonseed, and works by damaging immature sperm in the seminiferous tubules. A report in the *Chinese Medical Journal* claims that gossypol is 99.89% effective, is relatively safe, and is economical. Further research into its safety is being conducted.

## FEMALE CONTRACEPTION

One direction of research in female contraception involves attempts to inhibit ovulation. Included in this area are "brain contraceptives" (Camp and Green, 1978), substances contained in pills, tampons, or nasal sprays which act directly on the pituitary to interfere with the release of LH (necessary for ovulation). Also under investigation is Oocyte Maturation Inhibitor (OMI), a natural compound found in animals, which prevents the maturation of the egg within the ovary (Rodgers, 1977).

Another main focus of research is the development of new routes for delivery of progestin (which acts as a contraceptive). Tiny tubes or rods containing progestin that can be implanted under the skin (Hatcher et al., 1978), and bracelets soaked in progestin that can be worn tightly applied to the skin for absorption, are being investigated. The most promising of these devices seems to be the vaginal ring. One size fits every woman, and it is inserted by the woman herself, in the same manner as a diaphragm. The ring releases progestin which is then absorbed through the vaginal wall, thus bypassing the digestive system and the liver. The ring is left in place continuously, except during menstruation.

Other experimental methods are designed to interfere with fertilization. One of these is a sophisticated version of a very old method: the vaginal sponge (Camp and Green, 1978). Based on the same principle as the diaphragm, that is, to block the passage of sperm through the cervical os, these new sponges are made of collagen. Once it is inserted high in the vagina, the dry sponge expands and is held in place by the folds of the vaginal wall. It absorbs the ejaculate and, if saturated with acetic acid (which is like vinegar), the acidity will kill the sperm. Another variety of the sponge is made of plastic saturated with a spermicide. If these sponges are eventually marketed, they will be available without a prescription. One major advantage over other barrier methods is that the sponge can be left in place between menstrual periods.

Other attempts to block fertilization or subsequent implantation are being investigated. These include: a drug to prevent capacitation (final maturation) of the sperm once in the vagina (Goldstein, 1976); a drug that will interfere with the transport of a fertilized egg in the Fallopian tubes (Goldstein, 1976); "dummy sperm," that is, compounds that will cause the outer membrane of the egg to prevent penetration by sperm (Rodgers, 1977); an IUM, an intrauterine membrane, a more flexible version of the IUD (Wheeler, 1975). An immunological approach is also being studied, that is, the immunizing of women against sperm or against the hormones of pregnancy. Work in this latter area involves the use of a vaccine which causes the woman's body to form antibodies against human chorionic gonadotropin (HCG), a hormone produced by the placenta and necessary to sustain pregnancy (Camp and Green, 1978).

Methods to pinpoint the time of ovulation and thus avoid chemical manipulations are being developed. Known collectively as ovulation detectors, one such device is the Ovutimer, which measures the viscosity of cervical mucus and indicates the approach of ovulation (Seaman and Seaman, 1977). Another is the Ovutron, which measures the changes in the body's electrical field which accompany ovulation. The woman using this technique merely touches each index finger to an electrode on the Ovutron, which then flashes a reading (Millican, 1978). Such devices provide a sophisticated refinement of the rhythm method of birth control. To be truly effective, they will need to be able to predict ovulation three to five days in advance. Other methods to determine a woman's fertility period involve litmus-type tests for saliva and urine, taking advantage of the fact that the chemistry of these two fluids changes as the body prepares for ovulation (Seaman and Seaman, 1977). These methods are still in the speculative stages and have not as yet been extensively tested.

## STERILIZATION

Sterilization involves surgical procedures which interrupt the pathway of sperm in men and of the egg in women. Although in the past sterilization was considered an undesirable method of birth control, now the popularity of this method is growing.

## MALE

The male procedure is known as vasectomy, because it severs the vas deferens (see Chapter 5). Usually performed in a physician's office under local anesthesia, the procedure takes about 15 minutes. A small incision is made in each testis; the vas is located and drawn out. It is then tied at two points and snipped in between. The ends of the vas are returned to place and the incision closed. Discomfort is usually minimal. Fertility will remain for a few weeks because of the sperm stored in the tract beyond the site of surgery. Laboratory tests of seminal fluid can determine when sterility is assured.

The procedure of vasectomy involves no sexual side effects. Sperm are still produced; they remain in the testis and are reabsorbed. Testosterone production is not affected, nor are the processes of erection and ejaculation. The amount of seminal fluid remains essentially the same. There is no negative effect on the libido, and some men even report increased sexual feelings, presumably because the fear of pregnancy is eliminated.

The failure rate for vasectomy is 0.15%, and the rare failure can be attributed to incomplete surgery, spontaneous regrowth of the vas, or the presence of more than one vas deferens per testis. Recent research indicates that one-half to two-thirds of men who have undergone a vasectomy develop antibodies to the sperm which remain in the testes after the vasectomy (Stewart et al., 1979). It has been speculated that this stimulation of the immunological system may result in autoimmune diseases such as rheumatoid arthritis, but, as yet, there is no research to substantiate this suggestion (Stewart et al., 1979).

Men contemplating a vasectomy should consider it a permanent measure. Methods to reverse a vasectomy are being tried, but most still are considered highly experimental. One such method is microsurgery, using a high-power magnification microscope and suture thread one-thousandth of an inch in diameter to resew the severed ends of the vas. This technique is also known as "two-layer reversal" because the more delicate inner layer of the vas and its tougher, muscular outer layer are rejoined separately (Westoff, 1978).

Research is also proceeding on the use of plastic plugs or valves in the vas to control the flow of sperm (Boston Women's Health Book Collective, 1976). These techniques are still in the experimental stage.

## FEMALE

Sterilization procedures for women are more complex than a vasectomy. The Fallopian tubes are in the abdominal cavity and are not as readily accessible as in the vas. Tubal ligation, or tying the tubes, can be performed in a number of ways. The traditional method is known as a laparotomy. The woman is placed under general anesthesia and a two-inch incision is made in the abdomen. The Fallopian tubes are then located, tied at two points, and cut in between, or cauterized (sealed by burning). The incision is closed and the woman remains in the hospital for several days. This procedure is considered major surgery.

A newer technique, which can be done on an outpatient basis under local anesthesia, is called laparoscopy. About three quarts of carbon dioxide is infused into the abdomen to allow the tubes to be isolated. An endoscope, a small tube with mirrors and lights, is inserted through a small incision below the navel. Once the Fallopian tubes are located, they are cauterized with a second small instrument. A rubber band to be tied around the tubes has been developed as an alternative to cauterization (Hatcher et al., 1976). After the appropriate procedure, the incision is closed with sutures. The small size of the incision in this operation has given rise to the term "band-aid" surgery.

The mini-laparotomy is a recent variation of the standard laparotomy (Hatcher et al., 1978). Performed under local anesthesia, a small incision is made in the lower abdomen for direct visualization of the Fallopian tubes, which are then tied and cut or cauterized.

Tubal ligation is occasionally performed through other routes. A laparotomy or laparoscopy can be done through an incision in the cul de sac of the vagina; the instrument for a laparoscopy can also enter the body through the vagina and uterus. In some cases, these alternative routes result in higher complication rates. Complications for any of these procedures include reaction to anesthesia, infection, hemorrhage, and if cauterization is used, the risk of burning adjacent tissues (Hatcher et al., 1978). The theoretical failure rate for tubal ligation is 0.04%, and the use failure rate is slightly higher. Failure would most likely be a result of either incomplete surgery or the spontaneous rejoining of a tube.

Tubal ligation has no sexual side effects. The egg disintegrates and is reabsorbed into the body; hormone production, menstruation, and sexual response continue as usual. Libido may be increased because the woman is released from fear of pregnancy.

Hysterectomy, surgical removal of the uterus, is occasionally performed as a sterilization method. There is much controversy surrounding this practice because of its high rate of complications and the availability of other techniques (Hatcher et al., 1976). Additionally, it has been argued by Masters and Johnson (1966) that the uterus plays an important part in orgasmic response in some women.

Chemical sterilization is also being studied. When pellets containing the drug quinicrine are inserted into the uterus through the cervix, they cause permanent scarring and closure of the area where the Fallopian tubes join the uterus (Hatcher et al., 1976). Reversible sterilization is also being investigated. Two such techniques are microsurgery (Camp and Green, 1978) and the nonsurgical injection of a removable plug at the utero-tubal junction. Until these methods are proved successful and have widespread availability, tubal ligation should be considered permanent. In addition, it has been reported that the mini-laparotomy has more potential for reversibility than other methods because of its relatively nondestructive nature (Hatcher et al., 1978).

# ABORTION

Abortion, the termination of a pregnancy, has historically been the most widely practiced method of birth control. The induction of abortion by mercury was described in a Chinese medical text 5,000 years ago. Abortions were performed in ancient Egypt, Greece, and Rome. Aristotle reflected the majority position of Greek thought on the issue by declaring that abortion was acceptable until the soul entered the fetus.

The strongest opposition to abortion originates with the Catholic Church. From about the twelfth century on, except for the period of 1588-1591, Catholic law followed Aristotle and held that abortion was permissible up to 40 days for a male fetus and 80 days for a female fetus. Then, in 1869, the Pope declared that any abortion was murder. The current position of the Catholic Church is then only about 100 years old. In the United States, sanctions against abortion have stemmed from both religious and legal sources. Since the Supreme Court decriminalized abortion in 1973, response has been divided. While "right-to-life" groups assert the rights of the unborn fetus, others argue for a woman's right to control her own body.

Before the Supreme Court decision, it was estimated that one million illegal abortions were performed a year (Hatcher et al., 1976). Reports of such abortions were often accompanied by horror stories about "back-street" abortionists and a high rate of serious complications and death. Legal abortions are generally performed in a proper medical setting, and death is rare—one death per 100,000 procedures in 1976 (Stewart et al., 1979).

The discovery of an unplanned pregnancy can produce a mixture of feelings, such as fear and anger. "Problem-pregnancy" counseling, to become acquainted with the available options and to explore feelings, is very helpful. If an abortion is chosen, counseling at the time of the actual procedure can provide valuable support.

Women from all backgrounds seek legal abortions. A relatively high proportion are older women, 30% are married, and

Catholic women seek abortion at a slightly higher proportion than their percentage in the general population (Boston Women's Health Book Collective, 1976). Studies conducted on women who had legal abortions showed that the experience was not traumatic and that 90% of the women reported no negative psychological consequences. Rather, most women felt relief and satisfaction (Smith, 1973).

## METHODS

There are a number of different procedures for the termination of a pregnancy. Vacuum aspiration is the most common method used up to the twelfth week of pregnancy, dating from the beginning of the last menstrual period (LMP). This procedure is usually performed on an outpatient basis, often in an abortion clinic, under local anesthesia. The cervical os is dilated, and a thin tube is inserted into the uterus. The other end of the tube is attached to a vacuum aspirator which produces suction. The contents of the uterus, including the product of conception, are then sucked out through the tube. The procedure takes about ten minutes and involves mild discomfort. The woman stays in the medical facility for several hours and is watched for complications such as infection or hemorrhage.

Dilatation and curettage (D and C) is an older method of performing early abortions and is also a common procedure for various gynecological problems. For this procedure, the cervical os is dilated, and a curette, a metal loop attached to a long, thin handle, is inserted into the uterus. The physician removes the uterine contents with the curette. This method must be performed under general anesthesia; it causes more blood loss and may not be as efficient as vacuum aspiration (Hatcher et al., 1978).

A version of vacuum aspiration known as menstrual extraction is sometimes performed. This is usually done before sufficient time has elapsed for a pregnancy test to be conclusive. The cervical os does not need to be dilated; a thin, flexible tube is inserted into the uterus and attached to the vacuum apparatus. This procedure can be done without anesthesia. There is a risk that the procedure might not be complete; the fetal tissue at this stage would be so tiny that it is not always possible to determine if it was totally removed.

After the twelfth week of pregnancy, simple abortion procedures can no longer be utilized, because the uterine walls become soft and spongy, and perforation or excessive bleeding can result. Additionally, the fetus becomes too large to be removed by either suction or the curette alone (Boston Women's Health Book Collective, 1976). If an abortion is performed between the thirteenth and sixteenth weeks, the procedure used is dilatation and evacuation (D and E), which is an extension of both the D and C and vacuum procedures. General anesthesia is usually recommended, and both surgical instruments and a vacuum tube are used to remove the fetal and placental tissue. The procedure takes about 20 to 30 minutes and is considered to involve less risk than the abortion methods which are performed after sixteen weeks (Stewart et al., 1979).

In the sixteenth to twenty-fourth weeks, abortion can be performed by inducing labor and subsequent miscarriage. The most commonly used agents for this purpose are saline, prostaglandins, and urea. For a saline abortion, a needle or thin tube is inserted through the abdomen and into the amniotic sac in the uterus. About 200 cc. of amniotic fluid is withdrawn and replaced with an equivalent amount of saline solution. The uterus begins contracting within 8 to 24 hours. The labor will last 8 to 15 hours, at the end of which the fetus will be expelled.

Prostaglandins are hormonelike substances that cause contractions. The drug is administered by injection into the amniotic sac, or by vaginal suppositories (Stewart et al., 1979). Both the waiting period before the onset of labor and labor itself are shorter than with a saline abortion. However, there is a high incidence of nausea, vomiting, and diarrhea.

The complication rates for these procedures are higher than for early abortions. Excessive blood loss, infection, and cervical laceration are possible complications. Disadvantages of a saline abortion include shock and possible death if the salt solution is incorrectly injected into a blood vessel; on the other hand, prostaglandins have a higher rate of unsuccessful instillation (requiring a second dose) and present the likelihood that the fetus will show signs of life when it is first expelled.

Another procedure for late abortion which is rarely used is known as hysterotomy. This involves an incision through the abdomen and uterus to remove the fetus, much like a Caesarean section (see Chapter 7). Since this is major surgery, it carries the highest complication and mortality rate of all abortion methods (Boston Women's Health Book Collective, 1976). The main indication for this method would be a situation where induced labor has repeatedly failed.

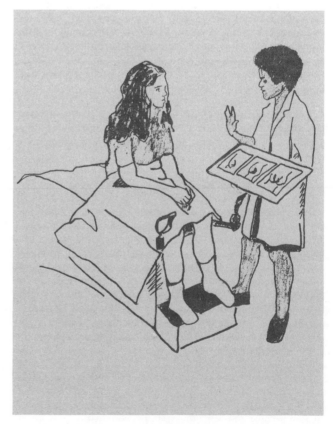

## POLITICAL PERSPECTIVES

In addition to the controversy surrounding the question of population control (see the section above on history of birth control movement), several other political issues have emerged with regard to birth control research and techniques.

One main concern is about research priorities. The funding available for contraceptive research does not approximate, in any way, the amount of funds expended for defense or space research. Moreover, the bulk of available funding is spent on "invasive" methods (hormones, IUDs, and so on); in 1976, only $50,000 of the $76 million spent worldwide went to investigation of "barrier" methods such as the diaphragm or cervical cap (Norsigian, 1978). Since the latter methods are safer, it can be argued that attempts to improve their effectiveness would be a worthwhile use of funds.

A second issue centers on the fact that the bulk of contraceptive research involves women. Of the $35.8 million spent on this research by the United States Agency for International Development over a recent seven-year period, only 5% was used to investigate methods for men (Rosenfeld, 1977). There appears to be two interrelated factors at work here: attitudes toward contraception for males, and the question of whether the male or female reproductive system is more susceptible to interference. We will deal with this latter issue first.

There are arguments that can be advanced to support either position. It has been suggested that the female system is easier to manipulate because it is simpler to stop one egg than billions of sperm (Bremner and de Kretser, 1975) and because there are more sites for possible interference: maturation of egg, ovulation, egg transport, or implantation (Arditti, 1976). The counter position claims that it may be easier to disrupt the continuous process of spermatogenesis than the discontinuous process of ovulation (Schwartz, 1976) and that the male system has the advantage of being less complex (Arditti, 1976). It is possible that an individual's attitudes and beliefs about the appropriateness of male contraception might influence the position she or he takes on this issue.

In 1976, 80% of the Federally funded birth control investigators were male (Norsigian, 1978), and it has been claimed that many researchers consider that it is the female who is responsible for contraception (Schwartz, 1976). The argument has been advanced that, since sociocultural male identity is closely linked to the reproductive system, the idea of male contraception provokes fears of castration and loss of libido (Rosenfeld, 1977; Arditti, 1976). The counter position stresses the significance of male participation and shared responsibility (Zilbergeld, 1978; Arditti, 1976). A recent study investigated whether men would be willing to take a contraceptive pill if one were available; 55.6% of the men said yes, and another 18.5% said they would probably be willing to do so. These two groups of men who thus expressed willingness to use the pill were more favorable to the idea of contraception in general, were less dogmatic in their beliefs and opinions, and were considered to be introspective, open to change, and sensitive to the feelings of others. The men who were less willing, the remaining 25.9%,

were seen as more assertive and forceful, resistant to change, and self-seeking (Gough, 1979).

A third concern focuses on the treatment of poor and minority group women. These women often constitute the subject population for testing new contraceptives (Seaman and Seaman, 1977). Additionally, the issue of sterilization abuse has attracted recent attention; it is claimed that poor and minority women are often sterilized involuntarily or without informed consent (Dreifus, 1975).

## INFERTILITY

As we have seen, many people practice birth control in order to reduce the probability of conception. On the other hand, many couples want to have children but are unable to do so for a variety of reasons. It has been estimated that 15% of the American population of childbearing age is infertile at any given time (Menning, 1977). Since this amounts to about one out of every six couples, this problem poses a more serious concern than many of us would imagine. Fortunately, in the past two decades, medical science has made significant advances in both the diagnosis and treatment of infertility; currently over 50% of the couples who receive proper diagnosis and treatment will be able to successfully conceive a child.

When a couple learns that they are unable to conceive, it can be a tremendous psychological shock. Additionally, the diagnostic and treatment procedures used are often threatening to both men and women, are time-consuming, and are sometimes uncomfortable or painful. Finally, most of the American public is very ignorant regarding the topic of infertility, with myths and misconceptions being much more prevalent than factual knowledge.

In this section we will consider the major reasons for infertility and the specific diagnostic and treatment procedures currently in use. Most of the information in this section is summarized from *Infertility: A Guide for the Childless Couple* by Barbara Menning (1977). This is an excellent book, available in inexpensive paperback, that we highly recommend as additional reading in this area.

Definitions of infertility vary. The most generally accepted criterion for infertility is the inability of a couple to conceive after a year or more of regular sexual relations without any use of contraception. (Also generally included in this definition is the inability, after conception, to carry a pregnancy to a live birth.) The term sterility is often incorrectly used interchangeably with infertility. Technically, the term sterility is reserved for those cases in which there is permanent, incurable infertility, for example, when the testes or ovaries have been removed because of disease.

Infertility has traditionally been considered a "female problem." In fact, however, the specific cause can be traced to the woman in about 40% of the cases, to the man in about 40% of the cases, and to the couple (for example, using ineffective coital techniques, such as having intercourse at the infertile times of the woman's menstrual cycle) in the remaining 20%. Of all cases, the direct physical cause of infertility or sterility can be reliably diagnosed approximately 90% of the time.

## CAUSES OF FEMALE INFERTILITY

Many different factors may prevent a woman from successfully conceiving. The most prevalent cause is some kind of infection. Infections cause inflammation of the tissues, which may lead to scars and adhesions in the uterus or in and around the Fallopian tubes or the ovaries. Syphilis or gonorrhea often leads to this result if untreated. Another generalized type of infection, termed pelvic inflammatory disease (PID), results when external bacteria gain entry to the reproductive tract, as sometimes occurs after an abortion or from the insertion of an IUD. Additionally, tuberculosis is a common cause of female infertility in those countries where this disease is still uncontrolled. Fortunately, the most common infections in women, trichomoniasis and monilia (yeast infection), do not cause infertility through direct damage to the reproductive system. They may, however, make intercourse painful and thus indirectly interfere with conception.

At times, conditions in the female reproductive tract may be hostile to sperm or may actually block the path of the sperm to the egg. In some cases, the vaginal secretions may be too highly acidic for the sperm to survive. Chronic cervical infection (cervicitis) may block the reproductive tract, as may thick, impenetrable uterine or cervical mucus and/or growths, polyps, or cysts. Another condition, a common cause of infertility, is endometriosis (see Chapter 7), in which the lining of the uterus (the endometrium) grows or spreads into the Fallopian tubes or ovaries. This tissue then reacts to normal hormonal fluctuations like the uterine endometrium, that is, it "bleeds" during menstruation. This process may lead to blockage of the Fallopian tubes or the development of scars or adhesions in the tubes or ovaries.

A variety of hormonal imbalances have also been implicated in female infertility. These conditions are, at times, difficult to diagnose because of the complex nature of the relationship between hormones and female reproductive capacity. Hormones from the ovaries, adrenals, hypothalamus, pituitary, and thyroid all play an important role and interact in a complex fashion. Hormonal problems may prevent a woman from ovulating or may cause irregular ovulation. Other hormonal imbalances can cause an inadequate build-up of uterine tissue, which normally occurs monthly in preparation to receive and nurture a fertilized egg. One complex disorder, caused partly by a hormonal imbalance, is Stein Leventhal syndrome. This disease is characterized by irregular or absent ovulation in addition to tough, fibrous growths surrounding the ovaries.

Many other conditions may cause fertility problems in the female. Congenital absence of the ovaries occurs in a few women. Other women may have a malformed or malpositioned uterus which interferes with reproductive capacity. The muscles around the cervix may be weak (an incompetent cervix) and may produce a miscarriage during late pregnancy. Finally, Menning (1977) suggests that poor diet, excessive alcohol or drug usage, and stress may also be related to infertility; the data in most of these areas, however, is only speculative.

## CAUSES OF MALE INFERTILITY

Several infections or diseases may cause fertility problems in the male. Venereal disease and tuberculosis may lead to damage and obstructions of the testicular duct system or the vas deferens. In over half of the post-puberty men who contract the mumps (see Chapter 5), the testes become inflamed. Depending on the severity of this inflammation and the effectiveness of treatment, in some men this process can lead to damage to the seminiferous tubules, where sperm are manufactured. Fortunately, very severe inflammation following a case of the mumps is usually limited to one testis; thus, the potential for fertility is usually retained. Other diseases which produce persistently high body temperatures can also decrease sperm production; however, recovery to normal levels of spermatogenesis usually occurs within a few months.

Excessive heat from causes other than abnormally high body temperature can also interfere with normal sperm production Effective spermatogenesis requires a temperature of 2.2 degrees Centigrade lower than normal body temperature. Sometimes male infants are born with undescended testes; that is, the testes remain situated internally in the lower groin. If the testes remain undescended up to the time spermatogenesis begins at puberty, the boy will be sterile. The reason for the sterility in this case is the fact that the temperature in undescended testes is body temperature, which, as noted above, is too high for effective spermatogenesis. Relatively simple surgery, usually performed on the boy before age eight, is an effective treatment in many cases. Even when the testes are normally positioned outside the body in the scrotum, however, excessive heat may still interfere with sperm production. Menning (1977) has reported one case in which a man was infertile because of excessive body heat caused by wearing an athletic supporter for long periods of time (he was apparently a fanatic tennis player). In such cases, normal spermatogenesis returns several months after elimination of the cause of excessive heat.

One relatively common cause of male infertility is a varicocele, a small varicose vein located near the testes. The process by which infertility results in these cases is unclear, although it has been suggested that the enlarged vein causes testicular temperatures to rise, thus affecting spermatogenesis. Surgery can restore fertility in approximately 80% of such cases.

Certain medications may reduce or otherwise interfere with normal spermatogenesis. Some antibacterial agents used to treat urinary tract infections, for example, cause a temporary reduction of sperm production. The drug methotrexate, used in the treatment of psoriasis, can produce irreversible chromosomal abnormalities of the germinal cells from which sperm are produced (Menning, 1977), leading to decreased fertility and an increased incidence of abnormal or deformed offspring.

## CAUSES OF INFERTILITY IN THE COUPLE

In approximately 20% of infertility cases, the problem lies with the couple as a sexual unit. Many of these difficulties may broadly be termed coital problems. For a variety of reasons (for example, health problems, work schedules, or general lack of interest), some couples engage in sexual intercourse relatively infrequently, thus lowering the probability of conception. Many of these couples miss the fertile period around the time of ovulation. Other couples may engage mostly in oral-genital activities or may use sexual positions in which conception is less likely to occur. The position with the highest likelihood of conception is that where the woman is on her back with her hips slightly raised: For optional opportunity for the sperm to reach the cervix, she should remain in this position for several minutes after ejaculation. Finally, several substances may be slightly spermicidal or may interfere with the sperm's movement toward the egg. Thus, the use of certain douches or lubricants such as petroleum jellies may interfere with fertility. In all of the above problems, simple counseling and education of the couple may produce conception.

One other major problem sometimes affects the couple in their attempts to conceive. Through continued exposure to semen, some women develop an immunological reaction to sperm. The woman builds up an antibody-based reaction to sperm, in the same way we all build immunity to diseases by contracting them or by vaccination. It is generally agreed that such a process does occur, and one estimate is that up to 20% of women build some degree of resistance to sperm (Menning, 1977). However, a considerable difference of opinion remains as to the specific mechanism by which such immunity may be developed, how to most accurately diagnose this condition, and whether or not the condition can be effectively treated. Currently, this is a very active area of research.

## DIAGNOSIS AND TREATMENT OF INFERTILITY

The diagnosis and treatment of infertility varies greatly. For some, this can be a relatively fast and inexpensive process. For most, however, the process requires several different tests administered over several months and may require major surgery and considerable expense. Typically, both members of the couple will be given specific diagnostic tests concurrently, and generally the tests begin with the safest and least complex procedure first. In the following section, we will describe the typical progression of diagnostic and treatment procedures. Some couples will learn the nature of their problem early in this sequence, while others may spend a total of several months in testing. In 10% of infertile couples, the specific reason for infertility, based on the knowledge we have today, will not be found (Menning, 1977).

Diagnosis begins by obtaining a detailed medical and sexual history of both partners. Specific illnesses which may have affected reproductive capacity may be discovered; if so, these findings may lead to the use of specific tests that confirm the causes of infertility fairly early in the diagnostic process. For example, a history of mumps during adulthood may lead to a semen analysis or a biopsy which may confirm that the infertility is related to testicular damage. While such a finding will undoubtedly create great psychological stress to the couple since it is tantamount to a diagnosis of sterility, early diagnosis such as this does eliminate the longer series of tests for both partners and subsequent suspense. The detailed sexual history may likewise indicate problems such as coital infrequency; here, simple behavioral changes may then produce conception, again eliminating the need for more prolonged and sometimes uncomfortable tests.

A complete physical exam is also undertaken as an early diagnostic procedure. Special attention is, of course, given to the reproductive organs. A complete pelvic exam is also done at this time for the woman.

The next procedure is for the physician to determine if the male's sperm are normal and if the female is ovulating. For a semen analysis, the man collects a semen specimen, preferably through masturbation. It is important that the entire ejaculation be collected in a clean container and that the specimen be delivered to the laboratory within one hour. The semen analysis (commonly called a "sperm count") is an investigation of several important factors: the number of million of sperm per cc. (the actual sperm "count"), their ability to move (motility), and whether or not their overall structure is normal.

The determination of ovulation in the woman may be measured in several different ways. Using a basal thermometer, the woman may chart her temperature over a period of several months (see the section above on Abstinence). At about the time of ovulation, her temperature will usually drop several tenths of a degree and then rise after the egg is released.

Another test for ovulation is the endometrial biopsy. This procedure, which causes discomfort in some women, may be performed in the physician's office. It can be conducted at any time between the point of presumed ovulation and the beginning of the next menstrual period. If ovulation has occurred, the endometrium will be under the influence of progesterone; if not, the influence of estrogen will be apparent in the tissues. With the woman lying in the typical position for a pelvic exam, her cervix is gently dilated. A small amount of the endometrium is then removed, and it is examined under a microscope to determine whether it is under the influence of progesterone.

Finally, the presence of ovulation can be determined by examination of the cervical mucus. Usually the mucus in and around the cervix is a thick, opaque substance. Around the time of ovulation, however, it changes into a clear, thinner solution. Thus, the mucus can be collected and examined for those changes which accompany ovulation.

If ovulation appears to be occuring and infertility is still present, several additional tests may be used. These are more expensive and cause more discomfort or pain than the tests previously described. One common problem in the normally ovulating female is that her egg never migrates from the ovaries through the Fallopian tubes where fertilization usually occurs. Diseases, infections, or scar tissue may actually block one or both of the tubes. One test to determine if the tubes are patent (open) is the tubal insufflation test. A special instrument is used to blow carbon dioxide through the cervical opening into the tubes. By using a stethoscope, the physician can determine whether the tubes are open and the gas is being passed through the tubes into the peritoneal cavity. Some physicians feel that this test may be unreliable and that it does not always tell whether either only one or both tubes are patent (Menning, 1977). For this reason, many specialists now prefer a special type of X-ray study, the hysterosalpingogram.

NAME  Jane Doe    ADDRESS  3560 N. MAIN ST  PHONE  723-6901

NORMAL OVULATORY CYCLE - BIPHASIC

| MONTH | FEBRUARY | MARCH |
|---|---|---|
| DATE | 7 8 9 10 11 12 13 14 15 16 17 18 19 20 21 22 23 24 25 26 27 28 | 1 2 3 4 5 6 7 8 9 10 11 12 13 |
| DAY OF CYCLE | 1 2 3 4 5 6 7 8 9 10 11 12 13 14 15 16 17 18 19 20 21 22 23 24 25 26 27 28 29 30 31 32 33 34 35 |

TEMPERATURE

MENSES ****

14 DAYS

OVULATION

MENSES ****

O: SEXUAL RELATIONS

D: DISCHARGE

A hysterosalpingogram is performed in an X-ray facility on an outpatient basis. Since some pain is involved, most physicians administer a mild analgesic before the procedure. A special dye is injected through the cervix, and a series of X-rays are then taken. If the tubes are patent, the course of the dye can be followed as it fills the uterus, flows through the Fallopian tubes, and spills out the ends of the tubes into the peritoneal cavity (the dye is later safely absorbed by the body).

Similar procedures are sometimes done in the male. If the semen analysis indicates any abnormality of the sperm, a small amount of tissue may be surgically removed from the testes and examined microscopically (a biopsy). X-ray studies can indicate if there are obstructions in the vas deferens or if there are other problems in the epididymis or seminal vesicles.

Another common diagnostic tool is the post-coital test. The couple is instructed to have intercourse (at around the time of ovulation). Within a few hours, the woman is then examined by her physician, and a sample of her cervical mucus is obtained and examined microscopically. The test can yield information about the number, motility, and structure of the sperm and about the quality of the cervical mucus.

If all tests are otherwise normal in the female or if tubal blockage has been indicated, a laparoscopy may be performed. This is usually an inpatient surgical procedure, requiring the woman to stay one to two days in the hospital. A small incision (about one inch) is made in the abdomen, and the laparoscope, an instrument through which the physician can observe the internal organs, is inserted. The physician can then carefully investigate all of the reproductive organs; endometriosis of the tubes, scars, or adhesions are often diagnosed in this manner. The physician may also inject a dye into the reproductive system and visually check to see if it passes out the ends of the Fallopian tubes, thus indicating whether they are patent. Final decisions regarding surgery to attempt correction of infertility are usually made only after a laparoscopy has been performed.

In those cases where the exact cause of infertility has been determined, there are a variety of medical and surgical techniques which may be employed in an attempt to restore fertility. In cases of a varicocele in men, a part of the spermatic vein can be ligated, or tied, thereby cutting off the blood supply to the varicocele and often resulting in significant improvement in both sperm count and motility. Obstructions in the ducts of the epididymis or vas deferens can also sometimes be corrected surgically, although the success rate of these procedures is highly variable and individualized.

A variety of procedures may be used to treat infertility in the female. Overly acid cervical secretions which create a hostile environment for sperm may be neutralized by simply douching with the proper substance. Other cervical conditions, such as chronic infections, are often successfully treated with medication. In other cases where some type of cervical barrier continues to prevent the migration of the sperm, a freshly masturbated semen specimen may be obtained from the male. The physician can then artificially instill the sperm through the cervical opening. In cases of endometriosis, hormones which prevent menstruation may be prescribed over a period of several months; improvement has been seen in a large proportion of such cases (Menning, 1977).

For women who are not ovulating, several new fertility drugs have been developed in recent years. Clomid stimulates increased FSH and LH production in the pituitary. These natural hormones then stimulate an ovum in the ovaries to ripen and be released in the normal fashion. Around 70% of women treated with Clomid will ovulate, and about 40% will become pregnant (Menning, 1977). Pergonal, produced from gonadotropins in the urine of post-menopausal women, is an even more powerful drug which stimulates an ovum to ripen; an injection of a substance called human chorionic gonadotropin must be given to then stimulate the release of the ovum. One risk of Pergonal administration is hyperstimulation of the ovaries, leading to multiple conceptions. Approximately 20% of the pregnancies occurring after Pergonal treatment are multiple, with most being twins (Menning, 1977).

Several surgical procedures are becoming common practice in treating female infertility. A dilatation and curettage (D and C) may be performed to remove polyps or excess uterine lining; this procedure sometimes provides an improved chance of pregnancy. In cases where ovulation has not been successfully stimulated by drug treatment, a wedge resection may be performed. In this procedure, a small, wedge-shaped piece of tissue is surgically removed from each ovary. The reason this technique stimulates ovulation is, however, unknown. Menning (1977) has reported success rates ranging up to 80% after a wedge resection. In cases where there are adhesions surrounding the ovaries or tubes or where the tubes are blocked internally, a tuboplasty is often performed. This procedure is considered major surgery and is indicated when all other reasons for infertility have been ruled out or other treatments have been unsuccessful. In a tuboplasty, scar tissue and adhesions are surgically removed. Often the tubes will be surgically opened to remove internal blockages. The success of this procedure is highly variable, depending upon the site, degree of blockage, and severity of the adhesions. It is not uncommon for this technique to be unsuccessful in restoring fertility, since in many individuals scar tissue or adhesions may quickly reform after surgery. Additionally, women who undergo these procedures have an increased risk of an ectopic pregnancy (a pregnancy in the tube rather than in the uterus). This occurs in 5% to 10% of women who become pregnant after a tuboplasty (Menning, 1977).

## SUMMARY

In this chapter we have reviewed a variety of issues and questions related to birth control and infertility. Throughout, we have emphasized the importance of recognizing that complete control over the process of conception is gradually becoming a reality for the first time in the history of human sexual relationships. The questions raised by these technological advances are indeed profound and revolutionary. Essentially, of course, the new information now available can provide women and men with the potential to plan for conception in a responsible and enlightened manner, rather than as a result of haphazard occurrence as was true in the past. Beyond these influences, however, this development has important and obvious implications for changing the traditional role of woman as "childbearer," for impacting on family relationships, and for ultimately affecting broad sociocultural issues, such as population control. Few individuals concern themselves with the broader philosophical implications associated with the technology of birth control. The history of humankind suggests, however, that the ethical questions that underlie each new advance in controlling our lives and destinies should be carefully considered by a responsible society.

# Chapter 9

## Other Dimensions in Sexual Behavior

# INTRODUCTION

Perhaps in no other area of human functioning do we reveal our versatility and ingenuity more than in our sexual behavior. The variety of practices in which humans have engaged in response to their sexual needs is limited only by their imagination. We have already described the more or less standard sexual behaviors that have been commonly defined by most members of our society as "normal" sex. There are, however, an almost infinite number of other sexual dimensions and "variations" that are also manifested by many members of our society over varying periods of time. As we saw in earlier chapters, some of these other behaviors have been regarded with misunderstanding, if not suspicion and outright hostility. Clearly, however, the changing climate of sexual opinion and the emergence of a more permissive sexual code provide us with a different standard for gauging these other dimensions in sexual behavior. In this chapter we will review those practices that represent solitary sex, or autoerotic activities, and several alternative dimensions of partner-related sex.

# AUTOEROTICISM

## MASTURBATION

Masturbation is another of the many sexual areas that are characterized by myths, ignorance, and paradox. Despite the commonplace nature of such behaviors, even so-called sexually liberated individuals are often embarrassed by discussions of masturbation. As we saw in earlier chapters, no doubt our contemporary attitudes toward masturbation are still influenced by religious doctrines which consider such practices to be sinful and immoral and by unverified Victorian medical claims that masturbation caused illness, insanity, and death. With the publication of the Kinsey reports, in which 92% of the men and 58% of the women interviewed reported having masturbated, the traditional antimasturbatory ethic began to change. Subsequent studies and social influences have further strengthened the position of those who questioned the older ethic. Recent studies, for example, suggest that the percentage of men and women who masturbate is greater than that reported by Kinsey (Hunt, 1974); the claim that masturbation can be physiologically harmful has been disproved (Gagnon, 1977); and sex authorities and therapists are now advocating masturbation as a means of enhancing body awareness, improving sexual gratification in general, and helping to overcome sexual dysfunctions

Despite these advances, traditional antimasturbatory values still prevail. In 1976, for example, an official statement from the Vatican maintained that masturbation is a seriously disordered act, despite "the force of certain arguments of a biological and philosophical nature" (Strong et al., 1978). Moreover, Masters and Johnson report that they are still frequently asked by physicians if masturbation causes insanity. Finally, a 1976 study analyzing the attitudes of male and female college students who reported having masturbated revealed the following (Gagnon, 1977):

40% thought that masturbation was immoral
10% thought that masturbation impaired study habits
20% thought that masturbation would affect their physical and mental health
50% thought that masturbation was immature
10% throught that masturbation would affect later sexual competence

Thus, although traditional views regarding the alleged dangers of masturbation are changing in the light of new knowledge and a new sexual ethic, there is still a climate of disapproval related to such behavior.

In terms of the development and acquisition of masturbatory behavior, it is probably the case that the final form of masturbation in the adult is the end result of a long series of experiences starting in infancy. In Chapter 7, we saw how early masturbatory behavior was a natural part of the psychosexual development in both sexes. Although such activities are often interpreted as a generalized form of self-stimulation, rather than as a specific sex act, there is little doubt that both young boys and young girls often experience orgasmiclike reactions during these episodes. With increasing age, the form, pattern, and frequency of masturbation changes in the light of parental attitudes, peer group influences, and general sexual knowledge. Adolescence brings with it a number of influences that further shape the form and patterns of masturbation. For boys, with the ability to achieve a clearly defined orgasm, masturbatory activities take on a more ritualized character with a beginning, an intermediate state, and an end (ejaculation). Peer group contacts may provide instruction and facilitate the acquisition of masturbatory behavior, especially in those elements of American society where adolescent masturbation is acknowledged. Male teenage jargon is replete with descriptive statements which represent direct recognition of masturbation, although in a somewhat disparaging tone. Further cultural refinements typically enter at this time. Thus, a male teenager may include pictures of nude women and/or engage in a sexual fantasy in his masturbation ritual. By the late teens and early twenties, those masturbatory practices that maximize stimulation are fairly well established for most males.

The situation is quite different for females. At every age more males masturbate than do females (or at least are more willing to report this activity), and this numerical difference persists into the later years. There is, however, an increase in the number of women who first start to masturbate during adulthood, in contrast to males. Moreover, Hunt (1974) reports that, while the frequency of male masturbation declines dramatically at certain later age levels, the frequency of female masturbation remains fairly stable through the middle ages and then gradually decreases in the later years.

Many men and women continue to masturbate even after they become involved in long-term relationships, for example, marriage, although masturbatory activities may occur, in some cases, as part of intercourse or other partner-related sex routines. Also, the incidence of masturbation among coupled individuals is probably influenced by inaccessibility of the partner. Thus, illness, physical separation, disagreements, fear of discovery by others, etc.—all may affect the rate of masturbation in partner relationships.

Most of what is known about actual masturbatory activities is the result of investigations by the Kinsey group and by Masters and Johnson (1966). The following description represents a summary of their findings.

Insofar as techniques are concerned, men and women masturbate by means of a number of genital stimulation procedures, although the variety of techniques is much greater in women than in men. The most frequently reported male technique involves circling the hand around the shaft of the penis followed by gentle stroking which increases in speed, intensity, and pressure as orgasm approaches. Many men discontinue stimulation at the point of orgasm. The entire sequence is usually accomplished as quickly as possible and takes from about one to two minutes after onset.

Although other male techniques have also been reported, for example, lying face down and rubbing the penis against an ob-

further complicated by the fact that female masturbation is, in some respects, considered by some to be even more deviant than male masturbation. It is certainly less well understood, even by females themselves. Until very recently, learning how to masturbate for women was not only impaired by this negative social climate but also by our general ignorance of what forms of stimulation are most satisfying to women. Even today, the topic is rarely discussed by women in the same manner that male masturbation is by men. For all of these reasons, fewer women, if they had not already masturbated as children, initiated the process of sexual self-discovery. If they did, they may have focused their efforts on the vagina, where the popular misconceptions suggested they should. Consequently, only a minority of women learned to become competent in masturbation. The significance of this observation is underscored by Kinsey's report that women who had masturbated to orgasm were more likely to enjoy intercourse than those who had had no masturbatory experiences, thus suggesting the significance of

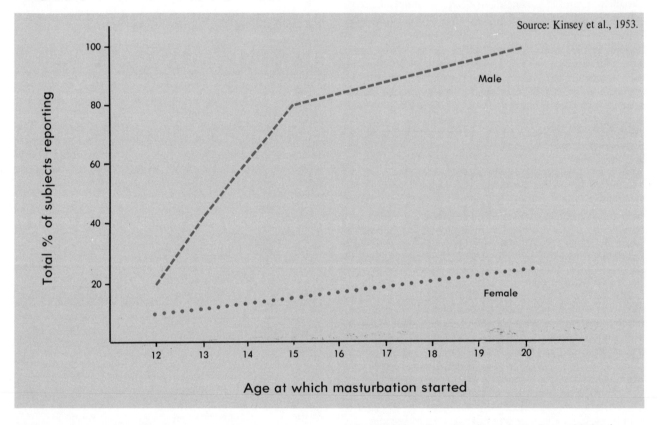

ject in order to simulate intercourse, apparently only a few men use more than just one favored technique. As suggested above, the final form for any one individual is usually the result of a series of masturbatory experiences that extended over a number of years.

Recently, vendors of sex paraphernalia have marketed a variety of mechanical rubber and vinyl devices for autoerotic activities that are ostensibly designed to serve as substitutes for manual stimulation, intercourse, and even fellatio. It remains to be determined whether such products will achieve any measure of popularity in our society.

As for female techniques, the situation is quite different and

such experiences for other dimensions of sexual behavior.

For those women who do masturbate, however, it seems reasonable to assume that a learning process similar to that for males gradually refined the technique in the direction of maximum pleasure. Manual stimulation of the clitoris and labia minora appear to be the preferred technique for many women. Typically these structures are rhythmically stroked or pressed with a gentle motion. Most women concentrate on the clitoral shaft and, as the glans retracts under continued stimulation, manipulate the hood and the glans together. As in the male, slow, gentle, and deliberate movements become gradually more intense until orgasm is reached, but, in contrast to the typical male pattern, most women continue stimulation through orgasm.

In addition to the above techniques, a substantial number of women report that manual stimulation of other parts of the anatomy, such as the breasts, thighs, torso, legs, etc., also provides erotic stimulation. Still others report that certain forms of muscle tension, in particular rhythmic thigh pressure to stimulate the clitoris, is also pleasurable and, under certain circumstances, produces orgasm.

Insertion of objects into the vagina as a masturbatory technique is evidently more of a male fantasy than an actual method employed by many women. Electrical vibrators used to stimulate the clitoral area have become a popular aid to female masturbation in recent years. These devices as an aid to stimulation are a far cry from the classical dildos inevitably shaped like a penis, under the mistaken assumption that such objects produced optimal stimulation.

It is interesting to note that virtually no studies have attempted to compare the quality of solitary sex with partner-related sex, yet, here again, important findings might emerge. Conventional wisdom holds that, given the option, the individual would prefer partner-related sex as being more pleasurable or satisfying. Yet, many women report experiencing more frequent and more intense orgasms (although not necessarily more "totally satisfying" orgasms) through masturbation than as a result of partner sex. Similarly, some men may actually prefer masturbation to partner sex on the grounds that under such circumstances they need not be concerned with "pressures to perform" or the need to delay ejaculation. Clearly, then, the relationships between partner sex and solitary sex are still in need of clarification.

In brief, then, the current climate of opinion with regard to masturbation suggests that such behavior is still generally considered to be, at worst, degrading and immoral and, at best, immature. As we shall see in subsequent chapters, however, there is some reason to believe that learning how or being able to masturbate has an important and beneficial impact on other dimensions of sexuality.

## Common Fantasy Themes During masturbation

| Theme | % Males Reporting | % Females Reporting |
|---|---|---|
| 1. Intercourse with a stranger | 47 | 21 |
| 2. Sex with more than one person at the same time | 33 | 18 |
| 3. Doing sexual things not done in reality | 19 | 28 |
| 4. Being forced to have sex | 10 | 19 |
| 5. Forcing someone to have sex | 13 | 3 |
| 6. Homosexual behavior | 7 | 11 |

(Source: Hunt, M. Sexual Behavior in the 1970's. Chicago, *Playboy Press,* 1974)

## FANTASY

By definition, fantasy constitutes a solitary activity since the mental images that make up the fantasy remain private until and when they are shared with others. Of the many different wish fulfillment fantasies that most people report (for example, achieving great wealth, getting straight A's, becoming a star athlete, winning a beauty contest, etc.), sexual fantasies are among the most prominent. These fantasies may include anything from undressing an erotically stimulating individual to recalling a prior sexual experience. Obviously, the content of a sexual fantasy is limited only by the fantasist's imagination. A fantasy can be a brief, fleeting image, or a detailed elaborate sequence of events. It can have little impact on the individual or produce a major physiological and psychological reaction. Some people, for example, report achieving orgasm solely as the result of fantasy. The finding that a substantial number of heterosexuals report homosexual fantasies and *vice versa* once again highlights the complex nature of human sexuality.

In reviewing the state of knowledge regarding fantasy activities, it is important to recall the limitations of sex survey research described in Chapter 4, since most of what is known about erotic fantasies is the result of these efforts. Briefly recapitulating what was said in this connection, the analysis of sexual fantasies in men and women typically involves retrospective accounts in limited samples of individuals. The extent to which valid conclusions can be applied to most people on the basis of such information is open to question.

Many men report experiencing a number of sexual fantasies (for example, having intercourse with an attractive woman) throughout the day. Although women apparently are less genitally oriented in their sexual fantasies than men, there is little doubt they share similar frequent experiences. This has led to what some writers have termed the "two levels of discourse" that characterize many human interactions, that is, the overt level and the covert, or fantasy, level. The two-levels phenomenon was beautifully illustrated in Woody Allen's movie *Annie Hall.* The female and male protagonists conversed, or interacted, with each other in a conventional manner (overt level). At the same time they alternately interspersed their speech or behavior with a dramatization or verbalization to the audience of their fantasies about the other person (covert level).

There are, of course, certain standard sexual fantasy themes that are evidently shared by many men and that represent perhaps the acme of sexual wish fulfillment. These include such themes as having sex with several women simultaneously, having sex with a sexually-aggressive woman who takes the initiative and complies with the man's every desire, and, for the middle-aged man, having sex with a much younger woman. Prostitutes, pornographers, and sex purveyors in general have catered to these sexual themes. As suggested above, female sexual fantasies are generally more highly individualized and less genitally oriented than male themes.

The complexity, vividness, and detail of a sexual fantasy may be enhanced if it occurs in connection with actual sexual behavior. Almost all men and at least two-thirds of all women who report having masturbated, for example, fantasized when

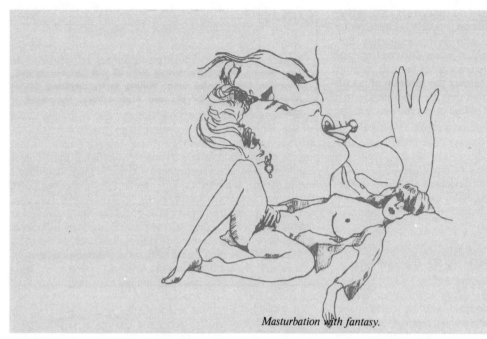

*Masturbation with fantasy.*

engaged in such behavior. Similarly, a substantial number of men and women also report having fantasies during partner sex. Again, the content of these fantasies is as wide-ranging and variable as the number of individuals who report them (Kinsey, 1948).

The association between fantasy and masturbation appears to be particularly strong, perhaps because the tendencies toward both of these behaviors emerge at about the same time in our psychosexual development. Thus, the adolescent boy or girl acquires the ability to construct organized and integrated fantasy themes at about the same time he or she has entered the first stages of mature sexual development. A sexually stimulating experience, for example, looking up a girl's dress, or catching a glimpse of a nude woman, may then be re-created in the boy's fantasy and provoke masturbation. The orgasm that accompanies the behavior serves to reinforce the fantasy. Later, with more sexual experience and maturity, the fantasy-masturbation ritual may become more sophisticated, involving elaborate sexual encounters (such as orgies) and other sexual acts (such as fellatio and cunnilingus).

Although women, no doubt, share a similar development in fantasy-masturbation relationships, as suggested above, most authorities report female fantasies are more individualized, of a more passive nature, and more romantically or emotionally oriented than male fantasies. These statements must be accepted with caution because of the difficulties involved in establishing general conclusions. Nancy Friday (1973), for example, in *My Secret Garden,* suggests that female fantasies are more lusty and active than had previously been reported. Obviously, then, female erotic fantasies remain a poorly understood phenomenon.

Although the study of sexual fantasies is still at the beginning stages, one thing that seems reasonably clear is that the differences in sexual themes reported by men and by women are related to those differences in socialization that emphasize different sex roles and different behaviors for males and females

(Barclay, 1973). Many authorities also argue that fantasies serve a useful function in that they enable us to prepare or "rehearse" for the actual events, they enrich our experiences, and they may even serve as a constructive incentive in achieving goals. When, however, the distinction between fantasy and reality breaks down, and the individual begins to react to the fantasy as a substitute for the real world, serious problems can arise. Thus, as long as we recognize these experiences as products of our imagination, and enjoy them for their own sake, our fantasies allow us to envision alternative ways of expressing our individuality and our sexuality.

## NOCTURNAL ORGASMS

Almost every man has experienced, at some point in his lifetime, an erotic dream that culminated in orgasm ("wet dream"). Such experiences occur most often during the teen-age years and in early adulthood, but a substantial number of both older and married men also report occasional nocturnal orgasms (also called nocturnal emissions). The incidence of nocturnal orgasms among women is apparently lower than it is among men, although about two-thirds of all women surveyed in various sex studies report having had dreams of sexual content (Kinsey, et al, 1953). There is a small percentage of both men and women who report having nocturnal orgasms as frequently as once a week.

Of all the socioeconomic groups represented in the Kinsey studies, college-attending males revealed the highest rate of nocturnal orgasms. Some authorities suggest that this finding may be related to the longstanding belief that nocturnal orgasms serve a "release" function. From this point of view, nocturnal orgasms provide for a release following a night of heavy petting without intercourse, or a sustained period of abstinence, in view of the fact that such experiences are relatively common for males attending college.

The climate of opinion regarding nocturnal orgasms has been less hostile than that of masturbation, possibly because nocturnal orgasms are considered to be of an involuntary nature. Both men and women occasionally report being disturbed by such events, especially women who are unaware of the fact that such experiences are not unusual. Whatever the function of nocturnal orgasms, it seems quite clear that they are a harmless form of sexual behavior and no index of sexual or psychological disturbance.

## OTHER DIMENSIONS OF PARTNER-RELATED SEX

Although there are an infinite number of departures from conventional partner-related sexuality, several examples have captured the attention of various authorities. In this connection, we will describe extramarital sex, group sex, and celibacy.

### EXTRAMARITAL SEX

Conventional adultery has a history as old as monogamy and since this issue has been discussed in previous chapters, here we will focus our attention on extramarital sex in the context of a "permitted" relationship (that is, acknowledged and accepted by both partners). Although "consenting adultery" is certainly not a new phenomenon, it has recently attracted the attention of social scientists and sexual authorities.

Sexual activity outside of an existing marriage relationship with the knowledge and consent of the spouse has been termed "consensual adultery" by Smith and Smith (1973). In such cases, partners engage in extramarital sex either individually ("open marriage," non-monogamous contract) or as a couple. Smith and Smith designate the latter case as "co-marital sex," to indicate its incorporation into the marriage relationship. It is also more popularly and perhaps pejoratively known as "swinging."

### How Swingers Meet

S-225
"Married couple, middle thirties. Wife 37 - 25 - 36, husband muscular, Los Angeles area. Willing to try anything. Interested in French, Greek, and Arab culture. No single men."

Much of the ad is self-explanatory. The references to culture hardly represents a hunger for international aesthetics. They represent a code: French culture signifies that the couple likes oral sex, the Greek allusion means that they are amenable to anal intercourse, and the Arab feature points to an appreciation of sado-masochistic practices.

(From: Murstein, B.I. *Law, sex and marriage through the ages.* New York: Springer publishing co., 1974)

A great deal has been written about such behavior; however, few of these efforts represent a scientific approach. One exception is a recent study by Gilmartin and Kusisto (1976). In this investigation, the personal and social characteristics of a group of middle class swingers was compared with that of an appropriate control group. Contrary to popular opinion, no meaningful differences between the two groups were found in terms of personal happiness. Some differences, however, emerged in terms of personal characteristics. Thus, swingers were less influenced by social control and were less concerned about conformity than was the control group. Smith and Smith (1973) also suggest that swingers differ from conventional partners in that they have engaged in a greater degree of premarital sexual experiences. They further suggest that consensual adultery may not necessarily impair the marital relationship, as is commonly assumed, but rather provides opportunities for individual growth and the satisfaction of needs that are not present in the traditional marriage relationship. Clearly, however, such

arguments remain in the realm of speculation and opinion in the absence of scientific documentation.

Given the strong interest in the topic of extramarital sex by most individuals, it is indeed unfortunate that so little substantive knowledge in this area has been forthcoming. Perhaps one of the most interesting issues raised by the emergence of such activities as consensual adultery and swinging is their relationship to the traditional double standard. The implicit acknowledgment of the male's "right" to engage in extramarital affairs while condemning the adultress is, of course, a phenomenon virtually all societies have struggled with since the dawn of civilization. Again, perhaps, such changes in sexual conduct have a variety of complicated implications and consequences that remain to be determined.

## GROUP SEX

Another topic of mystery and intrigue pertains to group sex, which includes anything from two or more couples to an orgy. Very little of a scientific nature has been established in this area and, therefore, we are restricted to self-reports. It is doubtful that a group sex pattern represents the kind of durable commitment reflected by such terms as heterosexuality and even homosexuality. Although there may be a small number of individuals who regularly participate in such events, group sex appears to be of a transient and episodic nature engaged in by a relatively few individuals perhaps only a few times. On such occasions, the individual may practice a variety of sexual techniques fulfilling the role of the heterosexual, the homosexual, the bisexual, or any combination of these orientations.

## CELIBACY

One additional departure from a conventional sexual relationship warrants discussion in this chapter, and here we refer to celibacy: the voluntary abstention from all partner-related sexual activities, although autoerotic behavior may continue (or perhaps increase) during a celibacy period. Celibacy, of course, has traditionally been practiced as part of a religious commitment, for example, by Catholic priests and nuns who are committed to abstaining from all sexual activities. In our discussion here, however, we are focusing on those individuals who have opted for a celibate status after having led an active sexual life, and despite the availability of partner-related sex.

Unfortunately, little is known about such examples of celibacy, inasmuch as this is a topic that has been virtually ignored by sex investigators. Most of what is know about celibacy is the result of personal observations by individuals who have adopted a celibate status; and, as we have suggested in earlier chapters, such information may be of limited scientific value.

The reasons for and the length of a celibate status apparently vary considerably. Most such decisions seem to occur after a dramatic change in a previously durable relationship, whereupon the individual's first priority now is to reassess his or her general life circumstances before returning to a sexually active status.

In other cases, sexual priorities may become less important than other concerns, for example, work on creative projects. Thus, a period of celibacy may serve as an opportunity to shift energy and affirmation to the self and to evaluate one's own needs and potentials independent of sexually determined priorities. It can also serve as a time to consider what one wishes to obtain from and contribute to a relationship.

For some individuals, celibacy may provide an opportunity to explore the dimensions of human relationships without sex. The need for physical contact, intimacy, and affection that are usually associated with sex can be satisfied in other settings, for example, with family and friends.

No data is available to determine what percentage of celibates engage in autoeroticism, although it is perhaps reasonable to assume that many do. In such instances, celibacy represents an opportunity to explore one's sexuality without the "distraction" of a partner.

Obviously, there are many questions related to celibacy that remain to be answered. It would seem to be of some importance to determine the incidence of celibacy in men and in women, the reasons for such decisions, how celibacy impacts on other sexual and social areas of human functioning, and how well the individual adjusts psychologically and sexually after a celibacy period.

## SUMMARY

Our understanding of the other dimensions in sexuality that were discussed in this chapter has lagged even further behind the study of conventional sex because of the stringent taboos that continue to operate in these areas. It is of interest to note that even the increased public acknowledgment of sexual topics still reflects this negative attitude. The term orgasm, for example, now appears in the popular media, but such references almost inevitably are used in conjunction with partner-related sex and rarely in the context of masturbation. Given the apparently much higher incidence of autoeroticism than of partner-related sex in a typical individual's lifetime (especially for males), it is probably the case that more orgasms are experienced in the former context than in the latter context.

Confusion and ignorance also characterize our understanding of such sexual dimensions as extramarital sex, group sex, and celibacy. What little information has been accumulated represents, again, a challenge to conventional wisdom. The finding that "swinging" does not necessarily impair personal adjustment, for example, is certainly incompatible with traditional morality. Of course, such observations require additional research before they can be accepted as valid findings.

Whatever the course of future investigation, it appears that each new dimension of sexuality that is investigated introduces new and challenging perspectives that remain to be clarified by further study.

# Chapter 10

## Variations in Sexual Orientation

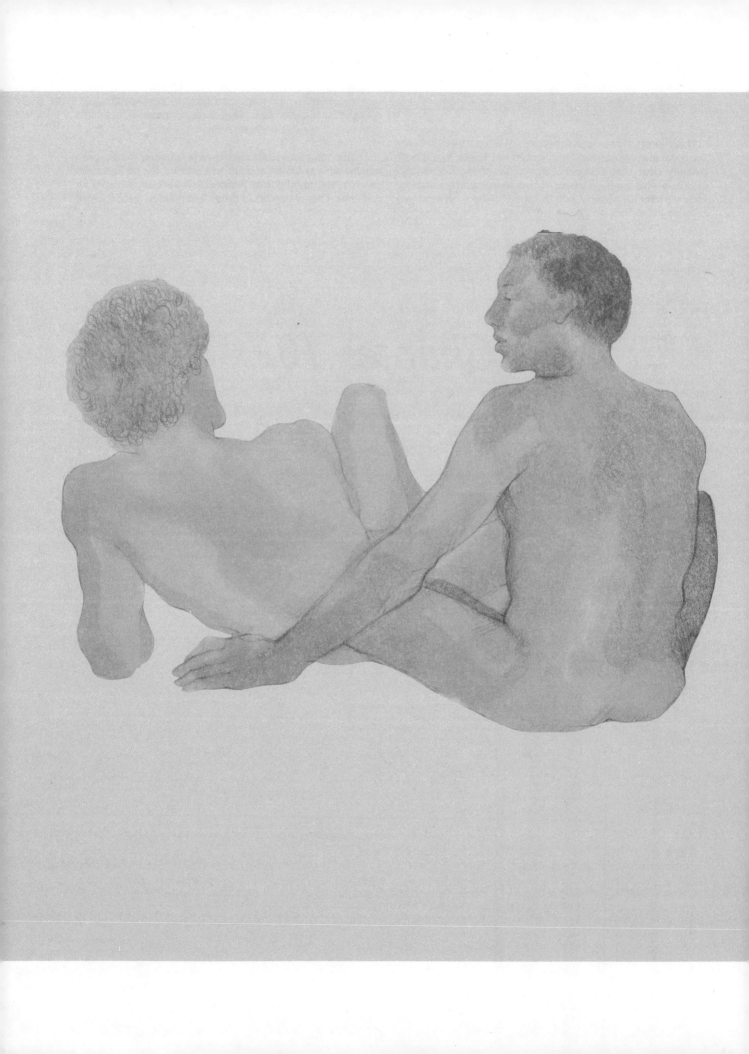

## INTRODUCTION

In addition to the several dimensions of sexuality beyond conventional intercourse that are described in Chapter 9, it is now patently clear that a substantial number of individuals also engage in what might be termed variations in sexual orientation. Here we refer to those patterns of sexual behavior between two or more individuals which are different from the heterosexual pattern, specifically, homosexuality, bisexuality, and transsexuality. Again, as we have seen, tradition has regarded these practices with hostility. Until very recently even the most progressive and enlightened of individuals considered these practices to be departures, at the least, from so-called normal sex, if not outright perversions. Increasingly, however, our sexual morality is reassessing some of these traditional values. The inclusion of these topics here as a separate chapter under the heading of variations reflects these recent changes in our sexual standards. Thus, for example, homosexuality has been traditionally regarded as abnormal behavior. As we shall see in this chapter, however, there is a growing sentiment in favor of regarding homosexuality as a variation in sexual orientation, rather than as abnormal behavior per se.

## HOMOSEXUALITY

It is an interesting commentary on our sexual values that probably as much has been written about homosexuality as about heterosexuality. Unfortunately, virtually all of these efforts, that is, writings about homosexuality, emerged from a background of ignorance and prejudice and were designed to bolster the moral superiority of heterosexuality, thereby reinforcing the myths that have evolved over the centuries. It has been only within the last few decades that objective scientific investigations into homosexuality have been conducted; and it has been only within the last 15 to 20 years that we have begun to derive an understanding of the physiological, psychological, and sociological dimensions of homosexuality to replace the pejorative and demogogic approaches of the past.

Kinsey (1948), of course, broke the ice with his challenging finding that a substantial percentage of primarily heterosexual men and women also acknowledged having had at least one earlier homosexual experience. More recently, with Laud Humphreys' (1970) sociological study of the manner in which some homosexuals use public facilities to contact other homosexuals, Bell and Weinberg's (1978) analysis of the diversity of homosexual life styles, and Masters and Johnson's (1979) recent report on the actual sexual behavior of homosexuals (Masters and Johnson, 1979), the veil of ignorance is slowly lifting.

There are also other forces at work which have impacted on the changing climate of opinion. The arts and the popular media continue to present new and challenging perspectives on homosexuality, some of which are clearly at odds with our traditional stereotypes. Several years ago, a popular Broadway play entitled "The Boys in the Band" later translated into a successful motion picture, offered a penetrating insight into the lives of several male homosexuals that was at considerable variance from our conventional wisdom. Similarly, a number of television programs have provided newer perspectives into homosexuality either through comedy or drama (for example, *A Certain Summer*) or through documentaries.

Finally, homosexuals themselves have taken the initiative in a number of ways in an attempt to eliminate the prejudice, inequality, and hostility that homosexuals have encountered for centuries. Thus, a number of prominent political leaders, entertainers, educators, and other citizens, both male and female, have "come out of the closet" (known as coming out) in recent years and acknowledged their homosexuality. Organizations such as the Gay Liberation Front and the Gay Activist Alliance project an open and forceful image in their efforts to achieve social, political, and economic equality in our society.

These advances have been accompanied by a gradual shift in our traditional hostility toward homosexuality. Hunt's survey (1974), for example, revealed that about half of his respondents favored the elimination of penalties for homosexual behavior between consenting adults, a far higher number than any previously reported by similar surveys. Men, in general, are less tolerant of homosexuality than are women, and they are more hostile toward male homosexuality than toward female homosexuality. Although Hunt's sample may not be representative of the public at large (see Chapter 4), it is of some importance to note that younger respondents were more liberal in their attitudes toward homosexuals than were older respondents

Nevertheless, it is a mistake to assume that these newer values signify any radical transformation of attitudes and beliefs. A substantial number of individuals in our society continue to regard homosexuals with great fear and suspicion, if not outright hostility. In the same year that Hunt reported the results of his survey, Weinberg and Williams (1974) found that 90% of their respondents continued to regard homosexuality as either an illness, a crime, or a sin. Furthermore, about 10% of the homosexuals surveyed in this study accepted the 'illness" viewpoint themselves. Finally, many people, homosexuals as well as heterosexuals, believe that homosexuality is something a person is "born with" and that once the behavior is acquired, it cannot be changed (Weinberg and Williams, 1974).

We can determine the validity of these and other beliefs about homosexuality by referring to the studies that bear on these issues. One limitation of the research in this area, however, is that most investigators have focused on male homosexuality. Consequently, whatever conclusions can be derived may not necessarily relate to female homosexuality.

### WHAT IS HOMOSEXUALITY?

Definitions of homosexuality differ depending on whether the focus is on behavior, attitudes, or such global concepts as preference and orientation. There are those individuals who claim that a homosexual is anyone who has ever experienced any sexual attraction toward a member of the same sex, a definition that would probably include the vast majority of individuals in our society. About one-half of all men and one-third of all women surveyed in various studies, for example, report having been sexually attracted to a member of the same sex at some point in their lives (McCary, 1973).

In recognition of the many different definitions of homosexuality and the wide variety of sexual orientations ranging from exclusively heterosexual to exclusively homosexual, Kinsey (1948) focused his definition on actual behavior by characterizing individuals in terms of their homosexual — heterosexual experiences on a scale of from 0 to 6. A rating of 0 meant that a man or woman had never had any homosexual experiences, a rating of 3 indicated those with an equal number of heterosexual and homosexual experiences, and a rating of 6 signified those whose sexual experiences were exclusively homosexual. (This technique was the one used by Masters and Johnson.) Those who fall at the low end of the range constitute the heterosexuals, the intermediate individuals were defined as bisexuals, and those with a rating of 5 or 6 the homosexuals. According to these criteria, about 8% of American males and 2% of American females at the age of 20 are primarily or exclusively homosexual (McIntosh, 1968). Other authorities estimate the rate of exclusively homosexual males to be around 2% to 3% of the population (Gagnon, 1977). Whatever the actual proportion, certainly the absolute number of homosexual men and women in our society is quite substantial. Some communities, of course, have a much higher proportion of homosexuals than do others, owing, no doubt, to a relatively favorable social, political, and economic climate. In any event, we will continue the use of these categories, that is, exclusively heterosexual, exclusively homosexual, and bisexual, in the discussion that follows.

Even a brief introduction to the issue of homosexuality immediately reveals one overriding fact: homosexuality is as variable as heterosexuality. Just as so-called straight (heterosexual) people differ in their sexual styles, roles, practices, and values, so, too, do homosexuals (referred to nonderogatorily as gay). Homosexuality is engaged in by individuals in every socioeconomic level, every ethnic and religious category, and every educational level. Some homosexuals exhibit a conventional public image, maintaining a job and a married life, while engaging in their homosexual preferences in secret (so-called closet homosexuals). In fact, according to Kinsey (1948), a substantial number of the married men in his survey continued to engage in homosexual activities after marriage; and 1% of this group were exclusively homosexual. Others dress in, act in, and, in general, adopt a more stereotyped homosexual life style, thereby openly acknowledging their sexual orientation. Still others shift from one life style to another from time to time.

As best as can be determined, closet, or covert, homosexuals make up the largest percentage of the total population of homosexuals. However, because the overt homosexual is so much more obvious, the public tends to equate all homosexuals with this life style. However, it is inaccurate to identify any one particular gay life style. Thus, the majority of homosexuals have probably never attended a gay bar or adopted a style of attire that could be called gay or worked in a career stereotypically associated with homosexuality. If these stereotypes exist at all, they are probably relevant to only some small percentage of overt homosexuals.

There are those homosexuals to whom their homosexuality is a matter of secondary importance. That is, their sexual orientation is of less importance than other aspects of their life style, for example, career, business, physical and recreational pursuits, and general life style. The impact of their sexual preferences emerges only on those occasions when sex is desired. There are others, however, to whom their homosexual identification is of considerable importance and dictates many of the other dimensions of their life style. Thus, their choice of job, place of residence, physical, recreational, and leisure pursuits, etc. are all more or less expressions of their homosexuality.

For all of these reasons, broad sweeping generalizations about homosexuality must be regarded with extreme caution.

## THE CAUSES OF HOMOSEXUALITY

What determines an individual's sexual preference or orientation? This is a highly significant issue and the subject of a considerable amount of speculation. Most of this speculation centers on the origination of homosexuality, to the neglect of the parallel question of what causes heterosexuality.

Historically, a great deal of effort has been invested in trying to learn the causes of homosexuality. Unfortunately, most of these investigations have been formulated under the assumption that homosexuality is inferior to heterosexuality. Thus, these efforts frequently took the form of uncovering the "quirk" or "infirmity" or "disease" that was responsible for this so-called perversion of normal behavior. It has only been quite recently that a more objective study of the causes of homosexuality has emerged. Generally speaking, investigations into the determinants of homosexuality have focused on three theories: heredity, hormonal functions, and social-psychological processes.

The earliest search for the "quirk" of homosexuality focused on the genes. This line of inquiry has continued up to the present time and still has numerous proponents, as witnessed by the fact that a substantial number of homosexuals themselves believe that they are "born" homosexuals. Despite the firmly held belief in this argument, no substantial evidence in support of the heredity position has ever been forthcoming. Conversely, a number of observations are actually incompatible with this argument (Miller, 1968). That is not to say that heredity can be totally discounted as playing a part in the cause of homosexuality. What is more likely the case, however, is that certain dimensions of homosexual behavior *may* be influenced by the genes. At the present time, however, explanations in terms of "being born with it" have little support outside of "conventional wisdom."

The hormonal theory has also attracted its adherents from time to time with, again, no conclusive evidence in support of this position. Some minimal hormonal differences between heterosexuals and a small number of men who are exclusively homosexual have been reported by several investigators (see Masters and Johnson, 1979), but the reasons for these differences have not been determined. It may be, for example, that these differences are the *result* of the homosexual orientation or life style rather than a cause. Various hormonal injections can, of course, produce certain sex changes; and, in fact, as we shall see, this knowledge is used in cases of transsexuality. However, this fact has no bearing on explaining the causes of homosexuality.

Perhaps the most popular theory attributes homosexuality to various child-rearing experiences. Beginning with Freud, a number of authorities have focused on impairment in parent-child relationships as the critical event in what were considered to be perversions in sexual preference, and this general approach is still very much in vogue. According to Freud, male homosexuality occurred as the result of a mother who was both overly domineering and subtly seductive while preventing her son from engaging in masculine pursuits and a father who was detached from his son, if not hostile toward him. Female homosexuality also occurred as the result of being raised under circumstances where the typical father-mother roles were reversed. By virtue of these inadequate parent styles, the child is prevented from identifying with and acquiring the appropriate sex role (Bieber, 1962). Without describing the serious flaws in Freudian theory, suffice it to say that efforts to substantiate these arguments have been almost totally unsuccessful (Sandler and Davidson, 1971). Thus, no such specific parent-child antecedents of homosexuality have been established. On the contrary, there is very good reason to believe that the relationships between sexual orientation per se, whether homosexual or heterosexual, and gender identification and sex-role behavior is far more complex than the Freudian model postulates. Thus, there are those whose sexual preferences are predominately homosexual but whose sexual self-identity is predominately heterosexual, and vice versa.

Although most of the psychoanalytic views remain to be verified, the importance of family relationships and other such experiential circumstances in determining sexual behavior has been emphasized by many social scientists. Again, no particular family pattern leading to homosexuality has been identified by these efforts. What does seem clear is that any child for a variety of reasons may, early in life, become more comfortable with a same-sex orientation than with an opposite-sex orientation. These early reactions may, in turn, be reinforced by actual sexual experiences during adolescence or even in early adulthood. The end result of these circumstances is a gradually emerging pattern leading in the direction of a homosexual orientation. Such an argument assumes that homosexuality is a learned or conditioned set of behaviors which may affect any one of us.

It is, of course, too soon to determine which of these various theories will ultimately prevail. As we shall see, the growing recognition that homosexual behavior can be modified for those who are motivated to change lends additional support to the learning theory position.

## HOMOSEXUAL LIFE STYLES

Regardless of one's actual sexual orientation, the need for social affiliation and sexual expression remains. Homosexuals, however, by virtue of the traditional hostility directed toward such behavior, have been denied the opportunity to meet those needs as openly as straight people. Public acknowledgment of homosexuality has often led to extortion, blackmail, and criminal charges (see Chapter 11). For these reasons, many homosexuals have been forced to develop a secret mode of com-

---

### The Jargon of the Gay Life

| | |
|---|---|
| λ | the Greek letter Lambda, a scientific symbol for activism, chosen by the Gay Activist Alliance |
| AC-DC | bisexuality |
| basket | male genitals |
| butch | a lesbian who adopts a masculine image |
| closet queen | covert male homosexual |
| cruising | the search for homosexual contacts |
| dyke | masculine appearing lesbian |
| femme | feminine appearing male homosexual |
| front marriage | marriage between a homosexual male and a homosexual female for the purposes of convenience |
| gay | homosexual |
| Humphreys | male homosexual contacts in public restrooms |
| Nellie | effeminate homosexual male |
| queen | effeminate homosexual male; a Nellie |
| size queen | gay male who desires a big penis on his partner |
| straight | heterosexual |
| tea room | public restrooms |
| to bring out | to initiate another into homosexual contact |
| to come out | to openly acknowledge one's homosexuality |

(From: Sagarin, E. Language of the homosexual subculture. *Medical aspects of human sexuality,* 1970, 4, 37.)

---

munication in order to pursue and gratify their sexual needs. A variety of more or less covert mechanisms have emerged over the years which enable homosexuals to identify one another. Various secret signals, cues, gestures, etc. have been used for this purpose. Ironically, these expressions are sometimes adopted by the straight society, at which time they no longer serve their original purpose. Certain dress styles, for example, serve as a clue for those in the know that the individual is a practicing homosexual. But when these same dress styles become popular, they lose their power of communication.

Another mechanism for providing contact, especially for male homosexuals, is the "tea room" (Humphreys, 1970). In each community, certain locations, usually of a public nature, serve as a meeting ground for men seeking a casual sexual contact with another male that will be consummated quickly and

"At shortly after 5 o'clock on a weekday evening four men enter a public restroom in the city park. One wears a well-tailored business suit, another wears tennis shoes, shorts, and a tee shirt; the third man is still clad in the khaki uniform of his filling station; the last, a salesman, has loosened his tie and left his sports coat in the car. What has caused those men to leave the company of other homeward bound commuters on the freeway. What common interest brings these men, with their divergent backgrounds to this public facility?

"They have come here not for the obvious reason, but in a search for "instant sex." Many men — married and un-married, those with heterosexual identities and those whose self-image is a homosexual one — seek such impersonal sex, shunning involvement, desiring kicks without committment."

(From Humphreys, R.A.L. *Tea Room Trade.* New York: 1970, pp. 1-2)

without any emotional involvement. Typically, but not exclusively, these facilities are used by married men concerned with protecting their reputation in the community. The locations may also be known to local law enforcement officials and tolerated as a "necessary evil" or subjected to periodic raids by the police.

Finally, of course, the gay life style serves the psychosocial needs of those individuals who are mostly exclusively homosexual and who more or less openly acknowledge their sexual orientation. Thus, it provides the individual with the means of peer identification and the development of a sense of community. Typically, gay life includes certain social and recreational locations, such as bars, that are frequented by homosexuals and serve as a meeting ground for casual or more enduring relationships. They may attract male homosexuals exclusively, female homosexuals exclusively, or both. Again, the existence of these locations is usually known and tolerated as a "necessary evil" since, from the standpoint of local law enforcement, they serve as a means of monitoring homosexuals.

Insofar as the characteristics of homosexual relationships may be described, conventional wisdom holds that one member of a homosexual relationship serves the "masculine" role and the other partner serves the "feminine" role. Such clear-cut role distinctions have been shown to be false (Hooker, 1968), and there is apparently at least as great a variety of gender roles and activities among homosexuals as there is among heterosexuals. Simon and Gagnon (1967), for example, found that about one-half of the homosexual men they interviewed practiced a wide variety of position roles depending on their own and their partner's desires. According to Lewis' research (1979), only 1% to 3% of lesbians incorporated stereotyped role playing into their sexual activities, and these are generally situations in which the women had no information about or exposure to alternative ways of patterning intimate life styles.

Among those who are exclusively homosexual, almost 25% of the males and 4% of the females report having had more than ten partners. Conversely, about 10% of the males and 50% of the females reported that their sexual relationships were restricted to only one partner.

## SEXUAL TECHNIQUES AMONG HOMOSEXUALS

The most extensive and detailed analysis of the sexual behavior of homosexuals has been reported by Masters and Johnson (1979). What follows is essentially a summary of their findings comparing, on the one hand, the sexual behavior and reactions of committed homosexual partners in which there was a longstanding relationship with, on the other hand, married heterosexual partners.

Perhaps the first observation to be made is that, except for the obvious fact that homosexuals do not engage in coitus, committed homosexuals are, in some respects, very much like married heterosexuals in their sexual techniques and in their reactions to sexual stimulation. For example, no differences in physiological reactions during sexual arousal and release between homosexual males and heterosexual males and between homosexual females and heterosexual females were observed. Moreover, similar patterns and frequencies of orgasmic dysfunctions between

homosexuals and heterosexuals were observed. And, perhaps most surprisingly of all, even the sexual fantasy themes of committed homosexuals were more like the sexual fantasies of married couples than they were different. Thus, contrary to popular opinion, both homosexual men and women report a high incidence of heterosexual fantasy activity, that is, lesbians sometimes fantasize about sex with a man, and gay men sometimes fantasize about sex with a woman. Finally, insofar as overall sexual orientation, male homosexuals, like male heterosexuals, are more genitally oriented during sex than are either female homosexuals or female heterosexuals.

In addition to these similarities between committed homosexual partners and married heterosexual partners, however, some rather interesting differences also emerged. The most prominent of these may best be identified as differences in lovemaking "styles." Both male and female homosexuals generally took more time during sex, and they appeared to be more relaxed and gave the impression of greater involvement than was true of the married couples. Moreover, there was more of a "my turn — your turn" pattern for the homosexuals, as contrasted with the mutual sexual release pattern of the married couples. Finally, the committed homosexual couples devoted more time to total pleasurable stimulation, whereas the married couples were more performance and goal (orgasm) oriented.

These differences emerged in both pregenital and genital lovemaking. For example, female homosexuals devoted more time to kissing, close body contact, and manual and oral breast stimulation than did the typical male partner of a heterosexual couple. Similarly, male homosexuals devoted more time to such pregenital activities, including nipple stimulation, than did the typical wife of a married pair.

The genital activities observed by Masters and Johnson included manual stimulation, oral-genital contacts (cunnilingus in the females and fellatio in the males), and anal intercourse in several male homosexuals and several heterosexual couples. During genitally directed sex, whether manual or oral, the typical lesbian couple devoted considerable attention to the labia, mons, inner thighs, and vaginal opening before the clitoris was stimulated directly. After initial contact with the glans, the clitoral shaft became the focus of attention. This was in contrast to the male heterosexual technique, which was characterized by a more direct approach to the clitoris, finger insertion into the vagina, and continued contact with the glans.

Genital activities in the male homosexual were characterized by a low-key, nondemanding style in which the areas adjacent to the penis were stimulated before the penis itself became the object of attention. More often than not a cyclical pattern of alternating high and lowered excitation emerged, thereby prolonging the onset of orgasm. Again, this was in contrast to the typical excitation pattern employed by the wives in the heterosexual pairs. Here, the penile shaft was the object of attention, and once penile manipulation began, it was continued and increased until ejaculation.

Aside from the "style" or pattern differences noted above, there were no important differences in fellatio technique between experienced male homosexuals and experienceed wives. With regard to cunnilingus, however, major differences between female homosexual and male heterosexual techniques did emerge. Again, the "style" differences noted above were reveal-

ed. In the female homosexuals this was manifested by a longer pregenital stimulation period involving the breasts, the lower abdomen and inner thighs, and greater inventiveness and variety in stimulation once the clitoris was approached. This was contrasted by the more routine and forceful techniques employed by the husbands.

Summarizing briefly from the Masters and Johnson studies, the most striking findings were in terms of differences in stimulative techniques between committed homosexuals and all other partner categories. Evidently, the characteristic pattern of homosexual lovemaking described above emerged after a relatively long period of interactions between the partners. In addition, another observed difference may also have contributed to these findings, thus:

> ... there was an observed tendency in homosexuals towards free flow of both verbal and nonverbal communication between stimulator and stimulatee. Information relative to sexual needs, levels of sexual involvement, what pleased or what distracted was usually exchanged openly during sexual activity or discussed without reservation after any specific sexual episode in anticipation of future sexual opportunity [Masters and Johnson, 1979, p 213].

## TREATMENT OF HOMOSEXUALITY PROBLEM CONDITIONS

As indicated, the rate and nature of sexual problems are essentially the same for homosexuals and heterosexuals. We will discuss in some detail in Chapter 14 the various treatment approaches for such disorders as premature ejaculation and orgasmic impairment. Since the procedures are the same, regardless of sexual orientation, the discussion in Chapter 14 will apply to both.

There is, however, one dimension of sexual dissatisfaction that is exclusively homosexual, and that is the desire to change from a same-sex orientation to an opposite-sex orientation. Numerous efforts to provide treatment for individuals desiring to change from a homosexual to a heterosexual orientation have been reported. They vary from traditional psychoanalysis to aversion therapy. Most of the clients in these studies were married male homosexuals. Unfortunately, the majority of these efforts have met with only limited success.

Recently, Barlow, Reynolds, and Agras (1973) described a treatment procedure for a male homosexual desiring to change to an opposite-sex orientation, that was essentialy a social learning procedure. A one-year follow-up revealed that the client was now functioning as a heterosexual and appeared confident and pleased with these changes. Despite the evident success of the approach, it is important to be cautious about generalizing from a single case.

Perhaps the most extensive treatment program for homosexuals desiring to change, however, has, again, been reported by Masters and Johnson (1979). Their approach is essentially an elaboration of the treatment methods employed for sexual dysfunctions. Since their procedures are described in detail in

Chapter 14, in this chapter we will only briefly summarize their efforts.

Clients may be dissatisfied with their homosexual orientation for a variety of reasons. For example, many of Masters and Johnson's participants were men who were sexually functional with other men but also had affectional ties with women. Clients are first carefully screened in terms of their sexual histories and motivation to change. Those who have never, or rarely, had any heterosexual experiences (5 or 6 on the Kinsey scale, for example) are considered to be appropriate candidates for "conversion" to heterosexuality. Clients with minimum to considerable heterosexual experiences (2, 3, or 4 on the Kinsey scale) are regarded as candidates for "reversion" to heterosexuality. Each client must demonstrate a strong commitment to change and enlist the aid of a cooperative opposite-sex partner. Of 54 male and 13 female homosexuals who participated in the treatment program, only 11 men and 3 women failed to register any benefits; that is to say, their sexual orientation remained essentially unchanged after treatment was terminated. All of the other clients experienced some change in the desired direction. As Masters and Johnson themselves suggest, these are only preliminary findings of the beginning stages in the development of treatment programs for those individuals who wish to change their sexual orientation.

Obviously, motivation to change is of critical importance in

such programs. Perhaps there will always be individuals who are unhappy with their sexual orientation and thus serve as candidates for such therapy. As society continues to acknowledge the sexual rights of individuals to engage in any activity as long as the rights of others are not violated, there may be less discomfort for the person with a homosexual orientation and an increase in the number of individuals who desire to be more comfortable in a committed homosexual orientation.

## BISEXUALITY

.As we have seen, sexual orientation varies across a broad spectrum of individual differences. It is true, of course, that many people are predominantly or exclusively heterosexual (0 and 1 on the Kinsey scale, for example) and many individuals also fall into the predominately or exclusively homosexual category (5 or 6 on the Kinsey Scale). Still a third category, however, is made up of those persons who are sometimes described as bisexual, that is, have sexual relations with members of both sexes (or, in commonplace terms, "swing both ways," "AC-DC"). The term bisexuality is potentially misleading because it suggests equal heterosexual and homosexual involvement, which may not accurately describe any given individual. We will continue to use this term, however, because of its popularity.

Despite Kinsey's caution that heterosexuality and homosexuality are not two discrete, exclusive, either/or orientations, sex researchers have generally tended to ignore bisexuality. Nevertheless, the number of individuals who actually or potentially fall into this last category is quite substantial. Thus, as we saw in Chapter 3, bisexual practices are quite common and even, in certain societies, widespread.

Similarly, most surveys suggest that a substantial number of men and women in our own society may also be considered bisexual. Kinsey (1948), for example, found that about 25% of the men and about 5% of the women he surveyed between the ages of 16 and 45 reported substantial homosexual experience even though their predominant orientation was heterosexual. Other investigators have reported even higher figures. Moreover, it is perhaps reasonable to assume that more people engage in bisexual practices than has been reported, since the definition of bisexuality is somewhat ambiguous. If the term bisexuality implies anyone who has engaged in both heterosexual and homosexual experiences, then clearly the incidence of such practices is substantial. Thus, a majority of heterosexual males report adolescent homosexual experiences. Furthermore, there are those individuals who have engaged in homosexual activity as an outlet as a result of sex-segregated circumstances (school, military, prisons), yet their self-identification is heterosexual. There are also those individuals with a primary heterosexual or homosexual emotional attachment who also engage in alternate sexual experiences out of curiosity or in a group sex setting.

These observations suggest that the relationship between one's own sexual identification and actual sexual behavior is quite complex. Blumstein and Schwartz (1974) investigated this issue, and their findings are relevant to the present discussion. In analyzing the sexual identification status in a large sample of

---

### Psychiatry's changing standards regarding homosexuality

A review of the American Psychiatric Association's definitions of homosexuality as revealed in their official classification manual (Diagnostic and Statistical Manual of Mental Disorders) reflects a series of changes over time from the view of considering homosexuality as seriously deviant to a position that is now quite different. Thus, early editions of the manual identified homosexuality as an example of pathological sexuality, or as a form of "sociopathic personality disturbance."

In the 1968 revision of the manual (DSM II), homosexuality was included in the less serious category of "personality disorders and certain other non-psychiatric mental disorders."

With the publication of the DSM III in 1979, homosexuality, per se, was no longer officially regarded as a mental disorder. Instead, a category of sexual orientation disturbance was formulated "for individuals whose sexual interests are directed primarily toward people of the same sex and who are either disturbed by, in conflict with, or wish to change their sexual orientation. This diagnostic category is distinguished from homosexuality, which by itself does not constitute a psychiatric disorder. Homosexuality, per se, is one form of sexual behavior and, like other forms of sexual behavior which are not by themselves psychiatric disorders, is not listed in this nomenclature of mental disorders."

(From: *Diagnostic and statistical manual of mental disorders, Third Edition,* DSM-111 Draft. Washington, D.C.: American Psychiatric Association, 1979)

bisexual women, Blumstein and Schwartz found that some of their subjects were ideologically bisexual. That is, while their own behavior may not have been bisexual, they identified themselves as bisexuals on the basis of their belief that bisexuality in humans was innate or natural and that this fact would be more apparent if social institutions did not suppress such practices. A second group of women identified themselves as bisexual although their sexual activities centered exclusively around other women. They rejected the homosexual label for several reasons: a sense of being in transition between different sexual orientations, a desire to keep their options open, fear of social stigma, etc. It seems clear, then, that there are no doubt many factors that determine bisexuality and many ways in which the individual manifests and interprets such an orientation.

There are, of course, those individuals whose bisexual behavior is congruent with their self-identification as bisexuals. Bode (1976) provides some further insight into a sample of women who fall into such a category.

In general, Bode's subjects reported that partner gender was less important than the partner's personal qualities. Their decision to engage in sex was based on emotional response or sexual attraction or on the context of an ongoing personal relationship, and the gender of the individual did not enter into such a decision. Some of the women in this study emphasized their need to relate to both men and women at a sexual level as well as at a nonsexual level. Thus, they had different emotional sexual needs and expectations, some of which could be satisfied with women, others with men. In their relations with other women, they could enjoy cuddling, caressing, and breast contact; with men they could satisfy their need for intercourse. Bode's findings are, at this point, tentative, and require further analysis by better controlled research.

It is perhaps of further research interest to note that some of the women in these studies who identify with a bisexual orientation reflect the characteristics of independence and ability to withstand social pressure that are also reported for lesbian women (Friedman, 1975).

Within the larger group of bisexuals, there are those individuals who view sex as purely a matter of physical release, who enjoy sex equally with both men and women but who have no interest in a durable emotional relationship. Masters and Johnson (1979) term such individuals "ambisexuals" and investigated the sexual responses of six male and six female ambisexuals in a laboratory setting. These men and women engaged in manual stimulation and oral-genital contacts with same-sex partners and in intercourse with opposite-sex partners. No obvious sex preferences emerged and each individual was capable of functioning effectively whether in a homosexual or heterosexual situation.

Although the significance of these findings for understanding human sexuality in general remains to be determined, Masters and Johnson suggest that the ambisexual individual differs from both the heterosexual and the homosexual in that partner gender is of no consequence and affectional involvement is of little importance.

Perhaps the one clear fact that emerges from these studies is the lack of research into bisexuality. Probably less is known about bisexuality than any other subject population in sex research. Some theorists, for example, Freudians, do not recognize the phenomenon of adult bisexuality; and, of course, the general public conception of such behavior is largely negative. Even certain elements in the gay community mistrust the bisexual, accusing him or her of being unwilling to accept a homosexual political commitment by keeping one foot in the respectable straight world. While there is no discernible bisexual subculture and no well organized political forum, some bisexuals are beginning to form ongoing discussion groups (Laws and Schwartz, 1977). These developments may result in a better understanding of bisexuality since such sexual orientations raise important questions about how people choose partners, about how people report or label their sexual identities, and about the impact of social pressure on sexual behavior in general. The phenomenon of bisexuality challenges our traditional view of the immutability of sex preference and sex identification (Blumstein and Schwartz, 1974) and begins to bring us closer to Kinsey's notion of human sexuality as existing on a continuum with many variations between exclusive heterosexuality at one end and exclusive homosexuality at the other (Kinsey, 1948).

## TRANSSEXUALITY

As we saw in Chapter 6, most people tend to equate gender and sex role with biological status. Departures from this "norm" tend to both bewilder and intrigue us, as in the case of transsexuality. The transsexual individual differs from this conventional norm in that she or he does not equate her or his sexual or gender identity with her or his biological status. On the contrary, the transsexual is convinced that she is a male or he is a female trapped in an opposite-sex body. Thus, the transsexual rejects her vagina or his penis, the typical mark of one's sexual status, since the transsexual believes she or he should possess the genitals of the opposite sex.

Typically, the transsexual's childhood is characterized by identification and preoccupation with the opposite-sex role (Stoller, 1976). The male transsexual, for example, may reveal little interest in masculine activities, preferring instead to join girls, even to the point of wearing girls' clothes and adopting a girl's name. Similarly, this same cross-sex identification is typically described by female transsexuals.

Despite the early expression of such cross-sex preferences, there is no evidence of biological factors as the cause of transsexuality; but, rather, the weight of current opinion favors an explanation in terms of early child-rearing patterns and other familial and social determinants.

Although adult transsexuals may engage in what would conventionally be regarded as homosexual behavior, since they are attracted to members of the same sex, the transsexual rejects this interpetation on the grounds that she or he is functioning as a member of the opposite sex. In the sense that most transsexuals wish to be loved by a straight person of her or his own gender, transsexuality thus differs from homosexuality. Moreover, transsexuals generally adopt the social mannerisms of the opposite sex, since these are the very attributes they wish to possess. The male transsexual, for example, often presents the stereotyped appearance and social behavior of a woman in order to achieve public identification with the female sex. Recently, however, some male transsexuals have expressed feminist values and choices (Feinbloom, 1976).

Transsexuality is certainly not a new or recent phenomenon. Transsexuals have appeared throughout history and in almost every society. As we saw in Chapter 3, certain cultures not only recognize and accept the transsexual but actually invest such individuals with special status. This recognition provides the transsexual with a clearly defined social role and a set of customs, thereby enabling him or her to adapt to the needs and the expectations of the group. This situation is clearly not the case in our society, however.

If the circumstances of transsexuality are confusing to the conventional heterosexual, they represent an even greater adjustment problem to the transsexual individual. Convinced that a biological mistake has occurred, forced by society to adopt a personal, social, and sexual role that is totally alien to them, and constantly frustrated in their desire to achieve a cross-gender identity, transsexuals often resort to extreme measures to reduce the conflict they constantly experience. It was often argued that therapy or counseling provided no relief for transsexuals since they had no desire to be cured of what others defined as an "aberration." The most direct way to reduce this conflict, then, was through a sex change.

Attempts by transsexuals to alter their biological status have taken a variety of forms (Pauley, 1965). Thus, a male transsexual might remove the facial hair and trim the hair in the pubic area to make it look more female. Some male transsexuals inject paraffin into the breast area. Both male and female transsexuals might take opposite-sex hormones in a further attempt to induce change in their physical characteristics. Cases of self-mutilation and other quasi-surgical attempts to modify the sex organs are surprisingly common. Pauley (1965), for example, reported that of 100 male transsexuals that he had studied, 18 had attempted or succeeded at amputation of their penis.

Even these extreme measures, however, may not provide the solution to the transsexual's continuing conflict, and the chronic state of personal unhappiness they experience leads to high rates of depression and suicide (Pauley, 1965).

Given this state of circumstances, it is understandable that the emergence of "sex reassignment" surgery came to be regarded by many transsexuals as the solution to their problems. Such procedures first captured major international attention in 1953 when Danish surgeons reported a sex reassignment procedure in the case of Christine Jorgensen, a former American serviceman. The approach of these surgeons involved surgically changing the penis into a facsimile of the female sex organs and providing the patient with hormone therapy and personal counseling in preparation for her new female status (Hamburger, Sturup, and Dahl-Iverson, 1953). Jorgensen subsequently became an entertainer and eventually married. In the years since then, the technology of sex reassignment surgery for both males and females has improved considerably, and several medical centers are now recognized for their work in this area.

The sex reassignment procedure, as it is typically implemented in most recognized centers, proceeds in the following manner. All applicants are carefully evaluated in terms of their sexual and social history in order to confirm the individual's transsexual status and to screen out those with a history of

psychiatric disturbances. Anywhere from 70% to 95% of the applicants are rejected on the basis of these criteria (Meyer and Peter, 1979).

Following this initial evaluation, the applicant is then administered hormone therapy and provided with personal counseling for at least six months as preparation for the anticipated changes. The male-to-female applicant is administered estrogen, which produces a gradual change in the direction of female physical appearance — the breasts enlarge, the hips become more rounded, and the male sex organs decrease in their erectile and ejaculatory capabilities. The female-to-male applicant is given androgens, which enhance the growth of facial hair, deepening of the voice, and enlargement of the clitoris and suppresses menstruation (Feinbloom, 1976). During this time, the applicant is encouraged to completely assume the identity of the opposite sex in all social and behavioral dimensions, for example, adopting opposite-sex clothing and mannerisms.

The last step in the procedure involves the sex reassignment operation. In males, the penis and testes are removed, except for the highly sensitive skin of the penis which serves as a lining for the newly constructed vagina. A clitoris is constructed from sensitive genital tissue. In addition, the urethra is shortened and positioned above the new vagina. A device is inserted in the vagina to prevent it from closing and remains in place for about six months. The new vagina may produce a small amount of natural lubrication during sexual arousal (Slavitz, 1976).

The female-to-male operation is considerably more difficult and risky. Typically, the clitoris is left in place and a penis and scrotum are formed from genital tissues (Feinbloom, 1976). Sometimes an artificial tube is implanted in the new penis for urination purposes, but since this tube is not self-cleansing, there is a continuing risk of infection. Inasmuch as the newly formed penis is incapable of spontaneous erection, a penile prosthesis that can be inflated and deflated is sometimes inserted. This device enables the individual to produce an erection as desired.

In addition, the breasts are removed, generally with little or no scarring so that the appearance of a male chest is achieved. Various components of the reproductive system such as the uterus and the ovaries may also be removed (Meyer and Peter, 1979).

Since the initial Danish procedure in 1953, it is estimated that approximately 2,000 individuals have undergone sex reassignment procedures (Slavitz, 1976); about 80% of them were men who wanted to be women. Until very recently, such procedures were generally accepted by authorities as a valuable treatment alternative for transsexuals. Benjamin (1966), for example, reported good to satisfactory results in terms of general social and sexual adjustment in 42 out of 51 male-to-female cases; only 5 cases had "doubtful" outcomes. Essentially, the same proportion of favorable results has been reported by other investigators. However, evaluation of a longer follow-up of applicants to the highly renowned Sexual Behavior Consultation Unit at Johns Hopkins Medical School casts some doubt on these findings (Meyer and Peter, 1979). Comparisons in life adjustment were made between 15 individuals who had undergone sex reassignment surgery and 35 individuals who had received only counseling; approximately 80% of both groups were men who wanted to be women. The study revealed that there were no signficant differences between the two groups in their general social and sexual adjustment.

The suggestion that emerged from this investigation was the following: There seems to be a period of time in the lives of transsexuals when they strongly desire surgery. With the passage of time, however, and in the absence of surgery, this desire diminishes and most of these individuals go on to make a reasonably adequate social and sexual adjustment. In view of these findings, the Johns Hopkins sex-change operation has been discontinued (Holden, 1979).

Although transsexuality has often been treated in a "freaky" or sensationalist manner in the popular media, the issues that are involved in such cases are far from trivial. It has been estimated that there are about 10,000 transsexuals in the United States, each of whom experiences varying degrees of stress and discomfort. Transsexuals such as Dr. Renee Richards, the tennis player, and author Jane/Jan Morris have described the problems such individuals encounter and focused public attention on transsexuality. Moreover, the phenomenon of transsexuality raises certain questions about our sexuality and highlights the complexity in determining "What is a woman?" and "What is a man?"

## SUMMARY

The analysis of human sexuality continues to reveal the wide range and diversity of sexual activities engaged in by large numbers of individuals beyond the so-called acceptable practices recognized by tradition. From the standpoint of sheer numbers alone, we know that a great many individuals have sexual relations with other than members of the opposite sex and that the capacity for sexual versatility is so great that the concept of a single sexual standard is simply unrealistic. Perhaps, then, we are beginning to accept Kinsey's admonition against considering heterosexuality, and especially heterosexuality in marriage, as the single best description of the sex life of most Americans.

In the process of expanding our recognition of these other variations of human sexuality, many of the time-worn superstitions and biases are gradually moderating. If mainstream America has not already established a new standard of what constitutes normal sex, at least we appear to be excluding certain sexual practices from what was previously regarded as abnormal.

There is, of course, much which remains to be done, especially in terms of a better understanding of the complicated relationships between sexual identity and sexual behavior in both homosexuality and heterosexuality and a better understanding of the parameters of bisexuality. As we continue to explore these and other questions, no doubt we will find even newer challenges to the myths of human sexuality.

# Chapter 11

## Sex and the Law

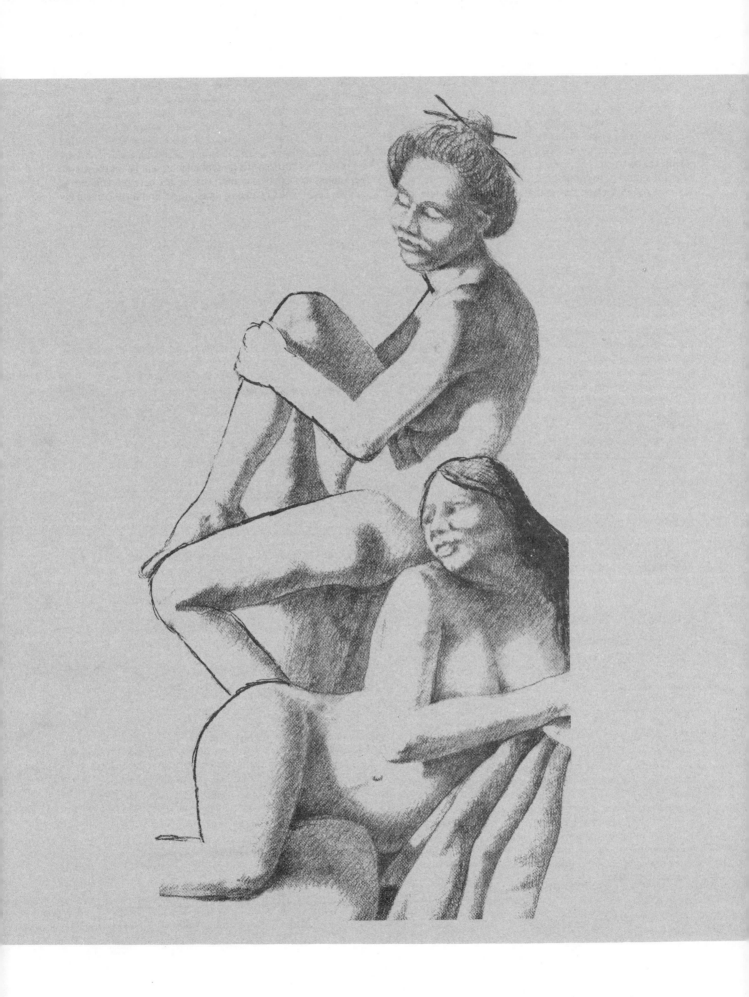

# INTRODUCTION

All societies have attempted to regulate sexual behavior by means of various social mechanisms, but no society has formulated as vast and confusing a patchwork of sexual laws and statutes as our own. The problems imposed on us by the maze of relevant statutes are compounded by the fact that most of our sex laws reflect archaic values that are often completely incompatible with contemporary sexual values. In the words of one authority, "the split between our society's permissive — even obsessive — sexual behavior and attitudes, and our primitive, puritanical statutes is indeed scarcely credible" (Pilpel, 1970, p. 61).

The status of our complicated and contradictory sexual law system has been a subject of debate for many years. With the advent of the so-called sexual revolution and the increasing pressure applied by various advocacy groups, however, professional and public recognition of the need to revamp our sex laws has reached new heights. Almost every aspect of our sexual law system has been called into question, from the definition of what is illegal to the determination of what methods should be used to enforce our sex laws. Although a complete analysis of the relationship between sexual behavior and the law is beyond the scope of this book, in this chapter we will briefly examine the range and variety of a number of our sex laws, point out the most salient issues that have resulted in controversy, and describe the manner in which our sexual statutes actually or potentially impact on the lives of each of us.

## SEX LAWS: A PRELIMINARY PERSPECTIVE

Generally, our sex laws have emerged from two related value systems:

1. There are those almost universal sex laws that are designed to protect the individual and society; and

2. There are those more specific laws that stem primarily from the Judeo-Christian ethic which considered anything other than procreative sex within the confines of marriage to be immoral, if not illegal.

Although the distinction which follows is certainly not a hard and fast one, generally speaking, statutes governing incest, pedophilia, bestiality, necrophilia, and sex-related violent acts (rape and assault) are examples of crimes that are almost universally condemned as threats to the social order. The laws governing adultery, premarital sex, oral-genital sex, homosexuality, nudity, prostitution, and obscenity more clearly reflect our own culture's basic Judeo-Christian tradition. Not all sex-related laws fit into this framework, but many are, rather, apparently the result of overlapping influences. Laws governing abortion and the dissemination of contraceptive information, for example, represent a concern for protecting society but also have obvious religious overtones.

Various authorities have also offered an alternative perspective for classifying our sex laws. In this context, laws are classified in terms of those illegal sex acts that involve victims (rape, child molesting, voyeurism, etc.) and those illegal sex acts that pertain to victimless crimes (premarital sex, prostitution, obscenity-pornography, homosexuality, etc.). Advocates of this perspective argue that laws in the latter group could be abolished without threatening society since these laws regulate private behavior between consenting adults and no victims are involved. Our focus in the present chapter will be on those laws pertaining to victimless crimes, that is, sex between consenting adults. Legal issues related to incest, rape, and birth control are dealt with in other chapters.

## LAWS GOVERNING SEX BETWEEN CONSENTING ADULTS

It frequently comes as a shock to many individuals that a wide variety of sexual activities between consenting adults are actually criminal offenses. Almost all States, for example, have laws prohibiting fornication, adultery, sex for pay (prostitution), oral-genital contacts (cunnilingus and fellatio), and anal-genital contacts (sodomy). The "crime" of adultery, for example, is apparently committed by more than one-third of our adult population (Pilpel, 1970) including, no doubt, some law enforcement officials themselves. Kinsey (1948) estimated that if all of the above laws were actually enforced, perhaps 95% of the male population of the United States could be tried as sex offenders.

Each State, of course, has its own brand of sex laws with the definitions and the penalties for the crime differing considerably. A married woman who engages in sex with an unmarried man, for example, will often be charged with adultery, whereas a married man who has sex with an unmarried woman is most often charged with fornication. Such discriminatory treatment can have important ramifications inasmuch as most States consider adultery to be the more serious offense. Thus, sentences for adultery range up to five years in prison, whereas fornication is usually classified as a misdemeanor and is punishable by a minimal fine. On the other hand, Arizona statutes define fornication as a felony punishable by life imprisonment.

In addition to the laws that define illegal heterosexual relationships such as fornication and adultery, many States restrict the nature of sex even within a marriage relationship. Thus, most States outlaw "unnatural acts," such as oral-genital sex and anal intercourse. In New Jersey, for example, consensual sodomy is punishable by a fine of up to $5,000 and/or up to 20 years in jail, and in other States, by life imprisonment at hard labor (Pilpel, 1970). One final example should suffice: An analysis of Michigan sex laws that appeared in the *Wayne Law Review* claimed that Michigan laws are vague enough to probably prohibit any and all sexual activity other than conventional petting or coitus.

## LAWS GOVERNING HOMOSEXUALITY

Many of the laws governing "unnatural acts" are, of course, actually directed at homosexuals, and most homosexual convictions are made on the basis of the violation of such statutes. Thus, although the law does not technically distinguish between heterosexual unnatural acts and homosexual unnatural acts, the vast majority of such prosecutions involve male couples.

Since homosexuality, like heterosexuality, typically occurs in private and because of the persistent belief that homosexuals aggressively pursue their sexual interests, various communities have employed questionable practices in their attempt to police such "crimes." Thus, police confederates are sometimes assigned to frequent known homosexual locations in plain clothes. If and when a sexual advance occurs, an arrest is made and the individual is charged with "lewd and lascivious" conduct. Such entrapment practices have been criticized by Gay activists and legal authorities alike.

Despite the persistent belief that homosexuals vigorously pursue a course of action to convert others and are a serious threat to the community, a number of studies prove the contrary. In fact, "the majority of homosexual solicitations are made only if the other individual appears responsive to the use of gestures and signals having significance only to other homosexuals" (Gall, 1966).

In general, there is little doubt that the law in these cases has been used in a discriminatory manner against homosexuals, that penalties for homosexuals are unduly severe, and that the methods often used to arrest homosexuals can be called into question themselves.

## LAWS RELATED TO PROSTITUTION

As with so many other dimensions of sexuality, our society's response to prostitution is paradoxical and inconsistent. Every State has enacted laws prohibiting sex for pay, and many communities vigorously enforce these laws. On the other hand, prostitution is not only recognized but even accepted under many circumstances. Camp followers, for example, are often recruited to "service" military personnel. Moreover, if civil authorities were genuinely serious about eliminating prostitution, arrest rates for male participants would equal those for female prostitutes. But, in fact, men who engage the services of prostitutes are rarely arrested. The "paradox" of prostitution has been tempered in those Western societies, such as Denmark and The Netherlands, which have legalized prostitution. But in the United States, where prostitution was and still is officially illegal except for certain rare exceptions (see later in this chapter), Kinsey (1948) found that perhaps some 70% of the total white male population had used a prostitute at least once. Furthermore, Kinsey estimated that more than one and a half million such contacts occurred each year in the United States — a total of more than 25,000 acts of prostitution each week.

Of the many laws relating to prostitution, those concerned with soliciting (that is, approaching someone for some immoral purpose) produce the majority of actual arrests. Most State laws regard soliciting as a misdemeanor punishable by a fine of perhaps $100 and/or a jail term of anywhere from several to ninety days. In fact, few convicted prostitutes spend more than several hours in prison for any one given offense before they are bonded out or their fine is paid.

Many arrests occur in the context of a solicitation to a police confederate. Since the knowledgeable pro is familiar with the laws prohibiting solicitation, she rarely mentions sex in her approach. More often than not sexual references are thinly disguised (for example, "Would you like to have a good time?", "Could you help me out with my sick mother?"). When the final arrangement is negotiated, the police confederate may acknowledge his official status and charge the woman with solicitation. Occasionally, law enforcement officials will make a concerted effort to eliminate prostitution by mass arrests at known prostitution locations. These efforts usually occur in response to local business concerns or offended individuals and are most often short-lived in their effect.

Beyond the little information provided by legal statistics and our conventional wisdom of prostitution, the sociology and psychology of prostitution is still only poorly understood. Strong, preconceived notions regarding the "typical" prostitute continue to persist although many of these views have not been supported by recent studies. For example, most of the earlier investigations into prostitution reported high rates of retardation, frigidity, homosexuality, serious emotional disturbance, and male hostility. More recent and better controlled studies provide us with a different perspective. Gebhard (1969), for example, found that most of the prostitutes he interviewed were of normal intelligence and led otherwise ordinary heterosexual lives, although most of them had only a limited education.

As to their reasons for entering the oldest profession, most women were influenced by simple economics. In the words of one prostitute: "You got it. You sell it. You still got it." For a young woman with a limited education and a restricted range of job options, the prospect of earning hundreds of dollars for one night's work has a strong appeal, moral and legal considerations to the contrary. Some, no doubt, are attracted to what may appear to the outsider as a glamorous life style, while others turn to prostitution to support a drug habit or to escape an unhappy home life. Again, contrary to public opinion, evidently very few women in the United States are actually forced into prostitution (Gebhard, 1969).

Once the decision to enter the profession is made, instruction in the skills and sophistication required in terms of dealing with clients, other members of the profession, and law enforcement is usually provided by an experienced pro during an "apprenticeship" period.

Most analyses identify several dimensions to prostitution, in terms of status level. The aristocrat of prostitution is the "call girl," who typically operates out of a single location. She has a so-called high-class clientele capable of meeting her relatively high fees. A second class of prostitution is characterized by the streetwalker, who is often much more blatant and aggressive in her activities and, therefore, more vulnerable to arrest. Many streetwalkers operate under the protection of a pimp or a procurer, representing activities which are also illegal.

Prostitution may also occur in the context of a "house" or commercial location. Through vigorous enforcement of the laws, the notorious brothel or bordello of the past has given way to today's massage parlor or escort service. Typically, manual stimulation or oral stimulation is provided as an alternative to intercourse in such locations since less of an arrest risk is involved in these practices.

## The Jargon of the Prostitute World

call girl - highest status level
streetwalker - lowest status level
hooker, whore, pro, hustler - synonyms for prostitute
John - a customer
turn a trick - a given sex act
cathouse - a brothel, bordello
pimp, madam, procurer - an agent for prostitutes
stable - a pimp's roster of prostitutes
outlaw - a woman who operates alone
"in the life" ⎫
"one of the girls" ⎭ the life style of the prostitute
"quickie" - a brief sexual encounter, usually no more than one
    hour
"local" - manual stimulation
"wet deck" - several brief coital encounters in succession
"going down," "blow job" - fellatio

*Solicitation by prostitute*

Prostitution may also be associated with a B-girl's role. Typically, the B-girl is a bar (hence the term B-girl) or lounge employee whose job is to entice men into buying drinks freely. Often, the B-girl operates in a striptease establishment (sometimes doubling as a striptease performer) where, implicitly if not explicitly, she promotes the idea of exchanging sexual favors for the purchase of drinks. Many communities have enacted special ordinances prohibiting B-girl activities, but, again, such statutes are almost impossible to enforce.

Although the preceding description is restricted to the most common form of prostitution, there are, of course, other types of sex for pay, such as homosexual prostitution and male heterosexual prostitution. Even less is known about these examples of sex for pay than about the more conventional forms of prostitution.

A number of scientific and legal commissions have analyzed our antiprostitution laws. Virtually every such effort has recommended radical reform of these laws. Benjamin and Masters' (1964) position is representative:

> Legislation aimed at suppressing prostitution may be challenged and criticized on a number of counts. The laws violate basic human rights; they have the effect of placing prostitutes in a special and unwarranted category in which their civil rights are often denied. They confuse vice with crime, and they inevitably have a damaging effect upon police and the courts, promoting crime and corruption while failing to achieve the desired objective of suppressing prostitution. [p. 69]

One further development that has recently emerged in our society is the legalization of prostitution. As of the present, prostitution is legal in only a few locations, all in the State of Nevada. This legalization represents, perhaps, the modern counterpart of the older "red light" district found in many American communities. The difference, of course, is that the older arrangement reflected the hypocrisy of the times; that is, prostitution was outlawed but operated under the covert protection of the authorities.

## OTHER SEX-RELATED LAWS

There are, of course, a whole host of additional sex-related laws in addition to those described above. Thus, there are laws prohibiting obscenity, nudity, abortion, the dissemination of contraceptive information, etc. The legal implications related to these issues are described in other chapters. Briefly, however, let us examine several examples of sex laws which show the extremes to which such regulation can be carried. Consider, for example, the following antinudity statute drafted several years ago for Alameda County, California: "Violation would consist of any female who exposes any portion of either breast below a straight line so drawn that both nipples and all portions of both breasts have a different pigmentation than that of the main portion of the breast and are below such a straight line." Enforcement of such a law could easily be carried to ridiculous extremes. Similarly, where contraception is illegal and abortion is not, a woman with a high risk pregnancy condition cannot prevent conception but must undergo an abortion if and when her life is threatened by a pregnancy. In Maryland, it is a crime to sell contraceptives from a vending machine except in those locations where liquor is sold (Pilpel, 1970). Far from being isolated examples, such peculiar regulations are representative of the irrational nature of many of our sex laws.

## REFORMING OUR SEX LAWS

During the past 3,000 years, the "abominations" of the Old Testament became the sins of the New Testament and the sex crimes of contemporary America. To the extent that these "transgressions" represent private acts between consenting adults, however, reformers increasingly argue that such behavior should be decriminalized. Moreover, advocacy groups, such as Women's Rights and Gay Rights, have condemned the discriminatory manner in which our sex laws are enforced, particularly with regard to prostitution and sodomy, respectively.

As we have seen, a number of study groups have been commissioned to review the status of our sex laws and to recommend changes as appropriate. Two of the most prestigious were the Wolfenden Commission in England and the American Law Institute Model Penal Code. In both cases, decriminalization of private sex acts between consenting adults was strongly recommended (Pilpel, 1970). With few exceptions, however, State and local legislatures have remained steadfast in their opposition to reforming our sex laws. Several States have revised their abortion laws within the last few years, and a few other minor breakthroughs have occurred. In the main, however, sex laws continue to reflect the archaic values and ethical concerns of the Victorian era. For these reasons, a number of individuals have challenged various statutes on the basis of their unconstitutionality. As a result of those efforts, the Texas sodomy law, the Florida fornication law, and the Massachusetts "crimes against chastity" laws have been found to be unconstitutional by the Federal courts. In the light of the continuing resistance at the State level, it would appear that the use of the Federal courts for reforming our sex laws represents the wave of the future.

# Chapter 12

## Pornography

# INTRODUCTION

As we have seen, in the past few decades, and particularly in the past few years, many sexually related topics and issues have been the focus of public attention in the United States. Abortion and the rights of unborn fetuses, the dissemination of birth control information and devices, and the value of sex education have all been recent topics of heated debate. While each of these issues has been the subject of serious scientific research, the major proportion of our public policy *decisions* regarding these topics have been based on other grounds. Personal, philosophical, moralistic, religious, and political factors have often been the deciding factors in the decision making, both for individuals and in terms of national policy impacting on all segments of our society.

Pornography represents one of the most controversial of these issues. It is a matter about which people have disagreed for centuries and which has been a concern in the United States since before the Revolutionary War. Pornography also appears to be a topic of pervasive concern in that almost everyone has some opinion on it. Recently the debate and controversy has extended from the local, neighborhood, grass-roots level all the way to the national political scene. The pornography issue has been examined at local town meetings, by various law enforcement agencies, by the United States Congress, by a Presidential Commission, and in numerous Supreme Court cases.

Many studies have investigated the possible effects of exposure to pornographic materials. By and large, however, this body of data has been ignored in decision making. This is not to imply that all decisions should be made purely on factual data without consideration of other important variables. In fact, each of us makes decisions daily based on our own personal preferences and on moral, religious, and political beliefs. Neither are we advocating the wholesale dissemination and use of pornographic materials in our society. Rather, we hope to provide a balanced presentation of the issues bearing on the pornography controversy, including a consideration of both the factual data and the personal variables that are relevant to the issue.

# DEFINITIONS

Pornography is a poorly defined and often misused term. There have been numerous attempts to define the term at several levels, ranging from personal opinions to legal attempts by the Supreme Court. The resulting definitions, however, remain imprecise and vague, and no consensus definition has emerged from these attempts. The terms *erotic, obscene,* and *pornographic* are often used (or misused) interchangeably. Let us consider each of these terms.

For the purposes of this chapter we will define *erotic* as any material which may portray sexual activity or arouse sexual feelings in an individual. There are many examples of such material in our society: passages from the works of Shakespeare, parts of the Song of Solomon in the Bible, works by Picasso and other famous artists, scenes from television programs and motion pictures, and magazine advertisements. By this definition some of the pictures and illustrations in this text may be erotic for some readers. The majority of erotica was not created expressly or primarily to arouse sexual feelings but rather for broader purposes, such as to entertain (motion pictures) or to sell products (advertisements). On the other hand, some materials produced primarily for arousal purposes (that is, pornography) may also be highly erotic by our definition.

*Obscene* will be defined as any material, including but not limited to sexual material, that is deemed personally abhorrent or objectionable for one or more of a variety of reasons. Material might be obscene because it conflicts with religious morals, because of its violent content, or because it displays excrement. One's own definition of erotic or obscene may vary greatly from individual to individual; this variation is based on a multitude of historical and environmental factors that are unique to each of us.

*Pornography* will refer to any material written, spoken, or expressed in pictures which was developed *primarily* to evoke sexual interest or arousal. As we shall see, attempts at highly specific and legalistic definitions, such as those offered in several court decisions, have often added only confusion and ambiguity. Our definitions are no better or worse than other attempts at interpreting these nebulous terms. However, we hope they will provide a useful and meaningful framework for the discussions in the remainder of this chapter.

# A BRIEF HISTORY OF PORNOGRAPHY

Two broad phenomena have for centuries been intricately intertwined in the pornography controversy. As we saw earlier, religious doctrines and beliefs have usually been of great significance in determining what is obscene or pornographic. Throughout history all religions have attempted to influence behavior by establishing certain rules of conduct. Some of these rules invariably have to do with sexual behavior. As these varied religious doctrines have evolved over time, religious beliefs have, for many people, had a significant impact on many aspects of behavior, including sexuality.

Political and legal variables have also had a significant impact on the regulation of sexual activities. Of particular importance in the pornography controversy in the United States has been a basic, constitutional issue. The first amendment to our Constitution guarantees a right to free speech and a free press. As we shall see, the bulk of the legal controversy in this country has revolved around this central issue: specifically, to what extent do State and Federal legal restrictions on pornography threaten or violate these First Amendment guarantees?

Related to the conflict are the numerous attempts since the time of the ancient Greeks to censor sexually related materials. The first legal attempt at limiting such materials in this country was a Massachusetts statute in 1711 (Lipton, 1976). The application of this law, however, was limited to sexual materials that were incorporated into religious materials; and, as such, the law was more a protection against an attacking of religious institutions and beliefs than a pure attempt at censoring sexual materials. However, by the early to middle 1800s, most States had legislated very broad obscenity/pornography laws. In 1865 Congress passed a law prohibiting dissemination of these materials through the mail. Many such laws passed in the 1800s remained essentially intact for the next century.

In 1957 the U.S. Supreme Court handed down a ruling in a suit that would become a landmark case regarding the pornography issue (*Roth* v. *U.S.*). Previous lower court decisions had declared that, with certain exceptions, the dissemination of a variety of printed and photographic materials was protected by the First Amendment. In *Roth* v. *U.S.* the Court essentially further restricted these exceptions by ruling that obscenity was not "within the area of constitutionally protected speech or press." The decision was based on two basic arguments. First, the Court pointed out that at the time the Constitution was written, many States had already passed laws limiting freedom of press and speech to some extent, for example, laws against libel and profanity. Thus, the Court argued that the writers of the Constitution did not intend to protect *every* statement, whether written or spoken. Secondly, the Court noted that there was "universal judgment that obscenity should be restrained" (Lipton, 1976); that is, over fifty nations and all the States already had enacted some types of obscenity law.

In addition to this ruling that obscenity was not protected by the First Amendment, the Court went on in the *Roth* v. *U.S.* decision to propose a legal definition of what is obscene. The test for obscenity became "whether to the average person, applying contemporary community standards, the dominant theme of the material taken as a whole appeals to the prurient interest" (Commission on Obscenity and Pornography, 1970). The Court further noted that such material must also be presumed to be "utterly without redeeming social importance." These basic components of the legal definition of obscenity remain essentially unchanged to the present. To be declared obscene, then, material must meet three basic criteria: (a) the dominant theme must appeal to a "prurient" (depraving or improper sexual) interests, (b) it must be judged offensive by "community" standards, and (c) it must be without "redeeming social importance or value."

This attempt at a legal definition of obscenity has suffered the same problems as other definitions offered: it is confusing and vague, and consequently there has continued to be much litigation concerning obscenity/pornography. Who is the "average" person? Is a "community" a neighborhood, or can it be construed to be a larger segment of society such as a city or state? How do we determine exactly what are a community's "standards"? How does one define "redeeming social value"?

In 1969 the Supreme Court added to this confusing state of affairs in its decision in the *Stanley* v. *Georgia* case. In this instance the Court ruled that the Constitution prohibits making private possession of obscene material a crime. Thus, an individual may legally possess obscene materials, but may not purchase them legally!

On June 21, 1973, the Supreme Court announced its decision on three separate pornography cases: *Kaplan* v. *California, Paris Adult Theatre I* v. *Slaton,* and *Miller* v. *California.* These rulings clarified some of the above issues while further complicating others. By a close five to four margin, the Court upheld the *Roth* decision that obscenity/pornography is not protected

by the Constitution (the minority advocated accepting the earlier recommendations of the Commission on Obscenity and Pornography that the legal ban on such materials be eliminated). The Court also removed the word "utterly" from the statement relating to social importance or value, substituting "serious literary, artistic, political, or scientific value." This has further been interpreted to mean that prosecutors no longer have to prove that material is obscene or pornographic; rather, the defendants must prove that the material in question is "serious" by the testimony of experts attesting to its literary, artistic, political, or scientific value. Additionally, the Court ruled that a State is included in the definition of "community" in the decision of what is obscene, although it did not define whether a city, town, or neighborhood also constitutes a community. Finally, the Court ruled that State laws against obscenity must specifically state which kinds of conduct portrayed in the materials in question are to be legally considered obscene.

These recent court decisions have been confusing and often contradictory. The arguments used in reaching these decisions have also been vague and unscientific. For example, in *Kaplan* v. *California* the Court decided that States may *assume* that there is a direct causal relationship between obscenity and antisocial conduct since this relationship is inherently unprovable. As we shall see later in this chapter, there is a large body of knowledge that runs counter to this argument.

## THE COMMISSION ON OBSCENITY AND PORNOGRAPHY

In October, 1967, Congress established the Commission on Obscenity and Pornography, whose purpose was "after a thorough study which shall include a study of the causal relationship of such materials to antisocial behavior, to recommend advisable, appropriate, effective, and constitutional means to deal effectively with such traffic in obscenity and pornography" (Commission on Obscenity and Pornography, 1970). In January of 1968, President Johnson appointed eighteen members to the Commission (President Nixon later appointed one member as a replacement). These Commissioners represented a variety of disciplines and occupations: five were judges or attorneys, four were concerned with the publication or dissemination of books, movies, etc., three were sociologists, two were psychiatrists, and one was an educator. There were also representatives of the Catholic, Protestant, and Jewish faiths (Lipton, 1976).

The Commission reviewed the available research material and also contracted with various investigators to carry out additional research. In 1970, the Commission made its report available to Congress, the President, and the public. Based upon its investigations, the Commission concluded that ". . . empirical investigation. . . provides no evidence that exposure to or use of explicit sexual materials plays a significant role in the causation of social or individual harms such as crime, delinquency, sexual or nonsexual deviancy or severe emotional disturbances. . ." (Commission on Obscenity and Pornography, 1970). Based on these conclusions, the Commission recommended that: (a) Federal, State, and local laws prohibiting the sale and distribution of sexual materials to consenting adults should be repealed; (b) a nationwide sex education program should be implemented; (c) a law should be passed prohibiting the mailing of unsolicited advertisements which might contain potentially sexually offensive materials; and (d) the sale of such sexually related materials to minors should continue to be prohibited.

It should be noted that these conclusions and recommendations were those of the majority of the Commission. However, six of the eighteen Commissioners did not agree with the above conclusions, and several wrote minority opinions castigating both the findings and the Commission itself. These dissenters pointed out flaws in some of the research and suggested there were found in some studies some negative effects which did not appear in the majority report. Several dissenters felt there was a causal relationship between pornography and many social or psychological pathologies, even though such a relationship has not been clearly demonstrated by the scientific method. One dissenting member wrote: "One can consult all the experts he chooses, can write reports, make studies, etc., but the fact that obscenity corrupts lies within the common sense, the reason, and the logic of every man." (Commission on Obscenity and Pornography, 1970).

The overall reaction to the Commission's report favored this minority position; President Nixon rejected the Commission's findings — according to some observers before he had ever actually read the report (Zurcher and Kirkpatrick, 1976). He called its conclusions "morally bankrupt" and supported his position by referring to "centuries of civilization and ten minutes of common sense." Mr. Nixon's position was also supported by Vice President Agnew and other high-ranking members of the administration. By a vote of 60 to 5, the Senate rejected the report, depicting it as an example of "marshmallow-headed thinking" (Zurcher and Kirkpatrick, 1976).

# EFFECTS OF EXPOSURE TO PORNOGRAPHY

It is clear then that the issue of obscenity/pornography has been a hotly debated topic and a focus of controversy at all levels of our American society. In recent years scientists in many countries have investigated the impact of exposure to pornographic or other sexually arousing, erotic materials. Let us turn now to the results of these studies.

## THE COMMISSION'S FINDINGS

The Commission on Obscenity and Pornograph both reviewed the existing literature and contracted for many new studies on the effects of pornography. The following is a brief summary of these data.

Several surveys were undertaken for the Commission. Interviews with 3,269 persons aged 15 and older, for example, indicated that only about 2% of the respondents felt that erotic materials were a "serious problem." Respondents were much more concerned with Vietnam, racial conflicts, and the economy. However, these results may be somewhat misleading and unreliable; a Gallup survey taken at approximately the same time indicated that around three-fourths of the population felt the need for stricter pornography laws (Lipton, 1976). These

apparently conflicting findings are probably the result of the different questionnaires and sampling procedures used.

The Commission also surveyed almost 3,500 psychiatrists and clinical psychologists. Of these, 80% reported that they had never personally seen a case in which pornography appeared to be an important factor in producing antisocial sexual behavior; 9% suspected pornography as a factor in one or more cases while 7% were convinced they had seen at least one such case. Similar findings were reported for other mental health professionals: for example, only 12% of those surveyed believed obscene literature was in any way implicated in juvenile delinquency.

The Commission thoroughly reviewed the available experimental data and found some very consistent reports (Commission on Obscenity and Pornography, 1970), including the following findings: A majority of both males and females (ranging from 60% to 85%) reported becoming sexually aroused or stimulated when reading or viewing erotic materials. Women appear to become more aroused by written material whereas men respond more to visually presented erotica. For both sexes, the amount of arousal resulting from exposure to erotic materials seems to decrease with age. Arousal was also found to decrease simply after repeated exposure to such materials — the so-called satiation effect. When individuals were placed in a room with many sexually stimulating books and movies available for daily viewing over a period of weeks, they very quickly lost interest and their total viewing time of this erotic material decreased rapidly. In one study, these behavioral changes were accompanied by a concomitant decrease in physiological measures of arousal.

Finally, the studies reviewed by the Commission indicated that exposure to sexually arousing materials did not produce any significant changes in the *patterns* of sexual behavior of the viewers. While certain specific behaviors (for example, masturbation, intercourse) usually increased in the hours or days immediately following exposure, individuals' overall basic patterns of sexual activity remained unaffected. For example, men or women without steady sexual partners were likely to report an increase in masturbatory activity (their common pattern) after exposure. Likewise, individuals with steady partners usually reported an increase in the frequency of their common sexual pattern, that is, intercourse. Taken as a whole, these studies suggested that exposure to sexually arousing materials often had an activating effect on sexual behavior. However, this activation was of short duration and, when it occurred, previously established patterns of sexual activity were maintained.

The Commission also reviewed several other lines of evidence, for example, the prevalence of past exposure to pornographic materials among convicted sex offenders. Since there have been more recent investigations of this and other variables since the Commission's report, the Commission's conclusions will be included, where applicable, in the following sections.

## LABORATORY EXPERIMENTS

Many of the Commission's conclusions were based on retrospective studies in which possible confounding variables were often uncontrolled. In recent years, there has been more of an emphasis on laboratory studies, where the actual exposure to arousing materials (and other variables) can be better controlled and where more accurate measurement of any effects of such exposure are possible.

The results of a study by Howard, Liptzin, and Reifler (1973) are supportive of similar data reviewed by the Commission. These investigators exposed young adult males to 90 minutes of sexually arousing material five days a week for three weeks. The subjects' patterns of sexual behavior were unchanged. Furthermore, the subjects quickly became satiated to the materials. These investigators reported this satiation to have been so great that many subjects actually became bored with the materials, and some of them would not have completed the experiment had they not been paid for their participation!

Mann, Sidman, and Starr (1973) investigated the longer-term effects of pornography. A group of married couples were asked to fill out daily questionnaires about their sexual behaviors for twelve weeks. During the middle four weeks, the couples viewed erotic films once a week. These couples reported the highest rates of sexual activities in the initial four weeks *prior to* exposure to the films. Those increases that did occur during the exposure period almost invariably were limited to the nights of film viewing only. Patterns of sexual behaviors generally were unchanged. Perhaps simple *anticipation* of erotic exposure stimulates or activates sexual activity just as much as the actual exposure to such materials.

The results of a study by Mosher (1970) are interesting because they suggested some sex differences in responses to erotica (Alfred Kinsey had hypothesized some 20 years earlier that such would be the case). In this study Mosher exposed college students to two sexually arousing films: one showing heterosexual intercourse, the other depicting oral-genital activities ending in orgasm. After viewing the films, both sexes reported approximately equal arousal to the coitus film, whereas males reported more arousal to the oral-genital film than did females. On the emotional level, females were more likely than

males to regard the behavior portrayed in the films as pornographic, disgusting, or offensive. It is interesting that many women had mixed feelings: they reported experiencing positive feelings of enjoyment and arousal along with their disgust. These investigators found similar but not identical results when the films were shown to married couples: the wives were significantly less aroused than the husbands by both films and rated them as more disgusting and offensive than did their husbands. Similar findings have been reported in other studies (Schmidt, 1975). However, in all of these investigations, while the reported differences have been *statistically significant,* the real, *absolute* differences between males and females have usually been rather small.

Related to these purported sex differences is the common stereotype that women are more aroused by romantic themes while men prefer "raw sex" or more sexually explicit materials. Heiman (1975) investigated this possibility by having sexually experienced college students, both males and females, listen to one of four different types of tape recordings: In the *romantic* tapes, a couple was heard expressing caring and affection but they did not engage in intercourse. In the *erotic* tapes, the subjects heard explicit descriptions of heterosexual sex, taken from pornographic materials and popular novels. The *erotic-romantic* tapes combined both the romantic and sexually explicit elements. The *control* tapes consisted of a discussion of the relative merits of choosing different majors in college. Two other variables were also manipulated: whether the male or the female in the tape initiated sexual activity and whether the description of the psychological and sexual responses depicted centered mostly on the male or on the female. Subjects made self-reports about their arousal. Additionally, objective measures of physiological arousal were taken through the use of either a penile strain gauge or a photoplethysmograph (see Chapter 4 for a description of these instruments).

The results of this study are both interesting and important. Descriptions of explicit sex (the *erotic* or the *erotic-romantic* tapes) were most arousing for both females and males. Contrary to the stereotype, women were more aroused than men by the *erotic* tape. Both sexes were most aroused by tapes in which activity was female-initiated and in which the female response was most vividly described. Perhaps the most significant finding was that a large proportion of the women subjects apparently were not aware of their own physiological arousal. Overall, there was a high correlation between arousal measured by self-reports and arousal measured by physiological methods. However, about one-half of the women did not report being aroused when the physiological measures indicated they were, indeed, sexually stimulated. It remains unclear as to whether these females were just unwilling to *report* their feelings or whether they really were unaware of their own physiological arousal.

These few studies may be taken as representative of the laboratory findings concerning the effects of sexually stimulating materials. Basically, while pornographic or erotic materials cause sexual arousal and may activate sexual activity, an individual's usual *pattern* of sexual expression is unaffected by exposure to such materials. And while there are reported differences of response between males and females, these differences are usually quite small; female and male responses to erotic material are generally much more similar than they are different.

## PORNOGRAPHY AND THE SEX OFFENDER

One of the most frequent arguments against pornography has been that exposure to pornographic materials is somehow strongly implicated in (if not the direct cause of) sexual offenses such as rape. There have been two extensive investigations of this possibility.

Workers from the Kinsey Institute for Sex Research interviewed 1,500 convicted institutionalized sex offenders, 888 criminals institutionalized for other than sex offenses, and a control group of 477 noninstitutionalized individuals (Gebhard, Gagnon, Pomeroy, and Christenson, 1965). Some experience with pornography was found for almost all the subjects in all groups. However, interest in and arousal from pornography were not found to be related to the sex criminals' commission of their crimes. In fact, as a group, convicted sex offenders were less interested in and less aroused by pornography than noninstitutionalized control subjects. Kinsey had previously found (Kinsey et al., 1948) that fantasy was not very important in the sex lives of less educated males from lower socioeconomic classes. Almost all of the sex offenders in this study were from the lower socioeconomic classes. Thus, cultural/demographic variables appear to be related to one's reaction to erotic materials. Nevertheless, exposure to pornography does not seem important in the making of a sex criminal.

Two specific subgroups of sex offenders did indicate a substantial interest in pornography. One such group were those individuals convicted of homosexual offenses against adults. This group, however, was from higher socioeconomic classes than the rest of the offenders, thus supporting the relationship between pornography and demographic factors. The other group of offenders who showed more interest in pornography were those convicted of aggressive sexual acts against minors. Gebhard et al. (1965) concluded that this reaction to pornography *per se* was not likely to have been influential in the committed offenses. Rather, this group of men had poor impulse control and seemed to overreact (often violently) to a variety of different stimuli. Their reaction to pornography was seen as simply a part of their life style of exaggerated overreaction to almost everything.

Goldstein and Kant (1973) studied more than 260 individuals from several noninstitutionalized groups in addition to convicted, institutionalized sex offenders; the entire group comprised male homosexuals, male transsexuals, active pornography users, black control subjects, and white control subjects. Their findings supported those of Gebhard et al. (1965). Sex offenders in general had *less* exposure to pornography earlier in their lives and currently than those who were not sex offenders. (Homosexual sex offenders were again the exception in this study.) Exposure to pornography was not cited by the sex offenders as important factors in the commission of their offenses.

The findings surrounding offenders convicted of rape were especially interesting. These offenders had extremely repressive and moralistic attitudes regarding sexuality in general (as a group, for example, they were highly opposed to premarital intercourse). They were also deficient in factual knowledge about sexuality compared to other groups in the study. Finally, they

had very little exposure to pornography, yet they engaged in more extensive and more varied sexual fantasies. Goldstein and Kant suggested that rapists use pornography differently from other people. Most individuals use pornography in an expressive fashion, that is, as an adjunct to heighten sexual arousal, whereas rapists, according to Goldstein and Kant, use pornography defensively. Their suggestion derives from the following: Rapists seem to choose strictly heterosexual pornography portraying conventional sexual activities. But their fantasies are often more unconventional and threatening to them, for example, transsexual or homosexual in nature. Thus, rapists may be using pornography to defend against or ward off their anxiety-producing fantasies.

These studies of convicted sex offenders do not support the popular belief that there is a causative relationship between pornography and sex crimes. On the contrary, sex criminals are less interested in and are less aroused by pornography than are non-sex offenders or normal individuals. Additionally, as a group they have had *less* exposure to pornographic materials throughout their lives than most people in our society.

## PORNOGRAPHY IN DENMARK

Recent social and legal changes within the Danish society have provided a unique, albeit unplanned, opportunity to investigate some effects of widespread and legal distribution of pornographic materials. In 1960, the availability of erotic literature, particularly paperback novels, began to increase markedly and reached a peak in 1967. For the next two years, until 1969, there was also a large increase in the availability of sexually graphic pictures (Commission on Obscenity and Pornography, 1970). These increases occurred in spite of the fact that the dissemination of such materials was illegal in Denmark at the time. Thus, the Danish situation in the 1960s was in many ways like the situation in the United States during the 1970s: a marked increase in the availability of pornography occurred even though these materials were illegal.

In June, 1967, the Danish Parliament removed the legal restrictions against erotic materials and in June, 1969, made it legal to sell pornographic pictures to individuals over 16 years of age. Since there are substantial data regarding the incidence of sex offenses during these years of increasing availability of pornography, it has been possible to look at the relationship between the availability of pornography in a society and the incidence of sex crimes.

Some interesting results emerge when we look at the incidence of Danish sex crimes over a period spanning three decades (Commission on Obscenity and Pornography, 1970; Kutchinsky, 1973). The overall rate of total sex offenses (excluding rape) remained very stable from 1948 until the mid-1960s. A large decrease in the incidence of such crimes was noted between 1966 and 1967 (remember that 1967 represented the peak in terms of availability of pornographic literature, and it was the year that the sale of these materials was legalized). This rate continued to decline into the early 1970s.

When we look at the decade of 1959 to 1969, we see a large decline in the rate of certain specific sex offenses. In Copenhagen, exhibitionism decreased by around 60%, voyeurism by 80%, and child molesting by about 70% during this decade. Kutchinsky (1973) has pointed out that public attitudes may have accounted for some, but certainly not all, of these decreases. Public and police attitudes toward exhibitionism appeared to have become more liberal and permissive during this time; thus, the incidence of this offense may not have actually changed, but rather such offenses were less likely to be reported or prosecuted. On the other hand, attitudes toward child molesting and voyeurism changed little during the 1960s, and the substantial decreases in these offenses cannot be attributed to attitudinal changes. It was also found that these changes in the incidence of specific sex offenses could not be accounted for by legislative actions, alteration of law enforcement practices, or modified police data-collecting or reporting procedures (Commission on Obscenity and Pornography, 1970).

Finally, it should be noted that the incidence of rape remained essentially unchanged during this period of time. The implications of this phenomenon, and especially its possible relationship to the availability of pornography, remain speculative at best. However, we do know that, among American populations at least, rapists are different in many ways from other types of sex offenders.

What can the Danish experience tell us about the effects of widespread availability of pornographic materials? To conclude that availability resulted directly in a lower incidence of sex offenses is premature and inappropriate. What is important is that widespread availability of pornography did not lead to *increases* in any type of sex offenses. Here, then, is additional data counter to the argument that exposure to pornography may be a direct cause of sex crimes.

## PORNOGRAPHY: GOOD OR BAD?

As we noted earlier in this chapter and elsewhere, a person's attitudes about sexuality are often very individualized, based on a set of unique learning experiences. One's personal *decisions* about sexual matters often are based on religious, political, or other personal beliefs rather than on scientific data. While the data reviewed in this chapter does not indicate that harmful effects may be expected from exposure to sexually arousing or pornographic materials, many individuals remain opposed to pornography on other grounds.

Drakeford and Hamm (1973) have suggested that there are a variety of non-data-based indictments against pornography. They point out that pornography has created what they term a "mythical woman," which is really a portrayal of a masculine wish fulfillment. The woman in pornography is seen as a lustful, promiscuous female who spends all her time tracking down men with whom she can satisfy her sensuous desires. Additionally, these writers suggest that the activities portrayed in pornographic material are actually counter to what we now about human sexuality. For example, they argue that women are involved in most of the pornographic representations of bestiality when, in fact, Kinsey and his associates found this behavior to be predominately a masculine one. They further contend that pornography divorces love from sex, may produce self-effacing attitudes and undue performance fears in both sexes, and generally misrepresents the true nature of human sexuality.

Those who have been exposed to any significant amounts of pornography will probably agree with these generalizations about the nature of much pornography available in the United States today. On the other hand, the data presented in this chapter does not suggest that pornography has any long-term negative effects on its users nor does it appear implicated in the commission of sexual offenses. Attitudes and decisions regarding the use of pornography will therefore probably remain highly personalized and individual in nature.

# Chapter 13

## Sexual Problem Behaviors

## INTRODUCTION

"We know that every actual thing we can do in an erotic context is also done by our nearest relatives among the mammalian animals and always has been done in every human culture from which our records survive. This, and a general swing in our own culture away from puritanism, from ascetism, from 'spirituality' and toward a warmer and more bodily way of being, has loosened the tourniquet which used to strangle many loves and caresses."

Wayland Young: *Eros Denied*

Abnormal sexual behavior is a matter of great concern to all of us. Unfortunately, as we saw in Chapter 11, the question of sexual deviancy in our society is complicated by our own unrealistic legal standards. Despite this source of confusion, there are certain forms of sexual misconduct which cannot be tolerated by any society, regardless of differences in history, tradition, and values. These forms of sexual misconduct are those behaviors such as rape and child molesting, which involve an obvious antisocial component. There are also a variety of sexual behaviors which have been traditionally regarded as deviant on the basis of conventional and social standards but are not necessarily antisocial acts in the sense that others are victimized as a consequence of the behavior. Transvestism and fetishism are examples of such behaviors. The standards related to such unconventional sexual behaviors, however, are in a constant state of flux. For these reasons, the title of this chapter connotes this shifting set of values, rather than referring to such behavior as pathological. In this context, we have reviewed the various definitions of sexual problem behaviors, several classification schemes, and a number of examples which have been traditionally included in these categories.

## DEFINING ABNORMAL BEHAVIOR

The question of defining abnormal or deviant sexual behavior has been a major concern since the dawn of history. As we saw in the preceding chapters, every age and every culture established its own standards of "normal" sexual behavior and designed various prohibitions to avoid deviation from those standards. In our own society, the definition of abnormal sexual behavior has been hampered by our lack of understanding of human sexuality in general. Thus, there is continuing confusion between what is publicly defined as sexually deviant, on the one hand, and what is actually practiced in private. Our conventional standards specifically reject a host of sexual practices which are evidently engaged in by many members of society. Perhaps the clearest example of this inconsistency has to do with masturbation, which many people still consider to be deviant yet which is practiced by the vast majority of males and a substantial number of females. At a personal level, this confusion regarding the definition of abnormal sexual behavior has convinced many individuals that they are deviant simply because their own sexual fantasies, impulses, and behaviors are out of keeping with public standards, even though they are quite normal by other standards.

Despite the continued difficulty in defining sexual deviance, one perspective of how such definitions emerge may be derived from an analysis of relevant cultural practices. A survey of the various social and cultural practices that have been used for the purpose of identifying sexual deviancy suggests that sexual abnormality has sometimes been defined directly, and sometimes indirectly or by inference. Examples of direct definitions are legal statutes, religious pronouncements, and official documents. Thus, as we saw in Chapter 11, incest, bestiality, pedophilia, necrophilia, etc. have been directly defined and universally condemned as abnormal.

Indirect definitions emerge from an attempt to define normal practices and then, by inference, a determination that departures from the normal are deviant and *ab*normal. This distinction is, of course, an arbitrary one, since, in the last analysis, any culture's value system regarding abnormal sexual behavior is ultimately shaped by both direct and indirect influences.

We have already reviewed direct legal definitions of deviant and outlawed sexual behaviors in Chapter 11. This chapter will focus on indirect definitions, as well as several attempts at direct definitions, especially as these pertain to Western society. We will start with an analysis of the various definitions of *normal* sexual behavior that have been proposed and that have had a profound influence on Western thought and practice.

## THE VARYING DEFINITIONS OF NORMAL SEXUAL BEHAVIOR

Although the definition of normal sexuality in Western society has varied from time to time, the basic concept has remained relatively constant. Thus, as we saw earlier, normality has been largely defined in the context of the marriage relationship. Some authorities, however, have proposed even more restrictive conditions. St. Augustine, for example, the early religious authority, formalized the longstanding Christian ethic which regarded celibacy as the noblest ideal of human attainment. Normal sexual behavior, in this context, was restricted to intercourse between a husband and wife for the exclusive purpose of procreation. Sex for pleasure, or sex under other circumstances, came to be regarded as deviant and sinful. In effect, then, many sexual activities fell into the category of deviancy by decree. This position influenced church doctrine and legal statutes for hundreds of years, and elaborate lists of penalties were devised to deal with those who deviated from these rigid standards.

Although contemporary values have moderated the Church's earlier position to some extent, the impact of this definition is still apparent in many areas of society. As recently as the early 1900s, for example, church officials argued that not only should sex be restricted to procreation between a husband and wife, but that it should be practiced only with the husband in the superior position. This pronouncement caused considerable embarrassment for missionaries attempting to convert primitive tribes to Christian values.

Recently, a newer and far more permissive standard has begun to emerge in our society which represents a radical departure from these earlier beliefs. This newer standard accepts the value of sex for pleasure and recognizes that traditional standards were unrealistic and impractical. The basic thesis of this approach is that any form of sexual behavior is normal as long as consenting adults are involved and no harm derives to the individual or to society as a result of the sexual behavior. Clearly, this viewpoint accepts as normal a variety of practices, including homosexuality, masturbation, and perhaps other forms of sexuality that would have been defined as abnormal by earlier standards.

## CRITERIA FOR DEFINING SEXUAL PROBLEM BEHAVIORS

There are, of course, various criteria that have been used for defining sexual problem behaviors. Generally speaking, these may be divided into formal and informal standards.

### Informal Criteria

The kinds of informal criteria that have been used to define sexual problem behaviors may be considered in the context of social mores, conventional practices, and community values. Thus, one may examine the general ethic of a given community or culture in order to identify that culture's sexual value system. In a country as complex and multifaceted as ours, this is no simple enterprise. In fact, it was just such an observation that prompted the Supreme Court to reject a general definition of pornography. Instead, the Court advanced the notion that pornography should be defined in terms of local standards.

In other words, the Court argued that, in a country as diverse as ours, and with an issue as complex as pornography, it was best to allow each community to define its own standards on the basis of local values. Thus, movies depicting explicit, hard-core sexual content might not be outlawed in New York or Los Angeles, but even the sale of *Playboy* magazine might be regarded as offensive in a small, sexually conservative Midwestern community. The Court's position was that local authorities such as clerical or legal officials could best reflect that community's sexual standards, rather than a general standard being imposed by others.

The opposite of this argument, however, suggests that any given culture, no matter how diverse and complex, may still be characterized by national sexual mores and values which, perhaps, reflect the general consensus of opinion for that culture. Such mores and values may be derived from a variety of sources, such as historical tradition, religious preferences, the mass media, political events, etc. Although conclusions based on such references are always open to serious question, perhaps some limited insights into our values regarding sexual deviance can be obtained by such an analysis.

As for historical tradition, our society has typically responded very slowly to new social influences. The "silent majority" is a popular expression referring to the broad mainstream of social, political, and probably sexual conservatism that exists in our society. Similarly, various examples from the media, such as ar-

ticles in popular magazines, newspaper articles, advertising strategies, etc., while clearly reflecting a more permissive and open expression of sexual topics, for the most part continue to present sexually related materials in the context of traditional values. The daily newspaper, for example, may carry a column on sexual inadequacy that might not have appeared a decade ago, but typically, such articles are presented in the context of improving *marital* relationships.

Finally, political events occasionally occur which provide further evidence of the strength of traditional values. Thus, in 1976 the Anita Bryant campaign to prevent homosexuals from teaching in the schools was strongly supported by the majority of citizens in the communities involved.

These various observations suggest that Americans continue to accept traditional standards in defining abnormal sexual behavior. Although there is clear evidence of greater tolerance for sexual expression, this change appears to be limited to those dimensions of sexuality which are the least threatening to tradition. For example, more and more married couples may be practicing a wider variety of sexual positions and techniques than were practiced a generation ago, but most Americans probably continue to consider homosexuality a sexual deviation.

### Formal Criteria for Defining Sexual Problem Behaviors

Of the various formal criteria that have been used in this connection, the most frequently relied upon are legal, medical-psychiatric, and statistical. Legal standards were reviewed in Chapter 11. Consequently, we will focus our attention on medical-psychiatric and statistical criteria in this chapter.

### Medical-Psychiatric Criteria

The criteria that have been used to define sexual problem behaviors in this context are an outgrowth of medical concerns with health-related conditions. In medicine, any condition that impairs the biological welfare of the individual is considered to be pathological. The psychiatric formulation of this principle is similar in that practices, including sexual practices, that impair the mental health or emotional status of the individual are also defined as pathological.

There is a long history that is relevant in this connection, starting with Krafft-Ebing's publication of *Psychopathia Sexualis* in 1886 and stretching, through Freud, to the present time. Here, again, the conventional emphasis upon sex between husband and wife was accepted as the norm; and almost any deviation was regarded as abnormal, although more recently psychiatry has moderated the deviancy implications for several sex practices that were previously defined as abnormal, especially homosexuality.

It was Krafft-Ebing who first described in any detail a variety of sexual deviations (fetishism, pedophilia, bestiality, necrophilia, transvestism, etc.). Freud elaborated on this position by classifying sexual deviations on the basis of abnormal sexual "objects" or abnormal sexual "aims." According to Freud, any given sex act involves an object and an aim or purpose. In normal sex, the object is an appropriate adult of the opposite sex, and the aim is intercourse. Thus, Freud considered homosexuality to be a deviation in the choice of sexual object, as was true of pedophilia, necrophilia, bestiality, and incest. Deviations in sexual aim included such practices as voyeurism, transvestism, exhibitionism, etc.

This tradition has been generally accepted by modern psychiatry with the exception of homosexuality. As we saw in Chapter 10, the current psychiatric position defines homosexuality as abnormal only in those cases where such a sexual orientation creates mental conflict for the individual. In addition to the deviations outlined above, illegal sexual practices such as rape are also considered to be pathological, since such behavior would necessarily produce emotional stress for the individuals involved.

## Statistical Criteria

The statistical approach to defining abnormal sexual behavior relies upon an analysis of the number of individuals who engage in a given practice, thereby defining normality in a statistical sense. Thus, if a majority of individuals have masturbated at one time or another, by definition such a practice would be considered normal. Conversely, if only a few members of society are transvestites, then, by definition, transvestism is abnormal. There are two problems with such an approach. The first refers to the manner in which the data are derived, since, as we have seen, it is difficult to obtain valid information regarding sexual practices. The second has to do with the degree of overlap between the data of a statistically derived norm and the data which are obtained through other criteria. For example, a majority of Americans may be cigarette smokers, but clearly, on the basis of medical criteria, this activity would be regarded as pathological. Similarly, incest may be the norm in a given subculture, in the sense that the majority of the members practice it, but criteria from other sources would consider such behavior to be clearly abnormal.

It should be clear at this point that no universal set of standards defining sexual deviations has been formulated. What is sometimes regarded as deviant in one framework is considered to be normal in another. In particular, when we turn from those few sexual practices that are universally condemned, for example, pedophilia, incest, or necrophilia, to all of the other sex-related behaviors, considerable confusion continues to exist. Even the psychiatric approach emphasizing emotional distress is not entirely satisfactory, since the criteria that define emotional conflict are also ambiguous and are usually determined by the judgment of individual practitioners. Although no entirely satisfactory resolution of this issue can be offered at the present time, it is important to recognize that different standards are used by different perspectives for different sexual practices. With this caution in mind, let us turn to a discussion of the various sexual practices that have traditionally fallen into the deviant category by most of the criteria described above.

The following discussions are ordered in terms of seriousness of the behavior as defined by social standards. Thus, the first

class includes sexual problem behaviors that have a damaging impact on others and are considered to be serious violations. In this category, we have included pedophilia, incest, and rape. A second class of sexual problem behaviors has also been traditionally outlawed by society, but these behaviors may not necessarily have a damaging impact on others. In this category we have included necrophilia, bestiality, voyeurism, and exhibitionism. A third category includes those behaviors that typically do not have a serious impact on others but are also frowned upon by most social standards. Transvestism and fetishism are included here. Finally, certain sexual "styles," such as sadism, masochism, and sexual excesses, that may cut across all of the above dimensions are also discussed.

## FIRST ORDER PROBLEM BEHAVIORS

### PEDOPHILIA

This term comes from the Greek "love of children" and refers to those individuals who derive gratification from one form or another of sexual activity with children. The magnitude of this problem behavior is reflected by several surveys which report that as many as 35% of the women (Gagnon, 1965) and 20% of the men (McCaghy, 1971) interviewed had been molested at least once during their childhood.

The public image of the pedophile is that of an older man who entices unfamiliar girls into his car by offering them candy and then forces his attentions upon them. In order to understand the nature and impact of pedophilia, however, we must look beyond this stereotype. Most of our information regarding this problem behavior comes from the arrest records of convicted pedophiles (Gebhard, Gagnon, Pomeroy, and Christenson, 1965). Although data from these sources may have little bearing on nonconvicted pedophiles, several important facts emerge from this information. First, the arrest records of convicted child molesters show a much higher rate of male than female pedophiles. Furthermore, most of these men were charged with sexually molesting a girl who was known to them (relative, friend, neighbor, etc.). The average age of the men at conviction was 35, but about 25% of the men in the sample were 45 or older. Psychological characteristics often revealed such problems as below average intelligence, emotional disturbance, and a drinking history. However, most convicted child molesters were not mentally retarded, and the vast majority led apparently normal lives prior to their conviction. It is of interest to note that the majority of convicted pedophiles revealed a highly moralistic attitude toward sex and had strong religious convictions.

As to the actual sexual activity, the typical convicted pedophile restricted himself to fondling the child's external genitalia, and the entire sexual encounter was usually quite brief. Gratification may be achieved by a "spontaneous" orgasm during the encounter, or by masturbation during or shortly after the sexual episode. Intercourse was rarely attempted, and, fortunately, the pedophile who engages in violent practices associated with child molesting is rare.

The homosexual pedophile is uncommon among the

homosexual population in general. Furthermore, such individuals are as vigorously scorned by the majority of homosexuals as they are by society at large. Psychological profiles of the homosexual pedophile typically reveal extremely deviant personality patterns.

A number of theories have attempted to explain pedophilia. The most popular of these attributes pedophilia to a fear of failing in normal heterosexual relationships. It is more probably the case, however, that such problem behaviors are the end result of a host of influences that are only poorly understood at the present time. In part, our limited knowledge of the causes of pedophilia stems from the universal revulsion that such behavior generates. Convicted child molesters are even scorned by the prison society, and very little effort has been directed at analyzing the reasons for this behavior or developing procedures to rehabilitate such individuals.

> One of the few efforts to treat pedophilia has been reported by a team of British practitioners. The patient in this case was a 25-year-old clerical worker who was being considered for brain surgery because of his severe pedophilia obsessions and compulsions. The patient's sexual interests were restricted to 9- to 12-year-old girls; and, although he had apparently not actually molested any, he spent a great deal of time watching, following, talking to young girls and masturbating to sexual fantasies of young girls.
>
> The treatment procedure involved aversion therapy, in which the patient was administered a brief, painful shock contingent on the pedophilia behavior. In this case, the patient was given photographs of young girls and asked to use them in creating a sexual fantasy. A plethysmograph (an instrument that measures changes in blood volume) was attached to his penis in order to identify erections in connection with this activity. When an erectile response occurred, the shock was administered to his arm. Interspersed with a series of such trials, other trials were administered in which the shock apparatus was disconnected and the patient was instructed to engage in normal heterosexual fantasies.
>
> A total of 200 pedophilia shock trials and 60 normal (no-shock) trials were administered over an eight-week period. The course of treatment revealed a gradual and continued decline in the frequency of erections to the pedophilia stimuli and an increase in normal sexual reactions. Although the patient continued to experience other sexual adjustment problems, one year after treatment he married, was free of obsessional symptoms, and no longer ran the risk of being convicted for child molesting.
>
> (From: Bancroft, J. H., Jr., Jones, H. G., and Pullan, B. R. A simple transducer for measuring penile erections with comments on its use in the treatment of sexual disorders. *Behaviour Research and Therapy*, 1966, *4*, 239-241.)

Recently, attention has been focused on the effects of the molesting experience on the child. Many authorities have argued that, except for those cases involving violence, the act, in and of itself, may be less traumatic than the parents' reactions to the experience. Thus, although the number of people who

report having had a sexual experience during childhood with an adult is surprisingly high, very few report serious psychological problems as a result of these experiences (Gagnon, 1965; Landis, 1956). It would seem, then, that when a child reports such an experience, the best response is to offer sympathy and understanding to the child, without overreacting to the possibilities of permanent damage.

## INCEST

Incest is most often defined as coitus between a parent and a child, although most societies also include and expressly forbid sexual relationships between other combinations of family members. Thus, there are various State laws (reviewed in Chapter 11) prohibiting individuals who are blood related (for example, siblings, uncle and niece, aunt and nephew) from marrying each other. Beyond these easily recognized circumstances, however, the definition of incest varies among States and among religions. The Roman Catholic Church and the Greek Orthodox Church, for example, prohibit marriage between first cousins, but some other religions permit such arrangements.

Accurate information regarding the frequency and character of incest is woefully lacking. Studies based on court findings suggest that incest is a very rare occurrence. Weinberg's (1955) survey of incest convictions indicates that only about two people per million are prosecuted for incest in the United States. By far, the vast majority of these cases involved sexual relationships between a father and his daughter. The second highest category of incest convictions involved coitus between siblings. Information from other sources, however, suggests that the actual incidence of incest may be considerably higher. The data from the study done by Gebhard and his associates (1965) suggest that as many as 4% of the population had been involved in an incestuous relationship at one time or another. Moreover, the majority of these cases involved sex between siblings, with incest between father and daughter as the second major category. Hunt's survey (1974) revealed a higher incidence of reported incest by his subjects (7%) with, again, the bulk of the cases characterized by sexual relationships between siblings or cousins. The fact that Hunt included cousins in his survey may have been responsible for the higher incidence reported in his study.

Whatever the actual incidence and character of the incest, there is some reason to believe that a substantial number of individuals in our society are exposed to incestuous experiences at some time during their lifetime. Again, however, an adequate understanding of incest is, no doubt, hampered by our traditional revulsion surrounding such practices.

Although much has been written about the dangers of incest, particularly in terms of the risk to society (Murdoch, 1949; Weinberg, 1955), it is only recently that a scientific perspective has been brought to bear on this issue. A number of authorities have described the risk to the offspring of such unions (Neel and Schull, 1975). Still others have focused their attention on the psychological impact of such experiences on the individuals involved, especially in terms of guilt and shame. A number of case studies, for example, imply that frigidity and impotence are the end result of such experiences. The recent concern and interest in sexual abuse in families is, evidently, a response to these concerns. Lester (1972), however, argues that conclusions regarding the damaging emotional effects of incest have not been well documented, and it remains for further research to better describe the cause and effect relationships between various incestuous practices and the emotional impact on the individuals involved.

Little is known regarding the relevant psychological characteristics of individuals who engage in such practices. What little we do known stems mainly from an analysis of the court records of men who were convicted of incest with their daughters. Generalizations to the population at large and to those who engage in other forms of incest, particularly of the sibling variety, must be regarded with caution.

Gebhard and his associates (1965) reported that most of the men arrested for incest were poorly educated, middle-aged, typically unemployed at the time of the offense, and possessed of a drinking problem. Most of these men came from an unstable family background and revealed a long history of inadequate social relationships. The vast majority of the convictions were for intercourse, and in only about 8% of the cases did the daughters resist. (It must be recognized that "resistance" is a relative term that may not adequately describe the extent to which coercion and other subtle pressures may be brought to bear in such circumstances.) The typical incestuous relationship continued over a long period of time and sometimes involved the silent consent of the wife/mother who, for a variety of reasons, chose not to intervene. Even less is known about brother-sister incest, which is evidently more common than father-daughter incest.

Theories regarding the causes of incest are based largely on speculation and poorly founded assumptions. There is, of course, a longstanding (perhaps morbid) fascination with the topic of incest as revealed by our major literary sources. Perhaps it was this tradition that convinced Freud of the significance of incest for understanding psychosexual development, in general. As we saw in Chapter 6, Freud argued that unconscious incestuous impulses were a universal phenomenon. Although the vast majority of individuals were able to resolve these impulses and thereby engage in normal sexual practices in adulthood, for Freud those individuals who were unable to resolve these impulses suffered from various neuroses later in life.

While few students of human behavior accept Freud's original thesis today, there is still no adequate theory to explain such behavior. Before such a theory can be offered, it would seem important to first distinguish between the varying forms of incest, on the grounds that each of these different circumstances is the result of different causes. Incest between siblings, for example, may be the result of sheer opportunity, curiosity, and the more or less normal sexual by-play and experimentation that occurs during childhood, especially where children share a bedroom and the usual parental controls are not exercised. Incest between a father and a daughter, however, may be more complex and perhaps best understood by examining the psychological characteristics of the father and the interactions between the various family members.

In addition to these perspectives, incest may also be regarded as occupying one end of a continuum, with normal familial interactions at the other end. Thus, behavior that may be regarded as incestuouslike in one context may represent wholesome affection in another. Similarly, the adult who interprets his or her childhood experiences as being incestuous may actually be misrepresenting them. Whether incestuous behavior is actual or fancied, one of the newer approaches to treating the problem of incest is family therapy in which all of the family members are required to examine the nature of their relationships and interactions.

## RAPE

The third problem behavior that we have included in this first category of sexual problem behaviors is rape. Although not a traditionally defined "perversion," rape is gradually being recognized by society as a sexual deviation, creating serious consequences for the victim as well as raising questions about the stability of the perpetrator.

As we saw in Chapter 11, the legal definition of rape varies from State to State, but all of the laws include the concept of the use of force or the threat of force on an unconsenting person for the purpose of achieving sexual gratification. The earliest definitions of rape were restricted to the use of force by a male on a female other than his wife. Over the years, this definition has been expanded to include a number of other circumstances, such as statutory rape (intercourse with a girl under the age of consent), homosexual rape, and, most recently, wife rape. Inasmuch as these legal issues were discussed in Chapter 11, the present discussion will focus on issues related to the typical rape offense, that is, the use of force by an adult male on an adult female.

Police records reveal that there are about 50 reported rapes per year for every 100,000 women in our society. Law enforcement officials estimate, however, that only one rape in five is actually reported. These statistics suggest, then, that rape is the most frequently committed violent crime in America today (Griffin, 1971).

With regard to the kind of man who engages in rape, there is no typical rapist. Police statistics compiled on convicted offenders reveal that most rapists were in their middle twenties at the time of their first offense and that most rapes were directed at a woman who was below the age of thirty and who was unknown to the attacker. However, about 40% of the cases involved a woman who was known to the rapist. The study done by Gebhard and his associates (1965) revealed that the majority of rapists in their sample were from a low socioeconomic background, were of below average intelligence, were raised under unstable family circumstances, and were physically unattractive. A substantial number of men in this sample, however, were of average intelligence, had a stable employment history, and led otherwise ordinary lives. Amir's study (1971) of 646 rapists revealed that the popular belief that rapists were insane had no basis in fact.

Because of the wide variability in background and characteristics of rapists, social scientists have attempted to classify different rape patterns. Cohen and his associates (1971), for example, have identified four rape categories which differ in terms of the typical rape patterns and the individual's motivation. The Aggressive-Aim rapist includes those individuals who engage in rape for the avowed purpose of injuring the victim beyond the rape act itself. Such men typically inflict injury to the victim's primary or secondary sex organs subsequent to the rape, for example, by inserting objects into the victim's vagina. The Aggressive-Aim rapist is often married but typically reveals a deliberate "masculine" life style and a derogatory or aggressive posture toward females in general. A second category, the Sexual-Aim rapist, is motivated more by sexual gratification rather than by aggression per se. Such individuals typically reveal a history of inadequate social relationships and a pattern of other sexual deviations, such as voyeurism and exhibitionism. The Sex-Aggression-Fusion rapist requires violence in order to become sexually aroused, and it is the struggle and resistance which he finds stimulating; however, such men are not aggressive after the rape has been completed. Sex-Aggression-Fusion rapists reveal a long history of impulsive acts and aggressive behavior even during childhood. Finally, the Impulse rapist differs from the other three types in that the rape act is more the result of sheer opportunity and less the expression of a longstanding pattern of deviant sexuality. Thus, the Impulse rapist may be involved in another criminal activity and, by sheer circumstance, discover that he is in a position to force a woman to comply with his sexual demands.

Many theories have also been offered in an attempt to explain rape. The traditional psychiatric position, for example, interprets rape as the expression of a disturbed personality which, in turn, is the result of an unstable childhood. Other authorities are more prone to explain rape in the context of the aggressive male role — passive female role that characterizes our society. Thus, the socialization process emphasizes sexual dominance for the male and reticence for the female as revealed in the popular sexual game in which the man, operating under pressure "to score," interprets the woman's no as a concealed yes. Such influences may foster an aggressive model for men and a rape-victim model for women. Still a third explanation views rape as an expression of nonconformist values. Thus, for certain individuals, rape is rationalized as a retaliation against an unjust society that practices discrimination and prejudice.

It is difficult to assess the validity of these theories in view of our limited knowledge regarding the causes of rape. The psychiatric position has the merit of face validity; however, defining a rapist as unstable tells us little about the causes of such behavior. The role model theory suggests that rape is a complex social phenomenon with multiple causes which makes good sense intuitively but is difficult to verify. The nonconformist theory can be criticized on the grounds that two wrongs don't make a right, that is, exposure to social injustice of one kind does not justify the expression of injustices of another kind.

Finally, all of these theories suffer from the simple fact that many men (perhaps most) are exposed to the kinds of influences described above, yet they do not resort to rape and do not develop aggressive sexual patterns. It would seem, then, that the status of these theories is questionable at the present time.

One further issue requires discussion in this context. There is a longstanding belief held by many individuals that many rape acts are, at least in part, caused by the female. Thus, law enforcement officials sometimes imply that the rape victim has provoked the attack by virtue of her dress, by her behavior, and/or by deliberately placing herself in a clearly dangerous situation. According to a newspaper account, in a recent case in Wisconsin, for example, the judge presiding over a rape trial commented that the man charged with the crime was not responsible for his actions because he had been exposed to women who dressed "sexually." (Later this judge was removed from office by a referendum approved by the voters in this community.) In addition to such examples, there are countless reports of rape victims who tell of questionable interrogation procedures and degrading treatment during the course of an investigation and during the trial. Aside from the obvious difficulty of defining what is meant by provocation (since, conceivably, any act can be so interpreted), the actual facts related to this issue contradict these widely held beliefs. According to the Federal Commission on Crimes of Violence, for example, only 4% of all reported rapes could be attributed to provocation on the part of the victim, even though the definition of provocation was broadly defined.

But of even greater concern than the difference between what is believed and what is true is the peculiar status that the crime of rape holds in our society. As we saw in Chapter 11, rape is the only violent crime in our society in which the victim is dealt with as if she were an accessory. Clearly, these are values that cannot be tolerated in an enlightened society if we are ever to come to grips with this serious problem behavior.

---

There are a number of steps you should take if you are the victim of a rape. First, get immediate medical attention. An extensive examination should determine whether or not injuries have occurred, even if you don't think there are any. In addition, tests for pregnancy and VD should be administered.

If and when your medical needs are taken care of, you will have to consider the question of reporting the rape and the possibility of subsequent prosecution against the assailant. The attack can be reported anonymously (check to see if your community has a rape crisis center) if you choose not to prosecute. If you want to prosecute, don't shower, change clothes, or douche, since evidence may be lost in the process, and call the police as soon as possible. If your case comes to trial and you will serve as a witness, familiarize yourself with courtroom and trial procedures.

Finally, you will have to consider the emotional consequences. Rape is almost always traumatic, engendering anger, guilt, shame, and disgust. Most rape victims have found that discussing their experience and their reactions to it in the presence of sympathetic friends and counselors has helped them to resolve the trauma. Many communities have formed informal discussion groups as a means of sharing experiences and offering emotional support to rape victims.

"One important thing to remember: although they can help, the police, the courts, or men will not finally stop rape. Women will stop rape."

(From: The Boston Women's Health Book Collective, *Our Bodies, Ourselves*. Second edition. New York: Simon and Schuster, 1976.)

What can be said then in summary about the problem of rape? First, the development of protective measures represents an important priority. Women should avail themselves of the many rape-awareness and self-defense programs currently being offered in many communities. Of equal importance is the development of effective treatment techniques for women who have been exposed to the trauma of rape. Such efforts are only at the beginning stages and much more needs to be accomplished in this area. One promising development is the recent emphasis upon rape-crisis centers which offer counseling to secondary rape victims (husband, boyfriend, parents, etc.) as well as assistance to the primary rape victim. Of a more long-range nature, more research should be directed at uncovering the causes of rape. The Cohen classification scheme discussed above represents an important step in this direction. If it can be demonstrated that different rape events can be organized into similar patterns, this breakdown will help in identifying the different causes of each type of rape. Identifying the causes of rape, in turn, will facilitate efforts to prevent the occurrence of rape. Finally, greater public awareness might help explode many of the myths which contribute to our cultural stereotypes regarding the crime of rape. It is important to recognize that our tolerance of rape and our failure to recognize rape as a violent act against another person has impeded efforts to eliminate the problem and has resulted in countless numbers of damaged lives.

# SECOND ORDER PROBLEM BEHAVIORS

As indicated above, a variety of sexual problem behaviors have been traditionally regarded as examples of deviations or perversions. A number of these problem behaviors are described in this section. Many of these practices would be defined as "paraphilias," a term that is used to indicate sexual pursuits that are atypical in a given culture.

## NECROPHILIA

Necrophilia is defined as sexual gratification in connection with the dead. The existence of a long history of laws and statutes prohibiting such practices suggests that necrophilia has represented a problem of varying degrees at different times. In our society necrophilia is apparently a very rare sexual practice and is generally considered to be associated with serious emotional disturbance.

## BESTIALITY

Bestiality (sometimes termed zoophilia) refers to sexual activity with animals. Like necrophilia, bestiality has been largely condemned, although surveys suggest that such practices are more common than necrophilia. Kinsey (1948), for example, reported that 17% of the male subjects in his survey who had been raised on a farm had engaged in bestiality. Most of these activities, however, occurred during adolescence and may reflect the generally exploratory and diverse nature of male sexuality which characterizes adolescence.

When animal contacts persist beyond this time frame, however, they are considered to be of a more serious nature. Thus, it is the small percentage of men and women who report a continuing pattern of bestiality that comprise the deviant category. The practices most frequently mentioned in this connection include copulation and oral-genital contacts with dogs. Such practices should be distinguished from exhibitions or sex shows involving prostitutes and animals.

Very little attention has been directed toward an explanation of bestiality, although it seems clear that at least some of these activities occur on the basis of opportunity.

## VOYEURISM

Voyeurism refers to those individuals who are more sexually aroused by observing sexually related stimuli, such as opposite sex nudes or strangers engaged in sex, than they are by the usual means of achieving sexual gratification. Furthermore, it is the danger and the excitement derived from "secret viewing" that contributes to the gratification and thereby determines the perverse nature of the act. This definition recognizes that it is normal to attend to and to be aroused by appropriate sexual stimuli, as in admiring a sexually attractive individual. Burlesque shows, topless acts, magazines such as *Penthouse* or *Playgirl,* and the recent increase in male strip shows represent additional examples of catering to the voyeur in all of us. It is only when such activities become ends in themselves and/or become the preferred sexual activity that they begin to represent a source of difficulty for the individual. Moreover, voyeurism is a serious offense when the individual commits a crime or violates the privacy of others in connection with the peeping Tom activities.

In view of what we know about sex differences in general (for example, men are evidently more aroused by nude women than women are by nude men), there are many more convicted male voyeurs than female voyeurs. Summarizing from the Gebhard and associates study (1964), the typical convicted voyeur was in his early twenties, almost always selected a strange woman as his target, and usually engaged in masturbation during or shortly after the voyeur activity. Although psychologically immature, the typical voyeur is not seriously disturbed and does not constitute a physical threat to women.

Theoretical explanations of voyeurism usually emphasize inadequacy in interpersonal relationships as a determining factor. Again, however, such an explanation provides little genuine insight into the causes of voyeurism. It seems reasonable to assume that some cases of voyeurism may be understood as special cases of normal viewing which, as we have seen, is an ordinary practice engaged in by many individuals. Why the voyeur begins to deviate from these normal practices to the point that "viewing" becomes more important than "doing," as it were, remains an unanswered question.

Insofar as treatment is concerned, several sexual retraining programs have enabled voyeurs to acquire more ordinary sexual outlets. Although the evidence is still limited, it would appear that this is a problem condition which is readily amenable to rehabilitation.

## EXHIBITIONISM

The obverse of voyeurism is exhibitionism, in which sexual gratification is derived from exposing one's genitals in clearly inappropriate circumstances. The popular stereotype is that of the older man, dressed only in a raincoat, walking up to an unsuspecting female and suddenly whipping open his raincoat, thereby exposing (or flashing) his genitals. Again, however, the actual circumstances are at some variance to this image; and furthermore, except for such relatively clear-cut situations, the criteria for defining exhibitionism are highly ambiguous. Thus, our society allows for, and in some cases promotes, many exhibitionistic practices. These practices may range from provocative modes of dress (or undress, as the case may be) through the use of erotically suggestive advertisements to full nudity and even sex acts which are presented in the context of art or entertainment. Ordinarily, the participants in such events would not be considered exhibitionists. Moreover, the exposure of the genitals under other circumstances, as in a medical setting, is considered appropriate. Finally, there is a much greater tolerance (and even encouragement) for female exhibitionism in our society than for male exposure. Thus, it is hardly surprising to find a much higher incidence of convicted male exhibitionists than female exhibitionists. Again, then, it is the pattern, the frequency, and the extent to which such practices begin to serve as a substitute for more normal sexual pursuits that, in the last analysis, defines the exhibitionist.

Most of what is known about this problem behavior has been gathered from reports by women who have been accosted by exhibitionists and from police records. As indicated above, the facts that emerge from these sources do not support the stereotype. For example, the average age of all men convicted for exhibitionism is thirty. About 60% of the sample are or were married, and a substantial number evidently engaged in normal sexual activities in addition to their exhibitionistic practices.

In terms of the impact on the women, typically the most serious consequence of such an experience is shock and embarrassment which is usually short-lived unless the event is overreacted to by other individuals.

Gebhard and his colleagues (1965) analyzed the pattern of a large number of convicted exhibitionists and divided them into three categories. About 50% of the cases (the first category) were characterized by a repetitive pattern, that is, the exhibitor had engaged in such activities over a relatively long period of time. The activities were planned and the individual went through a regular sequence on each occasion. In a typical case of this nature, the exhibitionist drives his car down a street, spots a women waiting at a bus stop, parks his car around the corner, approaches her to a distance of within six feet, rapidly exposes his genitals (often accompanied by an erection), and then races off after the woman has registered her shock and alarm.

A second category was made up of mentally retarded individuals who expose themselves largely as the result of poor judgment and a lack of social controls. The third category was made up of individuals who exhibited themselves while under the influence of alcohol.

In terms of understanding the causes of exhibitionism, some theorists suggest that the typical exhibitionist is a basically dependent, insecure individual who is "compelled to reaffirm his masculinity by publicly displaying his genitals." Alternative explanations emphasize the manner in which the usual shock reaction to the act of exposure serves to maintain such behavior. Thus, a neutral or controlled reaction would remove the reasons for the exhibitionist to continue his practice. This theory has led to a treatment program in which identified exhibitionists are required to practice their ritual in the presence of women who have been trained to "keep their cool" under such circumstances. The preliminary results of these efforts are quite promising in that a number of such men have been returned to society with an apparently normal orientation and without any further difficulty.

---

### Treatment Of Exhibitionism

Callahan and Leitenberg have reported one of the better controlled studies in the literature regarding the treatment of such sexual problems as exhibitionism. Two of the six patients who served as subjects in the study were exhibitionists, while the other four revealed a variety of diverse and individualized patterns of deviant sexual orientation. Arousal to deviant sexual stimuli was measured by the penile plethysmograph previously described. Based on each subject's own idiosyncratic history, a series of slides was prepared and presented to them.

One form of treatment employed a brief, painful shock to the fingertips. When the subject revealed an erection to the deviant stimulus, shock was administered. These shock trials were interspersed with no-shock trials in the presence of "normal" responses. A second form of treatment employed "covert sensitization." This technique requires the patient to imagine engaging in the deviant behavior and then imagining a highly unpleasant event occurring before completion of the act. For example, an exhibitionist might be asked to imagine an exposure act and then, just prior to the culmination of the act, to imagine being caught in the act by his wife.

All subjects showed marked reduction in deviant sexual orientation as a result of both treatment modes. These changes were maintained in five of the six subjects during a follow-up period after the patients were discharged from the program. In one case, for example, a 15-year-old boy was treated for a four-year history of repeated exposure. He had been institutionalized twice for this behavior and had not benefited from prior psychotherapy treatment. An 18-month follow-up of his case revealed considerable improvement in all measures. Appropriate erectile responses occurred in response to normal and deviant conditions; urges to expose himself had completely disappeared; and he had been engaged in normal heterosexual dating for eight months prior to the follow-up examination.

(From: Callahan, E. J. and Leitenberg, H. Aversion therapy for sexual deviation: contingent shock and covert sensitization. *Journal of Abnormal Psychology,* 1973, 81, 60-73.)

# THIRD ORDER PROBLEM BEHAVIORS

## FETISHISM

A fetish is an inanimate object which is considered to possess certain magical properties. Fetishism is a condition in which erotic feelings are aroused by a nonsexual object, such as a glove. Thus, the individual who "fixates" on an object which serves as a substitute for the usual stimuli in order to achieve sexual gratification engages in fetishism. This problem condition is almost entirely limited to men and represents, in an exaggerated form, the normal tendency in most males to become aroused by objects associated with the sex act. For example, many men are at least mildly aroused by women's underwear or by women's stockings. Moreover, any given man may be partial to a particular part of the female anatomy, hence the terms "breast man," "leg man," etc. It is only when the individual focuses on these inanimate objects exclusively and when they become necessary for him to achieve gratification that a fetish is indicated. The popular stereotype is that of the man who steals into a backyard and removes from a clothesline, women's underwear, which he then uses in a masturbation ritual.

*Shoe fetish, SM device*

Almost any object can acquire sexual meaning, depending upon circumstances, and, thus, in principle, any object can be fixated upon for fetishism purposes. In practice, however, most fetishes involve either a part of the female anatomy or an object of clothing. For example, much has been written about shoe fetishism and glove fetishism. In a typical object fetish, the individual handles the object and fondles it while masturbating. He may also require that the object be available during intercourse, in order for him to perform.

Explanations of fetishism have ranged from psychoanalytic statements in the context of castration anxiety, to learning theory based on conditioned responses. The latter position argues that stimuli which are present during highly rewarding experiences, as in orgasm, may acquire a rewarding status of their own.

Treatment of the fetishist may involve a series of reeducation experiences in which the fetish is gradually removed from the sexual events while more ordinary stimuli are gradually presented. Such efforts have been quite successful in most cases.

## TRANSVESTISM

Closely related to fetishism is transvestism, which is wearing opposite-sex clothes in order to achieve sexual gratification. The popular image of the transvestite is the "closet queen" who parades in private while wearing feminine attire. Such behavior is usually associated in the public's mind with blatant homosexuality. Once again, however, the actual facts are quite inconsistent with the stereotype. It is, of course, true that some male homosexuals dress up as "drag queens" and some female homosexuals present a "butch" image. Cross dressing to achieve sexual gratification is entirely distinguishable from homosexuality, however, in that the sex object is still a member of the opposite sex.

There are also socially accepted forms of transvestism, for example, stage roles in which an actor or actress wears opposite-sex clothes as part of the role portrayed, such as the character Klinger in the television series *M.A.S.H.* There are also entertainers who employ cross-dressing on a regular basis as part of their act, such as Flip Wilson's portrayal of the character Geraldine. We may even include female impersonators in this category, since each of these situations is designed to provide entertainment rather than to achieve sexual gratification.

Such instances are to be distinguished from the true transvestite, who periodically or regularly engages in cross dressing as part of a sexual ritual. Even in these cases, however, most studies reveal that the majority of such individuals are married men who have children and who lead otherwise ordinary lives. There are, of course, instances in which a transvestism stage precedes a sex-change operation, but these are relatively rare circumstances.

It is difficult to determine the incidence of such practices, probably because of the severe social stigma attached to transvestism. Pomeroy (1975) suggests that as many as one million males may practice some form of cross dressing in connection with sexual behavior, although this estimate has not been confirmed by other researchers.

The patterns of cross dressing differ widely among transvestites. In one instance, one man may turn completely to wearing women's underwear on a daily basis, while another may dress up as a woman only on special occasions. There are some men who may have cross-dressed several times simply out of curiosity. Whatever the particular pattern, transvestism, like most fetishes, is a harmless and victimless behavior which ordinarily does not interfere with social and sexual adjustment.

A number of theories have attempted to explain transvestism. Perhaps the most popular of them attributes this behavior to heredity, but there is no evidence to support this position. It seems far more reasonable to assume that transvestism is a learned behavior, and in this connection it is of some interest to note that many transvestites claim to have been dressed as girls during their childhood.

It is also apparent that transvestism is heavily determined by culture. Thus, the standards for identifying "deviancy" in cross dressing differ from culture to culture and within each culture. Traditionally in our society, the pressure for men to conform to the "masculine" model of attire is much greater than the pressure for women to conform to the "feminine" model. Women can wear typically masculine apparel such as work shirts, jeans, boots, etc. without arousing comment, but the male who adopts female attire is usually the target of censure. Several years ago, the fashion industry attempted to persuade men to carry handbags. Apparently, this effort was a failure despite a heavy advertising campaign. On the other hand, there is some reason to believe that at least some of these standards are changing. Many men are apparently now wearing silky, flowered underwear, and the necklace phenomenon has achieved considerable acceptance among the male public.

For those transvestites who desire to change their behavior (often because of the wife's distaste for such practices), aversion therapy has been quite successful. One such procedure involves the use of mild electric shock during the cross-dressing ritual. In addition, sexual reorientation procedures are also employed for the purpose of helping the individual achieve sexual gratification in more ordinary ways (Marks and Gelder, 1967).

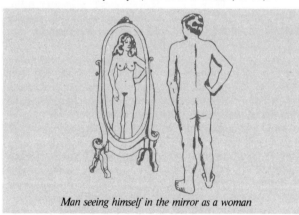

*Man seeing himself in the mirror as a woman*

# OTHER PROBLEM BEHAVIORS

In this last category, we have included several problem behaviors which represent deviations in sexual style. As such, they may occur in addition to the other problem behaviors already described or they may represent variations of more ordinary sexual practices.

## SADISM AND MASOCHISM

The term sadism stems from the writings of the marquis de Sade in the late eighteenth century in which he claimed that sexual gratification is best achieved by inflicting pain on others. The reciprocal of sadism is masochism, a term derived from the writings of Leopold von Sacher-Masoch in the nineteenth century, who reported being most erotically stimulated when he experienced pain in connection with sexual activity. Although both of these terms are now popularly used to describe individuals who respectively enjoy seeing another person suffer or

who themselves enjoy suffering, in the context here they refer to those individuals for whom sadism or masochism is a necessary part of their sexual style. (Despite the apparent similarities, sadism differs from rape in that the sadist typically restricts himself to consenting adults.)

A great deal has been written about both of these practices, but we still know relatively little about them. One explanation suggests that such peculiar preferences represent exaggerated forms of the kinds of experiences which many individuals describe as erotically stimulating. Information from a variety of sources reveals the often close relationship between sex and pain. Thus, Kinsey (1948), for example, reported that about 25% of both his male and female subjects were sexually aroused by biting and pinching and about 4% of his sample enjoyed experiencing mild pain in connection with sex. Given this background, an individual's own experiences may have advanced such conditioning to the point where clear masochistic or sadistic preferences emerge over a period of time (Sandler, 1964).

Neither of these sexual styles may constitute a difficulty unless they cross the threshold from mild pain to more extreme pain, for example, from gentle biting and pinching, which many people find sexually arousing, to slapping and the use of paraphernalia often associated with such practices, such as whips, belts, and the like.

Because of the difficulty in finding appropriate partners, sadists, masochists, and sadomasochists (individuals in whom sadism and masochism co-exist) often turn to prostitutes, some of whom specialize in such practices. In addition, sado-masochistic cults apparently exist in our society and are designed to match up individuals with there respective erotic preferences. Thus, a sex ad may refer to Bondage and Discipline (B and D) practices in which a male who is particularly aroused by physically restraining a female attempts to attract a female partner who will serve in the reciprocal role.

There are virtually no reports of individuals who have been treated for these practices. If the learning theory approach is correct in terms of explaining the causes of such behavior, it would seem reasonable to assume that a reeducation program in the same context would be successful.

## SEXUAL EXCESSES

As we have seen, individuals differ markedly in their desire for sex. When this desire becomes an all-consuming passion to the detriment of other aspects of social adjustment, the behavior is sometimes regarded as deviant. The terms that have sometimes been used to describe sexually hyperactive men and women are, respectively, satyriasis and nymphomania. Sexual hyperactivity may occur within the context of a relatively durable relationship where, for example, one of the partner's sexual desires far exceed that of the other partner; or it may take the form of promiscuity, that is, indiscriminate and casual sex with a large number of partners or in so-called one-night stands. Legendary examples of sexually hyperactive women from the past are the Roman empress Valeria Messalina and Catherine the Great. Prototypes of male hypersexuality include Casanova and the fictional Don Juan.

The term satyriasis is poorly understood and often misapplied, since there are no reliable criteria for judging normal sex frequency in males. Kinsey (1948) reported that the typical married man in his sample in intercourse two to three times a week, but a substantial number of men reported much higher sexual frequencies. Whatever the case, such facts are meaningless since limiting circumstances such as partner availability and erectile capabilities serve as a control over male sexuality. It is possible, for example, that many men would report higher rates of sexual activity if partner availability increased. Furthermore, as we have seen, the male sex role in our society supports the notion of aggressiveness. Thus, we are more inclined to portray male hypersexuality as a normal expression of this role.

For all of these reasons, it is impossible to stipulate when a man crosses the threshold from normal sexuality to satyriasis. As indicated above for other behaviors, perhaps it is only when a man's sexual style impairs other dimensions of social functioning (for example, marriage relationships) that we might begin to express concern, but this criterion is independent of sexual frequency.

This situation is even more confusing when the term nymphomania is considered. Again, perhaps we can achieve some understanding of how this label has been misapplied by considering the conventional female sex role in our society. Prior to the last two decades, when sex roles were more rigidly defined, a woman who deviated from the acceptable passive sexual style was considered "oversexed" and, in extreme cases, a "nympho." The conventional stereotype of such a woman was that she was "easy"; her name and phone number appeared on men's-room walls; her availability was happily communicated from fraternity brother to fraternity brother. Such women, however, probably existed more in men's fantasies than they did in real life. Thus, what determined a woman's reputation for hypersexuality was more often a comparison with the primarily masculine image of the proper woman's sex role, rather than the actual behavior of the woman. For these reasons, the concept of nymphomania cannot be separated from the double standard of sexual morality that still exists in our society.

There are, of course, women who come to the attention of practitioners because of their "compulsive need for sex", who rarely, if ever, realize sexual gratification and who are, in general, unhappy individuals. We might also include, in this category, those women who engage in "gang bangs," a rapid series of sexual encounters with several men in a single sexual episode. Again, however, such deviance is more a question of

general social and sexual maladjustment, rather than a function of sexual frequency exclusively.

In any event, as a result of changing standards, the question of what constitutes hypersexuality in females remains unanswered. From the one end of the continuum, that is, the conventional sexual pattern, to the other end of the continuum, the highly promiscuous female, there is an infinite variety of individual differences. Given the fact that an increasing number of women no longer accept the traditional passive role in sexuality and that many of them insist that the pattern and frequency of sex is as much their prerogative as the male's, it would seem presumptuous for society to set any arbitrary standards regarding sexual frequency. In this context, then, the term nymphomania, like its masculine counterpart, satyriasis, is a meaningless one.

## SUMMARY

In this chapter we have reviewed a number of sexual problem behaviors that have traditionally been termed deviations, perversions, and pathologies. The changing standards which have emerged in the last two decades suggest that these terms should be abandoned in the light of newer standards, in particular the consenting adult principle.

It also seems appropriate to classify sexual problem behaviors in terms of the damaging impact on the individual as well as on others. Thus, we have ordered these behaviors from those which most seriously victimize others to those which are usually victimless.

Several other points warrant attention. Popular notions characterize the sexually deviant as being clearly distinguishable from normal individuals. The facts, however, reveal that those stereotypes are grossly inaccurate. The majority of men who are convicted of sex crimes, for example, lead otherwise normal lives. It seems incomprehensible to the average person that a man who is most sexually aroused by wearing a blonde wig, an evening gown, and high-heeled shoes with sequins on them could still be normal in all other areas. Yet the evidence clearly supports such a perspective.

Finally, throughout this chapter we have seen how little is actually known about the reasons why people engage in such practices. There is a great urgency to direct appropriate research efforts in order to find the answers to such questions.

# Chapter 14

## Sexual Dysfunctions and Treatment

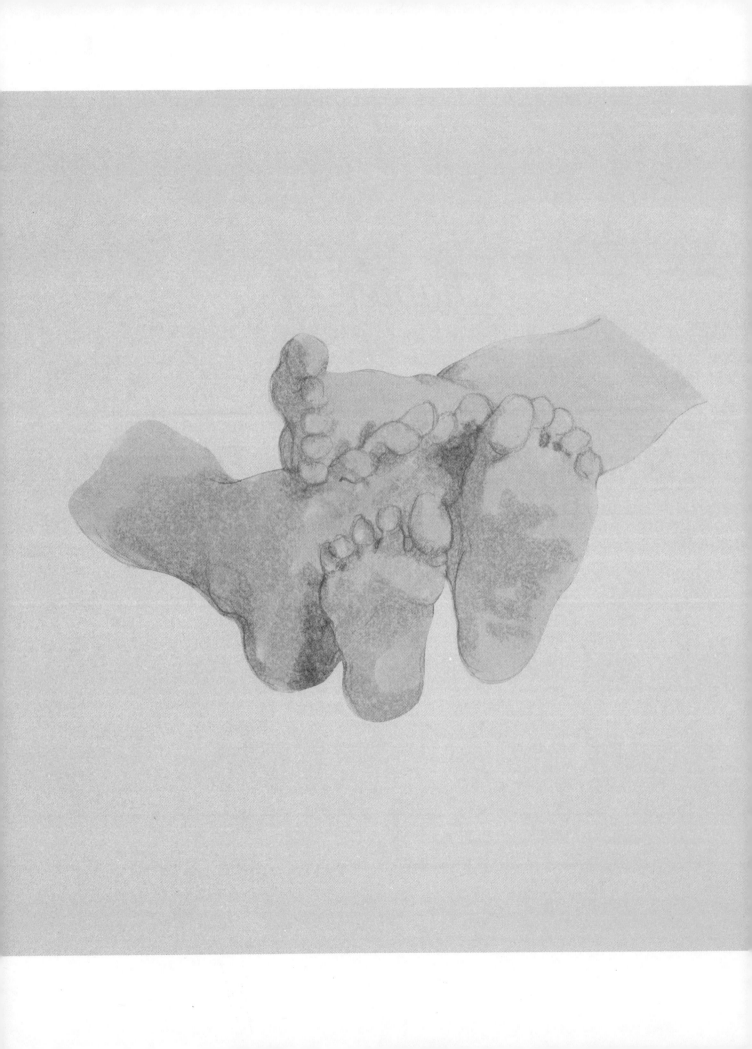

# INTRODUCTION

Sexual expression can be one of the happiest, most pleasurable, and most rewarding experiences in a person's life. Unfortunately, however, not all people are totally happy with this important aspect of their behavior. At some point in their lives, many people will become concerned about their own sexual functioning or that of their partner. For example, orgasms won't occur when we "want them to," or they happen too quickly.

Overt sexual expression occupies only a tiny part of our lives as far as actual time is concerned. Yet, when something goes wrong in this area, this difficulty can often have a substantial effect, sometimes influencing our daily routine to a great degree. A person may become obsessed with such an alleged failure and develop a poor self-image; relationships or marriages can become strained or terminated as a result.

Sexual difficulties have, no doubt, been with us since time immemorial, yet it is only recently that such topics have been openly discussed in our society. Several things have led to this current state of affairs. Freud and other early psychoanalytic thinkers gave much attention to sexual matters in their theories. While some of these concepts were later proved to be incorrect or misleading, Freud and his followers nevertheless began to bring sexuality out into the open and to make it a topic for legitimate discussion. The work of Kinsey furthered this process and added more factual data to our pool of knowledge in this area. People became more willing to openly explore and discuss sexual issues and, in the case of sexual dysfunctions, began asking for ways to alleviate these difficulties. The pioneering efforts of Masters and Johnson (1966; 1970) and other therapists can be seen as an outgrowth of these societal changes. Finally, in the past decade, the women's movement has been influential in changing the attitudes of both women and men. Women are now demanding a more equal place in all aspects of our society and are feeling free to express their own sexual needs and concerns.

Because of these cultural changes, many people today are seeking professional assistance in improving their overall sexual functioning and relationships. Masters and Johnson (1970), for example, have estimated that as many as one-half of the population will experience some degree of sexual dysfunction at some time during their lives. While this figure may somewhat overestimate the true incidence of these disorders (Masters and Johnson actually feel this is a conservative estimate), it seems safe to assume that a very significant portion of the population will experience some sexual difficulties at some point.

These numbers are not too surprising when we consider the impact of many factors on our sexuality. First, there are the cultural influences on our sexuality. Confusing messages such as "sex is dirty,"or "save it for the one you love" may create anxiety. Then there are other factors. The lack of adequate sex information, the lack of ability to communicate effectively with one's partner, and anxiety underlie many sexual difficulties or problems. Sexually disruptive anxiety may be fed by a host of factors: ignorance, unrealistic expectations of self and/or partner, fears about one's performance, overemphasis on technique,

fears of rejection, fears of intimacy, guilt. Difficulties with communication may also stem from many different sources. For example, many people believe that the only appropriate sounds in a sexual encounter are moans or words of endearment and that, further, talking will rob sex of its spontaneity. Such an approach may, however, actually sabotage getting one's needs met. Even if we believe that it's OK to talk, we may not be familiar with our own sexual responses and thus lack the appropriate information to convey to our partner, or we may simply not know exactly how to convey this information. Sometimes we believe that our partner is a mindreader (for example, "If he loved me, he would know how to stimulate me"), or we believe (erroneously) that is is our partner's responsibility to know everything about our own sexual response. Sometimes we are afraid that our partner will think we are being too assertive, or that our partner will feel threatened, or that we ourselves will somehow measure up poorly.

All of the above factors may contribute to a sexual dysfunction. As we shall see later in this chapter, many of the specific procedures for treating sexual dysfunctions are specifically focused on changing these factors. Let us now turn to a discussion of the common sexual dysfunctions of men and women and the treatment procedures that have been used in dealing with them.

# KINDS OF SEXUAL DYSFUNCTION

## IMPOTENCE

Impotence, or erectile dysfunction, is defined as the inability to obtain an erection or to maintain an erection. Further, this classification is broken down into either primary impotence or secondary impotence. Masters and Johnson (1970) have defined primary impotence as those cases in which the man has *never* successfully obtained and/or maintained an erection "sufficient to accomplish successful coital connection." This definition clearly emphasizes the importance most sex therapists place on the relationship qualities of sexuality in that the definition specifically relates erectile dysfunction to a "coital connection" (which can be either heterosexual or homosexual). Thus, a male with this problem might have morning erections or obtain erections by means of fantasy or masturbation but not with a partner. On the other hand, he might never have obtained an erection by any means in any situation. For example, some men born with endocrine disorders such as in Klinefelter's syndrome may never develop the proper steroid balance necessary for an effective erection. Such cases are rare, however.

Secondary impotence refers to those men who have completed intercourse successfully at least once. Of course, one "failure" to obtain or maintain an erection with a partner should not send a man running to his nearest sex therapist with fears of erectile dysfunction. Indeed, many situations such as fatigue or too much alcohol intake may cause a man to have an erectile problem on some occasions. Kaplan (1974) estimates that at least half of the male population has experienced one or more episodes of erectile dysfunction. In keeping with this general finding, Masters and Johnson (1970) recommend the clinical diagnosis of secondary impotence only when the failure rate approaches at least 25 percent of the man's total coital opportunities.

The causes of erectile dysfunction are many and varied. Diseases, such as diabetes or chronic renal failure, may precipitate an erectile dysfunction (the effects of various diseases and injuries upon sexuality are covered in detail in Chapter 16). Some antipsychotic medications (phenothiazines) and anti-depressive drugs (MAO inhibitors) as well as amphetamines and alcohol have also been found to cause erectile dysfunctions (Masters and Johnson, 1970). By and large, however, the over-whelming majority of erectile dysfunctions are caused by psychological variables. For example, of the 213 men treated for secondary impotence by Masters and Johnson (1970), actual physical causes were found to have been important in the onset of erectile dysfunction in only seven cases. Psychological reactions to environmental events are often implicated in the etiology of erectile dysfunction. For example, feeling degraded or "put down" by a prostitute during one's first attempt at inter-course was reported by several of the primary impotence men studied by Masters and Johnson. A very strict religious upbring-ing was reported by several men with the diagnosis of secondary impotence. Most importantly, a history of premature ejacula-tion or heavy alcohol usage was found in almost half of these men with secondary erectile dysfunction.

Masters and Johnson (1970) and others have stressed the im-portance of *fears of performance* in many men with erectile problems. A man may experience an erectile dysfunction on occa-sion, perhaps, as noted above, because of excessive alcohol in-take or extreme fatigue. Or he may have successfully obtained an erection but ejaculated very quickly. For whatever reason, the man begins to doubt his own ability to function properly and becomes obsessed with doubts like "Can I get an erection?" or "Will I last long enough?" This becomes, then, a vicious circle: the more he worries about his ability to perform, the more likely he is to "fail," thus reinforcing his fears and worries about his sexual functioning. As we shall see later, alleviating a man's fears of performance is an integral part of successful treatment modalities for erectile dysfunctions.

## PREMATURE EJACULATION

There are many difficulties in precisely defining premature ejaculation. In the most obvious sense, premature ejaculation refers to those situations in which a man ejaculates too quickly. Beyond this generality, several more specific definitions of what constitutes "too quickly" have been formulated. Older defini-tions emphasized the time element; thus, a man might be de-fined as a premature ejaculator if he ejaculated in less than 30 seconds after vaginal penetration or if he ejaculated prior to 20 penile thrusts. One obvious problem inherent in such definitions is that they are based on some subjective judgments; that is, do we choose 30 seconds, 60 seconds, or three minutes as our criterion for defining premature ejaculation?

In an attempt to depart from such a "stop-watch" approach, Masters and Johnson (1970) have defined premature ejaculation as a condition in which the man is unable to postpone ejacula-tion during intravaginal containment long enough to satisfy his partner in at least 50 percent of their coital encounters. On the one hand, this is an innovative approach, especially as it em-phasizes the interactional qualities of human sexuality. On the other hand, however, the time it takes a woman to reach orgasm is highly variable, both among different women and for the same woman on different occasions; in addition, some women are never orgasmic with intercourse. For these reasons, some authorities (for example, Kaplan, 1974) have considered the criterion proposed by Masters and Johnson as an unsatisfactory definition of prematurity.

Kaplan (1974) has pointed out that all these definitions basically conceptualize prematurity in terms of how long it takes a man to reach the plateau stage of sexual arousal. This is not the most important component in premature ejaculation accord-ing to Kaplan; rather, it is the absence of voluntary control over the ejaculatory reflex after the man attains heightened sexual arousal that is the crucial component of prematurity. Kaplan thus defines premature ejaculation as a condition when orgasm occurs reflexively, that is, when a man is unable to exert volun-tary control over this ejaculatory reflex once he has reached the plateau stage of arousal. Kaplan's definition is thus independent of both the time factor (for example, number of thrusts or seconds before ejaculation) and the factor of whether or not the female partner reaches orgasm.

Physical factors are less likely to be implicated in the etiology of prematurity than they are for erectile dysfunctions. Certain degenerative neurological disorders such as multiple sclerosis may cause damage to specific nerve pathways important for the ejaculatory reflex. Other localized diseases, for example, prosta-titis, sometimes may cause prematurity. However, such in-stances are extremely rare (Kaplan, 1974), and by far the majori-ty of cases of premature ejaculation are in no way related to physical causes.

The sexual histories of the premature ejaculators studied by Masters and Johnson yielded a very consistent pattern. While the specific situational events were varied, many of these men reported initial sexual encounters (or a series of early sexual en-counters) wherein there was some pressure to ejaculate quickly. For example, early sexual experiences were often with a prosti-tute, who wanted to "finish him off" quickly so as to get on to her next client. Or perhaps the early encounters were in the back seat of a car or on the couch in the parents' living room; in such instances, fear of discovery is certainly a motivating factor for rapid completion of intercourse. Thus, Masters and Johnson conceptualize premature ejaculation, in most cases, as a learned pattern of responding. Early sexual encounters establish a pat-tern of rapid ejaculation, a pattern that is then subsequently reinforced by later, similar sexual experiences. This general con-ceptualization of premature ejaculation is accepted by most workers in the field of human sexuality. However, it should be noted that the statistical validity of this theory has not been established and that such a conceptualization leaves unanswered the question as to why some men become premature ejaculators as a result of having been exposed to those hurried early sexual experiences while other men are not so affected (Kaplan, 1974).

## RETARDED EJACULATION

Also termed ejaculatory incompetence, retarded ejaculation is defined as a man's inability to ejaculate during intravaginal containment with his partner. Such men do not usually have difficulty in obtaining or maintaining an erection and indeed may ejaculate in other circumstances (for example, through masturbation, oral sex, or wet dreams). However, some men with retarded ejaculation experience severe fears regarding their sexual functioning and as a result may develop secondary impotence (Masters and Johnson, 1970).

Masters and Johnson view retarded ejaculation as a relatively rare phenomenon (it occurred in only 17 males out of the 510 couples they treated during an 11-year period). Others contend this is a much more common problem. For example, Kaplan (1974) states that milder forms of this disorder may be much more prevalent and reports a recent increase in the number of people seeking treatment for retarded ejaculation.

As in premature ejaculation, it is very rare for a case of retarded ejaculation to have an organic cause. Psychological reactions to environmental conditions or events seem to be implicated in most cases of retarded ejaculation. Among the males treated by Masters and Johnson, 12 had never been able to ejaculate intravaginally with their wives. Of these men, 5 were the products of a very restrictive religious upbringing which Masters and Johnson felt was significantly related to their disorders. Of those men who had successfully ejaculated for some time during their marriage, all began having problems after some specific episode which produced psychological trauma. For example, one man unexpectedly came upon his wife having intercourse with another man. Another began having problems when his two young children burst into the bedroom while he and his wife were engaged in intercourse. It seems apparent, then, that almost all cases of retarded ejaculation are the result of such psychological factors.

It may seem ironic to some readers that men (or their partners) would view retarded ejaculation as a problem for which they seek professional help. One might think that a man might be happy to be able to "last so long" and that his partner should be delighted to have a lover who can continue intercourse for long periods of time. In reality, this condition often becomes a very frustrating one for men; and many women express severe feelings of personal rejection when their partners are unable to ejaculate intravaginally.

## ORGASMIC DYSFUNCTION

Orgasmic dysfunction refers to a woman's inability to reach orgasm. This condition is further broken down into primary or secondary orgasmic dysfunction. Masters and Johnson (1970) define primary orgasmic dysfunction as the condition wherein a woman has never attained orgasm at any time during her lifespan though any type of sexual stimulation. In secondary, or situational, orgasmic dysfunction, a woman must have had at least one instance of orgasmic expression but currently experiences some orgasmic difficulties in some situations. For example, she might be orgasmic through masturbation or oral sex but not during intercourse (termed coital orgasmic inadequacy). Conversely, she might reach orgasm through intercourse but not through masturbation (masturbatory orgasmic inadequacy). The third type of situational orgasmic dysfunction has been called random orgasmic inadequacy. These women have been orgasmic at least once in both coital and manipulative (masturbation or oral) activities, yet orgasm occurs very infrequently by any means. Masters and Johnson report that these women are not usually aware of any physical need of sexual expression and that, on those rare occasions when they do attain orgasm, their reaction is usually one of surprise.

Several other terms have been used to describe orgasmic dysfunctions in women. For many years, the term "frigidity" was commonly used; the use of this term was unfortunate since the term carries negative or derogatory connotations. Additionally, the use of the word "frigidity" caused much confusion and ambiguity. Some individuals used the term to describe orgasmic dysfunctions as defined above while others used it to refer to women who showed little or no interest in sex or were sexually unresponsive, regardless of their orgasmic status. Fortunately, the use of the term "frigidity" has been replaced with more definitive descriptions. Recently, two additional terms have been used with increasing frequency. The term anorgasmia is now often used synonymously with orgasmic dysfunction. Additionally, Barbach (1974) has pioneered the term preorgasmic as an alternative label for primary orgasmic dysfunction. This term is a more positive description in that it implies a potential for more satisfactory functioning, that is, that although a woman has never experienced orgasm, she still may "learn" to do so.

Orgasmic dysfunction is a relatively common phenomenon (342 of the 371 women treated by Masters and Johnson received the diagnosis of either primary or secondary orgasmic dysfunction). Kaplan (1974) has stated that up to 10% of all women have never experienced orgasm and that, of the remaining 90%, only about one-half regularly reach orgasm during intercourse without some additional clitoral stimulation. If such is indeed true, this provides further evidence that the cultural stereotype of the coital orgasm as the only "normal" type of female sexual expression is clearly open to debate. Unfortunately, definitive statistics regarding the prevalence of female orgasmic patterns in American women are not currently available.

Orgasmic dysfunction is not likely to have a physical cause. Kaplan (1974) contends that, in general, the female sexual response is less likely to be affected by physical factors than is the male response. Thus, while certain conditions (for example, diabetes or the use of narcotic medications) may impair the female sexual response, the vast majority of orgasmic dysfunctions are not related to organic factors. Masters and Johnson (1970) found that psychological factors were almost always implicated in cases of orgasmic dysfunction. For those with primary orgasmic dysfunction, ignorance about sexuality was often reported. Religious orthodoxy was also an important factor in this condition. About one-fourth of the women treated by Masters and Johnson for primary orgasmic dysfunction were the products of very strict, rigid religious backgrounds. Similarly, psychological components, such as one's sexual value system and/or other, nonsexual relationship problems, were implicated in secondary orgasmic dysfunctions. Finally, women may be inorgasmic simply because they do not receive enough stimulation or appropriate stimulation. Thus, the majority of all orgasmic dysfunctions appear to be the result of prior conditioning in a variety of psychosocial situations.

## VAGINISMUS

Vaginismus is the condition wherein the muscle groups in the lower one-third of the vagina contract spastically. Penile insertion (or insertion of a speculum during a pelvic exam) may be difficult and in more severe cases impossible. This is a relatively rare condition, present to some degree in only 29 of the 371 women treated by Masters and Johnson. Kaplan (1974) suggests that vaginismus is basically a conditioned response in which pain or fear has been associated with attempts at vaginal penetration. For example, intercourse may have been actually painful because of a rigid hymen or some pelvic infection. After the initial condition has been ameliorated, the woman may continue to associate pain with penetration and therefore experience vaginismus. Masters and Johnson reported that vaginismus often occurred concurrently with primary impotence in the partner. Additionally, a significant number of women with vaginismus reported growing up in severely restrictive and religious home environments.

## DYSPAREUNIA

Dyspareunia, or painful intercourse, is usually thought of as a female disorder, although men, too, may suffer from this condition. In women, severe vaginismus may cause dyspareunia. Most cases are, however, a function of some physical problem. Any damage or irritation to the clitoris or vagina may cause painful intercourse. Pelvic infections, scarring after surgery, and allergic reactions to douches or contraceptive preparations may also produce dyspareunia (Masters and Johnson, 1970), as can a lack of vaginal lubrication. Infections and irritations of the penis may cause this condition in men. Another cause in uncircumcised men is phimosis, a condition in which the foreskin is so tight that it may not be retracted. For both men and women, dyspareunia typically disappears after symptomatic treatment of the physical problem.

## INHIBITED SEXUAL DESIRE

Hypoactive, or inhibited, sexual desire (ISD) refers to a persistent and pervasive inhibition of sexual desire and feelings. The person with ISD has little or no interest in sex, does not seek out sexual activities, and may have few or no sexual fantasies. Additionally, sexual feelings from genital stimulation may be absent or greatly reduced. For example, men or women with ISD may function "normally," that is, given adequate stimulation for example, a man may have an erection or a women may lubricate and/or be orgasmic. Nevertheless, these experiences may not really be very satisfying, with the pleasure obtained being of very short duration and often limited to the genitals. Some people with this disorder have described these experiences as being like eating a meal when one is not really hungry (Kaplan, 1979).

ISD is further broken down into primary and secondary inhibited sexual desire. Primary ISD is characterized by a lifelong history of a disinterest in sex, often so pervasive that the person has had no sexual experiences, including masturbation. Primary ISD is a very rare condition. Secondary ISD is characterized by a loss of sexual desire after a history of normal sexual development and experience and is the most common form of ISD. Many people with secondary ISD are appropriately characterized as having situational ISD; that is, they experience an inhibition of sexual feelings only in some situations. Kaplan (1979) has pointed out that these people tend to experience sexual feelings or desire under only those conditions that are psychologically "safe" for them.

ISD is a relatively common phenomenon. Kaplan (1979) has pointed out that perhaps as many as 40% of individuals seeking treatment for one of the other sexual dysfunctions (for example, erectile dysfunction or orgasmic dysfunction) may in fact be suffering primarily from ISD. Other sex therapists have reported similar findings, although the problem has not, until recently, been specifically called ISD. Kaplan has been the first to discuss in detail the phenomenon of ISD and to point out the added difficulties this disorder can present during treatment. Recent data (Kaplan, 1979) suggests that ISD is associated with many treatment failures when traditional sex therapy procedures have been applied to the other sexual dysfunctions.

ISD may be caused by a variety of factors. While the specific physiological mechanisms have not been clearly documented in many cases, clinical evidence suggests that a variety of drugs may produce lowered sexual desire. Narcotics, sedatives, alcohol, and certain antihypertensive medications all may produce ISD. Any condition which impairs androgen production may also be a cause of ISD. The majority of cases of ISD, however, appear to be caused by psychological factors. Reactions to severe stress, such as might be experienced after a traumatic divorce or job loss, are often associated with decreases in sexual desire. Depression is also a common cause of ISD. In cases where ISD is caused by psychological factors, Kaplan (1979) suggests that there is an active suppression of sexual desire (even though such suppression is unconscious and involuntary). Such individuals develop a variety of "turn-off" mechanisms, that is, they tend to suppress their sexual desire by evoking negative thoughts, thereby putting themselves into a negative emotional state. These negative thoughts may take a variety of different forms: some people may focus their attention on some negative aspect of their partner, for example, his pot belly or her bad breath; others may focus on some negative aspect of themselves, for example, "I am too fat." Whatever the specific "turn-off" mechanism, they all can have the same final effect—a decrease in sexual feelings and desire.

Several factors may be important causes of this active suppression of sexual desire. Anxiety, fears, anger, and power struggles have been enumerated by Kaplan as examples. Additionally, in many instances, ISD seems to be associated with fears of success or fears of intimacy. Typically, the underlying causes of ISD are much deeper, more complex, and more long-term than the causes of the other sexual dysfunctions. Thus, treatment of ISD usually requires the addition of more traditional psychotherapeutic techniques to deal with these underlying factors either before or concurrently with the more specific sex therapy procedures.

# TREATMENT OF SEXUAL DYSFUNCTIONS

Within the last century, a variety of different therapeutic methods have been used in attempts to treat sexual dysfunctions. In this section, we will describe the most commonly used procedures and discuss their effectiveness.

## PSYCHOANALYSIS AND PSYCHOTHERAPY

Freudian psychoanalytic techniques as well as other more traditional, insight-oriented "talk therapies" have been used to treat sexual problems. The basic assumption for these procedures is that the sexual dysfunction is a psychoneurotic symptom of an underlying, often deeply unconscious, motive or conflict that may have had its beginnings many years previously. The sexual problem can be ameliorated only when these conflicts have been dealt with. Thus, these psychotherapeutic procedures generally consist of helping the client recognize these conflicts at a conscious level and thus be able to deal with them more effectively and realistically. This method often requires for its success, substantial changes in the client's personality structure and may require a long period of time, often several years in the case of psychoanalysis.

The effectiveness of these procedures for treating sexual dysfunctions is much in doubt. There has been very little research in this area; most of the claims for the efficacy of psychoanalysis or other long-term psychotherapeutic procedures are based on case studies or relatively uncontrolled clinical observations (Reynolds, 1977). Briefer forms of psychotherapy (typically less than one year in treatment) have also not been found to be particularly successful. For example, in one study of men with potency disorders, or erectile difficulties, it was found that the sexual problem in approximately two-thirds of these men remained unchanged, either with or without psychotherapy (Johnson, 1965). Such findings have led many authorities (for example, Cooper, 1978) to suggest that traditional psychotherapeutic techniques should not be used in the treatment of male sexual disorders. To this point, we have even less data with respect to the effectiveness of these techniques for female sexual dysfunctions.

## THE SEMANS TECHNIQUE

This technique, also called the "start-stop" technique, was developed specifically for the treatment of premature ejaculation (Semans, 1956). Based on the knowledge that ejaculation is basically a reflex, this procedure enables a man to learn to maintain high levels of sexual excitement without reflexively ejaculating; that is, the man learns control over this specific reflex. The man masturbates to the point where he knows that any more stimulation will produce almost immediate ejaculation (called ejaculatory inevitability). At this point, he stops masturbation until this sensation subsides; he then repeats the same procedure. With each repetition, he will be able to tolerate longer periods of heightened stimulation. Initially, Semans

reported on eight men treated with this method; in all of them, the symptom disappeared within a month, during which time Semans had spent only an average of three and one-third hours with each of the men. This procedure is still used by many therapists in treating premature ejaculation and the "squeeze technique," developed by Masters and Johnson and described briefly below, is a variant of this method.

## KEGEL'S EXERCISES

Developed by the physician Arnold Kegel (1952), this technique (also see Chapter 5) is intended to strengthen the pubococcygeal muscle which runs along the sides of the vaginal opening. A woman may become aware of her pubococcygeal muscle by urinating and then voluntarily stopping the urine flow. When she does this, she is utilizing her pubococcygeal muscle. She is then instructed to practice tightening and relaxing this muscle several times a day, thus strengthening this muscle in much the same way other people increase muscle tone through lifting weights. This is an unobtrusive exercise that a woman may practice at any time and is used by many sex therapists as part of the treatment for females with orgasmic dysfunctions.

## THE MASTERS AND JOHNSON APPROACH

Masters and Johnson (1970) were, of course, the pioneers in developing a comprehensive therapy format for treating sexual dysfunctions for both men and women. For the most part, they do not view these disorders as symptoms of psychological disturbance but rather conceptualize them as learned patterns of behavior. We are born with the ability to be sexual. (Remember that Kinsey had earlier reported sexual responses in young infants that were essentially analogous to the adult sexual response cycle.) As time goes on, however, what happens is that sexually dysfunctional individuals have "unlearned" these patterns or that other certain "road blocks" have been placed in the way of the normal sexual response cycle, and the end result is a sexually dysfunctional individual. Thus ignorance, strict religious teachings, or culturally instilled attitudes may prevent a person from realizing his or her full sexual potential. If, as Masters and Johnson propose, sexually dysfunctional individuals have learned a dysfunctional sexual pattern, they can also learn (or relearn) how to respond more effectively. The Masters and Johnson format consists, then, of techniques through which individuals learn or relearn a different pattern of sexual responsiveness.

The Masters and Johnson treatment procedures, as conducted in their own setting, consist of a two-week program utilizing information dissemination and homework exercises practiced in the privacy of the couple's own motel room. The first three days consist of detailed history-taking interviews as well as complete medical examinations to rule out any organic causes. Throughout this time the therapists attempt to correct any misconceptions the couple may have about sexuality, a process that is of great importance throughout the therapeutic program. On the third day, a sensate focus homework assignment is employed. Sensate focus consists of stroking or massage exer-

*Male non-demand position for treating premature ejaculation.*

cises. During these first sensate focus procedures, touching of the sexual parts of the body (that is, the genitals or breasts) is prohibited. These exercises are designed to allow the couple to experience the sensual pleasures of their bodies without orgasm as the goal. Removal of this goal orientation to sexual activity helps to alleviate fears of performance so often associated with sexual dysfunctions. (Masters and Johnson prohibit intercourse throughout most of the treatment for the same reason.)

During the fourth day of treatment, a lengthy session is spent in discussing the anatomy of the genital organs and the specifics of the sexual response cycle. This is yet another opportunity to remove old misconceptions and to educate the participants about their own sexuality. Another set of sensate focus exercises is assigned, this time with the provision that the breasts and genitals may also be massaged but with the warning that orgasm is still not the goal of these procedures.

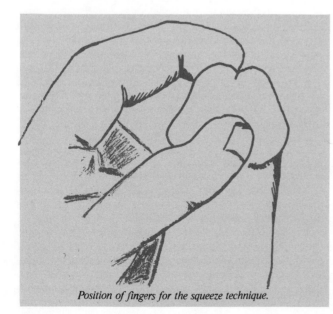
*Position of fingers for the squeeze technique.*

During the rest of the two-week treatment period, the specific homework assignments will vary depending upon the sexual dysfunction. In treating premature ejaculation, for example, the squeeze technique and other procedures are used. In this procedure, treatment begins with the man lying on his back with his partner sitting between his legs facing him. The woman directly stimulates his penis, either orally or manually, until he obtains an erection. At this point, the partner employs the squeeze technique, in which she tightly squeezes the head of his penis for several seconds. This procedure will postpone the man's urge to ejaculate and after the squeeze most men will lose 10% to 30% of the erection. This same procedure is then repeated several times, with the squeeze being applied just before the man reaches the point of ejaculatory inevitability. With each repetition, the man will be able to experience longer and longer periods of heightened sexual excitement without reaching the point of ejaculatory inevitability.

The next step in establishing ejaculatory control is what Masters and Johnson call "nondemanding intromission." With the man still on his back, the woman assumes the female superior position and inserts his penis into her vagina. The couple then concentrates on retaining this coital position but with no further movement to stimulate his penis. If the man feels he is about to ejaculate, he tells his partner, who immediately removes herself from his penis and again applies the squeeze technique. As the man progressively gains more control over his ejaculatory reflex, the couple can then begin pelvic thrusting or other coital movements. Through these simple procedures, Masters and Johnson have been quite successful in treating premature ejaculation within the two-week time period (their failure rate has been 2.2%). Upon completing treatment, the couple is encouraged to practice this squeeze procedure at least once a week for the next six months to help maintain this success in ejaculatory control.

A different series of exercises is prescribed for female orgasmic dysfunctions. After the sensate focus exercises have been completed, the couple assumes the "nondemand position" for female

*Female superior position used in "non-demanding intromission."*

stimulation. In this position, the male can easily reach and stroke all of the sexually stimulating areas of his partner's body. While the male manipulates his partner's genitals, she is instructed to place her hand lightly on top of his hand and to guide him; thus, the woman can "teach" her partner exactly what manner of stimulation is most arousing for her. After the woman has experienced heightened sexual tension in this position, the couple is instructed to assume the female superior position. As in the use of this position for premature ejaculation, initially there is no pelvic thrusting; rather, the woman is instructed to remain very still and to only absorb the awareness of this intravaginal containment of the penis. As she becomes more aware of these pleasurable feelings, pelvic thrusting is begun. Finally, the couple is instructed to assume the lateral coital position, a position Masters and Johnson state provides the most effective coital stimulation for both women and men.

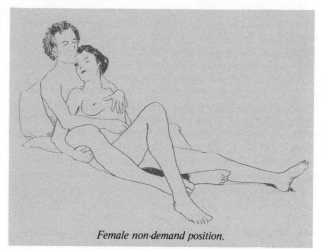
*Female non-demand position.*

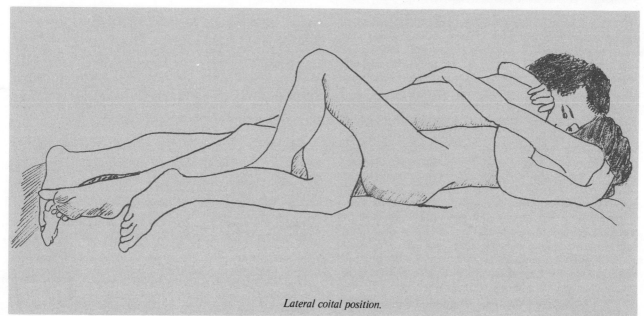
*Lateral coital position.*

Other types of exercises are prescribed for other dysfunctions, such as impotence or vaginismus. Regardless of the specific techniques employed, there are several other important components included throughout the Masters and Johnson treatment format. One such component is the use of cotherapists, one male and one female. This procedure has seveal important advantages, for example, each member of the couple in therapy will always have a therapist of his or her own gender available. Using cotherapists also probably increases the accuracy and completeness of information obtained from the couple since there are two people doing the interviewing. Another important component is the focus on the couple as a unit rather than on the individual with the "problem." This takes the pressure off the symptomatic individual, encourages open, honest, and active communication between the couple, and sets the stage for both partners' active participation in the treatment process. Finally, since individuals' fears and anxieties about performance are usually important aspects of sexual dysfunctions, the series of progressive exercises are arranged throughout treatment to eliminate goal-oriented performance.

The results of the Masters and Johnson treatment format indicate that this form of therapy was quite successful overall. Of the total of 790 dysfunctional individuals seen by Masters and Johnson (1970), 142 were considered to be initial treatment failures (that is, the symptoms were not reversed during the two-week treatment period). This yielded an initial failure rate of 18.9%. In other words, about four out of every five individuals seen were treated successfully. The failure rates varied from a low of 2.2% for premature ejaculation to a high of 40.6% for primary impotence. Five years after treatment, 226 of those treated were interviewed to determine the status of their present sexual functioning. At that point, the overall failure rate had risen to only 20%, suggesting that once these sexual dysfunctions were successfully treated, they did not tend to recur with any great frequency.

## THE KAPLAN APPROACH

Dr. Helen Singer Kaplan has been very influential in expanding upon the earlier work of Masters and Johnson. Dr. Kaplan and her colleagues at Cornell University utilize many of the techniques already discussed in this chapter, although there are several major differences between her approach and that of Masters and Johnson. Perhaps the most significant of these differences is her conceptualization of the therapeutic process itself. Kaplan (1974) takes a much more psychodynamic approach in dealing with sexual problems than do most sex therapists. While not denying that some sexual dysfunctions occur in otherwise "normal" individuals and appear to be basically learned responses, she feels there are deeper, underlying personality conflicts and/or other relationship difficulties in many people who seek treatment for sexual dysfunctions. For example, unresolved hostilities toward women may be implicated in some cases of premature ejaculation. Because of this conceptualization, Kaplan makes more use of traditional psychotherapeutic techniques in addition to a series of sexual exercises. Thus, the Kaplan approach is an integrated combination of the recognized sexual treatment exercises and other therapy procedures aimed at resolving personality problems and relationship conflicts.

Kaplan's approach is also different from that of Masters and Johnson in several other respects. Her treatment procedures are not nearly as time-limited as the two-week approach of Masters and Johnson. Some couples may require treatment over a longer period of time. Clients are not always seen for treatment every day; instead, they may be seen one to three times a week. Also, Kaplan and her associates do not always use cotherapists when treating a couple. Finally, rather than always using basically the same series of sexual exercises, Kaplan attempts to tailor this sequence, basing the exercises on the specific problem and the special dynamics of a specific couple's relationship. (It should also be noted that Kaplan prefers the start-stop approach of treating premature ejaculation rather than the squeeze technique.)

Kaplan has yet to report specific treatment outcome data, although she has stated that her results "to date support Masters and Johnson" (Kaplan, 1974). Nevertheless, her treatment procedures are promising and are indeed used by many sex therapists today. Kaplan's inclusion of more traditional psychotherapeutic techniques seems especially important here, since many couples seeking sex therapy also have other significant psychological problems which need to be resolved for sex therapy to be successful (Kinder and Blakeney, 1977; Kaplan, 1979).

## MASTURBATION

Several sex therapists have begun employing a series of masturbatory exercises in the treatment of both female and male sexual dysfunctions. For example, LoPiccolo and Lobitz (1972) have used a nine-step masturbation program in treating anorgasmic women. These women were first instructed to "get in touch" with their own bodies by viewing and exploring their genitals with the use of a mirror. Kegel's exercises are also prescribed early in the treatment process. The woman is then instructed to manually manipulate her genitals to become aware of exactly what kind of stimulation is most intense and pleasurable. She then attempts to masturbate to orgasm. If orgasm does not occur through the use of these procedures, she is instructed to increase the intensity and duration of her masturbation, to make use of fantasy, and to employ a vibrator. Once orgasm has occurred, the woman's partner is integrated into the treatment process. Here the woman begins by masturbating in her partner's presence; later he will stimulate her manually. Finally, the couple is instructed to have intercourse while he continues to stimulate her manually.

LoPiccolo and Lobitz (1972) have reported on the first eight women to have completed their program. None of these women were initially orgasmic and all were orgasmic by masturbation after a total of 15 treatment sessions. Six of the eight women also became orgasmic during intercourse with their husbands by the end of the treatment. Using a modification of the LoPiccolo and Lobitz masturbation program, Barbach (1974) has reported very similar results. Of 83 anorgasmic women treated, 91.6% were orgasmic through masturbation at the end of ten treatment sessions. Of those interviewed eight months later, about one-half were now orgasmic during intercourse in 90% to 100% of their coital encounters. Masturbation, using the Semans start-stop approach, has also been used in the treatment of premature ejaculation with equally positive results (Zilbergeld, 1975). While most approaches have focused on the couple as a treatment unit, these masturbatory exercises can be utilized for the treatment of individuals without steady partners.

## GROUP TREATMENT PROCEDURES

Traditional sex therapy has, for the most part, been done in an individual or couple therapy format. Thus, an individual or couple meets with a therapist or cotherapist team for several sessions and practices the sexual exercises between their therapy sessions. Several sex therapists have, however, been using a group treatment format. That is, several couples meet as a group with the therapist or cotherapists for part of the treatment procedure. The group is used to present information and instructions about specific exercises, which are then practiced in the privacy of the client's own homes, or, as in the case of an away-from-home treatment set-up, the client's own motel room. Perhaps one of the most unique of these group treatment procedures is the one developed by a group of sex therapists at the University of Texas Medical School in Galveston (Powell, Blakeney, Croft, and Pulliam, 1974).

After an extensive history-taking session and a physical exam, the couples taking part in the Galveston program then participate in an intensive, two-and-one-half-day treatment workshop. Three to six couples may be treated during each workshop. Multiple therapists from several different professional disciplines are used, with at least two therapists being available at all times. During the workshop, each individual couple has their own motel room in which to practice the sexual exercises. Couples meet as a group with the therapists, who provide factual information and instructions for the exercises. Couples then return to their rooms, where they practice the prescribed exercises. The workshop thus consists of an alternation of these group meetings and individual practice sessions in the privacy of their own rooms. Therapists are always available in the motel should any couple encounter difficulties at any point in the treatment process.

Beyond these basics, the Galveston program is unique in several other respects. First, the time in treatment is compressed into two and one-half days, a much more intensive procedure than commonly used by other sex therapy format. Couples in the Galveston program engage in essentially all the same exercises that would be prescribed by Masters and Johnson or by Kaplan, but within much greater time constraints. Additionally, the Galveston program therapists make much more extensive use of audio-visual materials than do most other sex treatment specialists, both as a means of presenting accurate and factual information and to desensitize the clients to sexually related topics. Finally, with few exceptions, the Galveston group treats all sexual dysfunctions in essentially the same manner. Rather than tailoring a series of exercises according to the specific sexual dysfunction as is done by Masters and Johnson, Kaplan, and others, these therapists expose all couples to essentially the same series of exercises, irrespective of diagnosis.

Of the 74 individuals treated for specific sexual dysfunctions, total symptom reversal was obtained in 63.5% of the cases (Blakeney, Kinder, Creson, Powell and Sutton, 1976). Because

of the brevity of this program, approximately one-half of the symptoms did not disappear until several months after the workshop. Presumably these couples required additional time to practice what they had learned during the workshop for complete symptom change to occur. However, two distinct groups of clients did not experience maximum benefits from this short-term, intensive workshop format. First, only about one-half of the premature ejaculators were treated successfully, a symptom with a much higher success rate when other treatment modalities have been used. Again, perhaps the brevity of this program did not allow for enough time to practice and benefit from the squeeze technique and other exercises. The second group that was not successfully treated consisted of those couples with other severe marital difficulties in addition to their specific sexual dysfunctions. Of those ten individuals who made little or no improvement during the workshop or during the next several months following treatment, nine reported severe marital difficulties which significantly interfered with the practice of prescribed homework exercises or with their marital relationship in general. Thus, while the Galveston program represents a unique approach with significant savings in time and money for the couples involved, certain types of individuals do not appear to benefit from this treatment format.

## SELF TREATMENT OF SEXUAL DYSFUNCTIONS

In recent years, many self-help books have appeared, covering a wide variety of adjustment problems. Glasgow and Rosen (1978) reported that one publishing company had 160 titles in its "self-improvement library." Kimbrell (1975) had earlier noted the publication of some 117 diet and weight control books. As might be expected, many of the self-improvement books are oriented toward enhancement of one's sexual functioning, leading to the possibility that a person or a couple might treat their sexual dysfunction by themselves, without professional help. While there has been almost no research in this area, preliminary data suggests that successful self-treatment of sexual disorders is a possibility for some people.

Lowe and Mikulas (1975) treated ten couples in which the man was a premature ejaculator. These investigators wrote an 80-page program which included instruction regarding the general problem of premature ejaculation, sensate focus, the squeeze technique, and the female superior and lateral coital positions. Subjects read this material and then performed a prescribed exercise. Depending upon the experiences in any given exercise, the couple either moved on to the next section of the instructions or repeated the same exercise with additional instructions. Before treatment, the mean time these men could engage in intercourse before ejaculating was less than two minutes. After treatment, these men had significantly increased their ability to control their ejaculation, with gains reported from 4.5 to 59 minutes. No similar changes occurred in control subjects who did not receive this treatment. However, this study suffered from several limitations. Subjects were all volunteers, they had relatively high educational levels, all had wives who agreed to take part in treatment, and there were no apparent interpersonal problems for any of these couples.

In the most comprehensive study of this type, McMullen and Rosen (1979) treated 60 anorgasmic women (half were married, half were single). One-third of these women viewed a series of six 20-minute videotape sequences in which an actress portrayed the steps to be taken to become orgasmic (modeling group). Another one-third received the same instructions in a printed booklet format (written instructions group). The remaining women served as a control group. Women in the first two groups met once a week to either view the videotapes or read the written instructions; they then practiced at home, before returning the next week, what they had learned. There were no significant differences found between the videotape or written instructions groups with respect to orgasms either during masturbation or intercourse. Twenty-four of the 40 women treated became orgasmic with masturbation, and 15 of these 24 also became orgasmic with intercourse. Interestingly, in this study those who failed to transfer this orgasmic capacity to coitus experienced intercourse less frequently, reported less vaginal lubrication, and their partners also showed a higher incidence of sexual dysfunctions. Follow-up after one year indicated no evidence of loss of orgasmic abilities; in fact, several women who had not become orgasmic during the initial six weeks of treatment had by then become orgasmic.

Self-treatment of sexual dysfunctions is thus an area of only recent concern and one in which further research is needed. However, these two studies suggest that self-treatment may be an effective method for some individuals and may represent a considerable savings of therapists' time and clients' money. Specifically, these studies suggest these procedures may be best suited for relatively well-educated individuals with no other severe problems in their relationship and whose partners are willing to take part in treatment and are not themselves experiencing a sexual dysfunction.

## RESEARCH IN SEX THERAPY CURRENT TRENDS

It should be clear from the preceding section that a variety of different therapy formats have been used to treat sexual dysfunctions in the past few years. Also apparent should be the fact that, with the exception of psychoanalysis and traditional psychotherapy, most of these sex treatment procedures have yielded relatively successful results. The overall effectiveness of sex therapy has recently been reviewed (Hogan, 1978; Kinder and Blakeney, 1977; Sotile and Kilmann, 1977); and all these studies supported the conclusion that sex therapy is effective in a large proportion of cases. They have also reached two other important conclusions. First, there remain some people for whom sex therapy does not work; there is a need to determine why treatment is ineffective in these cases and a need to explore new treatment alternatives for these individuals. Secondly, we know sex therapy is effective for many individuals, but we know very little about *why* it works. There are several factors, such as client variables (type of dysfunction, type of other relationship problems present), treatment variables (variations of structured exercises, use of audio-visual materials), and mode of therapy (individual versus group treatment, single therapist versus cotherapists), that may possibly influence treatment outcomes. While research concerning these variables is still in its infancy, researchers have recently begun investigating the potential impact of a variety of these possible components of sex therapy.

Some sex therapists (for example, Barach, 1974) have preferred to treat individuals without their partners being present. Others (for example, Masters and Johnson, 1970; Powell, et al., 1974) seem to hold to the notion that "there is no such thing as an uninvolved partner" and always try to treat the couple as a unit in all possible instances, even if one of the members does not have a specific sexual dysfunction. Recently, Ersner-Hershfield and Kopel (1979) treated primary anorgasmic women either with their partners absent or in the more traditional couples format. Those women treated with their partners present reported more satisfaction with the frequency of sexual activities and reported increased "total pleasure" as compared to women treated with their partners absent. However, few other significant differences emerged. For example, contrary to the suggestions of many sex therapists, those women treated with their partners, that is, as couples, were not superior on a number of different measures of couple activities or frequency of orgasm with their partners. These results suggest that treating the couple rather than just the symptomatic person is not always that beneficial and necessary.

This same study also addressed another important component of treatment. Most sex therapists extend treatment over a period of several weeks while some (for example, Powell et al., 1974) have condensed treatment into a much shorter time period. Ersner-Hershfield and Kopel (1979) investigated differences between massed versus distributed treatment by having some of their subjects meet twice a week for five weeks (massed) while others met once a week for ten weeks (distributed). Even though subjects in the distributed group rated their schedule as more helpful than those in the massed group, there were actually no significant differences between the groups on any of the outcome measures of treatment effectiveness.

This study by Ersner-Hershfield and Kopel (1979) is, it is hoped, characteristic of the future research to be carried out in this field. Given that we now know that sex therapy works for many people, the next task is to determine exactly which components of the sex therapy process are most responsible for this success.

## CHOOSING A SEX THERAPIST

Should a person have a sexual problem and wish to seek professional help, choosing a sex therapist who is well trained and competent can be full of perils and pitfalls. There has been a high demand for sex therapy in recent years and a shortage of adequately trained treatment personnel. All States regulate the practice of psychotherapy in some way (for example, by requiring licensure of psychiatrists, psychologists, or social workers); however, these procedures do not guarantee any "quality control" over sex treatment from a consumer standpoint. In fact, there appears to be a proliferation of nonprofessional "sex therapists" who are legally exempt from such current laws (LoPiccolo, 1978). Attempts from within the profession of sex therapy itself to establish and maintain guidelines regarding who is competent to offer his or her services as a professional sex therapist have not substantially improved this situation. The American Association of Sex Educators, Counselors, and Therapists (AASECT) began a licensing procedure for sex therapists in the mid-1970s. However, some authorities feel that these standards are too low to ensure competence. Additionally, AASECT certification is not backed up by any legal constraints on who can call himself or herself a sex therapist or who can practice sex therapy. Thus, many people represent themselves as sex therapists without even meeting these minimal AASECT certification standards and may do so legally in most States.

Given this relatively sad state of affairs, how does one go about choosing a well-trained, qualified sex therapist? While there is probably no totally reliable way to accomplish this, LoPiccolo (1978) has suggested that the following guidelines and principles be kept in mind:

1. Don't respond to any paid advertisements in any medium. Advertising is against the ethical codes of most professions whose members often practice sex therapy, for example, psychologists and psychiatrists.

2. Media coverage (for example, newspapers, television) of university, medical school, or other social agency sponsored clinics often provides a good way to locate qualified sex therapists in an area. These institutional clinics, geared toward education and training, often have higher standards of excellence than might be found in private practice. Additionally, the fees charged by these clinics are usually substantially lower than those charged by private practitioners.

3. Be sure that the therapist is licensed by the State (for example, as a psychiatrist, psychologist, or social worker). This license, of course, does not guarantee competence, but it does provide certain legal protections not present if the therapist is not regulated by the State.

4. Don't be afraid to check out the therapist's qualifications. Try to find a therapist who, in addition to being licensed, has had special training in marriage therapy and in specialized sex therapy techniques. LoPiccolo has stated, "A board-certified therapist who simply has read Masters and Johnson (1970) and has now decided to see sexual dysfunction cases is not the optimal choice" (1978, p.525).

5. LoPiccolo does not recommend seeking referral from the local medical or psychological society, since these organizations usually simply give the names of three or more of their members without references to their areas of special expertise. He does, however, suggest a call to the nearest university or medical school department of psychiatry, psychology, or social work. They may be helpful in locating a sex therapy specialist. One may also check the list of certified sex therapists published by AASECT (remembering, of course, the already mentioned reservations about the level of standards required by AASECT). Finally in this regard, LoPiccolo suggests that if the prospective therapist is a licensed professional in the State *and* is AASECT certified, these factors may provide some reassurance about that person's competence.

6. Do not uncritically accept referrals from family doctor or clergy. Rather, use them as a starting point, but still check out the therapist's qualifications as suggested above.

The above suggestions of LoPiccolo (1978) are reasonable guidelines and should serve to remind one to exercise caution in selecting a sex therapist. There are many competent sex therapists available, yet it is still not always easy to choose with reliability a good therapist rather than a poorly trained, incompetent one. It is hoped that in the future it will become possible to better regulate both the training and practice of sex therapists.

## SUMMARY

Perhaps more progress has been made in the area of treatment for sexual dysfunctions than in any other area of human sexuality. In one relatively short time span of 20 years, problems that had been resistant to change are now almost routinely ameliorated by a series of standardized treatment techniques. Certainly, many people have now achieved a higher level of sexual adjustment than was true before these developments emerged. That is not to say that all the problems have been resolved. On the contrary, as we have seen, much more remains to be done before a sophisticated and reliable set of treatment procedures has been scientifically documented. But we are well on the path to accomplishing this objective. Perhaps the time is nearing when treatment for sexual dysfunctions will be regarded with the same general level of acceptibility as is true for any other adjustment problem.

# Chapter 15

## Sexual Health

## INTRODUCTION

Any form of sexually related behavior from casual (kissing and petting) to intense (for example, coitus) is affected by the state of health of our bodies. The food we eat, the liquids we drink, even the clothes we wear, all may have an impact on those bodily processes which are related to our sexuality. Also relevant in this connection are the attitudes we develop which result from our contact with the medical profession. The exploration of these topics is the subject of this chapter. Specifically, we will consider such issues as sex and drugs, sex and health, in particular, nutrition and practical concerns related to the health of our genital organs, and common infections of the sexual system. Overriding each of these issues is the influence of the medical profession in determining sexual attitudes and influencing sexual behavior in our culture.

## SEX AND DRUGS

As we saw in earlier chapters, the many ways in which we express our sexuality involves a combination of physiological and psychological factors. Substances that affect physical and mental states can have a variety of influences on all dimensions of human functioning, including our sexual behavior. Given the widespread use of drugs in our society, it is important to explore influences of drugs on human sexuality. Unfortunately, research into the relationship between drugs and sexual behavior is only at the beginning stages, and few reliable results have been reported. One of the most difficult problems in this area is that the relationship between drugs and sex is a complex one, involving a variety of components, including general psychological variables, specific individual reactions, physical processes, sociocultural factors, etc.

It is the complex interrelationship between all of these components that makes it so difficult to conduct good, sound research in this area. Nevertheless, some preliminary observations can be made on the basis of information derived to date. In this section, we will discuss several categories of drug-sex interactions. In particular, we will review those substances that have been historically used in this context, such as aphrodisiacs, anaphrodisiacs, alcohol, etc. In addition, we will also discuss the role that mind-altering drugs and medications, in general, play in our sexual lives.

### APHRODISIACS

An aphrodisiac is usually defined as any substance that increases sexual desire or functioning, regardless of the specific mechanism involved, that is, whether the substance in question *actually* increases sexual activity or pleasure or only affects the subject's perception thereof. While most authorities disclaim the possibility that the usual aphrodisiacs actually enhance sexual desire or power, it is important to recognize that a *belief* in the sexual power of a substance is sometimes enough to produce, at least temporarily, an elevation in the individual's desire or capabilities. The search for such substances has long historical roots, with candidates offered from many different cultures.

The list of preparations recommended by various sources is indeed a long and exotic one, including such substances as the following: pine nuts, the blood of bats mixed with donkey's milk, root of the valerian plant, menstrual fluid, tulip bulbs, fat of camel's hump, salted crocodile, the powdered tooth of a corpse, wings of bees, the genitals of hedgehogs, swallow's hearts, powdered rhinoceros horns, and certain bones of the toad (Katchadourian and Lunde, 1975). Most of these are to be taken internally to restore and/or enhance male potency. A number of American and English medical textbooks published between 1890 and 1920 included references to a variety of other substances (Carter and Davis, 1976).

In addition to the above, certain foods have long been regarded as possessing sexually stimulating properties, due to the "doctrine of signatures," that is , their apparent resemblance to the external characteristics of male and female genitalia. Popular examples of such foods are bananas and oysters.

Although no evidence has ever been provided to support the belief in any of these so-called aphrodisiacs, one such substance holds a special status in our convential wisdom. The legendary stimulant *cantharides* (Spanish fly) is still regarded as a powerful sexual stimulant by many individuals. Cantharides is a powdered preparation made from dried beetles found in southern Europe. The substance is indeed a powerful systemic activator which, when taken internally, causes irritation and inflammation of the genitourinary tract as well as dilation of the blood vessels of the penis. These effects may produce a prolonged erection, though usually without a concomitant increase in sexual desire. More importantly, however, cantharides has toxic properties which, after prolonged use, may cause permanent penile damage and even death (Kaplan, 1974).

There are two general sets of circumstances often associated with the use of aphrodisiacs. In one case, aphrodisiacs are used by males to enhance their own sexual ability. In the other case, the aphrodisiac is slipped to an unsuspecting female by a male under the assumption that this will increase her sexual feelings and desire.

Although there is no evidence to support the popular belief in traditional aphrodisiacs, it is reasonable to assume that appropriate nutritional practices may enhance sexual behavior, just as poor nutritional practices may impair sexual behavior. It may even be the case that foods reputed to have sexually stimulating properties may actually provide dietary ingredients which influence sex hormones (Cheraskin, Ringsdorf and Brecher, 1976). Oysters, for example, contain zinc, an ingredient that is evidently important to the health of the prostate gland (Cheraskin et al., 1976; Rodale, 1978), which regulates certain male functions.

Despite these findings, it is important to recognize that the relationship between food or other substances and sex drive is a highly complicated one. Moreover, our current level of knowledge strongly suggests that there are no true aphrodisiacs which enhance sex drive or which directly increase sexual performance. Conversely, there is good reason to believe that unauthorized reliance on such substances can have serious consequences.

One final substance needs to be added to the list above, and here we refer to marijuana (*cannibus*). The popularity of marijuana is more a function of its reputed effect on enhancing sexual *pleasure,* rather than in terms of its enhancing the sex *drive.* In this sense, marijuana differs from the more traditional aphrodisiacs. Support for this argument is offered by Gawin (1978), who reported that experienced marijuana smokers claimed greater enhancement of sexual sensations than was true for those who did not smoke marijuana. Several qualifications must be advanced, however, before such a conclusion can be accepted. For one thing, marijuana often enhances sensations such as touch and taste which in turn may lead to a more intensely experienced sexual reaction. More importantly, however, a number of studies have clearly shown that marijuana reactions are strongly influenced by suggestibility, expectancy, and the placebo phenomenon. Furthermore, in several well-controlled studies, experienced users were unable to distinguish between real marijuana and marijuana in which the active ingredient of THC had been removed. Finally, it should be recognized that marijuana is still an illegal substance in most communities despite its apparent popularity.

## ANAPHRODISIACS

Paralleling the search for sexual activators, history reveals a continuing attempt to discover techniques which *decrease* sexual interest and behavior. Such efforts range from the famous cold shower to various chemical substances which are collectively identified as anaphrodisiacs. Perhaps the best known of these is saltpeter (potassium nitrate), the one time notoriously reputed addition to boarding school and prison fare. Medically, saltpeter is regarded as a diuretic (any substance which causes fluid reduction); and, while in and of itself saltpeter is not an anaphrodisiac, frequent urination may well produce the same effect.

A variety of other drugs have been used as anaphrodisiacs primarily because they act indirectly on sexual activity by depressing central nervous system functions or by blocking central nervous system arousal. Recent research with chronic sex offenders, for example, has focused on the antiandrogens, that is, substances that inhibit the action of androgens. Apparently, the most effective of these isolated to date is the steroid cyproterone acetate. Studies on male sex offenders undergoing treatment for hypersexuality have shown that cyproterone acetate decreases sex drive, erectile ability, and orgasmic capability (Laschet, 1973; Woods, 1979). Thus, at least while the drug is in effect, the level of sexual activity in these men was reduced to a level consistent with social norms.

In addition to the above substances, a variety of other drugs serve to decrease sexual functioning, in particular those which are known to affect hormonal processes. Individuals undergoing any form of drug therapy are well advised to determine whether or not the medication they are taking may exert such effects in their own case.

## ALCOHOL

Perhaps the one substance with the longest sex-related history is ethyl alcohol. Popular folklore recognizes alcohol's inhibition-reducing properties and/or its effects on reducing anxiety. The common aphorism "Candy's dandy, but liquor's quicker" illustrates alcohol's popular use as a seduction agent. What is probably less well known, however, is the paradoxical effect of alcohol on sexual behavior. While it may be true that a certain amount of alcohol will reduce inhibitions (and possibly facilitate sexual activites as a result), crossing that threshold may actually have the opposite effect. Shakespeare's porter in *MacBeth* has this to say of alcohol's paradoxical effects: "Lechery, sir, it [alcohol] provokes and unprovokes; it provokes the desire, but it takes away the performance." This threshold varies from individual to individual depending upon a variety of factors such as age, psychological state, physiological state, time of day, individual tolerance, and, for women, phase of menstrual cycle (the affects of alcohol are strongest premenstrually [Youcha, 1976]). Moreover, the rate of ingestion of alcohol also effects behavorial changes: the more rapid the ingestion, the greater the behavioral effects.

An understanding of the paradoxical effect of ethyl alcohol can be obtained by reviewing its physiological mechanisms. Alcohol is essentially a central nervous system depressant. In small amounts, it retards those processes related to anxiety arousal. In greater amounts, however, alcohol depresses judgment, visual-motor coordination, and brain function in general, including those brain functions related to sexual behavior. At still higher doses, the brain becomes narcotized, and loss of consciousness may result (Kaplan, 1974).

There is little doubt that continuous, heavy rates of alcohol consumption can seriously impair general sexual behavior (Kaplan, 1974), at least in males. Chronic alcoholism may result in atrophy of the testicles, impaired sperm production and, ultimately, total loss of sex drive and interest. Very little is known about the effect of chronic alcoholism on female sexuality.

In addition to these issues, there are other questions involved in the relationship between sex and alcohol. One important question pertains to the interaction of alcohol and other drugs (Ray, 1978). Such "poly-drug" interactions may result in a variety of serious consequences, depending upon the specific physiological mechanisms involved. For example, both alcohol and barbiturates function as central nervous system depressants, and, when taken together, the action of the combination can produce effects that are greater than those produced by each drug individually.

Finally, any analysis of the relationship between alcohol and sex must recognize the extent to which alcohol is a factor in rape and other violent asocial behavior.

## MIND-ALTERING DRUGS

Although supporting statistical data are not presently available, another major category of drugs used similarly to alcohol because of their reputed effects on sexual enhancement is that of the mind-altering, or "recreational," drugs. This category includes marijuana and the hallucinogens, such as LSD; in part, their effect on the user will depend on the particular circumstances under which use occurs (Woods, 1979).

We have already described the use of marijuana in this connection. Central nervous system stimulants such as cocaine and the amphetamines ("speed") have also received attention as sexual pleasure enhancers. There is, however, very little research on the sexual effects of these substances. It has been suggested that whatever sexual effects these drugs produce are a result of their action as central nervous system stimulants (Carter & Davis, 1976; Kaplan, 1974) or as euphoriants (Gawin, 1978). The euphoria generated by the drug might take erotic forms during sexual activity, which is them perceived as much more intensely pleasurable (Gawin, 1978). It has also been hypothesized that it may be the accelerated tactile, auditory, olfactory, and visual impulses generated by the use of the amphetamines which produces increased sexual feelings (Girdano and Girdano, 1976). It should be emphasized, however, that the effects of amphetamines on sexual interest and performance are as yet quite inconsistent (Woods, 1979).

Another parallel between these latter two categories of drugs and alcohol is the fact that overconsumption leads to decreased sexual interest and capacity (Woods, 1979). Similarly, long-term use of or addition to heroin, opium, or the barbiturates is usually accompanied by a loss of sexual interest (Kaplan, 1974; Woods, 1979).

Two other drugs which have obtained a subculture reputation as aphrodisiacs deserve mention here. Methaqualone was introduced in 1965 under the trade name Quaalude, as a nonbarbiturate, nonaddicting sedative-hypnotic. However, it has turned out to be addicting (Freedman, 1976). Meanwhile, it has gained fame as a powerful enhancer of sexual feelings. Functioning similarly to alcohol, methaqualone may reduce inhibitions and thus facilitate the sexual experience. However, large doses and continued use result in depression of sexual drive and inhibition of orgasm (Freedman, 1976).

Amyl nitrite, a vasodilator originally intended for the treatment of the heart condition angina pectoris, is reported to enhance orgasmic pleasure when inhaled or "popped" at the moment of orgasm (Freedman, 1976; Woods, 1979). This effect may be due to increased vascular response in the genital organs and/or to the production of an altered state of consciousness (Freedman, 1976). Despite its popularity, the use of this drug is medically dangerous, as coronary occlusions, some resulting in death, have been reported to follow the use of amyl nitrite during sexual activity.

## MEDICATIONS

The drugs discussed in the previous section have been deliberately utilized in a sexual context on the basis of the belief in their pleasure-enhancement properties. Another classification of drugs exists which can affect sexual functioning without the user's intent or ability to attribute these effects to the drug consumed. This category consists of those legally prescribed and/or over-the-counter medications which may produce effects on sexuality as a corollary to their primary use for indicated conditions. With one questionable exception, these drugs generally produce negative effects on sexual functioning.

The exception under question is L-dopa, or Levadopa, an agent used for the relief of Parkinson's disease. It has been observed that patients, especially elderly men, being treated with L-dopa experience increased libido. It is believed, however, that it is the relief of symptoms and improvement in general health resulting from the use of L-dopa that increases libido, rather than any specific mechanism of drug action on sexuality itself (Carter and Davis, 1976; Freedman, 1976; Woods, 1979).

Most drugs produce a variety of side effects, and side effects influencing sexual functioning are not uncommon. This fact is of importance to both the sex therapist concerned with those sexual dysfunctions that may have organic etiology and to the physician who prescribes or recommends medication. Adequate education about such influences will enable the clinician to alert his or her patients to potential side effects and to reassure them that subsequent sexual difficulties may be a normal reaction to the drug, thus allaying the patient's potential fear or feelings of inadequacy.

There are several types of drugs which can impair sexual functioning. The phenothiazines, for example, Thorazine, Mellaril, are known as the major tranquilizers. These drugs produce a sedative effect which may result in a decrease in interest in sexual activity. In addition, reports of erectile difficulties and ejaculatory disorders associated with these drugs have also been reported. For example, retrograde, or "dry," ejaculation (that is, ejaculation into the bladder rather than out through the penis) has been reported to occur in men using Thioridazine (Mellaril) (Kaplan, 1974; Woods; 1979). Chlorpromazine (Thorazine) may also influence sexual functioning by affecting the endocrine glands, possibly through its action on the hypothalamus. Animal studies show that phenothiazine derivatives can suppress hypothalamic and pituitary functioning, resulting in decreased secretion of hormones which affect the functions of the sex organs. For example, chlorpromazine blocks ovulation and suppresses estrus cycles in animals and has been shown to delay ovulation and menstruation in human female patients (Woods, 1979).

The so-called mild tranquilizers, for example, Valium, Librium, may increase sexual feelings or expression as a result of their action in reducing anxiety. On the other hand, these drugs have also been known to impair sexual functioning by causing decreased interest in sexual activity and ejaculation problems (Woods, 1979).

The use of various hypertensive (high blood pressure) medications occasionally results in a decrease in libido, erectile difficulties, retrograde ejaculation, and reduced intensity of orgasm. Several drugs of this type also affect reproductive functioning, for example, by blocking ovulation and suppressing menstruation.

Other agents of the type known as antidepressants may promote the development of erectile and ejaculatory disturbances, for example, the chemicals labeled as tricyclic compounds (for example, Elavil) and the monoamine oxidase (MAO) inhibitors (Woods, 1979).

Another type of drug compound in this category are the antihistamines (for example, Diphenhydramine, Benadryl, Chlorpheniramine, Chlortrimeton), which are very commonly taken to control allergy and cold symptoms. Continuous use of these drugs may result in interference with sexual activity by impairing erectile functioning and drying of *all* mucous membranes, including vaginal mucosa.

A final type of drug to consider here is the antispasmodics, which are used to produce relaxation of the smooth muscle of the gastrointestinal tract (for example, some ulcer medications); erectile difficulties may result from their use (Woods, 1979).

Given the large number and variety of medications covered in this area of discussion, it is important to reemphasize the responsibility of the physician to be aware of the possibility of drug-induced sexual problems and to effectively communicate this information to the patient. Additionally, the patient can take the responsibility of asking for this information. People who self-administer medication should also recognize the possible sexual ramifications of such substances.

As we stated at the outset of this section, research into the effects of drugs on sexuality is in its infant stage. In particular, the consequences of drugs for female sexuality are little known or understood. Most studies have tended to concentrate on male subjects.

# SEX AND HEALTH

The emphasis in this section is on achieving and maintaining the physical health of our sexual systems. Based on the understanding that the various systems of our bodies are interdependent and that our nutritional status affects *all* physiological processes, we will explore some dynamics of the relationship between sex and nutrition. We will also discuss the factors involved in maintaining the appropriate environmental balance of the healthy vagina.

## NUTRITION

Our bodies have the ability to maintain adequate functioning for many years on relatively poor nutrition before serious problems emerge. The standard American diet provides an overdependence on red meat, animal fat, and overrefined, overprocessed food products, along with an undersupply of whole grains and fresh fruits and vegetables. Many nutritional studies strongly suggest that a steady accumulation of such eating patterns, coupled with the lack of appropriate supplements to help counter the environmental stresses of life in our complex society, is partially responsible for the ever-increasing occurrence of degenerative deseases (for example, cardiovascular disease) afflicting people in their middle and later years (Cheraskin, Ringsdorf, & Clark, 1970).

It may also be the case that such a continued state of questionable nutrition will impact on our sexual systems. For example, new approaches to the study of menopause suggest that the estrogen production of the healthy adrenal glands increases as the estrogen output of the ovaries decreases, thus providing a gradual reduction in overall estrogen production and thus a smoother transition as the hormone levels seek a new equilibrium. Years of nutritional abuse and stress, however, can

deplete the adrenal glands to the extent that they will not be able to provide this buffer supply of estrogen (Heidi, 1976).

Nutritional circumstances can affect our sexual functioning at both ends of the continuum: nutritional deficiencies may cause specific sexual dysfunctions, and optimal nutrition may improve basic sexual functioning. Let us examine this latter assumption first.

Good nutrition can play an important role in ensuring good health and abundant vitality. For example, it has been suggested that adequate supplies of vitamin E may make people feel more sexually vigorous because their cell-oxidizing and circulation-stimulating properties can increase general vitality, muscular stamina, and cardiac efficiency (Cheraskin, et al., 1976). Significantly, as we have already stated, a number of the food substances which have been historically recommended as aphrodisiacs are foods which are rich in elements necessary to the proper functioning of the sex glands.

Just as optimal amounts of necessary nutrients provide a base for healthy glandular functioning, deficiencies of these essential factors may create sexual problems. For example, an undersupply or lack of vitamin E causes testicle degeneration and premature aging, while the lack of adequate protein can lead to lowered libido and lowered sperm count. General malnutrition, for example, an inadequate supply of protein, essential fatty acids, vitamin E, and several of the B complex vitamins, can diminish the body's ability to produce sex hormones. Overall nutritional deficiencies can similarly contribute to an underactive thyroid, which in turn leads to decreased libido and chronic fatigue, which definitely can be disrupters of sexuality. Hypoglycemia (a condition in which an excess of insulin is produced, causing lower than normal blood-sugar levels) sometimes may give rise to certain conditions both psychological (irritability) and physical (fatigue, erectile difficulties), which may inhibit sexual expression (Cheraskin, et al., 1976).

Just as sexual health may be vulnerable to poor eating habits, sexual health may be enhanced by nutritional therapy. As mentioned earlier, various difficulties associated with menopause can often be traced to nutritional deficiencies. Both vitamin E and the bioflavonoids, a substance that occurs along with vitamin C in foods, for example, the white pulp of citrus, have been reported to alleviate "hot flashes". Further, vitamin C is being studied currently to delineate its role in the maintenance of the health of the ovaries (Rodale, 1978).

One nutrient that is believed to play a major role in the health of the sexual organs is zinc. As previously stated, this mineral is essential for the health of the prostate gland in the male, yet it is undersupplied in the typical American diet. Prostate problems are fairly common in young men and quite endemic in men over 60. Studies have shown that many men with prostate problems have low levels of zinc in their prostate and that zinc supplements can improve the health of this gland. It is also the case that zinc appears to be essential for the metabolism of testosterone. One study has shown that the administration of zinc can restore erectile potency for some men on kidney dialysis who have low levels of zinc in their blood (Antoniou, Shalhoub, Sudhaker and Smith, 1977). In other studies, both zinc and brewer's yeast have been used with some measure of success in the treatment of erectile difficulties (Rodale, 1978).

Another factor that can have a negative influence on sexuality is stress—not only the stress of crisis situations but also the kinds of stress involved in daily living, for example, environmental air and noise pollution, poor nutrition, and psychological factors. Stess can cause physical changes (for example, decrease in testosterone production) which can lessen sexual desire. The acquisition and practice of relaxation techniques and other skills which reduce stress can thus have positive benefits for our sexuality. Proper nutrition can also contribute to stress reduction. There are a group of nutrients—zinc, again, and vitamins C, E, A, and D, and the minerals, magnesium, iron, and potassium which have been indicated as playing a role in resisting stress (Rodale, 1978).

## USE OF TOBACCO

The use of tobacco may be a further contributor to the impairment of sexual functioning. Cigarette smoking produces carbon monoxide in the blood, which in turn inhibits the production of testosterone. Further, nicotine constricts the blood vessels, the swelling of which comprise a central mechanism of sexual excitement (that is, vasocongestion). There is a documented statistical connection between tobacco use and erectile difficulties, lowered testosterone count, and sterility (Subak-Sharpe, 1974; Willenbecher, 1979).

Most attention has been focused on the smoking habits of pregnant women. Pregnant women who smoke are more likely to deliver infants with lowered birth weight and to have a significantly greater number of unsuccessful pregnancies that result in stillbirths and neonatal death (Subak-Sharpe, 1974). If a nursing mother smokes, the nicotine from her cigarette passes into her milk and also may possibly reduce the milk supply. However, studies also suggest that male smokers are more likely to father premature or stillborn babies, or babies with birth defects, even if the mother is a nonsmoker (Willenbecher, 1979).

Although most of the research into the effects of smoking on sexual performance has centered on the connection between smoking and erectile difficulties, the general consequences of (particularly heavy) smoking, for example, shortness of breath and constriction of blood vessels, may affect female sexuality as well (Subak-Sharpe, 1974; Ray, 1978).

## HEALTHY VAGINA

The last topic in this section involves issues related to vaginal conditions. As we saw in Chapter 5, the normal pH of the vagina is between 3.5 and 4.5, and it is this acid character which helps to maintain the health of the vaginal environment. We will now examine the mechanisms which maintain this acidity, its potential disrupters and preventive approaches to maintaining vaginal health.

One of the main mechanisms which produces the acidity of the vagina is the presence of non-disease-causing bacteria called lactobacilli or Doderlein's bacilli. These bacilli live on the glycogen normally present in the vaginal canal. Production of estrogen affects the presence of glycogen, that is, higher rates of

secretion of estrogen result in larger quantities of glycogen. This glycogen is food for the lactobacilli and also for the yeast organisms which also normally live in the vagina. The lactobacilli produce lactic acid as a waste product, and it is this lactic acid that maintains the acidic pH of the vagina, thus keeping it less susceptible to disease—a fine example of recycling.

The lactobacilli normally keep the yeast in check. However, there are several factors which can disrupt this ecological system by shifting the vagina to alkalinity and thus susceptibility to infection. These factors include orgasm, ovulation (because sperm need a more alkaline environment), menstruation (blood is alkaline), douching excessively or with alkaline substances, and physical exhaustion (Boston Women's Health Book Collective, 1976; Riddle, 1971).

The relationship between estrogen and glycogen is a crucial factor in maintaining the health of the vaginal environment. As estrogen increases, for example, if a woman is taking birth control pills or is pregnant, the glycogen level will also increase. As glycogen rises (and this might also occur if a woman has diabetes or consumes refined carbohydrates in excessive amounts), so does the yeast population since they "eat" glycogen more quickly than the lactobacilli do and thus outgrow the natural system of checks and balances. Overgrowth of the yeast results in a yeast, or monilia, infection.

At the other end of the glycogen-estrogen dependency is the diminished amount of estrogen resulting from increasing age (menopause). As estrogen lessens, so does the amount of glycogen. As this food supply dwindles, the lactobacilli population shrinks, and thus the amount of lactic acid and the protection it affords decreases.

Another important consideration is the use of broad-spectrum antibiotic therapy. Not only are the harmful bacteria that are causing the primary infection killed off by antibiotics, but so are the friendly lactobacilli. Thus, the yeast can flourish on the available stores of glycogen and, because lactic acid is not produced, the vaginal protection against infection by yeast or invading organisms is lowered.

Preventive measures, as part of a holistic approach to health care, include such practices as the use of cotton underwear, rather than nylon underpants or pantyhose, since nylon prevents the air circulation necessary to prevent the build-up of excessive moisture (and cotton absorbs moisture). Also recommended, if a woman is particularly prone to vaginal infections, is the addition of yogurt to the diet (Stewart, Guest, Stewart, and Hatcher, 1979) since this product contains lactobacilli. In general, checking the vaginal pH (with over-the-counter phenaphthazine papers) during the times of lessened acidity (for example, around ovulation) and attempting to restore the necessary balance (for example, with a mild vinegar douche) may help to hinder or avert vaginal infections.

## COMMON INFECTIONS

In this section, we will discuss common infections of the genitourinary system. This presentation will include both those conditions traditionally classified as venereal diseases as well as other prevalent ailments. The classic distinction between venereal diseases and other infections of the sexual organs is not necessarily appropriate since many of the organisms which cause the latter conditions can also be transmitted through sexual contact. Thus, the designation "sexually transmitted disease," where appropriate, is more accurate. Further, venereal diseases are often popularly associated with "illicit" sexual activity and thus carry a potential stigma. Unfortunately, this stigma may make some individuals feel uncomfortable seeking medical attention or notifying their sex partners about the disease. If a person has difficulty talking about sex in general, she or he will be embarrassed to discuss venereal disease with a partner, especially if such a discussion reveals or implies sexual activity outside of the relationship (Boston Women's Health Book Collective, 1976).

Sexually transmitted diseases are not new. For example, ancient Chinese and Egyptian manuscripts described a disease that was probably gonorrhea (Katchadourian and Lunde, 1975), and similar references appear in the Old Testament (Leviticus 15).

Throughout history, sexually transmitted diseases have been most common during wartime, and the first recorded significant worldwide epidemic of gonorrhea occurred during World War I (Bicher, Cherniak, Feingold and Gardner, 1977). World War II initiated another epidemic; after the war and with the introduction of penicillin, the incidence of gonorrhea decreased and the lowest rates of this century were recorded during the 1950s (Bicher et al., 1977). Starting in the early 1960s, however, the incidence of gonorrhea began to increase and has continued at epidemic levels through the late 1970s. Among communicable diseases in the United States, the incidence of gonorrhea ranks second only to the common cold (Stewart, et al., 1979).

Several factors are believed to have contributed to this epidemic. As we have already mentioned, infected individuals do not always seek treatment, and the disease can also be spread by people who are asymptomatic but nonetheless infectious. It is obviously important that a person know she or he has a sexually transmissible disease in order to prevent infecting others and in order to notify partners with whom she or he has come into sexual contact. Infected individuals do not always fulfill this latter responsibility, and public health agencies are generally ineffective in tracking down sexual contacts of infected persons (McCary, 1978). Another factor related to the epidemic has been the importation of strains of penicillin-resistant gonorrhea from Vietnam (Bicher, et al., 1977). Inadequate treatment might hide symptoms, and the infected individual, believing himself or herself cured, can continue to spread the disease. Additionally, the popularity of birth control pills has had an impact since this method of birth control increases a user's susceptibility to gonorrhea (Boston Women's Health Book Collective, 1976) and it also eliminates the potential protection afforded by such contraceptive methods as condoms.

Sexually transmitted diseases are not only unpleasant and potentially harmful in themselves, but they also represent a significant drain on our national health and resources. For example, 175,000 American women are hospitalized each year because of gonorrheal pelvic infections, at a cost of $212 million. Further, about 5,750 young women are truant each school day because of gonnorrhea (Stewart, et al., 1979). Mass education programs are needed to demystify the traditional venereal diseases ethic and to provide information about transmission, symptoms, and treatment as part of programs to eradicate these diseases (Bicher et al., 1977). Emphasis on methods of prevention can be taught from early adolescence on, as part of health education programs. Preventive measures focus on the use of condoms to avoid transmission of disease organisms between partners; and vaginal spermicides also offer some degree of protection against infectious agents (Stewart et al., 1979). It is also advisable to urinate after sexual activity and to wash the genitals with soap and water, though washing will not destroy organisms which have invaded the vagina or cervix. Sexually active individuals are well-advised to have tests for gonorrhea and syphilis at least twice a year.

## GONORRHEA ("THE CLAP")

In 1977, the *reported* rate for gonorrhea was 469 per 100,000 people in the United States (Stewart et al., 1979), or approximately 1,000,000 cases; the projected number of cases for 1979 was 1,010,000 (Center for Disease Control, 1979). The actual incidence is quite likely much higher; it has been estimated that only one in four cases are reported (McCary, 1978). This disease is caused by a bacterium, the gonococcus, or *Neissera gonorrhoeae,* which is transmitted only through sexual contact. The most common site of infection in women is the cervix where the disease may produce an unnoticed discharge (Bicher, et al., 1977). In general 80% of women with gonorrhea will be initially asymptomatic (Smartt and Lighter, 1971) and must, therefore, depend on an infected partner to notify them of the disease. On the other hand, 80% to 90% of infected men will develop noticeable symptoms. Within three to five days after exposure to the gonococcus, an infected man will experience discharge from his penis and pain or burning during urination. Depending on the site of contact, an individual may also develop an infection in the rectum, which may produce mild irritation, or in the throat, which usually produces no symptoms or occasionally a sore throat and a low fever (Bicher, et al., 1977).

Diagnosis for gonorrhea in men is made on the basis of a microscopic examination of penile discharge. For women, diagnosis is performed by a culture test of cervical secretions (Stewart et al., 1979). A small sample of secretions is placed in a special nutrient jelly to allow for the growth and identification of bacteria, the results of which are available in 48 hours. Treatment for the infected individual and his or her partner or partners, when possible, generally consists of injections of pencillin and a probenecid pill, which temporarily reduces the rate of excretion of penicillin by the kidneys. In this way, the antibiotic remains in the system longer in order to work more effectively. If a person has a history of allergic reactions to penicillin, other antibiotics, for example, tetracycline, can be used to treat the disease. After antibiotic treatment, the infected individual is advised to have a repeat culture test to ensure that she or he has been cured (Stewart, et al., 1979).

Untreated gonorrhea can lead to serious consequences. In women, the infection can spread to the uterus and Fallopian tubes and develop into a general pelvic infection. This generally produces pelvic or abdominal pain and tenderness, fever, and tired, achy feelings. Intensive antibiotic treatment will be necessary. Once the infection reaches the Fallopian tubes, there is a 15% to 40% risk of developing scar tissue which can obstruct the tubes and cause infertility; in fact, as we saw in Chapter 8, gonorrhea is a leading cause of infertility. If a Fallopian tube is only partially obstructed, an egg may become fertilized but, since the route to the uterus is obstructed, it may become implanted in the tube instead. As we saw in Chapter 7, such an ectopic pregnancy is a dangerous condition.

If a gonorrheal infection remains untreated in a man, within two to three weeks the bacteria may travel to the prostate gland, where they generally produce few symptoms. If the disease remains untreated, in about 20% of the cases, the bacteria travel through the vas deferens to the epididymis. Once the infectious process reaches this location, it will cause pain and local symptoms, for example, the scrotal skin becomes red and hot. At this point, the disease will leave scar tissue which closes off the passage of sperm. Usually only one testicle is affected, but if both become involved, sterility will result (Bicher, et al., 1977).

In 1% of cases that remain untreated for more than a few weeks, bacteria enter the bloodstream, causing symptoms such as fever, general ill feelings, and pain in the joints (arthritis). Antibiotic treatment is necessary to avoid permanent joint damage (Bicher, et al., 1977).

If a pregnant woman has gonorrhea at the time of delivery, the bacteria can enter the baby's eyes and cause blindness. Silver nitrate solution or penicillin drops placed in the eyes of the newborn immediately after birth will prevent infection (Bicher, et al., 1977).

## HERPES (GENITAL HERPES)

About 300,000 people a year develop genital herpes. This disease has reached epidemic proportions, and most experts concur that its incidence is rising (Callahan, 1978). The infectious agent is the Herpes Simplex Virus Type II, which belongs to the same family as Herpes Simplex Virus Type I. Herpes type I usually affects only the upper part of the body and is the organism responsible for cold sores or fever blisters around the mouth and lips. It has been estimated that there is an approximately 10% crossover between these two viruses, that is, that 10% of herpes infections in the mouth are caused by type II and 10% of genital herpes are caused by type I. This crossover is probably a result of virus transmission during oral-genital sex (Boston Women's Health Book Collective, 1976).

Although genital herpes may arise spontaneously, most cases are transmitted through sexual contact (Stewart et al., 1979). Within two to seven days after contact, an infected individual will develop the characteristic signs—small, extremely painful blisters. Some people complain of a tingling sensation before the blisters erupt. These occur at the site of contact, usually the vulva, penis, or anus. Women may also develop herpes on the cervix, which is usually painless and may, therefore, go unnoticed, though there may sometimes be a profuse, watery discharge (Kagan, 1978). The blisters soon break to form small open sores or ulcers. Some people also develop fever or have enlarged, tender lymph nodes in the abdomen (Stewart, et al., 1979).

Diagnosis for herpes can be performed by several methods. A culture test can be done with a specimen of material from the blisters, or a sample of cells scraped from the sores can be examined under a microscope. A blood test can detect antibodies for herpes, but this will indicate only whether an individual has had herpes in the past, not whether there is an active infection (Kagan, 1978).

There is no known cure for herpes; the only available treatment methods are directed at relieving symptoms. These methods include the use of pain-relieving pills or ointment, antibacterial ointment to prevent secondary bacterial infection of the sores, and sitz baths or cold compresses to relieve pain. The sores will heal spontaneously within one to four weeks, but the virus remains in cells in the nervous system. It is difficult to determine how long an individual is contagious after the sores have disappeared; laboratory studies have revealed infectious viruses several weeks after the sores have healed (Stewart et al., 1979). The virus can either remain dormant in the nervous system permanently or can cause recurrent attacks. Generally believed to be a result of stress, recurrent infections are neither as severe nor as lengthy as the initial bout. In some cases, a recurrent infection may be so mild as to go unnoticed but will nonetheless be contagious (Kagan, 1978).

A number of methods have been employed in attempts to provide a cure for herpes, but none have as yet proven effective. One such technique was photoinactivation; the sores were painted with dye and then exposed to fluorescent light. This technique has not been shown to be effective and may cause carcinogenic mutations of the virus (Stewart, et al., 1979).

Genital herpes may have serious consequences for women. It is suspected that the herpes virus may play a role in the development of cervical cancer. Research has shown that women with cervical cancer often have herpes type II antibodies in their blood and that women who have had genital herpes are more likely than other women to develop cervical cancer (Kagan, 1978). For these reasons, it is recommended that women who have had herpes have a Pap smear done every 6 to 12 months. Additionally, herpes can cause complications in pregnancy. Women with herpes have a higher than average miscarriage rate (Stewart, et al., 1979). If a pregnant woman has an active case of herpes at the time of birth, the baby can come into contact with the sores during its passage through the vagina. There is as much as a fifty percent chance that the child will become infected and, in a newborn, the virus can cause severe illness or death (Kagan, 1978). For these reasons, a Caesarian section is generally recommended.

## SYPHILIS

In 1977, there was a *reported* rate of 10 cases of infectious syphilis per 100,000 people (Stewart, et al., 1979), or approximately 20,000 cases. Syphilis is caused by a spiral-shaped bacterium called a spirochete, or *Treponema pallidum* (*T. pallidum* for short). Syphilis is transmitted only by sexual contact, or by skin contact with the infection. For example, the bacteria can enter the skin of a finger which touched the syphilis sore of an infected person (Stewart, et al., 1979). There is usually a period of three to four weeks between exposure and the development of symptoms, although this incubation period can range between 10 and 90 days (Bicher, et al., 1977).

Syphilis progresses through several stages. The first sign of primary syphilis is a chancre, a hard, red-rimmed, painless sore at the site of sexual contact, for example, the penis, vagina, anus, or lips. The chancre is not alway detectable because it is painless and it may also be hidden, for example, inside the vagina; nonetheless, during this stage, the disease is highly infectious. The chancre usually disappears spontaneously within two to six weeks (Stewart, et al., 1979).

Untreated primary syphilis develops into secondary syphilis, which is also very contagious. The symptoms of this stage usually develop somewhere between one week and six months after the chancre heals and may last for three to six months. The symptoms are variable and may include a rash, especially on the palms of the hand and soles of the feet, fever, sore throat, headache, nausea, or lack of appetite. Hair on the scalp may fall out in patches. Moist sores may develop around the genitals and anus (Stewart, et al., 1979).

Untreated secondary stage syphilis progresses into latent syphilis, which generally produces no symptoms. After about one year in this stage, the individual is no longer contagious except in the case of a pregnant woman who can pass the disease to her unborn child. During this latency period, which may last ten to twenty years (Bicher, et al., 1977), the spirochetes invade internal tissues and organs, including blood vessels, the spinal cord and brain, and bones.

Between one-third and one-half of all untreated cases will develop into tertiary syphilis. The complications of this stage include blindness, deafness, heart disease, loss of muscular control, and severe mental disturbances, and ultimately the disease can be fatal.

Diagnosis of syphilis can be made on the basis of observation of symptoms (for example, chancre), but the symptoms of secondary syphilis can be identical to many other diseases. Confirmation of the disease is usually done by testing the blood for syphilis antibodies, which appear six to seven weeks after the disease begins. The basic blood test is the VDRL, named for the Venereal Disease Research Laboratory of the U.S. Public Health Service, where this test was developed (Bicher, et al., 1977). If an individual suspects that she or he has syphilis but the blood test is negative, testing should be repeated about six weeks later. Syphilis can be cured by treatment with penicillin or other antibiotics.

Untreated syphilis in a pregnant woman can seriously damage or kill the fetus. For this reason, a VDRL blood test is an essential part of prenatal care (Stewart, et al., 1979).

## VENEREAL WARTS (GENITAL WARTS)

Warts that appear in the genital region are caused by a virus, similar to the virus that causes common skin warts. Venereal warts may follow a case of trichomonas or other vaginal infection. Venereal warts are generally dry and painless. In women,

they may occur on the vulva, around the anus, inside the vagina, or on the cervix. In men, they may appear on the penis, on the scrotum, or around the anus. They are transmitted by sexual contact and generally appear one to three months after exposure (Stewart, et al., 1979).

Venereal warts can generally be diagnosed on the basis of their appearance alone. If there is a question of a diagnosis between warts and other diseases such as skin cancer on the vulva, a biopsy for microscopic examination can be performed. The standard treatment consists of applications of podophyllin ointment or liquid to dry up the warts. This procedure is repeated once or twice a week until the warts disappear (Stewart, et al., 1979). If the warts are internal, that is, in the vagina or on the cervix, they can be treated by cautery (burning) or by freezing.

## PUBIC LICE (CRABS)

Lice in the pubic hair are tiny parasites much like the head lice which infect the scalp. The predominant symptom is itching in the pubic area, and an infected individual may be able to see the lice or feel their egg cases as tiny bumps on the pubic hairs. These lice are transmitted by sexual contact or by sharing the clothes or the bed of an infected person.

Diagnosis is done by a careful inspection of the pubic hair to find the organisms. The standard treatment to kill lice is the use of Kwell (gamma benzene hexachloride) in the form of cream, lotion, or shampoo, obtainable by prescription only (Stewart, et al., 1979). Removed from the environment of the human body, pubic lice can live for 24 hours and egg cases can survive for six days. Infected clothing and bed linen are safe to use after that time. If they are needed sooner, they should be boiled or dry-cleaned.

## YEAST INFECTION
## (MONILIA, CANDIDA, FUNGUS)

As we have already seen, yeast organisms normally live in the vagina; an infection is a result of an overgrowth of yeast. The symptoms of a yeast infection are a white, thick, vaginal discharge, which may resemble cottage cheese, and an itching red vulva. As previously noted, yeast infections result from many causes. The infection can also be transmitted by sexual contact; a male sex partner may harbor yeast organisms and pass them on during intercourse. It is unlikely that he would have symptoms, though irritation or infection may develop on the penis or scrotum. To prevent transmission or reinfection, condoms should be used during intercourse until a woman's infection is cured. A yeast infection (called "thrush") can also develop in the throat of an infected woman's sexual partner after oral-genital contact (Bicher, et al., 1977).

Diagnosis is performed by examining a specimen of vaginal discharge under a microscope. A yeast infection is generally treated with an antifungal vaginal cream or suppositories. As mentioned above, yogurt is a popular remedy. Some women recommend eating the yogurt; others insert it in the vagina. As yet, formal research has not confirmed yogurt's therapeutic effect (Stewart, et al., 1979).

## TRICHOMONAS VAGINITIS ("TRICH")

Trichomonas is caused by a one-celled protozoan, the trichomonad. Symptoms of this infection include a thin, frothy, white or yellowish-green vaginal discharge with an unpleasant smell, and a red, itchy, and painful vulva. Trichomonas is usually transmitted by sexual contact. Trichomonas in the male is usually asymptomatic and apparently harmless although some infected men experience a slight discharge and a tickling sensation in the penis (Bicher, et al., 1977).

Diagnosis of trichomonas is done by examination of a sample of vaginal discharge under a microscope, and sometimes trichomonas can be identified by a Pap smear. The most effective treatment drug is an oral antibiotic called metronidazole (brand name, Flagyl). This is a controversial treatment, however, because this drug can cause serious side effects, for example, decreased white blood cell production which can lower resistance to additional infection of any kind. Further, Flagyl has been demonstrated to be carcinogenic in mice and possibly in rats (Stewart, et al., 1979). A pregnant woman should avoid using this drug since it is not yet known if it can cause fetal abnormalities. The usual course of treatment with Flagyl runs for seven days; many experts now recommend higher doses for a shorter period of time, since a reduced exposure time to the drug may decrease the risk of serious side effects. An infected woman's sexual partner should also be treated at the same time. Some clinicians recommend an initial treatment with antibiotic vaginal suppositories or douches and reserve the use of Flagyl for cases where these treatments do not cure the infection (Stewart, et al., 1979).

## BACTERIAL VAGINITIS (NONSPECIFIC VAGINITIS, HEMOPHILUS VAGINITIS).

This type of infection is caused by bacteria and was labeled nonspecific before the particular infectious agents were known. If a woman has a bacterial infection of the vagina, her discharge will be yellow or greenish and may have an unpleasant odor. She may experience itching or pain during urination or intercourse. These infections may be transmitted by sexual contact, especially if the agent is *Hemophilus vaginalis*, or it may arise spontaneously (Stewart, et al., 1979).

Diagnosis is made on the basis of a microscope examination of a sample of vaginal discharge; the bacteria may also be detected on a Pap smear. There are a variety of treatment approaches. Antibiotic vaginal suppositories or cream may be used. Sometimes oral antibiotics are prescribed for use by the infected woman and her sexual partner or partners. An antibacterial douche is often prescribed for use as an adjunct to oral antibiotic treatment (Stewart, et al., 1979).

## CERVICITIS

Cervicitis is a general term referring to inflammation of the cervix. If the inflammation is mild, there may be no noticeable symptoms. Otherwise, symptoms include a profuse discharge with an unpleasant odor, pain during intercourse, and spotting or bleeding after intercourse. Cervicitis can be caused by infections, for example, gonorrhea, trichomonas, herpes, or yeast. Other causes include chemicals, for example, douche products, or an IUD string (Stewart, et al., 1979).

Some women have cervical erosion, a condition in which cells that normally line the internal cervical canal extend outward onto the surface of the cervix, where they appear as reddish areas. This is mucus-producing tissue, so the woman might experience a heavy mucous discharge. Since bacteria can thrive in mucus-producing tissue, cervical erosion increases the risk of infection. Erosion may be more extensive in women who take birth control pills and in DES daughters (see Chapter 8) (Stewart, et al., 1979).

Diagnosis of cervicitis can be done on the basis of symptom observation of the cervix (in severe cases, the cervix will be swollen and red) or the presence of inflammatory cells on a Pap smear. If cervicitis is caused by a specific infection such as trichomonas, it can be treated with the appropriate medication. Prolonged recurring cervicitis with abnormal mucus production may cause fertility problems by interfering with the ability of sperm to penetrate the cervical canal (Stewart, et al., 1979). Cautery (burning) or cyrosurgery (freezing) may be recommended for stubborn cases of cervicitis. These treatments destroy the abnormal areas of surface tissue to allow nearby normal cells to grow into those areas and replace the destroyed tissue (Stewart, et al., 1979).

## CYSTITIS

Cystitis is an infection of the bladder; and between puberty and about age 45, it occurs almost exclusively in women. The male urethra is comparatively long and thus bacteria rarely reach the bladder (Bicher, et al., 1977). Infections such as gonorrhea or trichomonas may cause a bladder infection, but the bacteria most commonly responsible for cystitis is *Escherichia coli* (*E. coli*). This organism is normally present in the large intestine and sometimes invades the urethra and bladder (Bicher, et al., 1977). Various factors can make the bladder more susceptible to infection, such as general low resistance or failure to urinate frequently enough (Stewart, et al., 1979). Sexual contact that injures or irritates the urethra can also result in a bladder infection. Very frequent and vigorous intercourse, especially after a long period of abstinence, may cause inflammation of the urethra or slight injury to the urethral opening. Bacteria can infect the weakened tissue and work their way up into the bladder. This condition is sometimes called "honeymoon cystitis," although this term is not always relevant (Bicher, et al., 1977).

Symptoms of cystitis include frequency of urination, burning during urination, cloudy or bloody urine, and possibly a feeling of pressure or pain in the center of the lower abdomen. Diagnosis is made on the basis of symptoms and a microscopic examination of a urine sample to detect the presence of bacteria and white blood cells (Stewart, et al., 1979). Treatment of cystitis is important since, not only is it uncomfortable in itself but additionally, if it is untreated, the bacteria can spread to the kidneys and can cause very serious infection (Bicher, et al., 1977).

The usual treatment is sulfa medication or a broad-spectrum antibiotic (Stewart, et al., 1979). However, sulfa drugs can be dangerous to the 10% to 14% of black people who have a hereditary blood enzyme (GGPD) deficiency. If this deficiency exists, sulfa causes a serious and potentially fatal form of anemia. GGPD deficiency can be detected by a simple testing procedure, which should be performed for blacks before sulfa is prescribed (Bicher, et al., 1977).

Sex-related cystitis can potentially be prevented by using ample lubrication, stopping if intercourse hurts, and urinating before and after intercourse. General preventive measures include drinking cranberry juice or taking vitamin C to keep the urine acidic, since these bacteria do not thrive in an acid environment (Stewart, et al., 1979).

## NON-GONOCOCCAL URETHRITIS (NGU)
## (NON-SPECIFIC URETHRITIS (NSU))

Non-gonococcal urethritis refers to inflammation of the male urethra that is not caused by gonorrhea infection and is as common as gonorrhea itself. NGU can be produced by a variety of infectious organisms though the causes have not yet been clearly established (Bicher, et al., 1977). While women do not get NGU, it is possible that they may carry the agents in their vaginas; thus, some cases of this disease may be transmitted by sexual contact. It has been also suggested that some cases are an allergic reaction to vaginal secretions of a sexual partner. Other possible causes are irritation from certain soaps, clothing dyes, or vaginal spermicides. NGU often develops after a case of gonorrhea, since the urethra, weakened by the original disease, is particularly susceptible to further infection (Bicher, et al., 1977).

The symptoms of NGU include a thin, usually clear discharge and mild to moderate pain during urination. Diagnosis is done by lab testing to eliminate the possibility of gonorrhea. Many cases of NGU disappear spontaneously within two weeks. Antibiotics, such as tetracycline, can eliminate symptoms and cure the disease sooner (Bicher, et al., 1977).

## PROSTATE PROBLEMS

Prostatitis refers to inflammation of the prostate gland which is usually caused by a bacterial or viral infection. The most common cause is gonorrhea, spreading from an untreated infection of the urethra. A bout of gonorrhea might also lower the body's general resistance, such that the prostate becomes susceptible to infection by other bacteria that would normally be unthreatening. The infected prostate will become swollen, hot, and painful. The pain will be experienced in the pelvic area, either intermittently or constantly, or only upon urination or defecation. The man may also experience fever and chills, or a feeling of heat in the perineal area (Rowan and Gillette, 1973).

Another potential cause of prostatitis is an abrupt change in patterns of sexual activity. This condition, known as congestive prostatitis, is characterized by burning on urination, rectal pain, and a slight urethral discharge and is a result of excessive ac-

cumulation of secretions within the gland. Because the prostate produces its portion of ejaculatory fluid based on a routine pattern of frequency of stimulation, sudden changes can cause excessive secretion. This condition may occur when a man abruptly changes his pattern of ejaculations to none. The reverse pattern can also cause prostate distress (Rowan and Gillette, 1973). numerous, frequent ejaculations to none. The reverse pattern can also cause prostate distress (Rowan and Gillette, 1973).

The usual treatment for prostatitis is the administration of antibiotics such as penicillin. If the condition is caused by a virus or is congestive prostatitis, antibiotic therapy will not work. In these cases, prostatic massage is performed. This is accomplished by insertion of the clinician's finger into the rectum and application of rhythmic pressure against the prostate, to empty out the extraneous material (Rowan and Gillette, 1973). Prostatic massage may also be used as an adjunct to antibiotic therapy when the prostate is considerably swollen.

The prostate gland sometimes shrinks somewhat in old age. However, it sometimes becomes enlarged, and its size can be determined by means of rectal exam. Enlargement occurs in 60% of men by middle age or thereafter (McCary, 1971). An enlarged prostate gland can encroach on the urethra and interfere with urination. Surgical remedy is often required, which does not necessarily interfere with either fertility or sexual response.

## SEX AND THE MEDICAL PROFESSION

Up to this point, we have considered a number of general health issues that relate to sexuality. Many of these issues have been heavily influenced by the medical profession, and no such discussion would be complete without considering the relationship between medicine and healthy sex in our society.

Historically, as we have seen, by the turn of the nineteenth century, scientific approaches to many issues began to replace religious doctrine. In questions related to health and sexuality, medical practitioners supplanted church officials as the chief authorities. Unfortunately, this development produced little, if any, significant advancement in knowledge for some years. Where church doctrine promised hell and damnation for those who violated the strict sexual codes, physicians claimed that disease and insanity would be the end result of certain sexual practices. Benjamin Rush, one of the most influential American physicians of the times, for example, wrote in *Medical Inquiries* in 1812, that masturbation caused insanity and that the excessive depletion of semen caused a variety of conditions including impotence, indigestion, epilepsy, and loss of memory. In addition to these mistaken beliefs, medicine continued the older view that men were driven by animalistic urges and that those urges must be controlled at all costs. Women, on the other hand, were increasingly regarded as being pure and untroubled by sexual desires (Corea, 1977). In order to reinforce this mythical image of the asexual female, a number of surgical techniques emerged, including clitoridectomy and ovariectomy which were supposed to "cure" female sexuality (Corea, 1977; Barker-Benfield, 1976).

With time and the advancement of knowledge, circumstances

improved somewhat. By the turn of the twentieth century signs of a more progressive approach to sexuality began to emerge, although medical schools continued to ignore the importance of sex education. The belief in the "asexual" woman was replaced by Freudian views, which, as we have seen, were still seriously inadequate (Scully and Bart, 1973).

Nevertheless, despite their limited knowledge, the medical profession continued to be regarded by the general public as the ultimate authority on all questions related to sexuality, and individual practitioners often presented themselves as guardians of sexual morality (Myers, 1976). No doubt, these outmoded values influenced many aspects of the doctor-patient relationship. It was the individual practitioner, then, within this limited perspective, who was often most heavily involved in decisions which had profound and far-reaching consequences for the sexuality of patients.

The situation with regard to female sexuality was particularly troublesome, first because so little was known about this area, and, secondly, because the almost total absence of women in the medical profession offered no mechanism for correcting invalid beliefs and questionable practices. The physician's attitudes regarding female sexuality very likely had a great impact on women patients, whether in the context of a routine gynecological examination or in terms of decisions regarding birth control and abortion.

During the 1960s the medical profession came under increasing attack from a number of quarters, especially from advocates of the women's rights movement (Boston Women's Health Book Collective, 1976). Particular criticism was leveled against those practices that were considered to be degrading to women (Robertson, 1979) and the lack of sex education and training in the medical profession in general.

As such concerns mounted, medical schools began to respond by introducing courses on sexuality and by adopting a variety of teaching techniques which were designed to upgrade the status of the physician as an authority in relation to sexuality. In this connection, a number of suggestions have been made. Thus, an adequately complete sex education curriculum for medical students would explore the broad spectrum and diversity of human sexual behavior and would serve three purposes — to provide basic sex knowledge, to develop clinical skills (treatment and counseling), and to promote and increase awareness and values clarification (Lief, 1973; Marcotte and Kilpatrick, 1976). An example of such a model program might involve both lecture format and small group discussion. Faculty and students who participate in such a course have an opportunity to deal with their own sexual concerns and problems, thus enhancing their personal and professional understanding (Marcotte & Kilpatrick, 1976).

Furthermore, the development of an understanding of and sensitivity to patients' concerns enhances the physician's ability to provide effective sex counseling. Frequently, the physician's previous lack of training in this area may have hampered his or her ability or desire to approach many sexually related topics, for example, in the case of breast removal, in the case of prostate surgery, and even in the case of patients who have had a heart attack or a colostomy. In effect, such a "con-spiracy of silence" on the part of the medical profession probably failed to meet the individual's needs for information and reassurance.

Medical education about sexual issues might also go beyond specific topics related to sexual functioning and present a broader perspective on the many factors which influence the patient's sexuality. For example, many nonsexual medical conditions may impact on the patient in such a way as to affect his or her self-image in negative ways, and this, in turn, might impair the individual's sexual functioning. Conversely, attention and concern directed to such issues by the physician may serve to alleviate sexual problems for the patient.

A positive direction that is being adopted in various medical schools around the country at the present time is the use of "professional patient-instructors" to teach the procedure of the pelvic examination to medical students and residents. In these unique programs, groups of community women (from academic, professional, or health-care related backgrounds) are trained in the art and science of pelvic exams and then are employed by the medical school to teach its students, acting in the roles of both instructor and patient. They are able to impart to the student the necessary physical skills and techniques, as well as appropriate interpersonal skills designed to treat the gynecological patient as a whole human being and to facilitate the physical aspects of the exam — for example, a relaxed woman is easier to examine than a frightened woman. In discussions with the authors, medical students in one such program report that the communication skills learned in this training can be very satisfactorily applied in other areas of physical diagnosis as well.

In addition to the already described changes in medical school curriculum, which may facilitate communication about sexuality in the doctor-patient relationship, we can also seek to increase our own knowledge about how we function sexually. Alternative descriptions of and perspectives on the subjective sexual experience presented in such books as *The Hite Report* (Hite, 1976), Zilbergeld's *Male Sexuality* (1978), books on fantasy, etc. can perform the valuable function of providing a forum for the reader to enlarge the context through which he or she comes to understand and appreciate his or her own sexuality.

## SUMMARY

As we have seen, there are many practical issues that concern us as we seek to maintain sexual health. To this end, it is important that each individual acquire that knowledge that will enable her or him to better understand her or his sexual functioning, to become more knowledgeable about the effects of various food and drug substances, to help identify common infections of the sexual system, and to facilitate being informed consumers of health care. Beyond these suggestions, however, many of our social institutions need to be examined in order to determine how they have failed to meet the sexual needs of the public and what steps must be implemented to overcome these shortcomings. The goal of this chapter has been to provide a framework for the reader and for society in general to approach these objectives.

# Chapter 16

## Sexuality in Special Populations

# INTRODUCTION

All of us hope to live long, healthy lives free from chronic illness or serious accidents. Unfortunately, some of us, at some time in our lives, will suffer long-term effects from an accident or a disease. But even if we ourselves do not ever have serious health problems, most of us know someone who is or has been seriously ill. It is important, then, in either case, to know how some of the more common serious diseases or injuries can affect a person's sexuality. That subject will be discussed in this chapter.

Just as optimal sexuality is associated with good physical health, it is often thought that illness or injuries inevitably impair sexual behaviors significantly. Although this is sometimes true, many people who have suffered from either injury or disease do not *necessarily* have to stop expressing their sexuality.

In addition to these specific medical problems, many other experiences and circumstances may significantly affect our sexuality because of changes in body images, attitudes, and values about ourselves. In this chapter we will discuss these circumstances and the ways in which they may affect us. Additionally, this chapter will deal with the sexuality of another group of people: the mentally retarded.

# SEXUALITY AND CHRONIC ILLNESS

Most of us know someone who has suffered from a chronic illness such as heart disease or diabetes. Sometimes we stop thinking of these people as sexual beings, and often they themselves expect their illness to significantly interfere with their sexuality. They are often placed in a "sick" or dependent role, which may cause them to feel depressed and to think less of themselves. These reactions, too, may affect their sexuality. Finally, many serious illnesses can at times affect one's sexuality because of actual bodily changes.

In this section, we will discuss briefly three of the most common of these illnesses: heart disease, diabetes, and renal (kidney) failure.

## CARDIOVASCULAR DISORDERS

Cardiovascular disease is the number one health problem in America today. Wagner (1975) reports that over fourteen million Americans suffer from some form of heart or blood vessel disease and that these ailments are found in individuals of all ages and socioeconomic levels. Of this group of diseases, heart disease, sometimes signaled by a heart attack, or myocardial infarction, is one of the most common forms (American Heart Association, 1974). A heart attack is not a chronic disease, or even a disease. It is an acute condition which sometimes informs a person that he or she *has* heart disease. A heart attack is often commonly referred to as a *coronary*, even though this term is really a shortened form for a specific kind of heart attack, that is, a coronary thrombosis.

Several studies (for example, Bloch, Maeder, and Hassily, 1975; Tuttle, Cook, and Fitch, 1964) have reported substantial changes in the sexual functioning of postcoronary individuals. Fear of another coronary or of death is common, and these indiviuals often limit their activities as a result, although the degree and type of these limitations are not always necessary from a medical standpoint. Decreased sexual desire and deceased frequency of sexual activity occurs in up to two-thirds of these people, with impotence being the most common specific dysfunction reported. About 10% of men who have had a heart attack have reported permanent·impotence. These decreases in potency are found in all age levels, but they are more common in older individuals. Such reductions in sexual activity are reported even in individuals who have returned to their otherwise normally active lives. Finally, there appears to be no correlation between the severity of the heart attack and subsequent sexual activity.

It should be noted that the above information pertains only to males; we still have little information regarding the sexual functioning of postcoronary females. In the one study to date (Abramov, 1976), 65% of postcoronary women were termed as "frigid" *before* their illness as compared to 24% in a control group. However, the definition of "frigidity" or dysfunction was very broad in this study; this category included women who reported "emotional dissatisfaction" as one result of sexual activity. Thus, these results are likely an overestimation of the incidence of such disorders among coronary-prone or postcoronary women.

Many of these changes in sexual activity among coronary patients are probably based on fear and misinformation (Tuttle, et al., 1964). Physicians are usually very specific in most of their recommendations to the coronary patient: typically they are encouraged to lose weight, stop smoking, reduce cholesterol intake, and engage in regular physical exercise. On the other hand, sexual counseling with these patients is less common. For example, Tuttle, et al.(1964) found that two-thirds of the males in their sample of postcoronary patients had received no specific instructions regarding sexual activity; the other one-third had received vague, nonspecific advice. Perhaps one reason for the inadequacy of sexual counseling is a lack of information within the medical community. Supporting this suggestion is the work of Hellerstein and Friedman (1969), who reviewed 33 cardiology texts and found a total of only about 1,000 words that referred to sexual activity in coronary patients.

In recent years, several studies have provided important information concerning the effects of sexual activity on the cardiovascular system. Perhaps the most significant of these investigations was that of Hellerstein and Friedman (1970), which provided the first real evidence regarding sexual activity in male coronary patients. These investigators questioned the validity of some of the findings of Masters and Johnson (1966), who had earlier reported heart rates of up to 180 beats per minute during intercourse. Hellerstein and Friedman suggested these results might be atypical because Masters and Johnson obtained their results from healthy individuals in a laboratory setting where their sexual activity had been photographed.

Hellerstein and Friedman set out to investigate the impact of sexual activity on the cardiovascular system of middle-aged, postcoronary men who engaged in coitus with their wives in the privacy of their own bedrooms. Forty-eight postmyocardial infarction men and 43 coronary-prone men were equipped with portable EKG recording devices and were studied for up to 48 hours each. During this time each subject kept a log, carefully noted as to the time, of the activities that he engaged in. No other specific instructions were given these men. A subset of 14 men engaged in intercourse during this recording period. By analyzing the data from the logs and EKGs, Hellerstein and Friedman were able to directly compare the impact of sexual activity and other normal, daily activities on this group of subjects.

Among these 14 men, the maximum heart rate ranged from 90 to 144 beats per minute during orgasm, with a mean of 117.4. Heart rate quickly dropped to a mean of 85 beats per minute two minutes after orgasm. On the other hand, the maximum heart rate during normal occupation or professional activities was 120.1, or just slightly more than the mean during orgasm. Hellerstein and Friedman concluded that sexual activity was not necessarily any more dangerous than normal, everyday activities and that the effect on the heart was roughly equivalent to climbing a flight of stairs or performing ordinary tasks in many occupations.

One of the most noted concerns of cardiac victims and their spouses is fear of a "coital coronary," that is, fear of another heart attack during sexual intercourse. While such events do occur, their incidence is very low (Massie, Rose, Rupp, and Whelton, 1969). These investigators also pointed out that such deaths usually follow a particular pattern: they occur in a male who is having intercourse with someone other than his spouse in unfamiliar surroundings (for example, a motel room), usually soon after food and alcohol intake. These are quite different circumstances from those surrounding the men studied by Hellerstein and Friedman (1970), thus leading to the conclusion that the chances of death from a coronary during intercourse is quite small within a stable sexual relationship (Friedman, 1978).

It appears, then, that sexual activities pose little risk for most cardiac victims as long as they have been physically rehabilitated to the point of resuming their otherwise normal daily routine. Of course, the patient should always consult his or her physician before resuming sexual activities or strenuous or physically demanding tasks.

## DIABETES

Some degree of impotence or erectile difficulty occurs in approximately 50% of diabetic males. Rubin and Babbott (1958), for example, reported impotence in 70% of the portion of their sample who had been diabetic for less than a year; this decreased to 45% among those who had been diabetic for five years or longer. These investigators suggested that this higher incidence of impotence among "new" diabetics occurred because the disease was not yet under control. In this sample, many men did report that their impotence disappeared when their diabetes was brought under better control. No relationship was found between either the age of onset of diabetes or the severity of the illness and the incidence of impotence. Similar findings have been found in several later studies (Woods, 1979). There have also been reports of ejaculatory problems, including retrograde

ejaculation, among diabetic men (Greene, Panayotis, and Weeks, 1963), although this phenomenon is apparently much less common than is impotence.

It has been known for some time that diabetes can cause damage to parts of the nervous system. This seems particularly important for male diabetics since sexual potency is dependent upon the integrity of the autonomic nervous system. Recently several studies have suggested that neurological damage may be implicated in a high percentage of those diabetic males suffering from impotence or ejaculatory disorders. For example, Ellenberg (1978) compared 45 impotent diabetics with a control group of 30 diabetics who were not impotent. Thirty-eight of the 45 impotent patients were found to have signs of some damage to parts of the peripheral nervous system; others had documented autonomic nervous system damage in the pelvic area. It has also been reported (Woods, 1979) that autopsy findings on a small sample of impotent diabetics indicated changes in the autonomic nerve fibers in the corpus cavernosa in four-fifths of the subjects studied.

Since impotence seems unrelated to severity or age of onset of diabetes, the reasons why some men become impotent while others maintain their potency are, as yet, unclear. It should be remembered that approximately one-half of male diabetics do not suffer from sexual difficulties. Attempts at treating impotence in those diabetics with evidence of hormonal changes or neurological damage have also yielded conflicting findings. Schoffling, Federlin, Ditschuneit, and Pfeiffer (1963) reported considerable success in the treatment of impotent male diabetics under 40 years of age who were administered testosterone. On the other hand, Ellenberg (1978) found no beneficial effects of testosterone administration for any of the 45 impotent diabetics in his study. Thus, the relationship between sexual problems in male diabetics and the possibility of treatment through hormonal replacement remains to be clarified by future research.

Sexual functioning in women diabetics also appears to be affected by the disease. Kolodny (1971) compared 125 women diabetics with a control group of 100 nondiabetic women. Orgasmic dysfunction (defined as absence of orgasm by any means in the preceding 12 months) was reported in 35.2% of the diabetic women and only 6% of the control group. Significantly, none of these nonorgasmic control subjects had ever experienced orgasm whereas the majority (40 out of 44) of the nonorgasmic diabetics had previously been orgasmic. These 44 diabetic women reported a consistent pattern of gradually becoming nonorgasmic over a period of about one year after the onset of diabetes. With respect to the possible neurological components of these sexual dysfunctions, Ellenberg (1977) compared a group of diabetic women with demonstrable neurological damage with a group of diabetics in which no neuropathy was clinically apparent. Around 80% of the women in both groups reported experiencing orgasm. Thus, while neurological impairment seems implicated in sexual dysfunctioning in male diabetics, similar findings are not reported for women. Ellenberg (1977) concluded that it was impossible to explain these apparent differences between male and female diabetics on the basis of anatomy, physiology, or neurology. It is possible that the measurement techniques used in diagnosing these kinds of neurological disorders are as yet imprecise, although such an explanation will remain purely speculative pending future research.

Diabetes has also been found to interfere with the reproductive capacity of both men and women. Among male diabetics, a variety of reproductive problems have been reported to occur, including low sperm counts, abnormal spermatogenesis, androgen deficiencies, and complete loss of ejaculatory functions (Woods, 1979). On the other hand, some of these same men have successfully fathered a child after treatment with gonadotropins and testosterone. Diabetic women have a higher incidence of ovarian and uterine atrophy than nondiabetic women as well as a greater than normal frequency of stillbirths and malformed offspring (Rubin and Murphy, 1958).

The overall effects of diabetes on the sexual functioning of both men and women is thus clearly documented. Nevertheless, the specific effects are extremely variable, with many diabetic individuals experiencing few or no changes in their sexuality. As yet, we cannot explain why or how some people are affected while others are not. However, given the higher than normal frequency of reproductive disorders among diabetics, and the fact that diabetes is genetically determined, diabetics who wish to become parents would be wise to seek medical counseling before attempting to conceive a child.

## CHRONIC RENAL FAILURE

The chronic failure of the kidneys to function properly represented, until the early 1960s, a terminal illness with no effective treatment available. Since that time, however, renal hemodialysis (the artificial cleansing of the blood's impurities) and renal transplants have become commonplace procedures for these patients. Currently, the mortality rate among hemodialysis patients is approximately 10% per year. The one-year survival rate for transplant patients is around 65%, unless the transplant is obtained from a homozygous (that is, identical) twin, in which case the survival rate is increased to around 94% (Abram, Hester, Sheridan, and Epstein, 1978). Thus, while hemodialysis and transplantation have significantly increased the likelihood of survival, chronic renal patients remain in a precarious state with a continued high probability of physical problems and death from the disease. It is not surprising, then, that this group of individuals often experience significant degrees of uncertainty and anxiety which can affect all aspects of their daily lives, including their sexuality.

Men with chronic kidney disease report decreased libido, decreased frequency of sexual activity, and an increased incidence of impotence. Women report a similar decrease in frequency of intercourse as well as a decrease in the ability to experience orgasm (Woods, 1979). Hemodialysis and/or kidney transplantation often leads to improved sexual functioning among these patients; however, the relationship of the disease and of these treatments to an individual's sexuality is extremely variable. The extent of this variability is illustrated in the study by Abram, Hester, and Epstein (1974) wherein extensive data were gathered from 32 male veterans who had been on hemodialysis for at least three months. Since about half of these men already had functioning renal transplants (and were no longer receiving hemodialysis), it was possible to compare their sexual activities before the onset of their kidney disease, during hemodialysis, and after receiving a transplant. Of these 32 patients: 7 had no significant decrease in sexual relations after the

onset of the disease or while on hemodialysis; 14 patients reported a decrease in sexual activity of at least 50% after the onset of the disease; and the remaining 11 patients reported no decrease after the disease onset but significant decrease while they were on hemodialysis. Among those in the group (about half of the 32) who received a kidney transplant, similar variability was found. Approximately 20% showed no significant changes in their sexual activities at any point during the disease process, including the time when they were on hemodialysis and after their transplants. The remaining 80% had experienced some decrease in their sexual functioning either after the onset of the disease or while receiving hemodialysis. Of this group, one half regained their potency after transplantation and the other half did not. The extent of this variability suggests that a combination of physiological and psychological factors are involved in the sexual functioning of patients with chronic renal disease.

Abnormalities in reproductive functioning, including abnormal spermatogenesis, have been documented in male renal patients (Woods, 1979), even after the men were receiving hemodialysis treatment. On the other hand, in one study (Elstein, Smith, and Curtis, 1969) 30% of the men evaluated became fathers even though semen analysis of this group of men indicated that paternity was not to be expected. Thus, chronic renal failure probably does affect a male's reproductive capacity; however, the specific effects are variable and unpredictable.

Similar findings have been reported for women. Chronic renal failure interrupts the normal menstrual pattern; however this pattern appears to return to normal, including resumption of ovulation, after several months of hemodialysis. More recently there have been several scattered reports of women becoming pregnant and delivering normal, healthy children after several years of hemodialysis (Woods, 1979).

Perhaps no other disease produces such an extensive combination of medical and psychological stresses as does chronic renal failure. Without treatment it is a fatal condition. Even with the recommended therapy, the mortality rate remains relatively high. In addition, the treatment procedures involved in hemodialysis often produce extreme dependency/independency conflicts (Abram, et al., 1978). The life of such a patient is literally dependent on the hemodialysis machine; typically patients spend about 30 hours a week connected to this equipment. Furthermore, these patients must cope with dietary and fluid intake restrictions, heavy economic burdens attendant to these treatments, and a variety of other medical complications such as infections and anemia. In addition to all of these factors, these individuals often feel the pressures of normal family life — supporting a family and/or living an otherwise productive and independent life while they are not on the hemodialysis machine. Abram and associates (1978) suggest that it is these kinds of conflicts — dependency/independency, sickness/health, passivity/activity — which underly any patient's adaptation to the disease. Given these stresses which invariably accompany chronic renal failure, we would expect that psychological components are implicated in the sexual difficulties experienced by many of these patients. How well a person deals with these stresses and anxieties seems to be a very important factor in his or her continued sexual functioning.

# BODILY TRAUMA AND SEXUALITY

Serious injury to the body often affects one's sexual functioning, even if the genital or reproductive systems are not directly injured. One particularly common type of bodily injury that affects sexual functioning involves trauma to the spinal cord. Such injuries often occur as a result of automobile and motorcycle as well as other accidents. Additionally, our society today has thousands of young men who sustained this type of trauma as a result of the Vietnam conflict.

Surgical procedures also represent a type of bodily trauma that may affect one's sexuality. Sometimes the genital or reproductive system is the direct focus of such surgical intervention, as in the case of a hysterectomy, for example. Other surgical procedures often have an effect on sexual behavior even though the genital/reproductive systems remain intact. In many of these instances (for example, a colostomy), the effect on sexual expression is most likely a function of changes in the person's body image. In this section, we will discuss briefly the effects of these traumatic events on human sexuality.

## SPINAL CORD INJURY

Men and women with spinal cord injuries have often been seen by many people as helpless, even pitiful, individuals who are confined to beds or wheelchairs and who are almost totally dependent upon others for their daily needs. However, recent advances in medicine, surgery, and physical rehabilitation have enabled those people with spinal cord damage to live longer and, in many instances, relatively normal lives. Many spinal cord patients are no longer confined to their homes or to hospitals but are instead making their presence known in all facets of our society. Recent Federal legislation requiring easy accessibility to public places for those in wheelchairs has also helped these individuals to take a more active and normal role in our society. Concommitant with these medical and cultural changes has been an increased awareness of the sexuality of those with spinal cord damage and the special sexual problems that may occur for some of these people.

Two variables are probably most important in terms of the potential sexual functioning of individuals with damage to the spinal cord: the site of the injury and the extent of the injury. Did the injury occur high on the cord closer to the brain (for example, cervical region), very close to the lower extremity of the cord (sacral region), or somewhere in between (thoracic or lumbar region)? Also, was the cord completely cut, or transsected, or was the lesion only partial? Generally, those people with incomplete lesions maintain more potential for sexual functioning; however, this effect can be extremely variable. Perhaps this apparent variability occurs because of the problems in diagnosing exactly the site and extent of these injuries.

Higgins (1978) has recently provided an excellent review of the sexual capabilities of spinal cord injured individuals. He has accurately pointed out that spinal cord damage can have very variable (and often unpredictable) effects at several different stages in the sexual response cycle for both males and females. Many males maintain some erectile capability, ranging from

48.2% to 91.7% of the individuals studied in the research surveyed by Higgins. Generally, erections are more likely to occur in those men with higher level lesions (that is, higher on the spinal cord) and with incomplete lesions. Variability is great, however, with erections occurring in some men with complete transsections of the spinal cord (Comarr, 1970). The ability to engage in intercourse varied from 5% to 56% of the men evaluated in these studies.

Higgins (1978) found that ejaculation occurred less frequently than erection, occurring in up to 50% of the individuals in one study reviewed. Those men with incomplete lesions and lower level lesions are more likely to maintain this capability. Variability is again apparent, with a few reported cases of ejaculation in men with complete lesions. However, even though ejaculation may occur in such cases, orgasmic capacity is often impaired because of sensory neuron damage. In other words, in some men, though the physical process of ejaculation occurs, the concomitant pleasurable feelings are not experienced. The ability to experience orgasm ranged from 2% to 16% of the individuals studied (Higgins, 1978). However, many of these men continue to experience varying degrees of nonorgasmic sexual tension or pleasure.

We know much less about the sexual functioning of women with spinal cord injuries. Specific physiological events such as vascular engorgement and vaginal lubrication have not yet been directly investigated. The limited data do again suggest much variability, with some women reporting essentially no pleasurable sexual feelings (Money, 1960) and other reporting vaginal lubrication (Bregman, 1975) and orgasm (Fitzpatrick, 1974). One reason for this lack of data may be the small proportion of women who have experienced spinal cord injuries. On the other hand, Griffith and Trieschmann (1975) have suggested that the continued societal biases against viewing women as sexual beings may also have contributed to this lack of knowledge. For whatever reason, our data remains incomplete, and future research into the sexual potential of women with spinal cord damage is clearly needed.

The reproductive capacity of spinal cord injured people is also varied. Successful impregnation has occured by males who have retained their ejaculatory capacity, although lowered sperm counts have been reported in some spinal cord injured males (Horne, Paull, and Munro, 1948). In other males electrical stimulation has been used to obtain semen from the seminal vesicle, which can then be used for artificial insemination (Bensman and Kottke, 1966). Among females, many experience disturbances in menstruation after injury; however, normal menstrual patterns typically return within six months to a year for most women (Comarr, 1966). Robertson and Guttman (1963) studied nine spinal cord injured females through eleven separate pregnancies. All these women delivered healthy offspring and all were able to breast-feed their infants. Furthermore, most were able to deliver normally through the vagina. One "positive" side effect of their injuries was that some women with lesions higher up in the spinal cord did not experience any labor pains whatsoever even though they had normal uterine contractions during labor and delivery.

In summary, injuries to the spinal cord have highly variable and unpredictable effects on the sexuality of both men and women. Many, perhaps the majority, of these individuals retain the potential for some degree of sexual functioning. Although reproductive capacity may be diminished, many spinal cord injured patients eventually do become parents.

## CHANGES IN BODY IMAGE AFTER SURGERY

A person's body image — that is, one's own mental picture of how one's body appears — can have a significant impact on many aspects of our daily lives. Body image is a highly individualized phenomenon and is subject to constant change either as a function of actual body changes or changes in one's perceptions or values. Body image seems especially important in the sexual functioning of members of contemporary American society. In our culture, we are constantly bombarded by media presentations and advertisements which leave little room for doubt about the most "desirable" body type — young, vigorous, healthy, and "well-built." Few of us fit this stereotype.

Many surgical procedures often lead to rather significant changes in body image and result in changes in one's sexuality. Let us now briefly review some of the more common of these procedures.

Hysterectomy consists of removal of the uterus and sometimes other parts of the female reproductive system, such as the ovaries. This is a relatively common procedure and often has a significant impact on a woman's sexuality and on that of her partner. Since parts of the sexual apparatus are removed by this technique, actual physiological changes may have an effect on sexual functioning. For example, removal of the ovaries may lead to hormone deficiencies which result in a thinning of the vaginal walls and a decrease in vaginal lubrication. Discomfort during intercourse may then occur. Additionally, of course, these women no longer have a menstrual period and are no longer capable of bearing children. Some authorities (for example, Morgan, 1978) have suggested that many other physiological changes resulting from hysterectomy can have major effects on sexual functioning; however, the consensus appears to be that such procedures generally produce only minimal changes to the vagina and pelvis, and by themselves they are not highly likely to lead to marked sexual dysfunction (Abitol and Davenport, 1974). Woods (1979) contends that the way in which the woman perceives herself (that is, her body image) is the most crucial factor.

Drellich and Bieber (1958) investigated several variables which might affect body image in 23 premenopausal women who had had hysterectomies. These women perceived the uterus as a very important symbol of their femininity, and many viewed the cessation of their menstrual periods with regret. Preoperatively, these women reported a variety of fears: that they would suffer a decrease in their sexual desire and in their ability to respond sexually; that they would be less sexually attractive to their husbands; that surgery would have a deleterious effect on their overall strength and their ability to perform their everyday duties. Others feared that removal of the uterus would lead to premature aging. A few of these women appeared to view the surgery as a punishment for activities (for example, extramarital sex or abortions) about which they felt guilty.

Thus, it is apparent that many women are fearful of the possible effects of a hysterectomy. These fears are often based on misconceptions and inaccurate information; nevertheless, a fear may have a significant impact upon an individual's body image and her subsequent relationship with her partner. Factual counseling for both these women and their partners may, in many cases, lessen the negative psychological impact of these surgical procedures on the lives of the people involved.

Prostatectomy, or the surgical removal of the prostate gland, is a relatively common procedure and can affect a man's sexuality both because of physiological reasons and because of changes in his values and perceptions about the way his body "ought to function." The prostate will become enlarged in approximately 60% of all men in middle age or thereafter; about 35% of these will require a prostatectomy (McCary, 1971). Because of damage to closely adjacent structures after such surgery, normal ejaculation is no longer possible for many of these men. During orgasm, retrograde ejaculation occurs in approximately 80% of these men (Gold and Hotchkiss, 1969). When this occurs, normal conception is not possible, although artificial insemination remains an alternative for these men. Although retrograde ejaculation does not necessarily decrease the pleasurable orgasmic sensations for all men, many are concerned by this occurrence. Some feel that their manhood is somehow threatened or diminished, and they experience sexual problems as a result.

Perhaps the major concern among men undergoing prostatectomy is that of impotence. Whether or not prostatectomies invariably produce impotence is an area of much controversy and one wherein a great deal of misinformation has probably been disseminated. For example, a recent human sexuality text that is used in many medical schools (Saddock, Kaplan, and Freedman, 1976) includes only a three-paragraph discussion of this issue and states that prostatectomy results in a "high incidence of impotence." The authors do not define "high incidence"; however, they encourage an open discussion with the patient of the risks involved and suggest the possibility of penile implants for these individuals. Given this frame of mind, it is likely that a self-fulfilling prophecy may occur for many men who undergo this operation. That is, having been counseled preoperatively that a high incidence of impotence results, the man may expect such an outcome and later actually experience impotence because of this expectation.

While impotency may occur because of damage to the genitourinary system or to the specific nerve tracts involved in erection, the real incidence of impotence in prostatectomy cases seems much lower than is commonly thought to be the case. Finkle and Meyers (1960) found that about 70% of prostatectomy patients retained their sexual potency one year after surgery. More recently, Gold and Hotchkiss (1969) studied 94 individuals who had undergone prostatectomies by several different types of surgical procedure. Of those patients who were 50 to 60 years of age, 80% experienced no changes in potency after prostate surgery, 10% reported a decrease in sexual potency (although none of these reported being totally impotent), and the remaining 10% reported improvement in potency following surgery. Among older patients, the incidence of impotency was higher: 62% of those aged 61 to 70 and 66% of those over 70 years of age reported some impairment of potency, ranging from minor changes to total impotence. For all men, the specific type of surgical procedure used was unrelated to diminished potency Relative age at surgery does seem to be important: younger men (less than age 60) were not likely to become impotent after this surgery and older men did seem at risk of some impairment of potency.

Impotence, then, is not always associated with prostatectomy. Younger men, it seems, run little risk of impotence following this surgery. Many men may have a set of inaccurate expectations surrounding this surgical procedure; others are troubled because of retrograde ejaculation. Thus, it is likely that psychological variables are implicated in those individuals who do experience diminished impotence after prostatectomy.

Mastectomy, the surgical removal of one or both breasts, often can have a devastating effect upon a woman's body image and overall self-concept. As we have seen, the breasts are part of the sexual anatomy and go through distinct physiological changes during the sexual response cycle. Most women find breast stimulation very pleasurable and incorporate such activities at some time during lovemaking. Many women breast-feed their infants, and breasts are often identified with the role of mother. Additionally, in our culture and in others, breasts have become *the* symbol for femininity and female sexuality and sensuality. The popular media constantly portray and reinforce these attitudes and values. Both women and men compare their own or their partner's breasts to the ideals presented in *Playboy*, in advertisements, on television, and in motion pictures. Thus, the breast is an integral part of our physiological sexuality and, in addition, has been invested with other values that have a psychological bearing on our sexuality.

Women who have other types of female surgery may see few outward signs of the operation, and thus their body image may be unchanged or may change very little. For example, the only external signs of a tubal ligation are two small, relatively unobtrusive scars. On the other hand, the woman who has had a mastectomy is immediately aware of actual, visible changes in her body. These changes may be very significant as in the case of a radical mastectomy in which part of the pectoral musculature and lymphatic tissue under the arm is removed in addition to the actual breast tissue. Such radical techniques can result in weakness and/or restricted movement in the arm. It is not surprising, then, that the body image and self-concept of women are often severely affected by these procedures. Men's perceptions of women who have had these procedures performed are often similarly affected.

When confronted with the possibility of a mastectomy, women are usually in a situation of conflicting feelings. On the one hand, they are fearful of the effects of possible cancer or other disorder for which the mastectomy may be necessary. On the other hand, they are anxious about and fearful of the disfigurement attendant to this procedure. Additionally, they are concerned about the effects on their sexuality and the impact upon their sexual relationships. Woods (1979) has reported the results of a survey of over 1,000 women conducted in 1974. When asked about their attitudes regarding breast surgery, over half felt they would lose a significant part of their feelings of femininity and believed that an unmarried woman's chances of later becoming happily married were significantly decreased.

In reviewing studies of women who had undergone mastectomies, Woods (1979) found that often there were overt changes in actual sexual attitudes, values, and functioning. These women have reported slight decreases in both sexual desire and in frequency of intercourse. They were also less comfortable about undressing in front of their husbands. Not surprisingly, the biggest change after surgery for these women was a significant decrease in the occurrence of touching the breast area, both by themselves and their partners.

It should be noted that mastectomies do not always produce these severe negative effects on one's sexuality and relationships with others. Recently, Woods and Earp (1978) studied 34 women four years after their mastectomies. The majority of these women reported no changes in either the frequency of sexual encounters or their overall sexual relationship, although some did report negative effects after the surgery. A comparison of women whose sexual activity decreased after mastectomy with those whose activity remained unchanged yielded several interesting and important findings. Those who maintained their previous patterns of sexuality were younger, were less likely to have had the more radical forms of surgery, had been better prepared for their operations, and were better satisfied with their overall relationships with their husbands. One of the most important factors associated with good sexual satisfaction was whether or not the husband was understanding and accepting of the woman's situation and whether or not the woman felt she could discuss the issue with and confide in her husband.

It is apparent that mastectomies represent a real threat, both physical and psychological, to a woman's self-concept, body image, sexuality and relationships with others. Nevertheless, one's adjustment to such a procedure is dependent upon a number of variables, and severe negative reactions are not invariably a side effect of such surgery. A supportive and understanding partner may be of great help to women who face adjustment to the changes caused by breast surgery.

Many other physical disorders can have an effect on our body image and our attitudes about ourselves. Severe burns and other types of physical disfigurements caused by accidents (such as the muscular atrophy often associated with spinal cord injuries) can have a significant impact. Furthermore, certain natural physical characteristics of our bodies affect our body image, for example, nose shape, hair texture, or height. Cosmetic surgery is often performed not because the body is dysfunctional in any way but to promote a better body image or self-concept. In some cases our body image in response to such surgery, injuries, or natural physical characteristics is very negative. In cases such as these, professional counseling may in many instances help us have a more positive body image and help minimize any resulting negative effects upon our sexuality.

## MENTAL RETARDATION

Approximately 3% of the American population is classified as mentally retarded. Historically, this group of individuals has been misunderstood and in the past was the target of treatment that would be unacceptable in our society today. For example, up until the last two or three decades, the institutionalized retarded were often sterilized routinely, sometimes as a condition for their release from the institution (Edgerton, 1967). Only in the recent past has there been a movement toward recognizing the full potential of these people, including the fact that they, too, have sexual feelings and are capable of appropriate sexual activities.

The popular stereotype of the retarded as individuals with extremely low levels of functioning and potential who must be institutionalized and must have the most basic of their needs (eating, dressing, etc.) taken care of by others is false for the most part, true of only the most severely or profoundly retarded. In reality, around 80% of the retarded are characterized by milder intellectual deficits, with IQs ranging from 55 to 70 (Hall, 1975). These individuals are termed *educable*, meaning they are capable of academic learning up to about the sixth grade level. They are also capable of being trained for a variety of occupations and of living outside of institutions. Many live relatively self-sufficient lives and are capable of achieving successful relationships and of becoming parents.

Nevertheless, the retarded are set apart, usually from an early age. Many myths and misconceptions surround the retarded, many of them relating specifically to sexuality. Examples of such misconceptions are: the mentally retarded are oversexed (or undersexed); the mentally retarded are infertile; the mentally retarded are incapable of "normal" relationships, including marriage and/or sexual relationships; offspring of the mentally retarded will themselves be retarded. While all of the above may be true for some of the retarded, there is as much variability among the retarded as there is among the nonretarded. When we examine the available data, we find that the retarded have much more potential for functioning in all areas of life, including sexuality, than most of us would imagine.

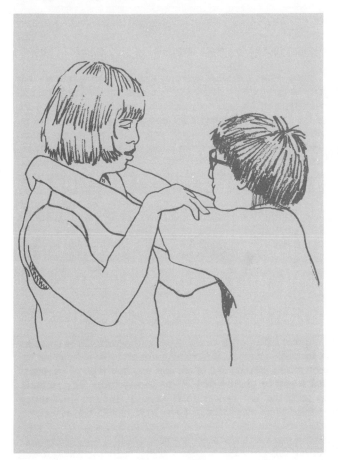

A positive relationship has been found between IQ and sexual maturation; that is, those with much lower IQs tend to mature more slowly (Mosier, Grossman, and Dingman, 1962). However, this relationship is very complex and variable. Many mature at a relatively normal rate; others, actually faster than the average. However, many parents of retarded children *believe* the children will mature slowly (or not at all) and thus put off any attempts at sex education. This delay can lead to disastrous results for the retarded individual. For example, the incidence of venereal disease among the retarded is three times that found in the normal population (Hall, 1975). Further, it has been documented that the retarded are deficient in sexual knowledge and that what little sex information they do receive consists of simple explanations about where babies come from and, for females, menstrual hygiene (Hall, 1974). Those people who work with the retarded have repeatedly encouraged comprehensive sex education procedures for these individuals, with the inclusion of parents and other family members, the school system, and related health professionals. However, as yet, few such programs have been initiated, and there is no data regarding the long-term effectiveness of such procedures.

Can a retarded individual be successful in "normal" adult activities, including marriage and sexual relationships, procreation, and parenting? Our cultural stereotypes and misconceptions would probably lead most of us to answer no to the above question. Recent data suggest, however, that the retarded are much more capable of these activities than had previously been thought. Hall (1975) has pointed out that the majority of the mildly retarded probably will marry (retarded women in this group are more likely than men to marry). Edgerton (1967) studied a group of married retarded people and found that the typical marriage pattern and life style was not all that different from nonretarded people in similar socioeconomic classes.

The incidence of retarded offspring from retarded adults is greater than that in the general population. For example, Reed and Reed (1965) found 40% of the offspring to be retarded if both parents were retarded. If only one parent was retarded, this incidence dropped to 15%. If neither parent is retarded, the incidence in the general population is around 1% to 3% of all live births. Thus, while this should be an area of legitimate concern for retarded adults, it is possible for them to produce normal, nonretarded offspring. With such advances in prenatal diagnosis as amniocentesis to detect certain genetic abnormalities (for example, Down's syndrome) and with increased sex educational opportunities, it may well be that these incidences of retarded offspring will decrease and that more retarded adults will become parents. Finally, while some people have suggested that "normal" children should be removed from retarded parents, Hall (1975) suggests that, given adequate information about parenting and additional supervision and emotional support, many retarded adults would be capable of being adequate parents.

In summary, retarded individuals have sexual feelings just like the rest of us. While there is much variability among this group, many of them are capable of much more normal functioning in all areas of their lives, including sexuality, than generally was thought to be the case. The removal of common myths and misconceptions about these individuals among the public at large, coupled with increased education regarding sex among the retarded themselves, may well help these individuals lead more normal lives and to be more accepted as functioning, productive members of our society.

## SUMMARY

In this chapter, we have considered several broad groups of individuals whose sexuality may, at times, have been affected by a variety of unfortunate circumstances. However, many of these individuals may maintain some degree of sexual functioning; indeed, many continue their normal sexual activities in spite of severe handicaps. In addition, as we shall see in Chapter 17, getting intimacy needs met is often more important than specific goal-oriented behaviors such as erection, genital contact, or orgasm.

Other conditions may also affect an individual's sexuality, for example, degenerative diseases, deafness, blindness, or speech disorders. Some of these conditions, like blindness, have no *direct* effect on sexuality but may change the character of sexual encounters (for example, placing more emphasis on tactile as opposed to visual arousal). Nevertheless, these conditions illustrate that almost anything *may* affect our sexuality, either directly or through changes in our body images. Continued education among these special individuals and the general public will, we hope, lead to more acceptance and a more successful integration of these people into our society.

# Chapter 17

## Sexuality: Personal Perspectives

## SEX AND VALUES

In the [illegible] chapters we have examined the many different d [illegible] human sexuality. Our discussion has taken us from [illegible] what sex has traditionally meant to Western socie [illegible] in the context of Judeo-Christian values, thr [illegible] sis of whatever scientific perspectives have bee [illegible] bear on these issues. The rationale of such an a [illegible] ightforward: the more knowledgeable we are, [illegible] an understand and appreciate the significance of [illegible] more meaningful and personally and socially [illegible] will our decisions be. Having examined sexuality [illegible] perspectives, it seems appropriate in this last chapter [illegible] now consider the question: "What *should* sex mean?"

This issue, is, of course, probably the most difficult sexual issue to deal with, since many different standards apply, each with its own philosophical and moral bias. As we have seen, standards relating to the meaning and value of sex have changed from time to time and from place to place. In the past, religious values predominated. As the conflict between religion and science evolved, many of these traditional values began to be called into question and were replaced by scientific perspectives. Science, however, can tell us only what "is"; it does not provide us with a system of values. Thus, science tells us, for example, that masturbation is not abnormal in the statistical sense; but only our own sense of morality can dictate whether such behavior is "right" or "wrong" for us. Again, science reveals that

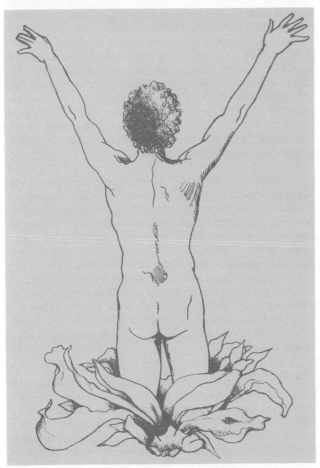

many people engage in sex outside of marriage, but only our own value structure determines whether or not we will condone such behavior. In terms of a contemporary sexual code, then, we seem to be at a point where our sexual standards are more divergent and variegated than ever before in the history of humanity. The emerging "consenting adult" principle seems to reflect, perhaps, only a pragmatic solution to the changing sexual scene. There is some reason to believe that despite our new sexual "permissiveness," many people continue to search for a new and more meaningful sexual code to guide their actions and to help make decisions.

There is, of course, no simple or final answer to the question of what sex should mean. Now that the new sexual morality has achieved a durable impact on our lives, however, such questions can no longer be ignored.

In this final chapter, we will attempt to focus on how our changing sexual morality and our expanding body of knowledge can be integrated into an individual's own personal value system as these issues bear on the sexual decisions and choices each of us must make. Within this perspective, we will first examine the ways in which our sexual dimension is alienated from other human dimensions and then examine those experiences that may facilitate "sexual synthesis." This discussion will also include the topic of sex and interpersonal relationships.

# SEXUALITY: ALIENATION
# AND SYNTHESIS

We have grown up in a society that advances conflicting messages about sexuality. On the one hand, we are openly bombarded with images that are explicitly or implicitly sexual in content; and on the other hand, official and traditional taboos limit effective sexual discussion in the home and at school. The lack of opportunity for open dialogue may impede our ability to make sense of our own sexuality. The typical sexual "role models" offered for public consumption by the entertainment and advertising media are young, beautiful, and exclusively heterosexual. Our fantasy heroes seem to be forever potent, and our heroines inevitably multiorgasmic. Sexual "cookbooks" and a multitude of sexological experts provide us with many ideas of how things *ought* to be in sex.

Thus, we have moved from a model of sexual repression in the Victorian era to a new cultural milieu in which male-female relationships are almost always sexualized. Whereas in the past sexual restraint was the ideal, today sexual technique is promoted as an end in itself. In the past we felt guilty for "doing it"; now we feel guilty if we do not do it (May, 1963). The view that sexual experimentation is more acceptable and justifiable than ever before — indeed, that one is deviant for *not* participating in this "sexual freedom" — applies complex and often subtle pressure on us to engage in sexual activity (Menninger, 1971). It seems as if sex now exerts another kind of tyrannical hold on us: there is a tendency to confuse quantity with quality and to equate promiscuity with sexual freedom, neglecting the perspective that "body counts don't count in war or sex" (Robinson, 1979). What may get lost in this welter of cultural images and demands is the individual's ability to clarify his or her own personal needs and desires.

A number of critiques have been directed toward this contemporary emphasis on sexual availability and adequacy. Rollo May (1963), for example, suggests that a simplistic preoccupation with technique can lead to a mechanistic approach to sexuality. Within this framework, sexual experiences can be dehumanizing, leaving an individual with feelings of emptiness and loneliness. May believes that the importance placed on "sexual freedom" and "salvation through sexual expression" constitutes a new kind of puritanism, in which participants are alienated from their bodies and their feelings, and their bodies are exploited as machines. As sex becomes an expected and ordinary routine, rather than a spontaneous and more humanly meaningful experience, it becomes impersonal. From this perspective, people find it easier and less risky to expose their physical nakedness in sexual encounters than to reveal their emotional nakedness and vulnerability (May, 1969). May cites the *Playboy* model as an example of the new sexual puritanism: the detached and empty expressions in the photographs suggest that the fig leaf has shifted from the genitals to the face.

Moreover, as we have already seen (Chapter 5), our cultural messages about sexuality include myths and misinformation which can cause us anguish, create "performance" anxiety, and undermine effective communication between partners. Experts' descriptions and laboratory models serve the purpose of teaching us more about sexuality. But when they are elevated as standards of perfection, they create confusion, especially if we attempt to measure ourselves against these standards and neglect to recognize the significance of individuality of form and expression. Expectations that sex will always be a mystical peak experience, that, in Hemingway's words, the earth will move, or that we will be consumed in a mighty blaze of fireworks, will more often than not create disappointment or blind us to the realities and varieties of our own experiences. Further, sexuality can work "bad magic" if we attribute to it the ability to solve relationship problems or the ability to create intimacy that has no foundation to begin with (Zilbergeld, 1978).

A central issue of concern in this discussion is the way in which our culture creates sexual alienation. It is as if our sexuality or our ability to know ourselves as sexual beings is first divorced from our other human dimensions and then handed back to us in prepackaged units (Marcuse, 1964, 1966; Steiner, 1974): here is an orgasm, here is a *Playboy* centerfold, and so on. This approach to sexuality is embodied in the basic plot of the linear, heterosexual scenario: kiss, touch breasts, touch genitals, exercise option of oral-genital contact, proceed to intercourse, have ejaculation-orgasm, fall asleep. The point is not that there is anything "wrong" with this model, but that it is defined for us as *the* basic sex model, rather than as one of many possibilities, including the establishment of meaningful interpersonal relationships in the absence of physical sex.

Several issues that have already been discussed in this book illustrate the need for a redefinition of "the sex act." The physical readjustments necessary in certain illnesses, for handicapped persons, and sometimes in old age all present situations in which the basic plot described above may have to be altered. Yet some of the valuable experiences potentially afforded by sexual contact—for example, touching, warmth, affection, closeness, intimacy—can nevertheless be realized in other ways. Eyes light up, partners cuddle, they massage each other, they hug and laugh together: are these ways of relating any the *less* sexual than the basic plot? If these activities are spontaneous expressions rather than mechanical performances, they can be equally valid expressions of sexual feelings.

The "American way of sex" is preoccupied with orgasms. Emphasis on orgasm as *the* goal of a sexual episode limits what is sexual and what is not and, in this way, can impose blinders between us and our experiences. Pressure to achieve an orgasm can interfere with our ability to appreciate and enjoy other good feelings (Myers, 1976), and this preoccupation with achievement can make sex seem more like work than play (Slater, 1974). More attention to the *process* and the sensations of the moment, and less to the "product," also opens the way to an appreciation of a broader sense of sexuality. From this point of view, there is a less rigid distinction between affectionate gestures and those episodes which specifically culminate in orgasm (Slater, 1974).

The basic perspective that we are suggesting here is that there is no single, unidimensional definition of sexuality (Bernard, 1966). Nor can the complexity of human sexuality be appreciated solely by intellectual or scientific analysis. Consider, for example, the distinction between sensuality and sexuality. Think of these activities: walking barefoot through new-mown grass, stroking a cat, dancing, singing, laughing, playing, sharing

intense conversation, admiring a beautiful sunset or a nude sculpture. These activities can appeal to our senses; the energy and delight we may experience in them is sensual: is it also sexual? Again, when our bodies and senses come alive in a special way, does it matter what label we attach to our responses? Indeed, the limitations of our vocabulary may prevent us from sensing an interplay between sensuality and sexuality in our experiences.

To add to this perspective, we can turn to the work of Norman O. Brown (1959), who pursues the idea of total body sexuality, and the significance of appreciating the sensitivity and responsiveness of the whole body for its own sake. Using several of Freud's concepts as points of departure, Brown discusses adult sexuality or concentration on the genitals as a narrowing of what in childhood was a broader capacity to delight in the pleasure of the whole body. A more diffused or generalized sense of sexuality can find expression and pleasure in a wealth of activities. Similarly, Brown speaks of children's taking pleasure in the active life of the body as *play*. Tumbling down a hillside, wrestling gently, taking a bath with a partner, giving and receiving back rubs and massage—all are examples of sensual and playful activities which can be satisfying in themselves (Teeters, 1977).

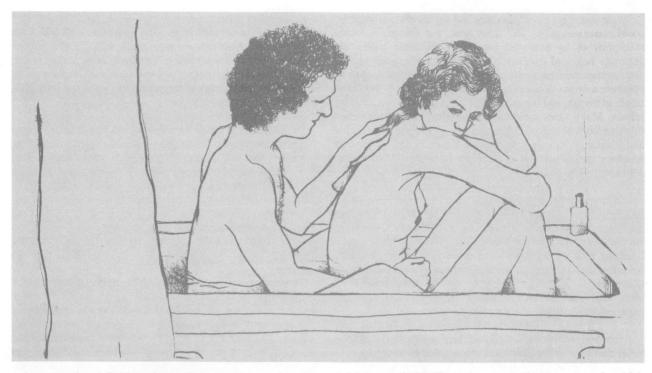

An expanding definition of sexuality must also consider the importance of "touching." The role of touching in sexual encounters is, of course, self-evident. As Montagu (1971) states, in no other aspect of interpersonal interaction is the skin so totally involved as in sexual union. Unfortunately, in our culture, touching, especially among adults, is often interpreted *solely* as a preliminary to or as part of sexual activity, and the more general sensual and pleasurable values of touching are neglected or even repressed.

It is interesting to note that the importance of touching as a means of personal communication, rather than solely as a prelude to a sexual encounter, has been recognized by Masters and Johnson (1975). Thus, they emphasize the manner in which touching bridges the separation between individuals and serves to have a person recognize, in a physically personalized way, affection and appreciation of another person.

The basic importance of touch and tactile activity in human experience has influenced even our language. Montagu (1971) explores various expressions involving the world "touch," such as "to keep in touch," or "to be touched by," that is, to be emotionally moved. He points out that the various meanings of this word often constitute the most extensive entry in a dictionary, as it does in the classic *Oxford English Dictionary*.

While touch is thus of fundamental significance in interpersonal relationships, at the same time, our culture is highly suspicious of its uses and expression. Whereas babies are generally held and cuddled, physical contact between parents and young children is often inhibited. Parents stop bathing children, a father decides that his son or daughter is too old to nestle in his lap, and the message of "don't touch" is a constant refrain. Many times parents avoid physical contact with each other in front of their children, and the media portray hugging and kissing as preludes to sex. Thus, the child soon learns that touching means sex and is therefore forbidden (Masters and Johnson, 1975).

We do engage in somewhat perfunctory embraces as a means of greeting, congratulating, or expressing comfort. Apart from these situations, however, affectionate physical contact between adults is frowned upon in our culture. The equation between touching and sex limits physical expression and is especially operative in our cultural taboo on touching between adult males (Zilbergeld, 1978). Zilbergeld suggests that these restrictions often lead men to interpret their feelings of warmth and closeness solely as a desire for sexual contact.

According to McCarthy, Ryan, and Johnson (1975), the belief that touching and physical expressions of affection must and should proceed to genital contact can result in the loss of valuable spontaneous experiences. If people refrain from touching because touching is laden with sexual connotations, they lose opportunities to express tenderness, intimacy, and delight in being together. Moreover, as we have seen in the discussion of Masters and Johnson's use of "sensate focus" or "nondemand pleasuring" (Chapter 14), nonsexual physical contact can provide a sensitive opportunity for partners to "be in touch" with each other.

In this section, we have attempted to indicate the diversity of meanings of sexuality. In some situations, what we want is genital contact. At other times, we may be interested in more general sensual contact or touching. Sometimes these inclinations merge, and we find ourselves wanting to extend sensual play into more focused genital activity. The perspective we have developed here suggests that human sexuality is flexible enough to encompass a wide range of expression, depending on the setting and the desire of the participants.

## SEX AND INTERPERSONAL RELATIONSHIPS

Sexual activity can be conceptualized as a language, as one of the vehicles by means of which we can express ourselves (Libby, 1974). Through fantasy, daydreaming, or masturbation, we engage in self-expression. Or we can enter into dialogue or conversation, that is, share sexual expression with others.

### ISSUES IN DECISION-MAKING

There are a number of important issues to consider in conjunction with our decisions to share our sexuality. Our motivations for being sexual, our choice of partner, and the situation can be simple or complex issues. The awareness with which we make these decisions can, we hope, enable us to develop a fuller understanding of our sexuality. The freedom to make choices about expressing our sexuality carries with it the concept of responsibility and a concern for our partner's and our own emotional vulnerabilities.

The situations in which we consider engaging in sexual activity can obviously vary. Sometimes we feel an immediate physical or sexual attraction to another person. At other times, sexual desire grows out of energies generated through other kinds of sharing: familiarity, closeness, affection. There are also situations which are potentially sexual because of personal or social expectations; for example: "We have been spending time together for several months; it must be about time to move into sex"; or, "If I don't make a move tonight, she [or he] will think I'm weird."

Sometimes people speak of having engaged in sexual activity because they felt "carried away" or overpowered by their physical sensations. It is helpful to distinguish the idea of being "out of control" from the concept of choosing to get caught up in the experience itself, to let go and savor the sensations of the moment. Often "I got carried away" is a way to rationalize to ourselves or to excuse our being sexual in a situation about which we were really doubtful.

It is important to remember that we do not necessarily have to *act* on sexual feelings. Sometimes we can just appreciate these feelings and sensations for their own sake (Zilbergeld, 1978), without having to proceed to engage in sexual activity. In some situations, not sex but a hug, a massage, or intimate conversation may most directly fulfill our immediate need for contact. On the other hand, it is important to keep in mind that when we do choose to act on sexual feelings, we do not necessarily have to have a specific justification, nor do we need to feel inappropriate guilt.

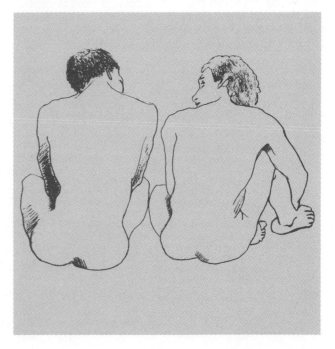

Although our cultural heritage emphasizes the reproductive aspects of sex, it is safe to assume that most instances of sexual activity involve other motivations. Sex can function on a number of different levels, to fulfill different kinds of desires: for physical release, to share sensual pleasure, to express a deep emotional connection. Very often, of course, a sexual episode will include a combination of these levels.

There may be times in our experience when sex may not have the same meaning for both participants. For example, one partner may be interested only in obtaining release from physical tension, while the other may be interpreting the sexual activity as an expression of love. If the situation is not clarified, misunderstanding, tension, or hurt feelings might follow. For this reason, it might be considered important that partners have an understanding and an ability to communicate about what the sexual experience means for each of them.

Additionally, the context in which people experience sexual activity can have considerable bearing on the significance or value they attach to it. A casual encounter, the beginning of a potential relationship, or a long-term union can each entail its own set of expectations or concerns about the nature of sexual activity. For example, a "quickie" to satisfy immediate physical needs may be quite acceptable to some couples who have been together for a long time and who have experienced a variety of different levels of sexual sharing. On the other hand, a couple who are just starting to explore their sexuality together may have different feelings about the kinds of sexual activity they want to pursue.

As we have already suggested, human sexuality is quite flexible and can meet a variety of needs (Zilbergeld, 1978). Beyond the obvious desires for physical release, pleasure, and intimacy, at various times, people also have other kinds of personal needs (conscious or not) which seek an outlet in sexual activity. Sex can be a way to overcome loneliness or boredom, to feel alive, to satisfy curiosity, or to seek adventure. At times people pursue sex in order to obtain status or bolster their sense of personal worth or competence, to express power or to exploit. Sex can also be a means of expressing rebellion against parental or social norms. These suggestions do not exhaust all the possible motiva-

tions for sex, and it is fairly evident that a combination of factors can exist in any given sexual experience. It ultimately rests with each of us to make the decisions about what circumstances are personally acceptable.

## LOVE AND INTIMACY

In the last analysis, each human being is fundamentally alone. Consciousness of our separateness and isolation creates anxiety and leads us to seek out and value those situations in which we feel close to or united with others (Fromm, 1956; May, 1969; Maslow 1970). The young child wants to be held and hugged. As we grow older, we seek friendship, affection, intimacy. Perhaps part of the natural value attributed to sexual activity resides in the fact that it can provide a nourishing sense of connection between two individuals.

The ultimate expression of such a relationship, that is, love or intimacy, can be one of the most effective ways of bridging the gap between two separate human beings (Maslow, 1970). Such emotional involvement carries with it the potential to provide many valued experiences: when all is going well, loving partners can share intense affection, caring, mutual acceptance, openness and trust, playfulness, and delight. Our approach at this point is not to supply a definitive analysis of love. Rather, we will explore some conditions of healthy, constructive relationships and some myths and unrealistic expectations about love.

According to such writers of classical works on love as Fromm (1956), May (1969), and Maslow (1970), the phenomenon of love presents a paradox: the lovers become one and yet remain two. On the one hand, the partners experience a sense of union, a merging of their two selves into one unit. Maslow (1970) describes this aspect of a love relationship as "need identification," that is, each person is so absorbed in the other that she or he is sensitive and responsive to the other's needs as if those needs were her or his own. And yet, at the same time, each partner's integrity or sense of self as an individual is strengthened.

The key to this paradox is perhaps provided by Maslow's (1970) discussion of the lover as respecting *both* his or her own self and the other's. To respect one's partner would mean accepting him or her as an equal, perceiving and appreciating his or her unique individuality, and valuing him or her as a person, as an end in himself or herself. Affirmation of the other's individuality also implies being eager for his or her growth and development. An example of this eagerness at its best is the feeling of ungrudging pride in the partner's achievements, even when they outshine one's own (Maslow, 1970).

According to Fromm (1956), love is not a mysterious quality that just "happens," but rather love is an ability to give of oneself. In order to develop this capacity to love and to have something to give, a person must have a productive orientation to life, that is, the desire to develop his or her personality and potentials as fully as possible. Preservation of one's integrity in a love relationship further implies developing an ability to love oneself and to be alone with oneself, as a condition for the ability to love others.

Up to this point, we have discussed several characteristics of what might be termed healthy love relationships. To repeat, it is not our purpose to establish a set of expectations or a list of correct *should's* that would be right for everyone, but rather to provide suggestions and food for thought. It is perhaps all too easy either to oversimplify or to present an abstract vision of ideal love. But human beings are not perfect: we do not always act according to expectation. If we pursue an impossible fantasy of perfect love, we may lose valuable relationship experiences that are more accessible to us.

Moreover, writers such as Fromm (1956) advance the idea that our contemporary social structure is not wholly conducive to love. The alienation we may experience in our society, while perhaps making us more eager to experience love, at the same time makes it more difficult for us to develop the capacity to be loving. On one basic level, our cultural conditioning often makes it difficult for us to explore and express our real feelings. If we grow up in an environment where demonstration of warmth and tenderness is restricted, for example, we may need time and motivation to learn to express such positive emotional responses. Again, intimacy presents certain risks. Letting down our barriers and moving toward openness and self-disclosure is often accompanied by fears. We may fear that our real selves are not worthy of being loved, or that we will be rejected. At the same time, the very experience of sharing these hesitancies and fears may enable people to grow closer.

Cultural myths and unrealistic images of romantic love present further barriers to the realization of personally satisfying relationships. If we search for the perfect lover or the ideal union, we will inevitably be disappointed, for such illusory projections fade when we get up close (Daniels and Horowitz, 1976). One of the main elements in the myth of romantic love is its lack of grounding in the concrete realities of our lives (Zerof, 1978). For example, the myth tends to focus on the extraordinary or peak experience. This is exemplified in the popular image of romantic love as a succession of idyllic scenes: lovers walking on a beach hand in hand into the sunset, or enjoying a champagne picnic by a secluded waterfall. These are presented out of context, rather than being perceived as ecstatic or

delightful moments which grow out of and, in turn, sustain the everyday, here and now experience.

Again, there is the idea that lovers can read each other's minds. While lovers may on occasion experience what appears to be telepathic communication, the myth leads us to expect this as an everyday occurrence. For example, we may make such assumptions as, "If you really loved me, you would know why I'm angry, what I like sexually," and so on. Dependence on this kind of intuition can undermine the growth of intimacy fostered by open and direct communication.

In the mythical version, romantic love never changes: in bliss it starts and in perfect bliss it continues. If we believe this aspect

of the myth, we might find ourselves trying to recapture some lost image of paradise, rather than perceiving the value of what we have at present and even welcoming changes the future will bring.

In this section, we have looked at different perspectives on the meaning of love. We must remember, however, that generalized descriptions cannot capture the core of the subjective experience. In the final analysis, what partners in significant relationships share is unique to them.

Communication in general and communication about sexuality are important components in relationships. There are four elements involved in verbal communication: what the speaker says, what she or he means, what the listener hears, and what the listener imagines the speaker's intent to be (Rush, 1973). Communication is also influenced by nonverbal factors, for example, tone of voice, facial expression, eye contact, body language. Wittingly or unknowingly, we often engage in communication "games" (Berne, 1964) in which we say one thing but mean another, or have hidden motivations or agendas. To be able to send direct messages and to listen clearly requires attention and awareness.

Brenton (1972) proposes several ways to facilitate communication that are applicable to discussions about sexuality and other sensitive issues. He suggests breaking the ice with "metacommunication," or talking about talking. In this way, the partners open a dialogue by exploring why it is difficult or embarrassing to discuss the specific issue of concern.

Another method is to practice "gradualism." By means of this approach, partners build up gradually to the problem at hand, by initially discussing the topic in general and, over a period of time, working up to the specific crucial issue. Similarly, disclosure of feelings can evolve from the most easily shared ones to the most difficult.

Brenton discusses several styles of communication and suggests that the style most conducive to effective problem-solving and growth is that of confrontation — confrontation of yourself and your feelings, and of your partner and his or her feelings. This style involves three rules of communication: speaking only for yourself, backing up what you say with examples, and getting and giving feedback. While confrontation is risky, since it involves openness and disclosure, it can create greater intimacy in a relationship.

## INTEGRATION

This is a book about sexuality. We have discussed physiological processes, the kaleidoscope of human sexual activities, and the cultural framework within which we express our sexuality. Yet book knowledge remains merely static words on paper until this knowledge is integrated in a personally meaningful and relevant manner. To this end, this chapter has focused on the personal aspect of the question, "What should sex mean?"

We have expressed the position that sexuality is an integral dimension of our personality. Yet the confusing and often negative attitudes about sexuality which pervade our culture can inhibit our ability to make sense of our sexuality. Either an intense preoccupation with sex, on the one hand, or a depreciation of sexuality, on the other, can impair our ability to integrate sexuality into our lives (van Kaam, 1976). But sexuality is not an external force beyond our control to which we must submit or against which we must fight. It is within our power to develop an awareness of our sexuality, and to shape its energies. Sexuality resides within us and between us: it is what we make of it. Sex is a very human activity: sometimes it is passionate, sometimes it is boring. Like everyday life itself, it is both ordinary and special at the same time.

In Maslow's (1970) study of psychological health, he presents a discussion of self-actualizing people, that is, those individuals who are developing their talents, capacities, and potentials to their fullest. Maslow suggests that, for such people, sexuality is both more *and* less important. It can be enjoyed intensely and, at the same time, be taken for granted. As Naranjo (Zaretsky, 1977) wrote, "People have to be free from sex in order to be free in sex."

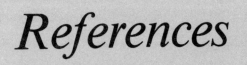

# References

Abitol, M.M., & Davenport, J.H. Sexual dysfunction after therapy for cervical carcinoma. *American Journal of Obstetrics and Gynecology,* 1974, *119,* 181-189.

Abram, H.S., Hester, L.R., & Epstein, G.M. Sexual activity and renal failure. In *Fifth International Congress of Nephrology* (Vol. III), Basil: Karger, 1974.

Abram, H.S., Hester, L.R., Sheridan, W.F., & Epstein, G.M. Sexual functioning in patients with chronic renal failure. In J. LoPiccolo & L. LoPiccolo (Eds.), *Handbook of sex therapy.* New York: Plenum, 1978.

Abramov, L.A. Sexual life and sexual frigidity among women developing acute myocardial infarction. *Psychosomatic Medicine,* 1976, *38,* 418-425.

American College of Obstetricians & Gynecologists. *Important facts about endometriosis.* Chicago: Author, 1979.

American Heart Association. *Heart facts.* New York: American Heart Association, 1974.

Amir, M. *Patterns in forcible rape.* Chicago: University of Chicago Press, 1971.

Anastasi, A. *Psychological testing.* New York: Macmillan, 1976.

Antoniou, L.D., Shalhoub, R.J., Sudhaker, T., & Smith, J.C., Jr. Reversal of uraemic impotence by zinc. *The Lancet,* October 29, 1977, 895-898.

Arditti, R. Male contraception. *Science for the People,* July 1976. Reproduced in C. Dreifus (Ed.), *Seizing our bodies: The politics of women's health.* New York: Vintage Books, 1978.

Arms, S. *Immaculate deception.* San Francisco: San Francisco Book Co./Houghton Mifflin, 1975.

Athanasiou, R., Shaver, R., & Tarvis, C. Sex. *Psychology Today,* 1970, *4*(2), 39-52.

Babbie, E.R. *The practice of social research.* Belmont, Calif.: Wadsworth Publishing Co., 1973.

Bandura, A., & Walters, R.H. *Social learning and personality development.* New York: Holt, Rinehart, & Winston, 1963.

Barbach, L.G. Group treatment of preorgasmic women. *Journal of Sex and Marital Therapy,* 1974, *1,* 139-145.

Barbach, L.G. *For yourself: The fulfillment of sexuality.* Garden City, N.Y.: Anchor Press/Doubleday, 1976.

Barclay, A.M. Sexual fantasies in men and women. *Medical Aspects of Human Sexuality,* 1973, *7*(5), 205-216.

Bardwick, J.M., & Douvan, E. Ambivalence: The socialization of women. In V. Gornick & B.K. Moran (Eds.), *Woman in sexist society.* New York: Signet, 1971.

Barker-Benfield, G.J. *The horrors of the half-known life.* New York: Harper & Row, 1976.

Barlow, D.H., Reynolds, E.J., & Agras, W.S. Gender identity change in a transsexual. *Archives of General Psychiatry,* 1973, *28,* 569-579.

Barry, H., Bacon, M.K., & Child, I.L. A cross-cultural survey of some sex differences in socialization. *Journal of Abnormal and Social Psychology,* 1957, *55,* 327-332.

Bart, P.B. Depression in middle-aged women. In V. Gornick & B.K. Moran (Eds.), *Woman in sexist society.* New York: Signet, 1971.

Beach, F.A. Factors involved in the control of mounting behavior by female mammals. In M. Diamond (Ed.), *Perspectives of reproduction and sexual behavior: A memorial to William C. Young.* Bloomington, Indiana: University Press, 1968.

Beach, F.A. Cross-species comparisons and the human heritage. In F.A. Beach (Ed.), *Human sexuality in four perspectives.* Baltimore: Johns Hopkins Press, 1976.

Beauchamp, G.K., Doty, R.L., Moulton, D.G., & Mugford, R.A. The pheromone concept in mammalian chemical communication: A critique. In R.L. Doty (Ed.), *Mammalian olfaction, reproductive processes, and behavior.* New York: Academic Press, 1976.

Bell, A.P., & Wienberg, M.S. *Homosexualities: A study of diversity among men and women.* New York: Simon & Schuster, 1978.

Bem, S. The measurement of psychological androgyny. *Journal of Consulting and Clinical Psychology,* 1974, *42,* 155-162.

Bem, S. Sex role adaptability: One consequence of psychological androgyny. *Journal of Personality and Social Psychology,* 1975, *31,* 634-643.

Bem, S. Probing the promise of androgyny. In A. Kaplan & J. Bean (Eds.), *Beyond sex-role stereotypes: Readings toward a psychology of androgeny.* Boston: Little, Brown, 1976.

Bem, S. Beyond androgyny: Some presumptuous prescriptions for a liberated sexual identity. In J. Sherman & F. Denmark (Eds.), *Psychology of women: Future directions for research.* New York: Psychological Dimensions, 1977.

Bem, S. & Bem, D. Case study of a nonconscious ideology: Training the woman to know her place. In D.J. Bem (Ed.), *Beliefs, attitudes and human affairs.* Belmont, Calif.: Brooks/Cole, 1970.

Benjamin, H. *The Transsexual phenomenon.* New York: Julian Press, 1966.

Benjamin, H., & Masters, R.F.L. *Prostitution and morality.* New York: Julian Press, 1964.

Bensman, A., & Kottke, F.J. Induced emission of sperm utilizing electrical stimulation of the seminal vesicles and vas deferens. *Archives of Physical Medicine and Rehabilitation,* 1966, *47,* 436-443.

Bernard, J. The fourth revolution. *Journal of Social Issues.* 1966, *22*(2), 76-87.

Bernard, J. Sex differences: An overview. New York: MSS Modular Publications, Inc., 1974, Module 26, 1-18.

Berne, E. *Games people play.* New York: Grove Press, 1964.

Bernstein, A.C. How children learn about sex and birth. *Psychology Today,* January 1976, pp. 31-36; 66.

Bibring, G.L. Some specific psychological tasks in pregnancy and motherhood. In *Premier Congrès International de Médecine Psychosomatique et Maternité, Paris 8-12 Juillet 1962,* ed. L. Chertok (Paris: Gauthier-Villars, 1965); reproduced in S. Hammer (Ed.), *Women: Body and culture.* New York: Perennial Library, 1975.

Bicher, M., Cherniak, D., Feingold, A., & Gardner, S. (Eds.) *V.D. handbook* (3rd ed.), Montreal: Montreal Health Press, 1977.

Bieber, I. *Homosexuality: A psychoanalytic study.* New York: Basic Books, 1962.

Blakeney, P., Kinder, B.N., Creson, D., Powell, L.C., & Sutton, C. A short-term, intensive workshop approach for the treatment of human sexual inadequacy. *Journal of Sex and Marital Therapy,* 1976, *2,* 124-129.

Bloch, A., Maeder, J., & Hassily, J. Sexual problems after myocardial infarction. *American Heart Journal,* 1975, *90,* 536-537.

Blumstein, P.W., & Schwartz, P. Lesbianism and bisexuality. In E. Goode & R. Troiden (Eds.), *Sexual deviance and sexual deviants.* New York: William Morrow & Co., 1974.

Bode, J. *View from another closet: Exploring bisexuality in women.* New York: Hawthorn Books, 1976.

Boston Women's Health Book Collective. *Our bodies ourselves* (2nd ed.). New York: Simon & Schuster, 1976.

Brayer, F.T., Chiazze, L., Jr., & Duffy, B.J. Calendar rhythm and menstrual cycle range. *Fertility sterility,* 1969.

Brecher, E.M. *The sex researchers.* New York: Signet Books (Paperback ed.), 1971.

Bregman, S. *Sexuality and the spinal cord injured woman.* Minneapolis: Sister Kenny Institute, 1975.

Breit, E.B. & Myerson-Ferrandino, M. Social dimensions of the menstrual taboo and the effects of female sexuality. In J.H. Williams (Ed.), *Psychology of women.* New York: W.W. Norton, 1979.

Bremner, W.J., & Kretser, D.M. Contraceptives for males. *Signs: Journal of Women in Culture and Society,* 1975, *1*(2), 387-396.

Brenton, M. *Sex talk.* Briarcliff Manor, N.Y.: Stein & Day, 1972.

Brown, N.O. *Life against death.* Middleton, Conn.: Wesleyan University Press, 1959.

Bruce, H.M. A block to pregnancy in the mouse caused by proximity of strange males. *Journal of Reproduction and Fertility,* 1960, *1,* 96-103.

Bullough, V.L. *Sexual variance in society and history.* New York: John Wiley & Sons, 1976.

Byrne, D. A pregnant pause in the sexual revolution. *Psychology Today,* 1977, *11*(2), 67-68.

Callahan, J. The herpes epidemic. *New Times,* June 12, 1978, 49-52.

Camp, S.L., & Green, C.P. Fertility control for the future. *The Draper Fund Report,* Summer 1978, No. 6, 14-15; 18-19.

Canter, N.F. *Medieval history: The life and death of a civilization.* New York: Macmillan, 1963.

Carpenter, C.R. Sexual behavior of free ranging rhesus monkeys (Macaca mulatta). *Journal of Comparative and Physiological Psychology,* 1942, *33,* 133-162.

Carter, C.S., & Davis, J.M. Effects of drugs on sexual arousal and performance. In Meyer, J.K. (Ed.), *Clinical management of sexual disorders.* Baltimore: Williams & Wilkins, 1976.

Casper, R.F., Yen, S.S.C., & Wilkes, M.M. Menopausal flushes: A neuroendocrine link with pulsatile luteinizing hormone secretion. *Science,* 1979, *205*(24), 823-825.

Cates, W., Ory, H., Rochat, R., & Tyler, C.W. The intrauterine device and deaths from spontaneous abortion. *New England Journal of Medicine,* 1976, *295,* 1155-1159.

Center for Disease Control. Gonorrhea—United States. *Morbidity and Mortality weekly Report,* 1979, *28*(45), 533-534.

Cerny, J.A. Biofeedback and the voluntary control of sexual arousal in women. Unpublished doctoral dissertation, Northern Illinois University, 1977.

Cheraskin, E., & Ringsdorf, W.M., Jr., with Brecher, A. *Psychodietetics.* New York: Bantam, 1976.

Cheraskin, E., Ringsdorf, W.M., & Clark, J.W. *Diet and disease.* Enmaus, Pa.: Rodale Books, 1970.

Cherniak, D., & Feingold, A. *Birth control handbook.* Montreal: Montreal Health Press, 1975.

Cherry, S.H. *The menopause myth.* New York: Ballentine Books, 1976.

Chevalier-Skolnikoff, S. Male-female, female-female, and male-male sexual behavior in the stumptail monkey, with special attention to the female orgasm. *Archives of Sexual Behavior,* 1974, *3,* 95-116.

Chodorow, N. Being and doing: A cross-cultural examination of the socialization of males and females. In V. Gornick & B.K. Moran (Eds.), *Woman in sexist society.* New York: Signet, 1971.

Clark, J.H., & Zarrow, M.X. Influence of copulation on time of ovulation in women. *American Journal of Obstetrics and Gynecology,* 1971, *109*(7), 1083-1085.

Cochran, W.G., Mosteller, F., & Tukey, J.W. Statistical problems of the Kinsey report. *Journal of the American Statistical Association,* 1953, *48,* 673-716.

Cohen, M.L., Garofalo, R., Boucher, R., & Seghorn, T. The psychology of rapists. *Seminars in Psychiatry,* 1971, *3,* 307-327.

Cohn, F. *Understanding human sexuality.* Englewood Cliffs, N.J.: Prentice-Hall, 1974.

Colen, B.D. Women turning away from the pill as contraceptive. *St. Petersburg Times,* November 4, 1979, 1,26.

Colligan, D. Tipping the balance of the sexes. *New York Magazine,* November 7, 1977. Reproduced in *Readings in human sexuality 78/79.* Guilford, Conn.: Dushkin Publishing Group, Inc., 1978.

Comarr, A.E. Observations on menstruation and pregnancy among female spinal cord injured patients. *Paraplegia,* 1966, *3*(4), 263-272.

Comarr, A.E. Sexual function among patients with spinal cord injury. *Urologia Internationalis,* 1970, *25,* 134-168.

Comfort, A. Likelihood of human pheromones. *Nature,* 1971, *230,* 432-433.

Comfort, A. *The joy of sex.* New York: Crown Publishers, 1972.

Commission on Obscenity and Pornography. *The report of the commission on obscenity and pornography.* New York: Random House, 1970.

Condoms. *Consumer Reports,* 1979, *44*(10), 583-589.

Cooper, A.J. Treatments of male potency disorders: The present status. In J. LoPiccolo & L. LoPiccolo (Eds.), *Handbook of sex therapy.* New York: Plenum, 1978.

Corea, G. *The hidden malpractice.* New York: Jove/Harcourt, Brace, Jovanovich, 1977.

Cristall, L., & Dean, R. Relationships of sex-role stereotypes and self-actualization. *Psychological Reports,* 1976, *39,* 842.

Daniels, P., & Weingarten, K. A new look at the medical risks in late childbearing. *Women and Health,* 1979, *4*(1), 5-36.

Daniels, V., & Horowitz, L. *Being and caring.* San Francisco: San Francisco Book Co., 1976.

Davenport, W.H. Sex in cross-cultural perspective. In F.A. Beach (Ed.), *Human sexuality in four perspectives.* Baltimore: Johns Hopkins Press, 1976.

de Beauvoir, S. *The second sex.* New York: Bantam, 1961.

Delaney, J., Lupton, M.J., & Toth, E. *The curse: A cultural history of menstruation.* New York: The New American Library, 1977.

Dick-Read, G. *Childbirth without fear* (2nd rev. ed.). New York: Harper & Row, 1970.

Dodson, B. *Liberating masturbation.* New York: Bodysex Designs, 1974.

Drakeford, J.W., & Hamm, J. *Pornography: The sexual mirage.* Nashville: Thomas Nelson, Inc., 1973.

Dreifus, C. Sterilizing the poor. *The Progressive,* 1975, *39*(12), 13-19. Reproduced in C. Dreifus (Ed.), *Seizing our bodies: The politics of women's health.* New York: Vintage Books, 1978.

Drellich, M., & Bieber, J. The psychological importance of a uterus and its functions: Some psychoanalytic implications of hysterectomy. *Journal of Nervous and Mental Diseases,* 1958, *126,* 322-336.

Edgerton, R. *The cloak of competence: Stigma in the lives of the mentally retarded.* Berkeley: University of California Press, 1967.

Eisenberg, G., & Kinder, B.N. The impact of sex education programs: A review of the literature. Unpublished manuscript, University of South Florida, 1979.

Elias, J., & Gebhard, P. Sexuality and sexual learning in childhood. *Phi Delta Kappan,* March 1969, *1*(7), 401-405.

Ellenberg, M. Sexual aspects of the female diabetic. *Mount Sinai Journal of Medicine,* 1977, *44,* 495-500.

Ellenberg, M. Impotence in diabetes: The neurologic factor. In J. LoPiccolo & L. LoPiccolo (Eds.), *Handbook of sex therapy.* New York: Plenum, 1978.

Elstein, M., Smith, E.K., & Curtis, J.R. Reproductive potential of patients treated by maintenance hemodialysis. *British Medical Journal,* 1969, *2,* 734-736.

Ersner-Hershfield, R., & Kopel, S. Group treatment of pre-orgasmic women: Evaluation of partner involvement and spacing of sessions. *Journal of Consulting and Clinical Psychology,* 1979, *47,* 750-759.

Erwin, J., & Maple, T. Arobisexual behavior with male-male anal penetration in male rhesus monkeys. *Archives of Sexual Behavior,* 1976, *5,* 9-14.

Fagot, B.I., & Patterson, G.R. An in vivo analysis of reinforcing contingencies for sex-role behaviors in the pre-school child. *Developmental Psychology.* 1969, *1,* 563-568.

*FDA Drug Bulletin.* Patient brochure for progestins warns against use in pregnancy. Author, 1978-1979, *8*(6), 36-37.

*FDA Drug Bulletin.* Update on estrogens and uterine cancer. Author, 1979, *9*(1), 2-3.

Feinbloom, D.H., *Transvestites and transsexuals.* New York: Delta, 1976.

Finkle, A.L., & Meyers, T.G. Sexual potency in aging males. IV. Status of private patients before and after prostatectomy. *Journal of Urology,* 1960, *84,* 152.

Firestone, S. On American feminism. In V. Gornick & B.K. Moran (Eds.), *Woman in sexist society.* New York: Signet, 1971.

Fisher, C., Gross, J., & Zuch, J. Cycle of penile erection synchronous with dreaming (REM) sleep. *Archives of Sexual Behavior,* 1965, *12,* 29-45.

Fitzpatrick, W.F. Sexual functioning in the paraplegic patient. *Archives of Physical Medicine and Rehabilitation,* 1974, *55,* 221-227.

Flaceliere, R. *Love in ancient Greece.* New York: Crown Publishers, 1962 (Translated by J. Clough).

Ford, C.S., & Beach, F.A. *Patterns of sexual behavior.* New York: Harper & Row, 1951.

Fosburgh, L. The make-believe world of teen-age maternity. *The New York Times Magazine,* August 7, 1977, 29-34.

Foster, A.L. Relationships between age and sexual activity in married men. *Journal of Sex Education and Therapy,* 1979, *1*(5), 21-26.

Freedman, A.M. Drugs and sexual behavior. In B.J. Sadock, H.I. Kaplan, & A.M. Freedman (Eds.), *The sexual experience.* Baltimore: Williams & Wilkins, 1976.

Freeman, J. (Ed.), *Women: A feminist perspective* (2nd ed.). Palo Alto, Calif.: Mayfield, 1979.

Freund, K., Sedlacek, F., & Knob, K. A simple transducer for mechanical plethysmography of the male genital. *Journal of Experimental Analysis of Behavior,* 1965, *8,* 169-170.

Friday, N. *My secret garden.* New York: Trident, 1973.

Friedan, B. *The feminine mystique.* New York: Dell, 1963.

Friedman, J.M. Sexual adjustment of the post-coronary male. In J. LoPiccolo & L. LoPiccolo (Eds.), *Handbook of sex therapy.* New York: Plenum, 1978.

Friedman, M. Homosexuals may be healthier than straights. *Psychology Today,* March 1975.

Fromm, E. *The art of loving.* New York: Harper & Row, 1956.

Gaer, J. *The love of the Old Testament.* New York: Grosset & Dunlap, 1951.

Gagnon, J. Female child victims of sex offenses. *Social Problems.* 1965, *13,* 176-192.

Gagnon, J. *Human sexualities.* Glenview, Ill.: Scott, Foresman & Co., 1977.

Gagnon, J., & Henderson, B. *Human sexuality: An age of ambiguity.* Boston: Educational Associates, 1975.

Gall, J.J. The consenting adult homosexual and the law: An empirical study of enforcement and administration in Los Angeles County. *UCLA Law Review,* 1966, *13,* 688-694.

Gawin, F.H. Pharmacologic enhancement of the erotic: Implications of an expanded definition of aphrodisiacs. *The Journal of Sex Research,* 1978, *14*(2), 107-117.

Gebhard, P.H. Misconceptions about female prostitutes. *Medical Aspects of Human Sexuality,* 1969, *3,* 24-30.

Gebhard, P.H. Human sexual behavior: A summary statement. In D.S. Marshall & R.C. Suggs (Eds.), *Human sexual behavior.* New York: Basic Books, 1971.

Gebhard, P.H., Gagnon, J.H., Pomeroy, W.B., & Christensen, C.V. *Sex offenders: An analysis of types.* New York: Harper & Row, 1965.

Geer, J.H., Morokoff, P., & Greenwood, P. Sexual arousal in women: The development of a measurement device for vaginal blood volume. *Archives of Sexual Behavior,* 1974, *3,* 559-564.

Gilmartin, B.G., & Kusisto, D.V. Some personal and social characteristics of mate-sharing swingers. In R.W. Libby & R.N. Whitehurst (Eds.), *Renovating marriage.* Reproduced in J.L. McCary & D.R. Copeland (Eds.), *Modern views of human sexual behavior.* Chicago: Science Research Associates, 1976.

Girdano, D.D., & Girdano, D.A. *Drugs: A factual account* (2nd Ed.). Reading, Mass. Addison-Wesley, 1976.

Glasgow, R.E., & Rosen, G.M. Behavioral bibliotherapy: A review of self-help behavior therapy manuals. *Psychological Bulletin,* 1978, *85,* 1-23.

Gold, F.M., & Hotchkiss, R.S. Sexual potency following simple prostatectomy. *New York State Journal of Medicine,* December 1969, 2987-2989.

Goldstein, B. *Human Sexuality.* New York: McGraw-Hill, 1976.

Goldstein, M.J., & Kant, H.S. *Pornography and sexual deviance.* Berkeley: University of California Press, 1973.

Golub, S. The magnitude of premenstrual anxiety and depression. *Psychosomatic Medicine,* 1976, *38*(1), 4-12.

Gordon, S. Freedom for sex education and sexual expression. In S. Gordon & R.W. Libby (Eds.), *Sexuality today - And tomorrow.* N. Scituate, Mass.: Duxbury Press, 1976.

Gordon, S., & Dickman, I.R. *Sex education: The parent's role.* New York: Public Affairs Pamphlets, 1977.

Gough, H.G. Some factors related to men's stated willingness to use a male contraceptive pill. *Journal of Sex Research,* 1979, *15*(1), 27-37.

Gould, L. X: A fabulous child's story. In M. Tripp (Ed.), *Woman in the year 2000.* New York: Dell, 1976.

Gray, H. *Anatomy of the human body* (27th ed.). C.M. Goss (Ed.). Philadelphia: Lea & Febiger, 1959.

Greene, L.F., Panayotis, P.K., & Weeks, R.E. Retrograde ejaculation of semen due to diabetic neuropathy. *Fertility and Sterility,* 1963, *14,* 617-625.

Griffen, J.A. cross-cultural investigation of behavioral changes at menopause. *Social Science Journal,* 1977, *14*(2), 49-55.

Griffin, S. Rape: The all-American crime. *Ramparts,* 1971, *10*(3), 26-35.

Griffith, E.R., & Trieschmann, R.B. Sexual functioning in women with spinal cord injury. *Archives of Physical Medicine and Rehabilitation,* 1975, *56,* 18-21.

Grimal, R. *Love in ancient Rome.* New York: Crown Publishers, 1967.

Grobstein, C. External human fertilization. *Scientific American,* 1979, *240*(6), 57-67.

Gross, L., & MacEwan, P. On day care. In D. Babcox & M. Belkin (Eds.), *Liberation now!* New York: Dell, 1971.

Haas, A. *Teenage sexuality.* New York: Macmillan, 1979.

Hafez, E.S.E. Transport and survival of spermatozoa in the human female reproductive tract. In H. Ludwig & P.F. Tauber (Eds.), *Human fertilization.* Stuttgart, Germany: Georg Thieme Publishers, 1978 (PSG Publishing Co., Mass.).

Hall, J. Sexual behavior. In J. Wortis (Ed.), *Mental Retardation and developmental disabilities: An annual review* (Vol. 6), 1974.

Hall, J. Sexuality and the mentally retarded. In R. Green (Ed.), *Human sexuality: A health practitioner's text.* Baltimore: Williams & Wilkins, 1975.

Hamburger, C., Sturup, G.K., & Dahl-Iverson, E. Transvestism: Hormonal, psychiatric, and surgical treatment. *Journal of the American Medical Association,* 1953, *152,* 391-396.

Haskins, G.L. *Law and authority in early Massachusetts.* New York: Macmillan, 1960.

Hatcher, R.A., Stewart, G.K., Stewart F., Guest, F., Stratton, P., & Wright, A.H. *Contraceptive technology 1978-1979.* New York: Irvington Publishers, 1978.

Hatcher, R.A., Stewart G.K., Guest, F., Finkelstein, R., & Godwin, C. *Contraceptive technology 1976-1977.* New York: Irvington Publishers, 1976.

Heidi, G. *Winning the age game.* Garden City, N.Y.: Doubleday, 1976.

Heiman, J.R. The physiology of erotica: Women's sexual arousal. *Psychology Today,* 1975, *8*(11), 90-94.

Hellerstein, H., & Friedman, E.J. Sexual activity and the postcoronary patient. *Medical Aspects of Human Sexuality,* March 1969, 70.

Hellerstein, H., & Friedman, E.J. Sexual activity and the postcoronary patient. *Archives of Internal Medicine,* 1970, *125,* 987.

Hellman, L.M., & Pritchard, J.A. *Williams obstetrics* (14th ed.). New York: Appleton-Century-Crofts, 1971.

Hennigar, G.R. Drug and chemical injury. In W.A.D. Anderson (Ed.), *Pathology* (6th ed.). St. Louis: C.V. Mosby, 1971.

Higgins, G.E. Aspects of sexual response in adults with spinal-cord injury: A review of the literature. In J. LoPiccolo & L. LoPiccolo (Eds.), *Handbook of sex therapy.* New York: Plenum, 1978.

Himes, N.E. *Medical history of contraception.* New York: Gamut Press, 1963.

Hite, S. *The Hite report: A nationwide study of female sexuality.* New York: Macmillan, 1976.

Hogan, D.R. The effectiveness of sex therapy: A review of the literature. In J. LoPiccolo & L. LoPiccolo (Eds.), *Handbook of sex therapy.* New York: Plenum, 1978.

Holden, C. Sex change operations of dubious value. *Science,* 1979, *205*(4412), 1235.

Hooker, E. Sexual behavior: Homosexuality. *International Encyclopedia of the Social Sciences.* New York: Macmillan, 1968.

Horne, H.W., Paull, D.P., & Munro, D. Fertility studies in the human male with traumatic injuries of the spinal cord and cauda equina. *New England Journal of Medicine,* 1948, *239,* 959-961.

Howard, J.L., Liptzin, M.B., & Reifler, C.B. Is pornography a problem? *Journal of Social Issues,* 1973, *29,* 133-146.

Hoyenga, K.B., & Hoyenga, K.T. *The question of sex differences.* Boston: Little, Brown, 1979.

Humphreys, L. *Tea room trade: Impersonal sex in public places.* Hawthorne, New York: Aldine Publishers, 1975.

Hunt, M. *Sexual behavior in the 1970s.* Chicago: Playboy Press, 1974.

Jacobsen, A. A woman's place - Her natural destiny: The social and sexual oppression of women. In S. Gordon & R.W. Libby (Eds.), *Sexuality today - And tomorrow.* N. Scituate, Mass.: Duxbury Press, 1976.

James, W.H. The incidence of spontaneous abortion. *Population Studies,* 1970, *24,* 241-245.

Jardine, J.O. Make him a better lover. *Playgirl,* 1979, *6*(11), 55-56, 64-66.

Jensen, G.D. Cross-cultural studies and animal studies of sex. In B.J. Sadock, H.I. Kaplan, & A.M. Freedman (Eds.), *The sexual experience.* Baltimore: Williams & Wilkins, 1976.

Johnson, A. The risks of sex hormones as drugs. *Women and Health,* July/August 1977, 8-11.

Johnson, J. Prognosis of disorders of sexual potency in the male. *Journal of Psychosomatic Research,* 1965, *9,* 195-200.

Jones, H.W., Jr. Development of genitalia. In A.C. Barnes (Ed.), *Intrauterine development.* Philadelphia: Lea & Febiger, 1968.

Kagan, J. Herpes: It can be treated—But not cured. *Ms.,* January 1978, 38-40.

Kantner, J.F., & Zelnik, M. Sexual experience of young unmarried women in the United States. *Family Planning Perspectives,* 1972, *4*(4), 9-18.

Kantner, J.F., & Zelnik, M. Contraception and pregnancy: Experience of young unmarried women in the United States. *Family Planning Perspectives,* 1973, *5*(1), 21-35.

Kaplan, H.S. *The new sex therapy.* New York: Brunner/Mazel, 1974.

Kaplan, H.S. *Disorders of sexual desire.* New York: Brunner/Mazel, 1979.

Karlson, P., & Luscher, M. 'Pheromones': A new term for a class of biologically active substances. *Nature,* 1959, *183,* 55-56.

Karmel, M. *Thank you, Dr. Lamaze.* Philadelphia: Lippincott, 1959.

Katchadourian, H.A., & Lunde, D.T. *Fundamentals of human sexuality* (2nd ed.). New York: Holt, Rinehart, & Winston, 1975.

Kegel, A.H. Sexual functions of the pubococcygeal muscle. *Western Journal of Obstetrics and Gynecology,* 1952, *60, 521.*

Kelly, J., Leavy, J., & Northrop, A. Who says athletes can't be pregnant? *Ms.,* 1978, *8*(1), 47-48.

Kimbrell, G.M. Note: Diet dilettantism. *Psychological Record,* 1975, *25,* 273-274.

Kinder, B.N., & Blakeney, P. Treatment of sexual dysfunctions: A review of outcome studies. *Journal of Clinical Psychology,* 1977, *33*(2), 523-530.

Kinsey, A.C., Pomeroy, W.B., & Martin, C.E. *Sexual behavior in the human male.* Philadelphia: W.B. Saunders Co., 1948.

Kinsey, A.C., Pomeroy, W.B., Martin, C.E., & Gebhard, P.H. *Sexual behavior in the human female.* Philadelphia: W.B. Saunders Co., 1953.

Kirkendall, L.A., & Rubin, I. Sexuality and the life cycle: A broad concept of sexuality. In SIECUS, *Sexuality and man.* New York: Charles Scribner's Sons, 1970.

Kish, L. *Survey sampling.* New York: John Wiley & Sons, 1965.

Kolodny, R.C. Sexual dysfunction in diabetic females. *Diabetes,* 1971, *20,* 557-559.

Komisar, L. The image of women in advertising. In V. Gornick & B.K. Moran (Eds.), *Woman in sexist society.* New York: Signet, 1971.

Krafft-Ebing, R.V. *Psychopathia sexualis.* New York: Pioneer Publications, 1939.

Kutchinsky, B. The effect of easy availability of pornography on the incidence of sex crimes: The Danish experience. *Journal of Social Issues,* 1973, *29,* 163-182.

LaBarre, W. Anthropological perspectives on sexuality. In D.L. Grummon & A.M. Barclay (Eds.), *Sexuality: A search for perspective.* New York: Van Nostrand Reinhold, 1971.

Larned, D. Caesarean births: Why they are up 100 percent. *Ms.,* October 1978, 24-30.

Laschet, U. Antiandrogen in the treatment of sex offenders: Mode of action and therapeutic outcome. In J. Zubin & J. Money (Eds.), *Contemporary sexual behavior: Critical issues in the 1970s.* Baltimore: Johns Hopkins Press, 1973.

Laudis, J. Experiences of 500 children with sexual deviation. *Psychiatric Quarterly Supplement,* 1956, *30,* 91-109.

Laws, J.L., & Schwartz, P. *Sexual scripts: The social construction of female sexuality.* Hinsdale, Ill.: Dryden Press, 1977.

Lerner, I.M. *Heredity, evolution, and society.* San Francisco: W.H. Freeman, 1968.

Levin, M.N. Let George do it: Male contraceptives. *Ms.,* January 1976, 91-94.

Levitt, E.E., & Lubin, B. Some personality factors associated with menstrual complaints and menstrual attitudes. *Journal of Psychosomatic Research,* 1967, *11.*

Lewinsohn, R. *A history of sexual customs.* New York: Harper Brothers, 1958.

Lewis, S.G. *Sunday's women/A report on lesbian life today.* Boston: Beacon Press, 1979.

Libby, R.W. Adolescent sexual attitudes and behavior. *Journal of Clinical Child Psychology,* 1974. Reproduced in S. Gordon & R.W. Libby (Eds.), *Sexuality today - And tomorrow.* N. Scituate, Mass.: Duxbury Press, 1976.

Lief, H.I. Obstacles to the ideal and complete sex education of the medical student and physician. In J. Zubin & J. Money, (Eds.), *Contemporary sexual behavior: Critical issues in the 1970s.* Baltimore: Johns Hopkins Press, 1973.

Lipton, M.A. Pornography. In B.J. Sadock, H.I. Kaplan, & A.M. Freedman (Eds.), *The sexual experience.* Baltimore: Williams & Wilkins, 1976.

Litewka, J. The socialized penis. In E.S. Morrison & V. Borosage (Eds.), *Human sexuality: Contemporary perspectives* (2nd ed.). Palo Alto, Calif.: Mayfield Publishing Co., 1977.

Lobsenz, N.M. *Sex after sixty-five.* New York: Public Affairs Committee, Inc., 1975.

LoPiccolo, J. The professionalization of sex therapy: Issues and problems. In J. LoPiccolo & L. LoPiccolo (Eds.), *Handbook of sex therapy.* New York: Plenum, 1978.

LoPiccolo, J., & Lobitz, W.C. The role of masturbation in the treatment of orgasmic dysfunction. *Archives of Sexual Behavior,* 1972, *2,* 163-171.

Lorenz, K. *On aggression.* New York: Harcourt, Brace, & World, 1966.

Lowe, J.C., & Mikulas, W.L. Use of written material in learning self-control of premature ejaculation. *Psychological Reports,* 1975, *37,* 295-298.

Luce, G.G. *Body time.* New York: Bantam, 1973.

Maccoby, E. Sex in the social order. *Science,* 1973, *182*(4111), 469-471.

Maccoby, E., & Jacklin, C.N. *The psychology of sex differences.* Palo Alto: Stanford University Press, 1974.

Malinowski, B. *The sexual life of savages.* New York: Harcourt, Brace, & World, 1929.

Mann, J., Sidman, J., & Starr, S. Evaluating the social consequences of erotic films: An experimental approach. *Journal of Social Issues,* 1973, *29,* 113-132.

Mann, T. The biochemical characteristics of spermatozoa and seminal plasma. In E. Rosenberg & C.A. Paulsen (Eds.), *The human testis. Advances in Experimental Medicine & Biology Series,* 1970, *10.*

Marcotte, D.B. & Kilpatrick, D.G. Persistence, planning, patience, and prevention: Aspects of sex education in medicine. *Journal of Sex and Marital Therapy,* 1976, *2*(1), 47-52.

Marcuse, H. *One-dimensional man.* Boston: Beacon Press, 1964.

Marcuse, H. *Eros and civilization.* Boston: Beacon Press, 1966.

Marshall, D.S. Sexual behavior in Mangaia. In D.S. Marshall & R.C. Suggs (Eds.), *Human sexual behavior.* New York: Basic Books, 1971.

Martin, J.C. Drugs of abuse during pregnancy: Effects upon offspring structure and function. *Signs: Journal of Women in Culture and Society,* 1976, *2*(2), 357-368.

Marx, J.L. The annual pap smear: An idea whose time has gone? *Science,* 1979a, *205*(4402), 177-178.

Marx, J.L. Dysmenorrhea: Basic research leads to a rational therapy. *Science,* 1979b, *205*(4402), 175-176.

Marx, J.L. Hormones and their effect in the aging body. *Science,* 1979c, *206*(4420), 805-806.

Maslow, A.H. *Motivation and personality* (2nd ed.). New York: Harper & Row, 1970.

Massie, E., Rose, E., Rupp, J., & Whelton, R. Sudden death during coitus — Fact or fiction? *Medical Aspects of Human Sexuality,* March 1969, 22-26.

Masters, W.H., & Johnson, V.E. *Human sexual response.* Boston: Little, Brown, 1966.

Masters, W.H., & Johnson, V.E. *Human sexual inadequacy.* Boston: Little, Brown, 1970.

Masters, W.H., & Johnson, V.E. *The pleasure bond.* Boston: Little, Brown, 1975.

Masters, W.H., & Johnson, V.E. *Homosexuality in perspective.* Boston: Little, Brown, 1979.

May, R. What is our problem? *Review of Existential Psychology and Psychiatry,* 1963, *3*(2), 109-112.

May, R. *Love and will.* New York: W.W. Norton, 1969.

May, R. *Power and innocence.* New York: W.W. Norton, 1972.

McCaghy, C.H. Child molesting. *Sexual Behavior,* 1971, *1,* 16-24.

McCarthy, B., Ryan, M., & Johnson, F.A. *Sexual awareness: A practical approach.* San Francisco: Boyd & Fraser, 1975.

McCary, J.L. *Sexual myths and fallacies.* New York: Schocken Books, 1971.

McCary, J.L. *Human Sexuality.* New York: D. Van Nostrand, 1973.

McCary, J.L. *McCary's human sexuality* (3rd ed.). New York: D. Van Nostrand, 1978.

McClintock, M.K. Menstrual synchrony and suppression. *Nature,* 1971, *229*(5282), 244-245.

McConaghy, N. Penile volume responses to moving and still pictures of male and female nudes. *Archives of Sexual Behavior,* 1974, *3,* 565-570.

McIntosh, M. The homosexual role. *Social Problems,* 1968, *16,* 182-192.

McLaren, A. The embryo. In C.L. Austin & R.V. Short (Eds.), *Reproduction in mammals: Embryonic and fetal development.* New York: Cambridge University Press, 1972.

McMullen, S., & Rosen, R.C. Self-administered masturbation training in the treatment of primary orgasmic dysfunction. *Journal of Consulting and Clinical Psychology,* 1979, *47,* 912-918.

Mead, M. *Sex and temperament in three primitive societies.* New York: Morrow, 1935.

Menning, B.E. *Infertility: A guide for the childless couple.* Englewood Cliffs, N.J.: Prentice-Hall, 1977.

Menninger, R.W. Decisions in sexuality: An act of impulse, conscience, or society? In D. Grummon & A. Barclay (Eds.), *Sexuality: A search for perspective.* New York: Van Nostrand Reinhold, 1971.

Merriam, A.P. Aspects of sexual behavior among the Bala (Basongye). In D.S. Marshall & R.C. Suggs (Eds.), *Human sexual behavior.* New York: Basic Books, 1971.

Messenger, J.C. *Inis Beag: Isle of Ireland.* New York: Holt, Rinehart, & Winston, 1969.

Meyer, J.K., & Peter, D.J. Sex reassignment: Follow-up. *Archives of General Psychiatry,* 1979, *36,* 1010-1015.

Michael, R.P., Bousall, R.W., & Warner, P. Human vaginal secretions: Volatile fatty acid content. *Science,* 1974, *186,* 1217-1219.

Miller, P. Review of homosexuality research and some implications for treatment. *Psychotherapy, Research, and Practice,* 1968, *5,* 3-6.

Millican, M.W. Family planning by electronics. *Tampa Tribune-Times,* October 21, 1979, 14-A.

Money, J. Phantom orgasm in the dreams of paraplegic men and women. *Archives of General Psychiatry,* 1960, *3,* 373-382.

Money, J. Destereotyping sex roles. *Society,* 1977, *14*(5), 25-28.

Money, J., & Ehrhardt, A.A. *Man and woman, boy and girl.* Baltimore: Johns Hopkins Press, 1972.

Monsour, K.I., & Stewart, B. Abortion and sexual behavior in college women. *American Journal of Orthopsychiatry,* 1973, *43,* 804-814.

Montagu, A. *Touching: The human significance of the skin.* New York: Columbia University Press, 1971.

Morgan, S. Sexuality after hysterectomy and castration. *Women and Health,* 1978, *3*(1), 5-10.

Mosher, D.L., *Psychological reactions to pornographic films.* (Technical report of the Commission on Obscenity and Pornography, vol. 8). Washington, D.C.: U.S. Government Printing Office, 1970.

Mosher, D.L. & Abramson, P.R. Subjective sexual arousal to films of masturbation. *Journal of Consulting and Clinical Psychology,* 1977, *45,* 796-807.

Mosier, H., Grossman, H., & Dingman, H. Secondary sex development in mentally deficient individuals. *Child Development,* 1962, *33,* 273-286.

Murdock, G.P. *Social structure.* New York: Macmillan, 1949.

Murstein, B.L. *Love, sex, and marriage through the ages.* New York: Springer Publishing Co., 1974.

Myers, L. The high cost of Milady's prudery. In S. Gordon & R.W. Libby (Eds.), *Sexuality today - And tomorrow.* N. Scituate, Mass.: Duxbury Press, 1976.

Myers, L. Orgasm: An evaluation. In S. Gordon, & R.W. Libby (Eds.), *Sexuality today - And tomorrow.* N. Scituate, Mass.: Duxbury Press, 1976.

Myerson-Ferrandino, M. *Patriarchy and biological necessity: A feminist critique.* Unpublished doctoral dissertation, State University of New York at Buffalo, 1977.

Naeye, R.L. Coitus and associated amniotic-fluid infections. *New England Journal of Medicine,* 1979, *301*(22), 1198-1200.

Neel, J.V., & Schull, W.J. *Human heredity.* Chicago: University of Chicago Press, 1975.

Nelson, W.E., Vaughn, V.C., III, & McKay, R.J. *Textbook of Pediatrics* (9th ed.). Philadelphia: W.B. Saunders Co., 1969.

Newton, N. Interrelationships between sexual responsiveness, birth, and breast feeding. In J. Zubin & J. Money (Eds.), *Contemporary sexual behavior: Critical issues in the 1970s.* Baltimore: Johns Hopkins Press, 1973.

Newton, N. Trebly sensuous woman. In S. Hammer (Ed.), *Women: Body and culture.* New York: Perennial Library, 1975.

Norsigian, J. Network seeks contraceptive reforms. *Network News,* April/May 1978.

Norwood, C. A humanizing way to have a baby. *Ms.,* May 1978, 89-91.

Oden, T.C. *Game free: A guide to the meaning of intimacy.* New York: Harper & Row, 1974.

Osofsky, J.D., & Osofsky, H.J. Androgeny as a life style. *The Family Coordinator,* 1972, *21*(4), 411-418.

Paige, K.E. Women learn to sing the menstrual blues. *Psychology Today,* 1973, *7*(4), 41-43.

Paige, K.E. The ritual of circumcision. *Human Nature,* May 1978, 40-48.

Pauley, I.B. Male psychosexual inversion: Transsexuality. *Archives of General Psychiatry,* 1965, *13,* 172-175.

Pembrook, L. Birth control: What's new, safe and foolproof. *Parents Magazine,* November 1977, 74, 113, 126.

Persky, H. Reproductive hormones, moods, and the menstrual cycle. In R.C. Friedman, R.M. Richert, & R.L. Vandewiele (Eds.), *Sex differences in behavior.* New York: Wiley Interscience Division, 1969.

Peterson, W. *Population* (2nd ed.). New York: Macmillan, 1968.

Pietropinto, A., & Simenauer, J. *Beyond the male myth.* New York: Quadrangle, 1977.

Pike, E.R. *Love in ancient Rome.* London: F. Muller, 1965.

Pilpel, H.F. Sex vs. the law: A study in hypocrisy. In A. Shiloh (Ed.), *Studies in human sexual behavior: The American scene.* Springfield, Ill.: Charles C. Thomas, 1970.

Pleck, J.H., & Sawyer, J. (Eds.). *Men and masculinity.* Englewood Cliffs, N.J.: Prentice-Hall, 1974.

Pocs, O., Godow, A., Tolone, W.L., & Walsh, R.H. Is there sex after 40? *Psychology Today,* 1977, *11*(1), 54-56.

Pohlman, E.H. Influencing people to want fewer children. Paper presented at the American Psychological Association Convention, Miami, Florida, September 1970.

Pomeroy, W.B. *SIECUS report,* 1976, *5*(2), 1-14.

Powell, L.C., Blakeney, P., Croft, H., & Pulliam, G.P. Rapid treatment approach to human sexual inadequacy. *American Journal of Obstetrics and Gynecology,* 1974, *119,* 89-97.

Proctor, E.B., Wagner, N.N., & Butler, J.C. The differentiation of male and female orgasm: An experimental study. In J.L. McCary & D.R. Copeland (Eds.), *Modern views of human sexual behavior.* Chicago: Science Research Associates, 1976.

Puner, M. Will you still love me? *Human Behavior,* 1974, *3*(6), 42-48.

Rasmuson, N. Men — The weaker sex? *Impact of Science on Society,* 1971, *21,* 43-54.

Ray, O. *Drugs, society and human behavior* (2nd ed.). St. Louis: C.V. Mosby, 1978.

Reed, E., & Reed, S. *Mental retardation: A family study.* Philadelphia: W.B. Saunders Co., 1965.

Reitz, R. *Menopause: A positive approach.* Radnor, Pa.: Chilton Book Co., 1977.

Reynolds, B.S. Psychological treatment models and outcome results for erectile dysfunction: A critical review. *Psychological Bulletin,* 1977, *84*(6), 1218-1238.

Rhodes, P. Sex of the fetus in ante partum hemorrhage. *Lancet,* 1965, *2,* 718-719.

Rich, A. *Of woman born.* New York: W.W. Norton, 1976.

Riddle, D. *What the doctors forget to tell you.* Pittsburgh: Know, Inc., 1971.

Rivers, C. Genetic engineers: Now that they've gone too far, can they stop? *Ms.,* June 1976, 49-50, 112-116, 120.

Robbins, M.B., & Jensen, G.D. Multiple orgasm in males. *Journal of Sex Research,* 1978, *14*(1), 21-26.

Robertson, D.N., & Guttman, L. The paraplegic patient in pregnancy and labour. *Proceedings of the Royal Society of Medicine,* 1963, *56,* 381-387.

Robertson, N. Conference criticizes gynecology methods. *New York Times,* March 26, 1979, C-16.

Robinson, W.R. *A cup of tea: Conversations.* Unpublished manuscript, Tampa, 1979.

Rodale, R. Sex and nutrition: A perfect marriage. *Prevention,* 1979, *3*(4), 73-77.

Rodgers, J. Other new frontiers in birth control. *Ladies' Home Journal,* August 1977, 62-64.

Rogel, M.J. A critical evaluation of the possibility of higher primate reproductive and sexual pheromones. *Psychological Bulletin,* 1978, *85*(4), 810-830.

Rorvik, D.M., & Shettles, L. *Your baby's sex: Now you can choose.* New York: Dodd, Mead & Co., 1970.

Rose, R.M. Androgen excretion in stress. In P.G. Bourne (Ed.), *The psychology and physiology of stress.* New York: Academic Press, 1969.

Rosenfeld, A. Controls on male fertility now seem to be within our reach. *Smithsonian,* July 1977, 36-43.

Rosenzweig, S. Human sexual autonomy as an evolutionary attainment, anticipating proceptive sex choice and idiodynamic bisexuality. In J. Zubin & J. Money (Eds.), *Contemporary sexual behavior: Critical issues of the 1970s.* Baltimore: Johns Hopkins Press, 1973.

Rowan, R., & Gillette, P. *Your prostate.* Garden City, N.Y.: Doubleday, 1973.

Rowell, T. *Social behavior of monkeys.* London: Penguin Press, 1972.

Rubin, A., & Babbott, D. Impotence and diabetes mellitus. *Journal of the American Medical Association,* 1958, *168,* 498-500.

Rubin, A., & Murphy, D.P. Studies in human reproduction. III. Frequency of congenital malformations in the offspring of non-diabetic and diabetic individuals. *Journal of Pediatrics,* 1958, *53,* 579-585.

Rubin, A.B., & Henson, D.E. Effects of alcohol on male sexual responding. *Psychopharmacology,* 1976, *47,* 123-134.

Ruble, D.N., & Brooks-Gunn, J. Menstrual myths. *Medical Aspects of Human Sexuality,* June 1979, 110-121.

Rush, A.K. *Getting clear.* New York: Random House, 1973.

Sadock, B.J., Kaplan, H.I., & Freedman, A.M. *The sexual experience.* Baltimore: Williams & Wilkins, 1976.

Sandler, J., & Davidson, R.S. *Psychopathology: Learning, theory, research, and applications.* New York: Harper & Row, 1973.

Sawin, C.T. Endocrine physiology. In R. Gordon (Ed.), *Essentials of human physiology.* Chicago: Year Book Medical Publishers, 1978.

Schmidt, G. Male-female differences in sexual arousal and behavior during and after exposure to sexually explicit films. *Archives of Sexual Behavior,* 1975, *4,* 353-365.

Schoffling, K., Federlin, K., Ditschuneit, H., & Pfeiffer, E.F. Disorders of sexual function in male diabetics. *Diabetes,* 1963, *12,* 519-527.

Schrader, S.L., Wilcoxon, L.A., & Sherif, C.W. Daily self-reports on activities, life events, moods, and somatic changes during the menstrual cycle. Paper presented at the 83rd Annual Conference of the American Psychological Association, Chicago, Ill., August 1975.

Schwartz, N.B. On contraceptives for males. *Signs: Journal of Women in Culture and Society,* 1976, *2*(1), 247-248.

*Scientific American.* Male pill. 1979, *240*(6), 104.

Scott, A.C. Closing the muscle gap. *Ms.,* September 1975.

Scully, D., & Bart, P. A funny thing happened on the way to the orifice: Women in gynecology textbooks. *American Journal of Sociology,* 1973, *78,* 1045-1050.

Seaman, B., *Free and female.* Greenwich, Conn.: Fawcett, 1972.

Seaman, B., & Seaman, G. *Women and the crisis in sex hormones.* New York: Rawson Associates, 1977.

Semans, J. Premature ejaculation, a new approach. *Southern Medical Journal,* 1956, *49,* 353-358.

Sharpe, J. The birth controllers. *Health/PAC Bulletin,* April 1972.

Sherfey, M.J. *The nature and evolution of female sexuality.* New York: Vintage, 1973.

Shettles, L.B. Conception and birth sex ratios. *Obstetrics and Gynecology,* 1961, *18,* 123-127.

Simon, W., & Gagnon, J. The lesbians: A preliminary overview. *Sexual deviance.* New York: 1967.

Simon, W., & Gagnon, J. Psychosexual development. *Transaction,* 1969, *6*(5), 9-17.

Singer, I., & Singer, J. Types of female orgasm. *Journal of Sex Research,* 1972, *8*(4), 255-267.

Skinner, B.F. *Science and human behavior.* New York: Macmillan, 1953.

Slater, P.E. *Earthwalk.* Garden City, N.Y.: Doubleday, 1974.

Slavitz, H. Transsexualism: A radical crisis in gender identity. In S. Gordon & R.W. Libby (Eds.), *Sexuality today - And tomorrow.* N. Scituate, Mass.: Duxbury Press, 1976.

Smartt, W.H., & Lighter, A.C. The gonorrhea epidemic and its control. *Medical Aspects of Human Sexuality,* January 1971, 96-115.

Smith, E.M. A follow-up study of women who request abortion. *American Journal of Orthopsychiatry,* 1973, *43,* 575-585.

Smith, L.G., & Smith, J.R. Co-marital sex: The incorporation of extramarital sex into the marriage relationship. In J. Zubin & J. Money (Eds.), *Contemporary sexual behavior: Critical issues in the 1970s.* Baltimore: Johns Hopkins Press, 1973.

Sommer, B. The effect of menstruation in cognitive and perceptual-motor behavior: A review. *Psychosomatic Medicine,* 1973, *35*(6), 515-534.

Sommer, B. Mood and the menstrual cycle. Paper presented at the 83rd Annual Conference of the American Psychological Association, Chicago, Ill., August 1975.

Sones, M. Giving birth. *Ramparts,* 1974, *13*(21), 36-54.

Sontag, S. The double standard of aging. In S. Gordon & R.W. Libby (Eds.), *Sexuality today - And tomorrow.* N. Scituate, Mass., Duxbury Press, 1976.

Sorensen, R.C. *Adolescent sexuality in contemporary America.* New York: World Publishing, 1973.

Sotile, W.M., & Kilmann, P.R. Treatments of psychogenic female sexual dysfunctions. *Psychological Bulletin,* 1977, *84,* 619-633.

Spanier, G.B. Formal and informal sex education as determinants of premarital sexual behavior. *Archives of Sexual Behavior,* 1976, *5,* 39-67.

Spence, J., Helmreich, R., & Stapp, J. Ratings of self and peers on sex role attributes and their relation to self-esteem and conceptions of masculinity and femininity. *Journal of Personality and Social Psychology,* 1975, *32*(1), 29-39.

Stannard, U. The male maternal instinct. Pittsburgh: Know, Inc., n.d.

Steiner, C. *Scripts people live.* New York: Bantam, 1974.

Stewart, F., Guest, F., Stewart, G., & Hatcher, R. *My body, my health: The concerned woman's guide to gynecology.* New York: John Wiley & Sons, 1979.

Stimpson, C. 'Thy neighbor's wife, thy neighbor's servant': Women's liberation and black civil rights. In V. Gornick & B.K. Moran (Eds.), *Woman in sexist society.* New York: Signet, 1971.

Stoller, R.J. Gender identity. In B.J. Sadock, H.I.Kaplan, & A.M. Freedman (Eds.), *The sexual experience.* Baltimore: Williams & Wilkins, 1976.

Streissguth, A.P. Fetal alcohol syndrome: Where are we in 1978? *Women and Health,* 1979, *4*(3), 223-237.

Strong, B., Wilson, S., Clarke, L.M., & Johns, T. *Human sexuality: Essentials.* New York: West Publishers, 1978.

Subak-Sharpe, G. Is your sex life going up in smoke? *Today's Health,* 1974, *52*(8), 50-53.

Sussman, N. Sex and sexuality in history. In B.J. Sadock, H.I. Kaplan, & A.M. Freedman (Eds.), *The sexual experience.* Baltimore: Williams & Wilkins, 1976.

Tangri, S.S. A feminist perspective on some ethical issues in population programs. *Signs: Journal of Women in Culture and Society,* 1976, *1*(4).

Tarvis, C., & Sadd, S. *The Redbook report on female sexuality.* New York: Delacorte Press, 1975.

Teeters, C. *Women's sexuality: Myth and reality.* San Jose, Calif.: Women, Inc., 1977.

Trause, M.A., Kennell, J., & Klaus, M. Parental attachment behavior. In J. Money & H. Mustaph (Eds.), *Handbook of sexology, procreation and parenthood* (Vol. III). New York: Elsevier, 1978.

Tuttle, W.B., Cook, W.L., & Fitch, E. Sexual behavior in postmyocardial infarction patients. *American Journal of Cardiology,* 1964, *13,* 140.

U'ren, M.B. The image of women in textbooks. In V. Gornick & B.K. Moran (Eds.), *Woman in sexist society.* New York: Signet, 1971.

van de Velde, T. *Ideal marriage: Its physiology and techniques.* New York: Random House, 1930 (Translated by S. Brown).

Van Gulik, R.H. *Sexual life in ancient China.* Leidan, Netherlands: E.J. Brill, 1961.

von Haam, E. Venereal diseases and spirochetal infections. In W.A.D. Anderson (Ed.), *Pathology* (6th ed.). St. Louis: C.V. Mosby, 1971.

Van Kaam, A. Sex and existence. In J.L. McCary & D.R. Copeland (Eds.), *Modern views of human sexual behavior.* Chicago: Science Research Associates, 1976.

Van Lawick-Goodall, J. The behavior of free-living chimpanzees in the Gombe Stream reserve. *Animal Behavior Monographs,* 1968, *1*(pt. 3).

Wagner, N.N. Sexual activity and the cardiac patient. In R. Green (Ed.), *Human sexuality: A health practitioner's text.* Baltimore: Williams & Wilkins, 1975.

Walfish, S., & Myerson, M. Sex role identity and attitudes toward sexuality. *Archives of Sexual Behavior,* 1980, *9*(3).

Weideger, P. *Menstruation and menopause.* New York: Delta, 1977a.

Weideger, P. Estrogen: The rewards and the risks. *McCall's,* March 1977b, 70-79.

Weinberg, M.S., & Williams, C.J. *Male homosexuals: Their problems and adaptions.* New York: Oxford University Press, 1974.

Weinberg, S.K. *Incest behavior.* New York: Citadel Press, 1955.

Westoff, C. Coital frequency and contraception. *Family Planning Perspectives,* 1974, *6*(3), 136-141.

Westoff, L.A. Vas deferens in vasectomies. *Esquire,* March 1, 1978, 25-26.

Wetter, R. Levels of self-esteem associated with four sex role categories. Paper presented at the meeting of the American Psychological Association, 1975.

Wheeler, R.G. The intrauterine membrane. In R.G. Wheeler, G.W. Duncan, & J.J. Speidel (Eds.), *Intrauterine devices.* New York: Academic Press, 1975.

Whiting, B., & Edwards, C.F. A cross-cultural analysis of sex differences in behavior of children aged three through eleven. *Journal of Social Psychology,* 1973, *91,* 71-188.

Willenbecher, T. Why the Turk can't get it up. *Mother Jones,* January 1979, 37-38.

Williams, J.H. *Psychology of women: Behavior in a biosocial context.* New York: W.W. Norton, 1977.

Willson, J.R., Beecham, C.T., & Carrington, E.R. *Obstetrics and gynecology* (3rd ed.). St. Louis: C.V. Mosby, 1966.

Wilson, E.O., & Bossert, W.H. Chemical communication among animals. In G. Pincus (Ed.), *Recent progress in hormone research* (Vol. 19). New York: Academic Press, 1963.

Wilson, S., Strong, B., Clarke, L.M., & Johns, T. *Human sexuality: A text with readings.* St. Paul: West, 1977.

Witters, W.L., & Jones-Witters, P. *Drugs and sex.* New York: Macmillan, 1975.

Witzleben, C.L., & Driscoll, S.G. Possible transplacental transmission of herpes simplex infection. *Pediatrics,* 1965, *36,* 192-199.

Woods, J.S. Drug effects on human sexual behavior. In N.F. Woods. *Human sexuality in health and illness* (2nd ed.). St. Louis: C.V. Mosby, 1979.

Woods, N.F. *Human sexuality in health and illness.* St. Louis: C.V. Mosby, 1979.

Woods, N.F., & Earp, J. Women with cured breast cancer: A description of women's experiences four years after mastectomy. *Nursing Research,* 1978, *27*(5), 279-285.

Youcha, G. How drinking affects women. *Woman's Day,* November 1976, 78-80; 228-230.

Young, W. *Eros denied.* New York: Grove Press, 1964.

Zaretsky, E. Toward a new form of sex. *In These Times,* November 2-8, 1977, 19.

Zelnik, M., & Kantner, J.F. Sexual and contraceptive experience of young unmarried women in the United States, 1976 and 1971. *Family Planning Perspectives,* 1977, *9*(2), 55-71.

Zerof, H.G. *Finding intimacy.* New York: Random House, 1978.

Zilbergeld, B. Group treatment of sexual dysfunction in men without partners. *Journal of Sex and Marital Therapy,* 1975, *1,* 204-214.

Zilbergeld, B. *Male sexuality.* Boston: Little, Brown, 1978.

Zuckerman, M. Physiological measures of sexual arousal in the human. *Psychological Bulletin,* 1971, *75,* 297-329.

Zurcher, L.A., & Kirkpatrick, R.G. *Citizens for decency: Antipornography crusades as status defense.* Austin, Texas: University of Texas Press, 1976.

# *Index*